I Could Have Been One

by

Donald Wm. Jeffries

The contents of this work, including, but not limited to, the accuracy of events, people, and places depicted; opinions expressed; permission to use previously published materials included; and any advice given or actions advocated are solely the responsibility of the author, who assumes all liability for said work and indemnifies the publisher against any claims stemming from publication of the work.

All Rights Reserved
Copyright © 2021 by Donald Wm. Jeffries

No part of this book may be reproduced or transmitted, downloaded, distributed, reverse engineered, or stored in or introduced into any information storage and retrieval system, in any form or by any means, including photocopying and recording, whether electronic or mechanical, now known or hereinafter invented without permission in writing from the publisher.

Dorrance Publishing Co
585 Alpha Drive
Pittsburgh, PA 15238
Visit our website at *www.dorrancebookstore.com*

ISBN: 978-1-6366-1183-9
eISBN: 978-1-6366-1773-2

This writing is dedicated to my best friend,
my wife, Anne,
who has always been my proofreader and guide.

Front cover photo by Anne Jeffries.

Acknowledgments

I wish to thank the following people for their unknowing contribution to the accomplishment of this project:

My freshman year college English Composition teacher, in whose class I learned skills that would serve me well the rest of my life.

My senior year college Business Communications teacher, who encouraged me to write a book on ethics, which was a subject that did not have much written concerning it at the time. She brought back attention to a dormant idea.

To others I learned from even in casual conversation, on related subject matter, who unknowingly gave me ideas, i.e. Rex.

I now wish to give thanks to those who had active participation in the accomplishment of this project:

Annie, for her encouragement and spending hours proofreading, after my dedicated hours of research and composition.

Marie and Michele, who are the two close friends who were my review team in the early days to give me feedback and ensure that I was getting the point of the writing across in a smooth manner.

Matt, for an interview, which included personal issues.

Ruth, who is a retired teacher, for being a review reader.

Christina, who enjoyed getting a "first look," by editing. She was my final influence, before the manuscript went to a publisher, for review.

I also wish to thank all those who knew of my project and gave me encouragement along the way.

And my thanks to Peter London, who is a man of principle, for taking the time to educate me on how the various aspects of obtaining permission to reference other publications relate to each other.

Preface

I discovered that I enjoyed writing back when I was in the military writing letters to Mom and Dad and girlfriends. Well,…they were friends, who were also young ladies. One time I got the wrong letter into the wrong envelope. Mom had a chuckle out of that. I thought of being a writer and, if I had had any sense, I would have set that goal for college. In any case, it has taken me a lifetime, to now, to do some serious writing. That is a good thing considering it took me all that time to research the subject matter, by living through it.

When I was growing up, my Stepdad would tell me stories of events that had happened to him. I considered them teaching stories. In my mid-20s, my Father told me a sampling of what military life was like for him during World War II, in the European Theater. It wasn't just history. It was his history.

This composition is part of my history, in that I use my personal experiences, from having lived the more recent history of this country and, by extension, the world. I also conducted research to ensure accuracy and expand on events beyond my own experience. This is both a composition and a compilation, as I have articles, in whole or in part, copied from online sources, in the book.

At times I have used what is now considered non-politically correct language. I do this to emphasize a fact of life, during that time period, in American history. To engage the reader in that time period.

Like many people I lived my young life not taking much of an interest in history or politics or the affairs of the world or even this country as I took it all for granted. Like others I was too busy making a living, being a professional, raising a family, being involved in activities and paying attention to family and household matters.

It was not until I retired that I became more interested in history and politics and the affairs of the world and this country. I became aware and I began to recognize parallels. I began to realize that I could have traveled a much different path, at the fork in the road.

Have you even wondered about the path not taken? What would your life have been like, if you had done something else instead of what you did? At what points, in your life, could you have gone this way or that? That has been a question within me since I reflected back over the paths I did take and therefore those not taken.

I once received a painting depicting a fork in a dirt road surrounded by woods, for my birthday. Okay…funny story. My wife had commissioned a co-worker to create the painting. On my birthday, upon escorting my wife back from lunch, to her office, she introduced me to the co-worker and simply said that my birthday gift was in the area of her cubical. At first I looked for a festive wrapped present. There was none. Then I searched for something not knowing what. Finally I looked at the co-worker as if to request, "Please give me a hint?" She replied to my unspoken request with, "It's not me!" In case you are wondering, the painting was hanging on the wall.

Life is full of twist and turns. Sometimes they are minor, but at other times they are major points in our lives. Some of them begin with options of at least two and sometimes more. Major points are obvious, while minor ones may not be so noticeable.

I was once in circumstances in which I could either attend college or find full-time employment. Employment it was and advance education was placed on the back burner for some time. That was obviously a major point.

I was physically secure. My emotional aspect was intact. Mentally I was upbeat. What few expenses I had as a single person were fulfilled, with enough to finance a social life. I even managed to save some.

However, what seemed like a minor decision later on, of moving into commission sales, turned out to be a very negative path to take. Due to stress my health declined. The doctor told me that I appeared to be ten years older than I was. I resigned the position in order to survive. My minor decision to not stay in salaried sales and transfer into commission sales, for the possibility of increased revenue, had a tremendous effect on me.

Minor points, which are not so noticeable, are ones in which the results on oneself may not be immediately observed. Just as with any major life event, these too may have physical, emotional and mental results. It is just that we are not aware such results will take place.

This composition involves history of social change and how, over time, such change can change us. Is this part of your own story?

It also includes some history that does not seem to have a relationship to the subject matter of social change. However, it does, in that it gives the atmosphere and background preceding the social change. It is my history and therefore my own atmosphere and background preceding my being involved in the social change. Everyone in this county was involved one way or another by either ushering in the change or being affected by it.

Since I had to pay attention to detail, as this writing is for generations from elderly to those just getting out on their own, I have included descriptions of items used during the mid-1900s, before the technology we know today. Those who are already familiar with such items may take a reminiscing journey down Memory Lane. And if you are not old enough to do so, then it will be either an introduction or a refresher of stories by older relatives or from visiting a museum.

Giving my history also serves the purpose of giving the background to the present. From history we learn how the present developed. From the present we learn options for the future. Our ancestors' present is our past. Their future is our present. Our present is our future generations past. Our future is their present. History is a lot more than dates, places and events recorded in a book. It is people's lives; their environment and lifestyle and hardships and enjoyments.

Have a meaningful read.

Bibliography

This writing is not fictional, but factual.
I do not have the imagination to compose fiction.
Therefore it is well referenced.

All references are given within the text itself.

Contents

Title	Page i
Dedication	Page ii
Acknowledgments	Page v
Preface	Page vii
Bibliography	Page xi
Table of Contents	Page xiii

Chapter One Twentieth Century

1940s	Page 1
1950s	Page 13
1960s	Page 33
1970s	Page 58
1980s	Page 63
1990s	Page 76

Chapter Two Twenty-First Century

Retirement Years	Page 83
Communist Manifesto and Related Research	Page 84
Agenda 21	Page 100
What Am I?	Page 103
The Connection	Page 111
The Parallel	Page 115
Christianity	Page 126
The Differences	Page 164
Communism Manifested	Page 178
Communism/Socialism Today	Page 240
Socialism Manifested	Page 269

Was He or Wasn't He	Page 323
America and Israel	Page 341
World Upside Down	Page 344
Additional Thoughts Referencing	Page 366
It Had No Fancy Name	Page 387
In Closing	Page 411
Addendum	Page 415
Other Publication's Credits	Page 425

Chapter One

Twentieth Century

1940s

I was born in the middle of a war. Not that my mother gave birth to me in the midst of a battle. Well…there was the struggle to get me out, of course. I was born in the regular fashion, at a hospital. The battles were going on around most of our world, to the east of us on the Atlantic Ocean, in Europe and on the Africa Continent and to the west of us on the Pacific Ocean and in the South Pacific countries and Asia. At some time or another, I read those born in war will themselves go to war. In my case and that of my generation, that would prove to be a true theory. It does seem each generation has its own major event(s).

As the beginning of peacetime settled in post-World War II (WWII), surviving military personnel, of the Allied Forces consisting of America, the British Empire, France and Russia, returned home, to warm welcomes of gratitude and love. Some personnel decided to remain in the military. However, each one had their own form of post-traumatic stress disorder (PTSD), which was not called PTSD, but battle fatigue. Each had to learn how to live with it, while not talking about what they had lived through. They wanted to forget.

And they all carried war guilt. The guy next to me got killed, why wasn't I? That soldier lost his legs. Why am I in one piece? They were wounded. How is it that I wasn't? Jones sure did a brave thing. I wish I was like him. It is not logical. But it is there just the same. I know a person, who served during the Viet Nam War, whose duty was to brief the deploying troops and get them loaded onboard the aircraft, which would take them to Nam. That person knew she was sending some to their deaths. It wasn't her. It was the military, which she and they were serving in. But she has had to deal with that personal guilt. Mine? Mine is I did not do enough. I should have done more. I did volunteer for duty with a high death rate. In looking back on it though, when I was not accepted due to my job specialty not being required, they did me a favor.

During the war taking place, when I was born, a much older Cousin than I had found a restful place, with his unit in the French countryside, by a lake. He was able to have momentary peace. After returning home, he painted a canvas from memory and it always hung in his living room. While I am sure he must have accomplished other paintings that was the only one he kept and hung. That was the only memory he wanted to remember, from his war experience. It was as though the tranquility of the smooth water pushed all the damaging memories down into its depths.

My Father had been with the forces that liberated a concentration camp, in Germany. The only statement he could bring himself to make to me concerning the liberation was that what he saw was the worst thing he had ever seen. I once met a Jew, who had been in such a camp. My head was filled with questions to ask about his experience. When I asked if I could see his number, he rolled up his shirt sleeve. I saw the identifying black tattoo, of a long number, on his left forearm. My mind emptied as it filled with respectful knowledge that he had suffered greatly of human inhumanity to humans. He and I just sat in each other's presence, in silence. It would not be until much later I would wonder if my father had liberated him.

I Could Have Been One

Both my Cousin and my Father tried to wash their memories away with alcohol. Both were in serious relationships with women, who loved them. In my Father's case, that was after he and Mom were divorced not long after he returned home, from the War. Both were asked which they loved more; alcohol or their future wife. They made the transition and became good husbands, but the memories were still there deep down inside. They, as did all others, died with those buried memories.

The Greatest Generation consisted of our parents, older relatives and their friends and neighbors. Our older siblings had conducted paper drives and remember ration books for food, gas and any product manufactured with materials required for the war effect. They also remember the absence of fathers and older brothers and sisters in the military. Sometimes they had to live with only stories of their fathers and relatives, who did not return home. Most of us born during World War II did not have any kind of an awareness of a father, during our very first years. Mine was in England, with the Third Armor Division, preparing for DDay, when I was born. My own connection to my Father would not be until I was an adult.

There were also those men who served onboard merchant marine vessels. I knew a man who had begun his life on the water working with his father on a New York tugboat. During WWII, he served in the Merchant Marines and was on a few ships due his previous ships being torpedoed by German U-boats (submarine). So it was not just military personnel involved in the war. There were thousands of civilians, including partisans in various countries fighting the German army and the Nazis. Thousands more civilians were affected by the invading armies of Germany and Japan.

Not all men went to war. My Stepdad was rated, by the military, as 4F or physically unfit for military service. It was due to a damaged ear drum. He did serve though, by working the San Francisco shipyards, in support of the war effect. Decades later I would live in university married student housing, which had been purchased and relocated from San Francisco. It had been built originally for the shipyard workers, during WWII, as small apartments. Much later I would wonder if my Stepdad had lived in them.

A couple of years after WWII the Army Air Corps morphed into its own separate branch of the military services as the United States Air Force.

The victorious United States of America, and the British Empire and the world began a period of prosperity as peacetime production replaced wartime production. The iconic, factory worker, poster woman Rosie the Riveter and the women like her returned to home life, with their returning husbands, who went back to work in the factories. Some husbands did not return home, but the women had to find other work. By the time I was born, there were 310,000 American women working in wartime factories. After the War, single women had to find employment elsewhere or perhaps marry a prior G.I., which is short for Government Issue, by the way. Women who served in the Armed Forces did the same. The Baby Boomer Generation was begun. (Online reference for Rosie the Riveter on "History" website.)

After WWII, Russia, who had been our ally, may have continued military production and buildup, in view of their aggression against what became known as the Soviet Block Eastern Countries.

The aftermath of the War also began as surviving torn and displaced Jews found their way to Palestine (now the State of Israel) which was occupied by the British. Some Jewish factions did not want any more foreigners in the country of their heritage and attacked the British military. While many of those Jews had immigrated to Palestine and were new to that country, the British were occupiers having been there post World War One. The Jews wanted their own country, with their own government and with no prejudice or persecution as they had suffered in Europe not only during the war, but also before the War; long before the War. The British did decide to leave the country. The new Israeli government and military had to establish itself and face new situations such as interactions with the Muslim countries, which surrounded them. I remember the "6 Day War" of 1967, when Israel defended itself against Egypt and invaded that country to win the war. And that was 22 years after WWII. The online reference has a good overall review of both what lead up to the State of Israel being proclaimed and what occurred afterward. (Online reference History.com "State of Israel Proclaimed".)

In Europe, the Nuremberg Trials took place deciding the degree of guilt of twenty-two Nazi war criminals, for the slaughter of approximately six million Jews and other unwanted human beings. Jewish Nazi hunters later discovered more Nazi war criminals in hiding and brought them to justice, in the following decades.

Israel was not the only location Jews traveled to during post WWII. Many Jews sought life with family and friends who had either escaped the Nazis or had settled in other nations before the war began in Europe such as America. I read, in an article some time ago, that for the most part, people did not want to hear their stories, including their relatives. People did not want to think that such a thing as the Holocaust, of humans, could happen.

By the way, the term "holocaust" is Biblical Old Testament as in the sacrifice of many animals to God.

People who had survived in war torn countries like France took action against their own who had cooperated with Nazi/German personnel, in any way. Those countries had to recover from aspects, of the war that countries, which the war did not take place in, did not have to recover from and the results of victory were much more intensely felt both east of the Atlantic and west of the Pacific. To this day, the effects of that War are still felt, including by those here in America, although more and more of the affected are leaving this life.

The world started a period of follow-up and cleanup and pickup and straighten-up and adjusting and reorganizing and rebuilding, of nations and communities; the rebuilding of interrupted lives, with some being more interrupted and damaged than others.

No words can describe fully the human condition of physical, mental, emotional and spiritual aftermath of war. Nor of any life changing tragedy natural or otherwise. Nor can a scientific study. That human condition can only be manifested, in its many forms, and observed. However, counseling can assist one.

The adjustment from war torn to victory or defeat brought the settling into the recovery process, with each person finding their place and some taking longer than others to do so. For my Father it took a divorce, discovering another woman who loved him, giving up drinking, marrying and living the rest of his lifetime being responsible for a family and to his profession. Like many others he returned to his employment, moved up into management and spent the rest of his life with that company, before he passed over from this world due to stress related health problems caused by the War.

In general, the men of the Greatest Generation continued to be great, by taking whatever employment they could such as factory work, and working in it until retirement, to support their family. They purchased a house and took a second mortgage on the property to finance college education for their children. They wanted a better life for their children than they had.

In general, the women of the Greatest Generation supported their husbands and children by tending to them and the household. They supported them not just physically, but also mentally and emotionally and sometimes spiritually. In general, the husband was the family provider and protector and the wife was the heart of the family.

History is made during our own lifetime.. It becomes the historical road into the future and the history of future generations to study in school both primary and advanced. Our history is the road back to and of previous generations. We are not so far removed from those previous generations and our own ancestors. During my own lifetime, I had an aunt who was born in the 1890s, over a hundred years ago.

I recently read an account of a War Between the States soldier written by his great-grandson. From the great-grandfather to the grandfather, who was a very young child during that War, to the father and to the son are four generations; four generations covering from the mid-1800s to the early 2000s covering one whole century plus half of a century worth of decades.

My grandparents were born in the late 1800s not long after America's War Between the States also known as America's Civil War, War of Northern Aggression and War of the Rebellion. My great grandparents were involved one way or another in that War. I grew up hearing stories of local events and people of that War. Sometimes stories of such involvement are passed down from generation to generation. One such story was passed to me, from my stepfamily. My city Grandma also told me stories of her life, when she was a child, in the late 1800s. My country Step Grandma was still living that life style to some degree.

By the way, I use the term "War Between the States". Yes, by some from that time, it was called a civil war. However, I offer the following:

In a civil war, one portion of a nation's populace is trying to defeat the forces of that nation's government so they may, in turn, establish their own government in place of the defeated one. This was not the case during America's mid-1800s. Before the War, the Southern States seceded from the United States of America. They formed their own government for the Confederate States of America complete with its own constitution and government institutions. This was legal under the Tenth Amendment of the United States Constitution, in that if the Federal government has not established a law concerning a subject matter, then the States themselves may do so. Secession had never been a subject matter of an established law, by the U.S. Government. Therefore....

The War itself came over a dispute of a Union island fortress that was within a Confederate State. However, it is actually not that simple nor is it complicated. There are just other aspects involved.

My grandparent's generation were adults during World War I (WWI), which included the Russian Revolution and the beginning of Socialism/Communism being brought from written word and spoken ideas to the manifestation of government control.

In the 1940s, some grocery stores had fruits and vegetables, which came from local farms, displayed outside of the store, in the open air. No store, of any kind, had the variety of merchandise there is today, which made selection a lot easier. Milk might be delivered to the home, by a milkman. Refrigeration was by a block of ice brought by an iceman, who carried it inside, with large tongs, and placed it in an icebox, which was equipped with an ice compartment and a drip water pan. There was no air conditioning and the furnace was coal burning. Electrical transformers, lines and cords, connectors and switches were very different from what they are today being crudely made as the early items of a relatively new industry. In those early days, wiring could be on the outside of the wall. Mainstream America had passed through the end of its transition from the Victorian Era lifestyle, with all of its positives and negatives, and well into an era of improvements and innovation, with all of its positives and negatives.

I have come to believe that, in general, inventions and developments have their spinoff side-effects, which are not so good. For example, the automobile gave people faster transportation. However, it has been the instrument of death and debilitating injury. And now automobiles are being developed in which the human does not have to drive it or even think about what traffic itself is doing. The thinking is done, for the human, by a computer developed by humans. I am not saying vehicles should be done away with, but I do not care for computers replacing the human brain.

The world itself, of the 1940s, was getting ready to develop into a modern culture of convenience, entertainment and consumptive commercialism against a backdrop of Socialism and Capitalism; Democracy/Republics and Communism forward movement. I had been birthed, raised and would be grown into and during that transition.

We arrive in existence through the action of a man and a woman. These days that may be either directly or indirectly; usually directly. Hopefully that action was through their love for each other and both parents are involved when a child is born. Hopefully both remain involved during their lifetime providing both are worthwhile parents. However, sometimes any of the above is not the situation.

Through our parentage, we arrive into the circumstances of their personal and family life as well as social, economic/material, political conditions, including those conditions beyond our immediate environment which may affect us such as state, national and global. And we are raised and grown according to all of those conditions and situations, beyond our control as a product of our environment, to a point. Hopefully we learn how to think for ourselves.

I have read a child's raising is completed during the very early years of their childhood. Not only have they basically learned a native language and been introduced to their physical environment, but also they have been taught by example, word and action what is permissible and not permissible; is unsafe, beginning social graces and even the beginnings of what is right and wrong.

There was a little person, but a little bigger than me, in my life. I did not know then she was my sister; just that she was there with me. She had to begin school and I had no idea what school was or why she had to go there and not be with me. I adapted to her coming and going just as I had to Mama's going to work. Then the day came when something happened and Mama told me my sister had gone to some place called Heaven.

She was in the children's choir down the street and had come back home holding sheet music in her hand. It was a new song she had learned. The church was on the other side of the street and Mama would watch the traffic and tell her when to safely cross, which she did that day. Then the wind came and blew the sheet music out of her hand and into the street. Before Mama could grab her, she ran back into the street and in front of the car. My almost seven years old sister had beautiful, curly, red hair. She was thrown over the car and came down on the back bumper, which was metal. Her hair was torn off and she was buried in a wig.

She had been killed by a drunk driver as he hit and ran. I could not understand. She was just gone and I would not see her again. But once again I adapted. I adapted to her not being in my life, but I have always missed her; even when I did not know it. I was two years old.

The driver…he was found, prosecuted and imprisoned. Both he and my sister became statistics.

As I grew, Mama would take me on walks and I discovered my environment. Saturday was a walk downtown. If it was the Christmas Season, we would view department store window displays and visit my favorite Aunt, who was always a seasonal employee at Macy's, and she would give me a treat.

Mama introduced me to the corner movie theater, where we would see a film sometimes. There was the bakery, where I enjoyed a donut. Next was the shoe repair shop, with the Cat's Paw advertisement in the window. These were all places Mama had known as a child, when the owners had been young. One hot summer day I had my first A&W Root Beer float. And there was the hot, roasted, peanut vendor down at the park. Both humans and birds were fed. Happy times of learning and innocence, with Mama.

Children have their life firsts. The first person I knew with a disability was the blind neighbor lady. She was very gracious and still lived in the family home. We lived in what had been a family home, but was broken up into apartments. Every Halloween she would host a party on her front lawn. It was an event to look forward to. I saw my first drunk one Halloween. Mama took me down to the local block party. The streets were blocked off, for a fun family time with all of the activities. The police were there for safety reasons. They observed and removed the drunk man quickly.

By the end of the 1940s, I had been raised and had little idea of what I had been born into. Only that I had a mother and her family. Our residential environment was apartment living. Mama went somewhere most days and did not return until the day was done. Grandma gave me food and a comfortable, secure feeling. There was an aunt, whose company I enjoyed; not that I realized what an "aunt" was. Or the reality of what a mother and grandmother was for that matter. They were all just big people in my life.

I became acquainted with the seasons of the year and seasonal events. Christmas became my favorite because it brought family together and was joyous. I suppose receiving presents also had something to do with it. And special food we did not have the rest of the year.

I even received presents from my Father, although I did not know he was my Father. He was just some man who came at Easter and Christmas and brought things for me. I did not know why. We never interacted. He would bring things and leave. Later I would learn who the man was in relation to me and that he and his wife would select and purchase the gifts and she would wrap them beautifully. I do remember a time when he was at the same funeral Mama and I were. A mutual friend had died in a house fire. Father asked Mama if I could spend the day with him. She replied she did not believe it would be a good idea.

Two years after WWII ended the British Empire downsized and the beginning of the end came to Britannia's majestic world influence, while the world influence of the United States of America grew. The British released rule of India and India was divided into the Muslim country of Pakistan and Hindu India and the world came to know the names of Mahatma Gandhi and Nehru.

The People's Republic of China also known as Communist China was established by Mao Zedong (Tse-tung), after he defeated the Chinese Nationalist Party leader Chiang Kai-Shek not by election, but by civil war in 1949 post WWII. I once heard someone say both men were war lords. I personally have not conducted research on such and therefore do not really know if such is true. It doesn't really matter. What does matter is the Nationalist took refuge on the island of Taiwan, after their defeat. The Chinese Nationalist and the

Communist had been in conflict since 1921 shortly after the beginning of a formalized Communist movement of the Russian Socialist Democratic Labour Party, in 1912, and the 1917 October Bolshevik Revolution. The Bolsheviks were the majority faction of the Russian Socialist Democratic Labour Party lead by Vladimir Lenin. The Russian revolution occurred during World War I. (Online reference Wikipedia "Chinese Communist Revolution".)

By the time the final New Year's Eve came for the decade, I was in school and Grandma had quiet time at home.

1950s

This decade literally started off with the Korean Conflict, which was the first time the United Nations became involved in such a matter. The Communist country of North Korea invaded the country of South Korea. Once again families of the world became involved in supporting with aid and or military members, but this time under the United Nations' action whereas The War to End All Wars of World War I, which produced the League of Nations, and World War II had been under alliances of countries. The same countries involved, in both World Wars, realigned themselves, between the two World Wars, so that some fought for the opposite side, in relation to Germany, the second time around. During WWI, Japan was allied with the countries against Germany such as United States, which it would attack, during WWII in being allied with Germany, bringing the United States into that War. The Korean Conflict ended several years later, with a truce. There is no victor in a stalemate and that truce is still formally in effect, with Communist North Korea rattling its saber every now and then. Tensions with that country have increased. (Online references Office of the Historian "The League of Nations" and Throughtco "History and Principles of the United Nations".)

My favorite Aunt met and married my favorite Uncle, who had served in the Korean Conflict, in the Coast Guard, which also operated off the coast of North Korea as well as our coastlines. My Father-In-Law served in both WWII and Korea. He was one of those sailors on duty at Pearl Harbor the Sunday morning of December 7th of 1941. Neither my favorite Uncle nor my Father-In-Law wanted to talk about their experiences.

There was plenty of work to be had and even poor families were existing better, including my own.

Although there were credit and installment plans, at stores such as furniture stores, and bank loans for purchasing, credit cards were just beginning to exist. They were called by such names as Diners Club card and travel and entertainment card. To entice shoppers to purchase their product, Cracker Jacks, with the Navy uniformed sailor boy on the package, offered gifts inside ranging from toy whistles to adjustable rings.

My Mother collected Green Stamps. Participating grocery stores, of the S&H Green Stamps Operation Company, issued to the customer a stamp for a certain amount of money spent, for groceries. A customer could go home with at least a handful or a purse full. In those days a grocery store was just that; a grocery store, without drugs and clothing and camera film and coffee shops and housewares and…etc. All of that other stuff could be purchased at the corner drug store or the five and ten store down the street or at a department store or a regular cafe. Anyway…the stamps were licked and pasted into small booklets. A catalog was provided, by the store, and the customer could choose an item and save up the required number of stamp filled books to obtain the item. Seasonal "Idea Books" were also available, at Christmas. Items ranged from small appliances to toys. There was no "Internet" and therefore no online catalog or website. Everything was accomplished through the grocery store itself. Those stamps were collected and books filled from the 1930s, of the Great Depression, to the Recession of the 1980.

I COULD HAVE BEEN ONE

The exception to the rule of store singularity was Woolworth department store, which had a restaurant.

When we lived in the "big city", Mama introduced me to Woolworth's lunch counter. When she said we were going shopping, on a Saturday, I looked forward to having a lunch that would be special.

Walmart had not been founded yet. There were no "super" stores, although big city stores such as Macy's and Gimbals were quite large. There were lots of family owned business and some company small stores and franchises. Military personnel had returned home and began some of these small businesses.

Some "chain" franchise businesses we know today such as "fast food", were started with just one location back during that time period.

People still handwrote hardcopy letters on stationary and the only way to mail them was via the United States Postal Service (USPS), which was established by Ben Franklin, during the early days of our country. Mother wrote letters using a pen she would dip into a small bottle of black ink. She'd wipe the excess on the side of the bottle and repeat that process to keep ink in the pen's nib, at the end of the handle. Once she was finished writing, she would blot the stationary to absorb any excess ink with a blotter, then rinse the nib with water and ensure the lid of the ink bottle was on tight.

Parcel shipment was also via the USPS. FedEx and those UPS men in brown shorts were not thought of yet. But there were men in grey uniforms driving Greyhound Buses used for the shipment of large packages. Some prior Army Air Corps and Air Force pilots began flying civilian cargo aircraft as well as passenger aircraft and farming crop duster aircraft.

The United States Congress composition was unlike today now that a prior military person serving in Congress is rare. Most of the Post WWII Congress was filled with those who had served in the military. Prior military personnel also became politicians at the state, county and local levels. And we had an Army General elected to the Presidency; President Eisenhower. Congress was composed of men. Now many politicians are women. In fact, there are more women in Congress today than there ever has been.

Alexander Graham Bell's invention called the telephone, which is the ancestor of the cell phone, allowed people to contact others via women employed as switchboard operators. Direct dialing, on rotary phones, had not been established yet as an improvement. By the early Fifties, the party-line type of operation, which involved more than one household being on the same connection line, was being phased out. This type of operating system sometimes caused situations in which the operator had to tell the first party to end their conversation with their person on the other end of the call, so the operator could contact the number requested by the second party. There were also situations when people silently listened on another person's conversation, which would also happen later, when a household had more than one of the new modern dial telephones, which was not a party-line outside of the household. Yes, it did offer temptation, to busybodies, at times and parents listened in on their teenagers.

There was also Samuel F. B. Morse's invention of the telegraph. An operator would receive the message to be sent, from the customer, tap out the message, in Morse Code involving a series of taps on a metal key system creating the long and short configuration for each letter. The key was connected to electrical wiring. Such wiring would pass out of the building and onto telegraph poles, which were placed one after another from city to city and town to town just like the telephone. The receiving operator would listen to the incoming electrical tapping of their key and translate the code into the written message, to be either picked up by the receiving person or delivered by a telegraph courier. Money could even be wired.

Such communication inventions created decades earlier, or even in the 1800s, were related to industry which continues to improve and expand our lives today.

During America's War Between the States, President Abraham Lincoln ordered his Generals to ensure that telegraph lines were installed as much as they could be when their armies advanced into enemy territory. It was quite common to find the President in the central telegraph office, of the Union Army, in Washington, District of Columbia (D.C.). This was a large asset in his management as the Commander in Chief of the Union Army.

During the World Wars, the telegraph had been used by the military services, to inform the next-of-kin of their loved ones being killed in action (KIA), missing in action (MIA) or captured as a prisoner of war (POW). Families feared the unexpected knock on the front door.

Although Western Union still exists as a financial services transfer company, it discontinued the service of the telegraph for which it was an icon, as the company name itself was synonymous with the service product. As residents obtained household telephones and services expanded between cities and towns into every nook and cranny of America, the telegraph became more and more unneeded; just as two-way "walkie talkies" developed into mobile phones, for use in vehicles, and now cell phones replaced them and have all but phased out landline telephones.

For the following, please keep in mind I grew up in a small town and these are generalities.

Many people had checking and savings accounts, at a bank, which did not conduct business concerning mortgages or investments. Those were handled by specialized institutions. However, there were also people who did not use checking accounts and dealt only with cash. Paychecks could be cashed at some businesses such as neighborhood grocery stores and bars. Many families lived financially from week to week.

My first experience with banking and check writing was as a young boy. A schoolmate invited me over to his house one Saturday. It was warm weather and we were playing outside, where a large cardboard box sat. He turned it upside down and stated, "Let's play bank." I replied, "Okay, I'll rob the bank." He responded by saying, "No, you have to come into the bank and write a check." I stated, "Okay…then after that I'll rob the bank." Frustrated he replied,

"No. Bank robbing is violent. We are going to just play banking." I conceded and wrote my first check. I never went back over to visit as I found his idea of play boring. Maybe his parents worked at one of the two banks in town or maybe he had learned check writing from his parents, when he was with them in a bank.

Saturday was for shopping, having lunch at a restaurant and maybe taking in the latest Hollywood film and socializing while doing so. Sunday was for attending church, socializing and relaxing. There were Blue Laws, which were State and local laws prohibiting businesses from being open on Sunday or for alcohol to be sold on Sunday and other related laws. Such laws date back to the founding of our country. (Online reference The Free Dictionary "Blue Laws".)

Schools were functioning only from September through May. Every school day began with the Pledge of Allegiance and prayer, in the classroom such as the Our Father. School rooms had framed pictures of Presidents George Washington and Abraham Lincoln. Some school rooms, in older rural buildings, held more than one grade. Part of my own schooling was in classrooms holding two and three grades. Middle school also known as junior high was developing, in the late Fifties.

At the beginning of summer vacation, we kids somehow believed summer was forever. In any case, it was a time to just be a kid and have fun, although farm kids always helped with chores and some worked the fields. As we grew older some of us kids also helped our parents in the family business or assisting their independent contractor dads. I began learning house painting, at the age of twelve. Only I was free labor as it was considered that I benefitted from the income as a family member. Later I would be paid. Older teenagers could obtain seasonal or part time jobs, for spending money.

We were taught to respond to adults with, "Yes Madam/Sir." and "No, Madam/Sir". For that matter we were taught to address adults as Madam and

Sir, including our parents at times. A gentleman would open a door for a lady, tip his hat to her, walk with her on the inside of the sidewalk, give her his handkerchief (which a gentleman always had available), pick up items she had dropped and carry items she had purchased.

Walking with the lady on the inside of the sidewalk may have been to protect the lady from street puddle water being splashed onto her, by a passing vehicle.

There were certain customs of etiquette applied during a date such as walking her to her front door. There were also table manners during the eating of a meal and not having one's elbows on the table. Such etiquette rules had practical reasons supporting them, if elbows are on the table, then the hands are either up in the air in front of the person's face or out across the table possibly interfering with space required for dishes and glasses, which might cause an accident and that could cause stained or water soaked clothing and embarrassment as well.

In general, we were taught to be courteous, polite and respectful of both people and property. The Golden Rule of "Do unto others as you would have them do unto you." was repeatedly taught to us. In church, we all learned the Ten Commandments. We were taught at home, in school, in church and by family, friends, neighbors, and others what was right from wrong. "It takes a village to raise a child" was already being practiced here long before that African saying was ever publicly used here in America. I remember the saying from the 1980s. (Online reference Afriprov.org, African Proverbs, Sayings and Stories.)

However, human nature being what it is, I shoplifted a fifteen-cent Classic Novel, in comic book form, from a drug store. It may have been *Rob Roy*. Kids would also play pranks or steal pumpkins out of a garden knowing, if caught, punishment would be given. However, whoever thought they would be caught?

Teachers were allowed to punish students, including getting a student's attention by use of a paddle on the backside for high school boys. There were no dress codes as pride in personal appearance was taught and fashions were modest. Clothing was neat, clean and ironed. If the reader does not know what ironed/ironing is, Google it. There were no security guards or school police officers on campus. Boys carrying a pocket knife was commonplace as it was used as a tool, for a variety of functions. Lockers were not searched as there was no reason to search for anything. Illegal drugs had not filtered into schools. Since the internet and social media had not been thought of yet, bullying was in person. Cell phones had not replaced public phone booths, on the street as well as in stores. While fighting was frowned upon, standing up for one's self or another was taken into consideration.

In rural areas, people did not lock their doors even when they were away from home. Kids could securely run around town, go on bike rides and be out until a reasonable hour at night without the parents being in fear for them. Most kids followed the rule, "Be home before dark." This not only got kids home for supper, during the winter season, but also give the kids plenty of time to play, after supper, during the summer. There was also "Come home when the street lights come on."

Halloween was safe for children to receive treats from neighbors and people they knew or did not know. Only decades later would it be a scary time, when it was rumored that a razor blade was found inside a candied apple that had been given to a child during their "trick or treating". Hospitals began to announce they would X-ray the treats as a community service and churches began to host family safe events. Dutiful parents began to examine all treats and loving people began to give only treats that could not be tampered with. I would inspect my children's candy that was commercially wrapped for any tears or puncture marks. If the razor blade incident did occur, then a real live mentally deranged human monster had come out and changed children's and parents' joy and delight into horror and restriction. If the incident did not actually occur, the result of the rumor was the same.

If one dropped out of high school, one was expected to have some form of economic life support either by family employment or independent means. If one completed high school, a person either went on to college, which was mainly a four year institution, a trade or professional school or found gainful employment. This included enlisting in the military.

For men, enlistment was instead of waiting to be drafted into the Army. For us poor boys, it could be a kick-start into adult life and we could earn benefits such as the G.I. Bill, for education. For women, enlistment was an option, since there were women's auxiliary counterparts to the service branches such as Navy Waves, although young women more than likely would find civilian employment, attend college or marry. Back then the top professions for men were doctor, lawyer, and business. Nursing was a top one for women. Teaching was both men and women. In the business world, generally men were managers and women were secretaries or bookkeepers. In retail stores, men were managers and clerks, but women were usually clerks. Banking was the same. Bottom line is that one was taught responsibility.

During that time, a person without much education could start in a low-level position, with a company, and work their way to a top-level position by gaining experience. One could also change work positions moving around as circumstances mandated or the desire to travel outweighed the desire for stability. Now all of that has changed and just interviewing for a job is an exercise in scientific methodology.

One thing I could not understand at the time, was what I later learned to be Jim Crow equal-but-separate-laws. I would sit at the lunch counter looking at the "colored men" who worked downtown in menial positions, placing their order at the back door, receiving their food and sitting on the ground in the alley, to eat. That was at a small restaurant. There were at least a couple of larger restaurants that did have inside dining facilities at the back of the restaurant separate from the regular dining. I could not understand why they could not come in the front door and sit down. It made no sense to me.

As for the "colored side" of town, that was just where they lived and the "white side" was just where we lived. I did not think about why they were there and we were here.

In reading the hometown newspaper a while back, I came across an article written by a now older man. His grandfather had moved to town to operate a company business back in the 1950s. The writer's father was one of the sons who worked at the business. The writer begin working at the business when he was ten. There, he learned lessons of life about honesty and the Golden Rule. That was the real education he received, at the family business.

In the article, he wrote of how his father treated people with fairness and going beyond the expected service. Long story short is many customers received free service because they could not afford to pay, but having the service was a necessity for the survival of their family. Charge accounts were established, for payment when the customer could. However, for some customers, their economic condition never did improve. Their charge accounts were marked "Paid In Full" as if they had paid it off. That was just for the record. To the operator and his sons, it was not just a business for earning their living, it was community involvement and assisting those less fortunate.

There was also another aspect of the business. It did not matter if a person was white or colored. All were treated the same, including the colored man who was an employee at the business and became like a second father to the white grandson, of the original owner. The colored man relocated to California. While the grandson was serving his country, in the Navy and stationed in California, he visited and spent days at the man's home. When some of his white shipmates discovered what he was doing, they no longer associated with him. That was in the 1960s. Upon writing about his father's death, he stated his mother told him if Segregation had not been in place, there would not have been enough room in the streets for the number of cars in the funeral processional.

Later I learned the why as far as the history behind Segregation and Jim Crow laws, but I still view it as wrong. At the time, I just knew it existed and that was the way things were; just as the writer also expressed. By the way, whites also had to obey such laws, although I believe a white person would suffer peer pressure more than actual punishment, while the black person would be arrested, prosecuted and punished.

This is a good point to say that in viewing history, even one's own, one should not view it with the eyes of the present, which gives a false view because it contains the conditions of today and does not take into account the conditions of the past. One may say something should not have happened or something was wrong or ask why did they do that? Those are valid comments and questions. However, one should also examine what was life like at the time. What was the world like at the time? What events had previously taken place, to cause what took place later? What was the mindset of people at that time that caused them to do what they did? What side effects occurred that caused other effects? Who, when, why, what and how? For example, the mid 1800s were not our second decade of the 21st Century in a whole lot of ways.

Another mistake is using the events of the past to blame people of today, who are far removed from that past. Yes, some cultures have not changed that much, but those of the past are not those of today. They may still live in a basically unchanged situation, but the situation of the world around them has changed and therefore affected their own world, to some degree or another. Each culture of today should be viewed by the present, for it is in the present.

One cannot erase the past. It happened and it is there in existence to stay in reality. One should learn from the past. What was positive? What was negative? Should Jim Crow laws have been established? No, but they were and for a reason; wrong reasoning thought to be good reasoning by those of limited understanding caused by their prejudice and the attitudes of the time they lived in, with a past of limited understanding based on practices of one human dominating another. Such practice have been part of history beginning with the early civilizations; civilization of warring countries and tribes dominating the defeated.

Were Jim Crow conditions better than the conditions of actual slavery? Yes. Are integration conditions better than the conditions of Jim Crow? Yes. Is the condition of actual acceptance better than the condition of forced integration? Yes. But BOTH races have to actually accept. Both have to have mutual understanding and acceptance. Both have to stop the prejudice, which runs both ways. Both have to learn from the past, but with the future in mind. However, with human nature being what it is, I suppose there will always be people who want to be a victim and blame others for their own situations and think with an entitlement philosophy. Just as there most likely will always be those who believe they, for some reason, are better than others.

Just because one has more education than others, a higher IQ, more money, a higher professional status or social status does not mean one is better than others. What it does mean is that one was able to take advantage of life's opportunities, study and work hard and make something of themselves. By doing so they accepted responsibility for themselves and took on more responsibility as they rose in position and status. But as a human being they are not any better than any other human being. They are different than some human beings because of their intelligence and developed potentials, but they are not better than other human beings, as a whole. They just have some differences from others. And that is all. There will always be those who do better than other people. There will always be those who achieve, while others do not. Sometimes those who can achieve do not due to circumstances of one kind or another. Then there is that student who obtains high grades without having to study hard. There is the student that has to study hard for their grade range from average to high. And there is the student who no matter how hard they study they get only average and below. But the important issue is how each of them use what they have to work with.

In *The Haunted Fifties 1953-1963*, by journalist I.F. Stone, his entry for May 17, 1954 states that United States Supreme Court Justice Warren read the opinion in *Brown v. United States*.

Background: Certain states had put into place segregation laws, also known as Jim Crow, of so called "equal, but separate"; equal facilities, but totally separate locations. Louisiana had passed legislation, in 1890, to have equal, but separate railroad carriages. Only nurses caring for children, of the other race, could ride in a carriages designated for the other race. Plessy was a man of seven eighths white and one eighth black and appeared as a white person. In 1892, he purchased a first class ticket and entered a carriage designated for whites, only to be arrested and imprisoned. Upon appeal to the Louisiana Supreme Court, Judge Ferguson upheld the lower conviction. Plessy had contested based on violation of the Equal Protection clause of the 14th Amendment as well as violation of the 13th Amendment, which banned slavery. Ferguson based his decision on the 14th Amendment protecting political and civil rights such as voting and sitting on juries, but not social rights, and that the 13th Amendment concerned only the actual institution of slavery itself. (Online reference "Supreme Court First One Hundred Years" *Plessy v. Ferguson* 1896.)

The *Brown v. United States* case concerned segregated schools and if black children could receive the same equal education opportunities. Chief Justice Warren read that to separate black children from others of similar age and qualifications solely because of their race generated a feeling of inferiority as to their status in the community that may affect their hearts and minds in a way unlikely ever to be undone. That ruling not only ruled for "Brown", but also reversed *Plessy v. Ferguson* and provided a major catalyst for the Civil Rights movement itself, of 1955 to '68.

Back to that small cafe. It was at that same small cafe my interest in history was perked. I met a descendant of one of the town's founding families. She was a reporter for one of the newspapers. My first day there I sat by her and she began a conversation. From then on, I would sit by her as she informed me of events that had taken place in the area going back to the Civil War. I missed her when she was not there. History became my favorite subject in school.

Although it was my favorite subject, the seed had only been planted. It would be long into the future before I would actually realize the importance of history and of knowing it and of why past events had happen.

Another aspect of society of the 1950s was the role of married women, which was mainly to care for the household and children. In general, the men had the responsibility of earning the family revenue, which was one reason the better paying positions were held by men, in my opinion. My own Mother worked as needed to support our family. Women staying at home would not be questioned until the next decade.

Most couples also had only one car. I believe, in most situations, the wife would drive the husband to work, if the wife could drive. In the case of contractors, who were men, they required the family transportation to transport not only themselves to the job site, but also their equipment and supplies.

The first time I ever heard of murder and suicide was the day after Mama and her coworker were instructed to leave their evening shift by the clothing store owner. His wife was the evening manager. Once Mama and her coworker left, he took his wife to the upstairs office, where he shot his wife and himself. My innocence began being removed. Bad things could happen. I was nine years old.

As part of the learning of social graces my parents took me with them to say goodbye to an elderly lady who had once been a neighbor as she was about to depart from this life.

Stepdad was the one who taught me about people being different in background, race, family origin, education, social status, etc. He would point out a person and tell me their story. So I had begun learning something of my place and relationship to others.

My socioeconomic status was never an issue growing up. I was just where I was and others were where they were. No big deal. There were only a couple times I realized my place. One summer I was working with my Stepdad painting the outside of a house. The owner of the house was a doctor, whose son was my classmate. The son was quite uppity and delighted in making a poor boy like me feel beneath him. I felt as though I was not painting his parents' house, but I was painting his house and therefore serving him. He was not at home at the time and I hoped he would not come home while I was there, which he did not. I was glad when that job was done. The other time I was a sophomore in high school. A freshman girl invited me to a country club dance. I knew she lived in a nice neighborhood and the country club was for rich people and the one suit I had was a wee bit too large. I declined the invitation and stayed within my own environment.

Stepdad also taught me that Communism was bad. However, I do not remember being taught about Socialism. For that matter, I do not remember being taught that we lived as a Capitalist nation, under a free Republic. It would take me decades for that.

Children were to be seen and not heard. This meant not interfering with, disrupting or disturbing adults and staying out of the way. For the most part, we entertained ourselves both inside and outside of the home. However, there were naturally times of interaction with adults as we got older.

We were in what was called a Cold War, with Communist Russia, who had been our ally during WWII against Socialist Germany. Besides spying on each other, Russia and the United States were in competition on everything such as space race, nuclear buildup, foreign aid, etc. I remember a *Life* magazine cover, with the printing on it concerning who was better academically; Ivan or Johnny, with Ivan being the Russian student and Johnny being the American student.

I Could Have Been One

The first President I remember is Dwight D. (Ike) Eisenhower, who served in the office from 1953 to 1961. I had heard adults say he was elected due to his having been the highest ranking general in World War II, who succeeded in defeating the Nazi's. Therefore he would be a leader to bring peace and security to our Nation. The only thing I actually remember about him is his taking many trips to Florida to play golf, which the news media seemed to always give a full report of. Later in a college class we were studying about our Nation's Presidents. Each one fell into one of the basic presidential categories. Ike was in the do-nothing category. Well…maybe he was, but then did he have to do anything except represent our Nation during the time of post WWII rebuilding? And how many deals were made on the golf course?

Haunted Fifties entry for June 13, 1953 is as follows:

> "Elisenhower" is as much and no more to the left than were Landon, Willkie and Dewey. In a two-party system, under normal conditions, both parties play as close to the center as possible. This leaves both the Republican right and the Democratic left dissatisfied but since they have nowhere else to go they exercise no leverage. At the moment, while the Republicans are thus 'left,' the Democrats are 'right.' In fact some of them are shopping around for a more conservative candidate…."

While the *Haunted Fifties* is a good study on the political movements and ideas of the time, I am not going into such a study in this writing of that time as it is my purpose to present only what I remember from growing into adulthood. I do believe the writer, Stone, tried to view all aspects of a situation.

In schools, we were trained to "duck and cover", in preparation for a nuclear attack or the resulting fallout of one. We would duck down to the floor and move under the cover of our school desk. Not so sure that would have really helped though. I guess it was a case of some kind of action was better than none at all and gave some sense of security in light of the conversations we kids heard between adults about a possible attack from Communist Russia during the Cold War. However, young kids did not dwell on such things or know the seriousness of it all.

Another aspect of the Cold War was action within our own country. United States Senator Joseph McCarthy, who obtained the position of Chairman of the Senate's Committee on Government Operations, began investigations into Communist activities within the United States. At the same time, FBI Director J. Edgar Hoover authorized such investigations. As a side note, in I.F. Stone's September 5, 1953 entry, he uses the term "antiliberal" in regards to Hoover. So even back in the 1950s the term "liberal" was being used to describe a political position and it was not a good position, in respect to conservative. I remember McCarthy going after Hollywood personalities claiming they were Communist.

In 1956, the so-called Russian Satellite Country also known as "Iron Curtain Country" of Hungary saw a rebellion by its citizens against its Soviet Russian ruling occupiers. Decades later I would read a small paperback book titled *Bridge at Andau* by James Michener. It was published the year following the failed Revolution. Hungarians were interviewed after they had crossed over the bridge connecting Hungary with Austria, outside the village of Andau. Michener changed the names of the people involved. Sometimes he combined stories of more than one person. This was all done to protect not only the person he interviewed, but also family that had to be left behind. I found it to be a fascinating read of real people committing real acts of bravery. Even Russian occupation solders fought beside the Hungarian people. In one case protecting the Hungarian citizen fighters from the Russian KGB also known as State Secret Police. It was after that the Russian government decided to place its occupation soldiers on two year rotation tours of duty so they would not come to view the occupied as humans to be treated as they themselves would want to be treated. In searching for information on the book, for this writing, I found it for sale and ordered it.

There was also a saying of "Better dead than Red" meaning it was better not to live at all than to live under Communist totalitarian rule. Communist China was also called Red China. "Red" was used for the Communist due to the red star worn on the military uniforms and the red of their flags, with the hammer and sickle on it. Later I would learn the saying also meant it was better, for American military, to commit suicide than to be captured by Communist forces, who would torture and conduct brainwashing to turn one against their own country by controlling their mental thinking process through stress coercion, drugs and psychological techniques. (Online reference Dictionary.com "Brainwashing".)

The 1960s film *Manchurian Candidate* staring Frank Sinatra was based on such mind control of American Prisoners Of War, by North Korea during the Korean Conflict of the 1950s.

Boy and Girl Scout Troops were available to enjoy learning opportunities, which might last a lifetime, as well as leadership development and achievement abilities. I held my first leadership position in the Boy Scouts. One of the things we could learn was the Morse Code. Girls did not want to join the Boy Scouts and homosexuality was not spoken of and therefore not taught or learned.

For boys who wanted to earn some cash, one could mow lawns or be a paperboy. My first professional position was that of paperboy. It was also my first business position as I established a customer base and grew the business of both residential women and professional men as well as hawking my papers on the downtown street. One winter, when my Stepdad could not get work, I supported us on the revenue from my paper route.

Radio stations delivered the news at certain times of the day early morning, at lunch and in the evening. Television stations were not aired twenty-four hours a day and seven days a week. I do not remember when the broadcasting time began, except that it was early morning with the news, but do remember after-school and weekend broadcasting. Teens rushed home to watch televised *Dick Clark's American Bandstand*. Westerns and other shows aired after school, which were advertised by school kids' tin lunch boxes. Most of those TV programs I saw parts of through a paper customer's front screen door. Television airing ended at midnight. Every station formally signed off of the air with the instrumental playing of our Country's National Anthem and the television screen was filled with the off-of-the-air logo and emitted static sound. That logo is forever implanted into the minds of many of us older generation.

Between the television, radio and newspaper, people kept up on current events such as Fidel Castro's revolutionary progress, Communist Russia's actions, the latest from Washington, D.C. and the tactics of the Republicans and the Democrats. Locally it was which church was having what activity and the same with service organizations, what business was opening, closing or changing and who was in what vehicle accident, where and the results of the accident along with public announcements of marriage, birth and death, etc.

Oh…television was first in black and white, only later did color come into view. Same thing with the movies, which began with no sound and the actors being very animated. Before the movie was the latest news and a cartoon.

During the '50s, Fidel Castro led Communist revolutionaries, in Cuba, against the forces of Cuban President Batista and finally won victory in 1959. He established the first Communist country in the America's. (Online reference Wikipedia "Fidel Castro".)

Involvement in one's community was also taught. Stepdad was a member of a service organization. I was a member of a church organization and volunteered for both school and church activities. Both Mom and Dad would at times volunteer their time for church or school activities.

Long story short is I grew up in a post-world war, Christian, conservative, patriotic, earn one's way, be of value, contribute to the community, anti-Communist environment, in a Southern atmosphere. Times were simpler, less confusing and straight forwardly uncomplicated. One knew about cause and effect, taking responsibility for one's actions and not being entitled except to what was earned. There were sayings such as "Buyer beware.", "There is no such thing as a free lunch.", "For God and Country." and "As American as apple pie".

Folklore had it George Washington admitted to his father he could not tell a lie and he did indeed chop down the cherry tree and Abe Lincoln was known as Honest Abe.

In 1959, Nikita Khrushchev stated, "You Americans are so gullible. No, you won't accept communism outright, but we'll keep feeding you small doses of socialism until you'll finally wake up and find you already have communism. We won't have to fight you. We'll so weaken your economy until you'll fall like overripe fruit into our hands." (Online reference azquotes.com)

1960s

I remember seeing, on television, a news report showing Nikita Khrushchev, who was then the General Secretary of the Communist Party of the Soviet Union and the leader of Communist Russia or U.S.S. R., banging on the table during the United Nations General Assembly meeting with his shoe and shouting, "We will bury you from within!!!!!" He was addressing America. That is what I remember. (Online reference Nova Online "Khrushchev at the United Nations….")

However, I researched the incident online and all I could find was confusion, but it is all about his shoe banging and not one mention concerning what he said. But I remember what he said as do other people of my generation. It was a memorable moment during the Cold War. The confusion is if he did actually take off his shoe and bang it on the table, if he had a third shoe he banged on the table, if he simply had a slipper he symbolically waved in the air and slapped down on the table, did he actually have no shoe or slipper and banged his fist instead or did he not do any of that.

I could care not what he did as the important issue is what he said. "We will bury you from within!!!!!"

It was not until I enrolled in a basic law class in 2002, that I learned the 1960s was a time of Federal Civil Rights laws being passed down to the States. During the 1960s, I was in the military and afterwards drifting around and pretty much out of the news loop.

It was the decade of the Cultural Revolution, in which the drug culture began, with the youngest generation revolting against what they saw as the hypocrisy of parents having had instructed them to do as they were told and not what the adults did and against the sins of both law enforcement and a warring government.

San Francisco, at Height and Ashbury, became a "flower child" center of so-called hippies enjoying an existence of independent communal lifestyle, with no obligations as free spirits, with free love, in expanding the mind with LSD, while floating free feeling the vibrations of Rock music and psychedelic art. According to a magazine article I read some time ago some of those hippies now own businesses in that community and some joined "The Establishment".

An interest grew in both the martial arts and religions of the Far East, including discovering and activating one's metaphysical third eye and chakra centers of the body.

The 1960s was also the decade of the Viet Nam War, which would go into the 1970s lasting a decade worth of years, for the United States. For South Viet Nam, war was longer than that, for they had previously defeated the French occupiers. They had done so as a country. Then the Viet Cong revolutionaries of South Viet Nam rose up against the United States supported South Vietnamese government. Their goal was to overthrow that government and replace it with a Communist government. Now that was a civil war, a revolution. Like many others, I was involved before the American populace even knew we were involved.

It was also a time of political revolution in the United States, as demonstrated by the anti-war riot at the 1968 Democratic Convention in Chicago. Anti-war protests were prevalent on college campuses. However, the one held at Kent State University on May 4, 1970 by approximately five hundred students, resulting in the shooting and deaths of students, by the Ohio Army National Guard, was the most noted because of its tragedy. Now all of those involved, both student and Guardsmen, including their families, have to live with that day for the rest of their lives. In the words of Forrest Gump, "That is all I am going to say about that." (Reference movie *Forrest Gump*, with Tom Hanks.)

The Registration, for the Draft, resulting in military service was in full operation. Unlike WWII there was a much higher percentage of men drafted, than those who volunteered. Exemptions were made for college students and employees working for a company with a government contract. In 1970, the exemption for college students was removed. There were cases of young men receiving their draft notices and deciding to escape into Canada.

Even Elvis Presley was not exempt. He was assigned duty with an armor unit stationed in Germany. The same armor unit that my Father served with, during WWII. *Life* magazine published a feature article on his induction into the Army, including a photo of his hair being cut off. But he was Elvis. He was still "Cool". The news media still paid attention to him even among all of the war and anti-war attention.

However, when the boxing champion, Mohammed Ali also known as Cassius Clay, received his draft notice he did not follow Elvis' example in performing his obligation to his country. There was a black pattern of thinking concerning why should they fight for a country which did not appreciate them, saw them as unequal to whites and had enslaved their ancestors. In this case, he was also a Black Muslim, which was why he had changed his name. This American black religious group claimed to be Islamic, however, it is my understanding the group was not accepted by the actual Muslims of the Middle East due to differences in beliefs. The black religious group also was a Separatist group wanting to live completely in isolation, from the whites. They and the Ku Klux Klan had common ground as they both agreed on total separation.

Mohammed Ali filed as a Conscientious Objector, to military service, based on his religious beliefs as well as his anti-American involvement in Viet Nam beliefs. He was denied the status, prosecuted and stripped of his championship title. Eventually the United States Supreme Court overruled the decision of the Draft Appeal Board based on the fact the Board had not given him a reason for the appeal rejection. (Online reference Biography On Line under name.)

In 1961, the Berlin Wall was constructed while Berliners were fast asleep. When they woke the next morning, whatever side of the wall they went to sleep on was where they were to stay. West Berliners, in the American, English and French sectors of post WWII Germany could no longer travel into the Russian sector to visit relatives and friends. Likewise East Berliners could no longer travel into West Berlin for visiting and attending cultural and sports events. There was travel between the East and West, but it was highly limited and controlled. One had to be traveling on official business. (Online reference ThoughtCo "Rise and Fall of the Berlin Wall".)

Although the Cold War, between the United States of America along with other western countries such as England, and the Union of Soviet Socialist Republics also known as Communist Russia now known as the Commonwealth of Independent States, began as soon as WWII ended and Russia began to isolate their occupied sector of East Germany. Soon the Wall presented both a physical and symbolic separation between Communist Russia and the "Free World". Later it would be torn down.

While I was living in the Los Angeles area, I met a German man. He had lived behind the Wall, on the East German side. He joined two or three families being led by another man in escaping through no-man's land and into a spot between two watch towers. However, the group leader was shot down and killed before reaching the Wall. This man took the lead and got those families to and over the Wall and into the hands of U.S. soldiers.

Amidst all of this turbulence of Cultural Revolution, I began to drift away from the teachings of my growing up years. Not because of the war in Nam or the cultural movement, but because I did not use those teachings to guide my thought processing, which guided my behavior. I did not question the right or the wrong of situations and I abided by a live and let live philosophy. I also began drinking and killing my conscience bit by bit, by performing small acts of lying, cheating, stealing, which led to more serious acts. Little by little I damaged the connection to my conscience. I no longer prayed or attended church. I had drifted away. I did not plan to. It just happened. Happened because of my thoughtless, undisciplined actions.

After enlisting in the military, I attended church during basic training. Doing so was encouraged by training commanders and there were other Christians in the training unit. However, once graduated from basic training and I was attending the basic school for my future military service specialty, my mind was on spending the weekend off base. Sometimes I attended church and sometimes I did not. Mostly I attended because of a young lady. Later, in the advance school, I did the same. Once I was assigned to a unit, to serve the rest of my obligated time with, I sometimes attended church. Attendance depended first of all if I had the duty that weekend and secondly if I felt like going. It did not occur to me that I was forming a habit. I was replacing the habit of attending church with the habit of not attending. It was that simple. Eventually I was not interested in church any more. Once I turned twenty-one, I graduated into the bar and night club life. The only thing I wanted to do on Sunday morning was to have a Bloody Mary, for my hangover.

I had always been the good kid; most of the time. I was dedicated to church life. That was my growing up. However, in looking back, it is as though that was what I was expected to do, by a Christian/Conservative raising. Not that all Conservatives are Christian or that all Christians are Conservative; just that it was my raising. It gave me purpose and a lifestyle, for my teen years.

I believe this same process occurs with a great many young people. They are away from home and on their own. They find other interests. If one is in college, there is of course study time and college activities. Plus one must find a church off campus unless it is a Christian college. If one is not away from home, it is a matter of finding their own space and activities and going into their own as adults. There is also one's social life and love attraction influence and the influences, in general, of people and places and things such as social media of the day, entertainment.

Both teens and young adults are impressionable and do not have a lot of life experience. They live in the here and now sometimes not giving a care to the future, but just going through the process of trying to be independent and go one's own way. Some fail to realize their parents and grandparents and those of the older generations do have life experience to learn from. But sometimes one does not think about that, for it is as though the offspring never thinks about the fact the older generations were not always such; they were once young too. Even if the younger generation does factually realize it, they do not think about what that actually means.

Going to church was just something a family did, but why is that important to continue? What does all of that stuff really mean anyway? I needed a break. I wanted to just do my own thing. Therefore it needs to be taught why it is important. The child cannot just learn about Christianity. They have to be taught the meaning of Christianity and why they should follow Jesus.

When I did go home, after being released from military active duty, Saturdays were hard for me. Mom and Dad expected me to go downtown shopping with them. It actually was more than an expectation, it was verbally forceful. Upon meeting someone, Dad would declare that I had arrived home from the military and had been in Viet Nam. Saying I was home from the military was okay, but not the declaring I was in Nam. I would get compassionate looks and statements indicating sympathy for me. There were a great many more young men who had served in a much greater capacity than I did. I did not want to be felt sorry for. I know people meant well, but it embarrassed me. I would always politely acknowledge their concern by answering any questions or replying to any comments.

Maybe Dad was proud of me and wanted to show me off. Maybe he wanted the attention by extension. Whatever the reason even if subconscious, I did not want attention. And being made to go shopping with them gave me the feeling of being a kid; like when I was growing up. I began to purposefully not be home around the time they would leave for shopping, which would be commented about when I did get home. I did not stay back home very long. I broke away.

I do not believe I am unique. The preceding is a part of my story and an example of how young people want to break from the growing-up years and even their parents.

While I was in the military, we received word Russia was sending ships loaded with long-range missiles, to Communist Cuba. This was a threat to American peace and welfare. President John F. Kennedy communicated with the U.S.S.R. President Khrushchev and finally issued orders for the US Navy to blockade Cuba against the Russian ships. If the Russian ships continued to sail for Cuba, they would be fired upon under the authority of the Monroe Doctrine, which states protection of the Americas from non-North, Central and South American sources. Khrushchev waited until the last minute to recall the ships back to their own country.

There was also a 1960s incident between the U.S. Navy and Communist China. International waters begin at three miles from a country's coastline, at least at that time. One of our naval ships was sailing outside the three miles, off the coast of China, but within eleven miles of its coast. China contacted the ship and claimed coastal waters started at the eleven-mile mark. It instructed our ship to leave and sail beyond the eleven mile mark or be fired upon. Three Naval aircraft carrier task forces were assembled and sailed toward China and passed the eleven mile mark. They commenced to sail between the eleven and the three mile mark waiting for China's shore batteries to fire on them. The batteries did not. The task forces sailed such a pattern day after day, for some time. After a decent amount of time of challenging the Communist Chinese without incident, we sailed away to continue routine operations.

During that sailing around, booklets titled "What To Do If You Become a Prisoner Of War" were passed out. And that was when reality set in. I had joined the Navy to get away from home and see the world, but I had also taken an oath to protect America from enemies both foreign and domestic.

The next incident was the South Viet Nam revolution, by the Communist Viet Cong supported by Communist North Viet Nam supported by Communist China. We were told if we did not stop Communism there, we would have to stop it at our back door. That justified the war to us.

It was during the '60s that Fidel Castrol established a Communist Cuba and began to influence Central and South America. And those freedom-loving Cubans were braving the waters between their home country and the United States, to continue to live in freedom. It was the tide of freedom loving Cubans fleeing to the United States, from the tide of Communism in their home country.

Post military I began to just exist, while moving from one situation to the next without thinking of others and my relationship with them. I was floating through life meaninglessly not knowing what I wanted to obtain or where I wanted to go. At least for the most part, I had no educational or professional goals and therefore no objectives. My only goal was to have a roof over my head, clothes on my back and food in my stomach, which did not always happen. I did not like myself much less love myself and therefore I was incapable of loving anyone else. I destroyed what relationships I did have until I had none.

During the '60s, the beginning of the evolution of "Colored People" into the "Black People" was a correct course of action; even the development of the original Black Panther Party to protect their people from injustice seemed to be good. Now…in reading the exact wording of writings of a War Between the States Union soldier, he refers to black people as…well…"black.". So that term is not new. It was a term used by at least some white people long ago. Most likely it depended on what area of the country a person was from and their education level as to how a black person was addressed.

Also during that time period, I came across a non-Christian religion that made sense to me as I had drifted away from my own Faith. One of its major teachings was the acceptance of all people; White (European descent), Black (African descent), Brown (Hispanic descent), Red (American Indian/Native American descent), Yellow (Oriental descent). It is interesting how we give color names to races, when we are all some shade of the same flesh color from a very fair tone to a very dark tone. I suppose it is easier that way, to identify one another. If one places a sheet of white, black, brown, red and yellow construction paper up against a member of that so-called color race, none of the construction paper looks anything like the skin tones of those races.

I phased in and out of that religion for about twenty years. It did hold within it what seemed to make sense and the equality of blacks and whites. That was satisfactory for me, but I had become a fallen-away Christian as I was not practicing Christianity. I was not only a drifted-away Christian, but also a fallen-away Christian.

Because of its One God, One Planet, One People belief, my Stepfather asked me if I was sure it was not a Communist front. At the time, I had no idea why he was relating that belief to Communism. I only knew I needed to back him off in such a way that he would understand. I stated, "I did not kill Communist in Nam only to come home and join them." He was satisfied.

When I enlisted, he had tried to talk to me about what a person may go through in the military, in war. He could not. He had only observed the effects of such service. He had not served in war. He told me that I might change, but he was not talking about maturing.

When I was selling newspapers downtown, one of my customers, who worked at a laundry business, always liked my smile. She instructed me to never lose it. I did, during my military service.

It was not my hometown that I immediately went to once my active duty military service was completed. With the exception of my parents, I felt I did not have a reason to go back home. Also Mom and I had not been getting along very well, when I had been home, while I was in the military. She did not care for my bar life. This was the person who had went nightclubbing during her young days. A longtime friend would much later refer to me as being somewhat on the rough side back then, as it was during my drinking and running around days. Upon being released from military duty, I decided to first go and visit some people I had met in California, when they were on vacation. So I went to their home state and town instead of my own.

My second day there I was taken over to some friends of my friends. We had no sooner arrived, when the mailman arrived. Among the mail was an item the lady of the house was confused about and had no idea what it was or why it was been mailed to her. My friends looked at it and did not recognize the item either. It was passed to me and I had an emotional reaction to it. It was a Communist newspaper. I had killed Communist only to come home and discover they were operating openly in my own country. They had come above ground.

The newspaper had been produced locally by a Communist cell. It was a bulk mailing most likely using the telephone book to send to random people. It was legal under our freedom of speak. I had fought for that freedom. I had fought for Communist to use our own freedom against us.

When I was a very young child, in the late 1940s, my Mother would tuck me into bed, on a Sunday night, and turn the radio on. I remember three shows broadcasting over the airwaves, *The Shadow*, *I Was a Communist for the FBI*, and *The Blackwood Brothers*, who were Gospel singers. *I Was a Communist for the FBI* told the adventures of an FBI agent who had infiltrated an American Communist Party underground spy cell. (Online reference *I Was a Communist for the FBI*.)

While I was in the military and post-military drifting around status, from one place to another, our society continued to change. The United States Congress and Presidents enacted legislation as the Supreme Court interpreted the meaning of the wording of the United States Constitution as challenges were presented. Federal law began to be passed down to the States mandating that this and that would or would not be done.

Much of this was due to various society changing, counterculture movements such as Civil Rights, Feminism. It is not my intention to give a history of those movements, with relevant legislation, but only to demonstrate events which challenged our thinking causing some decision points in our lives. Those of us of the older generation lived that history and the younger generations learn it in school, at least I hope they do. But just what did we believe and why? Did our traditional thinking require adjustments?

Civil Rights covered not only law enforcement actions, from stating what became an individual's Miranda Rights to anti-police brutality, but also destroyed those Jim Crow Laws as a result of the Black Civil Rights Movement spearheaded by Reverend Martin Luther King, Jr. General overall legislation was developed, under the Civil Rights Act of 1964, with the Equal Employment Opportunity Commission implementing it. No one was to be discriminated against due to race, color, sex, religion or national origin. The Civil Rights movement and legislation was long overdue, in my opinion. (Online reference History.com "The Miranda Rights…".)

While the Black Civil Rights Movement centered on the Southern States because of the Jim Crow laws which were instituted there post-America's War Between the States/Reconstruction, it also went to Washington D.C. Such legislation was required not only in the Southern States, but also all across the United States. (Online references: History.com "Civil Rights Movement", The Free Dictionary "Jim Crow Laws", National Archives "Civil Rights Act of 1964…".)

Although the Movement was by large majority a black movement, with some white people joining in to support, there was another aspect involved; that of police brutality against not only black people, but also against whites; poor whites. A black boy might be beaten worse, in a back room of a police station, with a rubber hose, but a white poor boy could suffer the same fate. This happened in the good, old days, where I grew up. Oh…Southern environment does not just include the Deep South, but also those States directly above the Deep South as well as some immediately west of the Mississippi River.

White prejudice against black people was not only in the Southern States, but also in Northern States; just as black prejudice against white people was. As a teenager I witnessed the development of suburbs. Whites relocated from inner-city housing and apartments out to the edges of cities, in brand new, housing developments; suburbs. This was part of the post-war growth, of our Nation. Black people took advantage of the opportunity and relocated out of their traditional neighborhoods and into traditional white neighborhoods, where whites had vacated. Whites still living there had a choice; either move or adjust to living beside blacks.

Remember the 1970s television series *All in the Family* with Archie Bunker? Remember when the black family of George Jefferson moved in next door? (Online reference IMDB *All in the Family*.)

The saying, at the time, was if black people moved into a white neighborhood, then the real estate would go down. Another was that black people were trashy. I cannot verify the real estate saying, but I can verify the one about being trashy as I witnessed it. Therefore I will accept that, in general, that aspect of the situation was true, at least at the time, just as there was/is "white trash". In either case, there is a lack of respect for one's self and surroundings and the actions of the adults are passed on to the children. The trashy aspect was counteracted later on as black professionals and those with self-respect relocated into predominately white neighborhoods. The trash aspect may be what caused the real estate to go down. Also, if white people were shown a house to purchase in a neighborhood, they might not purchase once they discovered that coloreds lived there. Therefore the price of the housing would have to be lowered, in order to sell the property, including to blacks of lower income. This occurred in a Northern State, where my Mother had family, whom we visited and sometimes lived.

At that time I also heard of white neighborhood action being taken against black people, in the form of an unofficial neighborhood watch, with the intent of keeping an eye on black people just driving through the neighborhood, in case of trouble.

What I did not know and would not discover until much later in life is the city of my Mother's family was a center for the Ku Klux Klan. The Klan was also known to be in California, in the '80s. So the Klan was not just in Southern States, although it had been first established in the Deep South.

A couple issues require mentioning here. One, when the slaves began to be imported from Africa to the Americas, they were also imported to the northern States of this Country. However, because of the harshness of the northern winters, the slaves would die. The slaves imported to the southern States fared better and adapted. Therefore slavery in the North was not a profitable investment. Only later, after generational adapting in the South, was the runaway slave able to survive in the North. Two, ever heard of white slavery? England enslaved the Irish and sent them here to be worked. There were also indentured servants, who for one reason or another, had to work for a master to pay off a debt. This included children sold into debt by English parents. Sometimes both a wife and children, who had no rights.

Also in the '60s were the Black Race Riots. Everyone heard about them, including me. Black people rioted in some major cities, with one of the most notable being the Watts Riots, in Los Angeles. A peculiar aspect was that they were race riots, in which grievances against white treatment of blacks were being protested against, but the black people did not attack white people. They attacked their own neighborhoods and burnt them. Both emergency services, of fire and police, were called into action. The Army National Guard was activated, by the respective State Governors, to maintain the rioters within their own burning neighborhoods as well as to protect the emergency services personnel. It was through the black church communities that peace was established and maintained, in some future situations even into the 1990s. Such rioting accomplished nothing positive except to let the negative element know that the positive element would not allow their own to be destroyed. On the one hand it damaged the black movement, while on the other hand it did bring respect to the black Christians and their leaders.

As stated earlier there was also the Feminist Movement, which was nothing new in the Twentieth Century as it began in 1848, which was before the

War Between the States. Since I feel it is important to show the progression, I am presenting their time table of events as follows:

1848: The first women's rights convention is held in Seneca Falls, New York. After 2 days of discussion and debate, 68 women and 32 men sign a Declaration of Sentiments, which outlines grievances and sets the agenda for the women's rights movement. A set of 12 resolutions is adopted calling for equal treatment of women and men under the law and voting rights for women.

1850: The first National Women's Rights Convention takes place in Worcester, Mass., attracting more than 1,000 participants. National conventions are held yearly (except for 1857) through 1860.

1869:
May: Susan B. Anthony and Elizabeth Cady Stanton form the National Woman Suffrage Association. The primary goal of the organization is to achieve voting rights for women by means of a Congressional amendment to the Constitution.

November: Lucy Stone, Henry Blackwell, and others form the American Woman Suffrage Association. This group focuses exclusively on gaining voting rights for women through amendments to individual state constitutions.

December 10: The territory of Wyoming passes the first women's suffrage law. The following year women begin serving on juries in the territory.

1890: The National Women Suffrage Association and the American Women Suffrage Association merge to form the National American

Woman Suffrage Association (NAWSA). As the movement's mainstream organization, NAWSA wages state-by-state campaigns to obtain voting rights for women.

1893: Colorado is the first state to adopt an amendment granting women the right to vote. Utah and Idaho follow suit in 1896, Washington State in 1910, California in 1911, Oregon, Kansas, and Arizona in 1912, Alaska and Illinois in 1913, Montana and Nevada in 1914, New York in 1917; Michigan, South Dakota, and Oklahoma in 1918.

1896: The National Association of Colored Women is formed, bringing together more than 100 black women's clubs. Leaders in the black women's club movement include Josephine St. Pierre Ruffin, Mary Church Terrell, and Anna Julia Cooper.

1903: The National Women's Trade Union League (WTUL) is established to advocate for improved wages and working conditions for women.

1913: Alice Paul and Lucy Burns form the Congressional Union to work toward the passage of a federal amendment to give women the vote. The group is later renamed the National Women's Party. Members picket the White House and practice other forms of civil disobedience.

1916: Margaret Sanger opens the first U.S. birth-control clinic in Brooklyn, N.Y. Although the clinic is shut down 10 days later and Sanger is arrested, she eventually wins support through the courts and opens another clinic in New York City in 1923.

1919: The federal woman suffrage amendment, originally written by Susan B. Anthony and introduced in Congress in 1878, is passed by the House of Representatives and the Senate. It is then sent to the states for ratification.

1920: The Women's Bureau of the Department of Labor is formed to collect information about women in the workforce and safeguard good working conditions for women.

August 26, 1920: The 19th Amendment to the Constitution, granting women the right to vote, is signed into law by Secretary of State Bainbridge Colby.

1921: Margaret Sanger founds the American Birth Control League, which evolves into the Planned Parenthood Federation of America in 1942.

1935: Mary McLeod Bethune organizes the National Council of Negro Women, a coalition of black women's groups that lobbies against job discrimination, racism, and sexism.

1936: The federal law prohibiting the dissemination of contraceptive information through the mail is modified and birth control information is no longer classified as obscene. Throughout the 1940s and 50s, birth control advocates were engaged in numerous legal suits.

1955: The Daughters of Bilitis (DOB), the first lesbian organization in the United States, is founded. Although DOB originated as a social group, it later developed into a political organization to win basic acceptance for lesbians in the United States.

1960: The Food and Drug Administration approves birth control pills.

1961: President John Kennedy establishes the President's Commission on the Status of Women and appoints Eleanor Roosevelt as chairwoman. The report issued by the Commission in 1963 documents substantial discrimination against women in the workplace and makes specific recommendations for improvement, including fair hiring practices, paid maternity leave, and affordable child care.

1963: Betty Friedan publishes her highly influential book *The Feminine Mystique*, which describes the dissatisfaction felt by middle-class American housewives with the narrow role imposed on them by society. The book becomes a best-seller and galvanizes the modern women's rights movement.

June 10, 1963: Congress passes the Equal Pay Act, making it illegal for employers to pay a woman less than what a man would receive for the same job.

1964: Title VII of the Civil Rights Act bars discrimination in employment on the basis of race and sex. At the same time it establishes the Equal Employment Opportunity Commission (EEOC) to investigate complaints and impose penalties.

1965: In *Griswold* v. *Connecticut*, the Supreme Court strikes down the one remaining state law prohibiting the use of contraceptives by married couples.

1966: The National Organization for Women (NOW) is founded by a group of feminists including Betty Friedan. The largest women's rights group in the U.S., NOW seeks to end sexual discrimination, especially in the workplace, by means of legislative lobbying, litigation, and public demonstrations.

1967: Executive Order 11375 expands President Lyndon Johnson's affirmative action policy of 1965 to cover discrimination based on gender. As a result, federal agencies and contractors must take active measures to ensure that women as well as minorities enjoy the same educational and employment opportunities as white males.

1968: The EEOC rules that sex-segregated help wanted ads in newspapers are illegal. This ruling is upheld in 1973 by the Supreme Court, opening the way for women to apply for higher-paying jobs hitherto open only to men.

1969: California becomes the first state to adopt a "no fault" divorce law, which allows couples to divorce by mutual consent. By 1985 every state has adopted a similar law. Laws are also passed regarding the equal division of common property.

1970: In *Schultz v. Wheaton Glass Co.*, a U.S. Court of Appeals rules that jobs held by men and women need to be "substantially equal" but not "identical" to fall under the protection of the Equal Pay Act. An employer cannot, for example, change the job titles of women workers in order to pay them less than men.

1971: *Ms. Magazine* is first published as a sample insert in *New York* magazine; 300,000 copies are sold out in 8 days. The first regular issue is published in July 1972. The magazine becomes the major forum for feminist voices, and cofounder and Editor Gloria Steinem is launched as an icon of the modern feminist movement.

1972:

March 22: The Equal Rights Amendment (ERA) is passed by Congress and sent to the states for ratification. Originally drafted by Alice Paul in 1923, the amendment reads: "Equality of rights under the law shall not be denied or abridged by the United States or by any State on account of sex." The amendment died in 1982 when it failed to achieve ratification by a minimum of 38 states.

Also on March 22: In *Eisenstadt* v. *Baird* the Supreme Court rules that the right to privacy includes an unmarried person's right to use contraceptives.

June 23: Title IX of the Education Amendments bans sex discrimination in schools. It states: "No person in the United States shall, on the basis of sex, be excluded from participation in, be denied the benefits of, or be subjected to discrimination under any educational program or activity receiving federal financial assistance." As a result of Title IX, the enrollment of women in athletics programs and professional schools increases dramatically.

1973: As a result of *Roe* v. *Wade*, the Supreme Court establishes a woman's right to safe and legal abortion, overriding the anti-abortion laws of many states.

1974: The Equal Credit Opportunity Act prohibits discrimination in consumer credit practices on the basis of sex, race, marital status, religion, national origin, age, or receipt of public assistance.

In *Corning Glass Works* v. *Brennan*, the U.S. Supreme Court rules that employers cannot justify paying women lower wages because that is what they traditionally received under the "going market rate." A wage differential occurring "simply because men would not work at the low rates paid women" is unacceptable.

1976: The first marital rape law is enacted in Nebraska, making it illegal for a husband to rape his wife.

1978: The Pregnancy Discrimination Act bans employment discrimination against pregnant women. Under the Act, a woman cannot be fired or denied a job or a promotion because she is or may become pregnant, nor can she be forced to take a pregnancy leave if she is willing and able to work.

1984: EMILY's List (Early Money Is Like Yeast) is established as a financial network for pro-choice Democratic women running for national political office. The organization makes a significant impact on the increasing numbers of women elected to Congress.

1986: *Meritor Savings Bank v. Vinson*, the Supreme Court finds that sexual harassment is a form of illegal job discrimination.

1992: In *Planned Parenthood v. Casey*, the Supreme Court reaffirms the validity of a woman's right to abortion under *Roe v. Wade*. The case successfully challenges Pennsylvania's 1989 Abortion Control Act, which sought to reinstate restrictions previously ruled unconstitutional.

1994: The Violence Against Women Act tightens federal penalties for sex offenders, funds services for victims of rape and domestic violence, and provides for special training of police officers.

1996: In *United States v. Virginia*, the Supreme Court rules that the all-male Virginia Military School has to admit women in order to continue to receive public funding. It holds that creating a separate, all-female school will not suffice.

1999: The Supreme Court rules in *Kolstad v. American Dental Association* that a woman can sue for punitive damages for sex discrimination if the anti-discrimination law was violated with malice or indifference to the law, even if that conduct was not especially severe.

2003: In *Nevada Department of Human Resources v. Hibbs*, the Supreme Court rules that states can be sued in federal court for violations of the Family Leave Medical Act.

2005: In *Jackson v. Birmingham Board of Education*, the Supreme Court rules that Title IX, which prohibits discrimination based on sex, also inherently prohibits disciplining someone for complaining about sex-based discrimination. It further holds that this is the case even when the person complaining is not among those being discriminated against.

2006: The Supreme Court upholds the ban on the "partial-birth" abortion procedure. The ruling, 5–4, which upholds the Partial-Birth Abortion Ban Act, a federal law passed in 2003, is the first to ban a specific type of abortion procedure. Writing in the majority opinion, Justice Anthony Kennedy said, "The act expresses respect for the dignity of human life." Justice Ruth Bader Ginsburg, who dissents, called the decision "alarming" and said it is "so at odds with our jurisprudence" that it "should not have staying power."

2009: President Obama signed the Lily Ledbetter Fair Pay Restoration Act, which allows victims of pay discrimination to file a complaint with the government against their employer within 180 days of their last paycheck. Previously, victims (most often women) were allowed only 180 days from the date of the first unfair paycheck. This Act is named after a former employee of Goodyear who alleged that she was paid 15–40% less than her male counterparts, which was later found to be accurate.

2013: In Jan. 2013, Defense Secretary Leon Panetta announced that the ban on women serving in combat roles would be lifted. In a Jan. 9 letter to Panetta urging the change Joint Chiefs of Staff Chairman Gen. Martin Dempsey said, "The time has come to rescind the direct combat exclusion rule for women and to eliminate all unnecessary gender-based barriers to service." The move reverses the 1994 rule that prohibited women from serving in combat. The change will be gradual; some positions will be available to women immediately but each branch of the military has until 2016 to request exceptions to the new rule. By now women have been and are serving in combat.

(Online reference InfoPlease "Timeline – U.S. Women's Rights".)

Of course, now there are college studies on both the Civil Rights and Feminist movements as well as a treasure trove of publications.

Legislative action lead to the Affirmative Action Plan, which came out of the Civil Rights Act of 1964 and President Lyndon B Johnson's Executive Order 11246 and the Equal Protection Cause of the Fourteenth Amendment of the United States Constitution. The Amendment was ratified in 1868 and states in Section One as follows:

> "All persons born or naturalized in the United States and subject to the jurisdiction thereof, are citizens of the United States and of the State wherein they reside. No State shall make or enforce any law which shell abridge the privileges or immunities of citizens of the United States; nor shell

any State deprive any person of life, liberty, or property, without due process of law; nor deny to any person within its jurisdiction the equal protection of the laws."

The pros and cons of Affirmative Action have long been spoken sometimes with great assertion and aggression. Personally I have found it to be what was conceived as a positive action for the betterment of some people, but turned out to be reverse discrimination against white males and even more importantly a no-win situation for anyone for this reason. Quotas, for the hiring of minorities and women, were formulated. This meant employers had to hire a certain number even if the people were not or barely qualified. Therefore the best person, for the position, was not necessarily hired. The same applied to education. Colleges had to operate by human numbers. The Plan also dealt with minority business owners who were to be given special treatment, where Federal contracts were concerned. Therefore the best business, for the work to be performed, was not always contracted. (Online reference United States History "Affirmative Action".)

I was in a situation, which involved the advancement of a young, black man. Our white supervisor was all for Affirmative Action. He first saw to it a young, white woman was advanced into management training. In her case, it was deserved and she was qualified. When he wanted to advance the black man, the man hesitated, to give the proposition thought as he would be in a junior management position. He did not feel ready for such a position. The supervisor called in a young, black woman, who had recently been advanced into such a position. She talked the man into accepting the offer. I happened to overhear some of the conversation. She promoted the idea to him that he was obligated because of his race. She made him feel guilty. I felt then that I knew what would happen and hoped it did not as I liked that young man.

In some ways, he was qualified for the advanced position, but in some he was not. He tried and failed. I did not blame him. I blamed the white supervisor who wanted a "Look at me. I 'm an Affirmative Action supervisor." He wanted another feather in his cap. I blamed the woman, who used both the race card and the guilt tactic. I was the one who ended up cleaning out that man's desk and mailing his belongings to him. I hated that assignment.

He did not win. The only thing he gained was a temporary higher status that led to embarrassment and disgrace. The supervisor did not win, in the end. The woman did not win, in the end. The employer did not win as they had to hire and train another person, which cost money. And in the words of Forest Gump, "That is all I am going to say about that." (Online reference Wikipedia *Forrest Gump* and the 1994 movie *Forrest Gump* starring Tom Hanks.)

Was there need for enforced change? Yes! However, there is a proper way to conduct implementation. Congress has always been the subject of ridicule, but over time the justified rational, for such ridicule, has increased. It has increased to the point of the coming of the Death of Common Sense. And that is not just my opinion. I once read a poem on the subject that was floating around the email waves; the death of common sense, in general.

Not all protest movements and corrective legislations dealt with race and gender. There was also Freedom of Religion. The issue of prayer and Bible reading in public schools arose. While the final decision seems to have hung on the most noted case of atheist Madalyn Murray O'Hair, to draw out the pros and cons of Supreme Court Justices, it was actually hers and that of *Abington v. Schempp* combined in 1963. Schempp's was in Pennsylvania, while O'Hair's was in Maryland. The arguments dealt with both the First and Fourteenth Amendments and the issue of the separation of Church and State. (Online references Beliefnet "Who Was Madalyn Murray O'Hair?" and Scroll Publishing "Supreme Court: Ban on Prayer in Public Schools".)

The First Amendment is as follows: "Congress shall make no law respecting an establishment of religion, or prohibiting the free exercise thereof; or abridging the freedom of speech, or of the press, or the right of the people peaceably to assemble, and to petition the Government for a redress of grievances."

Prayer and Bible reading were removed, from public school classrooms and any school sponsored event such as school sports games. As in no public official could lead a prayer or read the Bible, before a sports game. However, there was a school principal announcing at the first football game of the season that government did not allow her to lead prayer, but anyone attending the game could. The whole stadium stood and prayed.

I had pretty much been out of the loop news-wise, during my military and drifting/lost years. I remember Civil Rights marches and sit-ins and demonstrations, but I do not remember what legislation was signed into law when. I remember the feminist movement, without really knowing what occurred. At the time, I did not have either a radio or television, nor did I subscribe to a newspaper. I also missed the Beatles and the Rock movement.

1970s

This time period was basically my lost decade.

Due to my moving around and not caring much about what happened to me, I did not maintain an employment position for very long. I had the G.I. Bill education benefits coming to me, but I did not have sense enough to go to a Veterans Affairs office or a college to check out the conditions of the benefits and what I could or could not do; even when a friend advised me to. I did not even think about the fact there were conditions. I just did not think. I was lost and drifting with the wind.

It took a man at an Employment Office enquiring if I would be interested in a government sponsored training program; a program for those of seemingly very little job skills. They were starting up a drafting program in partnership with the local college.

During my freshman year of high school, after asking about my interests, which I had an interest in art, my science teacher loaned me his monthly issue of *Architecture Digest*. I discovered Frank Lloyd Wright and that I had an interest in architecture. I wanted to be an architect. That was my college goal. I began to take as much math in high school as I could and a drafting course. However, when I enlisted in the military, that dream faded away.

I thought I could at least be an architectural draftsman. To my disappointment, the actual drafting portion of the course, which also included math, physics and English, was the same old mechanical drawing I had in high school, which I did not do well in. Then one night there was an industry speaker, who gave a presentation on what to expect after the course. All was well until he stated we would be working in a large office space, with a lot of other draftsmen. Each of us would be working on a different portion of the same project. I did not care to be just another draftsman. I never went back to the course after that night. Later I was contacted by the man at the Employment Office for an in-person interview. I was resigned from the course and placed back into the general unemployment pool. Much later I did obtain a drafting position, in which I worked at home performing architectural design modification. I really enjoyed it. It did not even seem like work and I would spend sometimes twelve to sixteen hours at the drafting table. Now it is all computerized. I suppose it is still fun as the creative aspect is still involved.

Another issue, which does concern gender, is abortion. When I was growing up, abortion was illegal as it was seen as taking a human life, except for medical reasons in saving the mother's life. It did happen for the pragmatic reasons of shame and embarrassment though. "What will people think if they know my teenage daughter is pregnant out of wedlock?" "What will my parents say, if they find out?" "What will people think of me if I have a baby and

I am not married?" One of the reasons used to support legalizing abortion was that deaths, of some women, had occurred. Some of the abortions had been in unsanitary, make-shift, operating rooms also known as back alley rooms.

In 1973, a decision was made, by the United States Supreme Court, in the case of *Roe v. Wade*. The name of Jane Roe was an alias. The defendant, Wade, was a Texas District Attorney. It became the landmark case granting abortion rights to women and leading to the Pro-abortion, Pro-life selections, of position, on the subject.

A lower court had used the Ninth Amendment to support their position on continued banning of abortion, which is as follows: "The enumeration in the Constitution, of certain rights, shall not be construed to deny or disparage others retained by the people."

However, the Supreme Court made its decision based on the Fourteenth Amendment.

(Online reference Thoughtco "*Roe v. Wade* Supreme Court Decision".)

While in my mid-twenties, I had the opportunity to visit Iceland. The non-Christian faith I was following at the time had a program for missionaries to other countries. I was talked into going to Iceland with another missionary and joining one already there. I figured it was a place I had not been to and it sounded interesting. It is the old settlement territory, of the Vikings, where the old Viking language was still spoken without much of it having changed. Not liking the black rioting situation and wanting to leave, before the whole nation went up in flames, I entertained the idea of living in Iceland or Europe. Upon hearing of my resignation to travel to Iceland, the Union Steward came to me and enquired about my doing so. The conversation went something like this:

You're going to Iceland?

Yeah.

Do you know that Iceland is a Socialist country?

No. Why?"

Socialism is Communism.

But Iceland is not a Communist country.

But it is a Socialist country. You might want to rethink what you're doing.

I had no idea about Socialism or why he said it was Communism. I went and enjoyed the Icelandic winter, on the edge of the Arctic Circle, followed by a western European winter of self-guided touring using Arthur Frommer's *Europe on Five Dollars a Day* and a thirty day Eurail Pass.

Upon returning to the States, I pretty much continued my drifting around, with nothing but survival objectives. At one point, I made use of the Food Stamp program. I did not think about if it was Socialism also known as Social Justice program. I required food. Not wanting to commit a crime to obtain money, I did what others were doing.

Around the beginning of this decade, I started to go through a process of moving toward trying to settle down. I still drifted, moving from one situation to another, having acquaintances here and there of whoever cared to have their life intersect with mine. I had left hard liquor behind having kind of drifted away from it, having only beer now and then. For one reason, beer was less expensive. I still had no goals and therefore no objectives and certainly no plan of action. My birth Father once called me a "will of the wisp", which today has many definitions, but he meant I wandered wherever circumstances led me, without discipline. I did begin to pray as I wanted to repair that communication line with God. I did begin to at least try to live a right way of life…sometimes. Looking back on it all maybe I realized, on some level, I was lost, in more ways than one.

Toward the end of the decade, I started to go through a process of praying more and deciding what I wanted in life. I wanted to stop drifting and have stability. The thought of education entered my mind.

At one point, when I was in between employment. I figured I could go to college, on the G.I. Bill, or I could find another job. I took the entrance test to a four year institution and figured I would do whatever presented itself first; college or employment. Employment it was and education was placed on the back burner.

I first became aware of the Chicano Civil Rights Movement, during the mid-1970s. However, that movement had its roots in the 1940s as the Mexican American Civil Rights Movement, which moved on into the '50s and '60s. It concerned Hispanic empowerment, in standing up and fighting for the betterment of life not only for farm workers, but also in taking on issues such as the restoration of land grants. (Online reference Wikipedia "Chicano Movement".)

There is still a Restoration or Reclamation movement wishing to take back American lands which were gained from Mexico, in the American Mexican War, of 1846-48. After Mexican forces were defeated in Mexico and a new Mexican government was formed, all lands north of the Rio Grande through what is now the American Southwest and on up into Utah and over into the mid and lower parts of California were sold by Mexico to the United States. While I have not studied the full history concerning such land grants at that time, it does not make sense to me that those lands would have been taken away from their owners. The land would have simply been in whatever territory existed at that time and therefore under the laws of that respective territory. Therefore the land would have been left to the families who had settled and developed the land. (Online reference History,com "Mexican-American War".)

The history of the City of Pleasanton, California and the Kottinger Family, who received a Mexican land grant for service to early Mexico, is a good example of this. I served with and am still a close friend of a Kottinger descendant.

In fact, I have learned giving land grants, for military service, was common practice, including for both the American Revolution and the War of 1812 to American soldiers, who then settled lands west of the original thirteen States.

Other issues taken up, by the American Hispanic movement were educational, voting and political rights as well as the education of America beyond the Mexican stereotype as seen in Hollywood movies or as only farm workers.

1980s

After marriage, I was around my wife's college friends, I noticed how knowledgeable they were and that they most likely would be advancing professionally. They had a profession. During my teen years, my Stepdad had informed me about educated fools as he called them; people with an education, but no common sense. When I talked about college to my Mother, she only offered reasons why I could not achieve such a dream; they could not afford to pay for college and working my way through college would really be hard. But I decided it was time to take advanced education off of the back burner.

The G.I. Bill benefits were only available for a ten year period. I began college right after the benefits had expired. Government guaranteed student loans financed my advanced education. It was a low interest rate and low monthly payments, but it seemed like forever to pay off.

When my wife became pregnant and I wanted to obtain increased revenue, I enlisted in the military again, by way of the National Guard and began to actually set goals and objectives. I began to live. I began to think. I was also working a fulltime night position and attending college part-time in the mornings. That was after I had a year of fulltime attendance, for my freshman year.

In the Random House College Dictionary, 1975 revised edition…oh… hard copy, the definition for *feminism* is "1. the doctrine advocating social and political rights for women equal to those of men, 2. … an organized movement for the attainment of such rights for women." It also has the definition for *women's liberation* as "a modern movement to gain full educational, social, and economic opportunities for women equal to those which men are traditionally understood to have." And below that for *women's rights* as "the political, legal, and social rights equal to those of men, claimed by and for women." Very similar definitions. However, in my opinion, *feminism* is being defined by the Feminist Movement itself. There should be more to the definition not involving the Movement.

I married a feminist, who did not associate herself with the formal Women's Liberation Movement, but who has always stood for equal rights of both women and men, while recognizing the differences between the two. I concur. A move, for me, from Conservative to Liberal?

When we met, she had recently graduated from college. We attended a private gathering, for some social occasion. This was during our courtship days. She warned me ahead of arriving at the event that I would be checked out and opinions would be formed by her lady college friends, who were also feminist. I passed.

After we were married, one of those friends spent so much time at our place that my wife gave her the title of "my other wife".

One Saturday as we were leaving our Married Student Housing apartment at the university, I discovered a Communist newspaper on my doorknob. Again I had an emotional reaction, which lasted all day, but it was much less reactive than sixteen years before.

After classes one day, some friends and I had gone into the cafeteria, for refreshments. I was approached by a young woman I assumed was also a student there. She tried to interest me in the newspaper she was promoting. It was Communist. I simply said I was not interested and she tried to further engage me in discussion concerning world affairs. Again I stated I was not interested, at which she tried to shame me. I told her in no uncertain terms to leave me alone. By then, my friends had joined me and we turned and seated ourselves at a booth. The woman followed us and began speaking to my friends. They began to answer her questions and I told her to leave. She stated she was not speaking to me, but to them and that she had a right to be there. I almost hit her! I got up and left instead. I have never hit a woman in my life.

My friends were foreign students. We were together on another occasion, when some other students, of my friends' home country, were having a promotion for the Communist cause, in their home country. They were also fund raising. That was when I learned that people, of such a cause, are not necessarily Communist in reality. They do not like the political/social conditions of their country and would accept the financial and other assistance from either the United States or Communist Russia, who competed for alliance throughout the world. Their home country was Iran and it was only a few years after the Iranian Revolution against the United States supported Shah. My friends could not go home.

I still had not learned the difference between Communism and Socialism though.

During my college days, working nights and weekends in commission sales, I was once again on the Food Stamp program since I was not able to bring in a proper amount of revenue for supporting a family.

It was during that time period I began to actually think about my actions, with increasing awareness of consequences. I began to think of other people and our country.

We moved into our starter house, which was a small bit of property good for a young family, in a new development. I felt guilty. I had achieved the American Dream, of home ownership, but around the corner from me in rental property were poor families. I had achieved what others had not. I had private property. I was a poor boy, who had achieved the American Dream, but who had begun to think as a Socialist, who do not believe in private property ownership. This made me an easy victim, of one of the less fortunate family men around the corner, who borrowed money from me.

As I settled in I did counter the guilty feeling by realizing I had achieved what I had by earning it. I had taken the goal of higher education off of the back burner, studied and worked day, night and weekends. I had both paid my own way and been on government assistance. I had been poor and had worked my way out. I had earned that little bit of the American Dream.

My wife began to stimulate my thinking concerning social issues. But she was not the only woman to do so. When "Pro-Life" and "Pro-Abortion" stimulated the third choice of "Pro-Choice", there was much general discussion on the issue of, "Which are you?" I had not really given any serious thought to the issue. I was just too busy making a living and raising a family.

By my raising, abortion was wrong because it took a life. However, pragmatic thinking allowed it. Such pro and con beliefs concerning the practice of abortion go back to Ancient Greece. So it has not been and is not now a new issue. It has only continued into our time, for us to decide for our own selves what we believe. (Online reference Abort73.com "Ancient Abortion History".)

It was a woman supervisor, who actually stimulated me into considering "Which am I?" She was pro-choice. I began to consider the "what if's" and got personal about it. In facing the reality of possibilities of what could happen to us that sometimes happened to parents because of choices their children make, the wife and I had discussed both sides of the "what if" issue. What if our son got a girl pregnant? What if our daughter became pregnant?

I extended that in my consideration. What if she became pregnant through rape? What if she did not want to carry the child in her body? That last one got me. I decided I was Pro-Choice. Since Pro-Choice is actually an element of the Pro-Abortion Movement, I had become pro-abortion. Come to think of it I remember President Obama stating his pro-choice stance and support of Planned Parenthood using the same rational. (Online references

WND "Obama uses daughters to lobby for abortion..." and All About Popular Issues "History of the Pro-Choice Movement".)

California passed a law permitting its high schools to assist a student in receiving an abortion, without parental notification. The argument against notification was the girl's parents might tell her to move out of their house. The law did pass by vote. I have not been able to find the law itself, but I did find a website stating that California does not require a minor to have parental consent. I voted no on that one. There are also IUDs given out to high school girls, by the high school, without parental consent. (Online reference FindLaw.)

Other material I came across online told of the South Korean "drop box" in which babies are abandoned by teen mothers or because the baby is a girl, has disability or the parents are poor. Here in the United States mothers can drop off babies at a hospital or police or fire station. At least there are options to having an abortion such as legal adoption.

Sometimes murder is performed by poor parents, who are looking to the future. In India there is a tribe in which baby girls are killed so a marriage dowry will not have to be given, when parents are poor. In some places due to cultural belief or dead conscience, life is cheap, including by some in America. Pragmatic thinking is involved. The baby's life is low priority compared to either selfish or survival reasons.

Like the Southwest States, California is rich in Spanish history and influence having had the European colonization, by first the Spanish advancing up from the bottom of North America and into the mid portion of what is now the United States. Later the French traveled from Canada down the Mississippi River Valley, while the British of course took the American Northeast and down the Atlantic coastline and inland. The Russians traveled from the American Northwest down the Pacific coastline to just above the San Francisco area leaving evidence of their existence by way of the still standing Fort

Ross, which is the fortification the Russians built. However, they could not survive the hardships of the location and returned to the Northwest later returning to Russia.

In California, the Spanish did survive due to better conditions. This was partly due to the Spanish Catholic Missions, around which settlements grew and roads between mission settlements developed. There was widespread community. Land grants were given by the Spanish King. Later generations of both Spanish and Mexicans, who are descendants of both Spanish and Native Americans, were born in the New World. The descendants born in early California became Californios. However, Californios were not only Spanish and Mexican descendants, but also other Western European settlers, who had made their way to the area.

It was Californios who signed the original California State Constitution. The State was heavily influenced by the early Spanish/Mexican settlement, but over time there was influence by other cultures of Western Europe. Americans from the East sought new lives of opportunity in the far-most western territory. Then the Gold Rush of 1849 happened, during which my own family, on my Father's side, went and became established.

Southerners who saw a war between North and South coming and did not want to be part of it conducted a lateral transfer from the South to Southern California. The Chinese came to earn a living offering services such as laundry, as well as working on the construction of the Transcontinental Railroad heading east. The Portuguese came and established fishing fleets as they had in the home country. The Swedish came and worked the forest for lumber. The Italians came and grew grapes and developed wine. Of course these are generalities as there was work for all in many industries. And the California Central Valley became the largest food production area for the world. This is the story of America. This is the "Melting Pot". And that was just in California.

Therefore Mexicans are not new on the scene of America. My own introduction to them was during the harvest season back home. Migrant workers, under the Bracero Program, from 1942 to 1964, came to America, under temporary agricultural contracts. There were pros and cons to this program.

I had heard of Cesar Chavez and the United Farm Workers Union. I had heard, from a career law enforcement officer, that Chavez was successful partly due to being protected by the Mexican organized crime leaders, in a hard core California prison. Depending on who one talks to one may hear pros and cons concerning him both as a person and his union organizing. However, it was not until I began researching him, for this writing, that I discovered his connection to the Bracero Program.

In my own opinion, I feel his organizing the farm workers and conducting non-violent protesting and political action for farm workers' rights was a required necessity. I witnessed his union members boycotting stores. I do not know the specifics of the boycott or remember exactly when it was. I just remember seeing the boycotters holding their flags.

As for the Bracero Program connection, he was, at least in part, responsible for Congress ending the Program. He and Dolores Huerta, who was the union co-founder along with Chavez, believed that the Program undermined the U.S. workers and exploited the migrant workers. The migrant workers of the Bracero Program worked for less pay, could not protest how they were abused and could easily be fired and replaced.

Chavez was very active politically fighting for farm workers' rights through the decades of the 1960s, '70s and '80s. He also influenced the 1986 Immigration and Reform Control Act, on related issues of U.S. farm workers. (Online reference Wikipedia "Cesar Chavez".)

I also remember televised news stories reporting how Mexican farm workers legal and illegal were abused. They were given non-habitable shacks to live in, in areas that had no running water or toilet facilities, no roads and was located away from everything and everyone. Government inspections began to be conducted and conditions improved.

I visited a local migrant camp. It is actually a compound of well-constructed buildings, in very good condition, with full facilities. If one did not know it was there, one would think that it was simply a gated community complex, which it is.

From a friend, who some time ago worked at the camp caring for the children, I learned that when she was there, the camp was very rundown and unhygienic. State health inspectors came in and closed the camp until it could be greatly improved. That took three years. All shacks were erased.

Now there are one level apartment complexes built around small court yards. They look better than most government housing projects I have seen. The apartments are one to four bedrooms, with a combined living and dining and kitchen area. Toilet and shower facilities are inside. A heater is in the combination area. Swamp coolers are on the roof of each apartment. Linoleum flooring is throughout. Beds are provided, but no other furniture.

Over time I have learned from various people that some of the migrants at this camp have been coming here for many years. Once they have registered and been assigned to an apartment, they drive over to a storage locker business and retrieve the furniture and household effects they left there the previous year, from when they went back to Mexico or Texas or Southern California. Some have a worker visa, while some have a resident visa.

It is not only men farm workers, but also their families. I saw grandparents. Maybe the grandmother watches after the children, while the parents and grandfather work the fields or orchards, but she may work those as well. They also work the canneries, after harvest season. The pay is decent and some may receive a higher wage in the canneries depending on their position.

However, the work is seasonal. I can relate to seasonal. My Stepdad was a painting contractor. For exterior painting, the weather has to be from warm to hot and not rainy or cold with snow or ice. People wanted the interior painting done during the summer as well. Schools had to be painted when the children were not there, which meant during the summer vacation. It was not until Dad managed to build up a good reputation and obtain county and city contracts that he was able to have bad weather work, of painting inside, which was sometimes at night after business hours.

I know about seasonal work and not being able to save money, for the seasonal non-work period, because of expenses during the work season.

So migrant workers do not have it easy just as many American citizens do not. Move-in day, at the camp, also brought representatives from various government agencies such as county assistance. One offered free training, for positions in most likely very low level jobs related to agriculture and also forestry. That one was a tri-county outreach, under a State university. A city agency offered assistance and training in various aspects of family related concerns. There was also representation from an employment agency. Not sure if that one was government or private. There were only two men, with no material and I did not ask for a business card.

During the time I was gaining firsthand knowledge of the local camp, I went to a presentation given by the County Sheriff. Questions were asked of him concerning illegals in reference to migrant workers. He stated there is a small percentage of illegals who manage to work their way into the migrant system. However, they are here to work and do not contain a criminal element. In fact, they and legal migrants are victimized by their own people, who are the criminal element such as scam operations.

During my inquisitiveness at the migrant camp, I was told since the illegals stay low and do nothing to draw attention to themselves, they most likely will not obtain residence at a camp. They will stay somewhere around the outside of the camp and do not have easy access to social services like the legals do. However, I was also told in conversation with a person living in another area that their local camp was full of illegals. How the person knew this I do not know as our conversation was interrupted. I am thinking all camps are not managed the same.

When I had the opportunity I did ask local people, with knowledge of the situation, why the illegal workers do not come into the country legally as the other workers did. The response was time and cost. It can take four years to obtain a worker visa and six years to obtain a resident visa. While some people are in an employment situation, in their home country, that allows them to wait the respective time period. Others are not employed. They are barely surviving where they are and are willing to take the chance of being discovered here illegally. And they do not have the money for the visa applications. So they come here to work and have some kind of a better "poor" life. This has also been confirmed, by people who have gone through the process of legal immigration to this country. I also learned in some countries, a fee is charged for the application to leave that country and live or work in America. In the case of Mexico, that fee is in the thousands. There are legal resources in this country, to assist with obtaining a visa, if one has the time and money.

Remember this is the situation at the time of writing this. By the time you read this, it may have changed.

California is one of the States of the Union, in which immigration is a major issue; undocumented workers also known as illegal immigrants also known as illegal aliens. I first became aware of the issue because of the first amnesty, in 1982, under prior California Governor, President Ronald Reagan. It was the first time such a political move had been made.

The background of illegal immigration, for this country, begins in the late 1800s, with the situation worsening in the mid-1900s. In 1875, the first federal law was passed prohibiting convicts and prostitutes from entering the country. In the mid-1880s, most Chinese were prohibited along with paupers, criminals and the mentally ill. Of course, there were still those who entered illegally.

On June 27, 1952, Public Law 414 dealing with national immigration was established being as much as possible an all-inclusive document. (Online PDF reference.)

The mass problem with illegal Mexicans seems to have begun in the 1950s. By the time Reagan was elected, there were over three million illegal immigrants, with the large majority being Mexican.

However, Mexicans are not the only Hispanic people who have received special attention. Since the Immigration and Nationality Act of 1965, Congress has passed seven amnesties as follows:

1. Immigration and Reform Control Act (IRCA), 1986: A blanket amnesty for over 2.7 million illegal aliens
2. Section 245(i) Amnesty, 1994: A temporary rolling amnesty for 578,000 illegal aliens
3. Section 245(i) Extension Amnesty, 1997: An extension of the rolling amnesty created in 1994
4. Nicaraguan Adjustment and Central American Relief Act (NACARA) Amnesty, 1997: An amnesty for close to one million illegal aliens from Central America
5. Haitian Refugee Immigration Fairness Act Amnesty (HRIFA), 1998: An amnesty for 125,000 illegal aliens from Haiti
6. Late Amnesty, 2000: An amnesty for some illegal aliens who claim they should have been amnestied under the 1986 IRCA amnesty, an estimated 400,000 illegal aliens
7. LIFE Act Amnesty, 2000: A reinstatement of the rolling Section 245(i) amnesty, an estimated 900,000 illegal aliens.

(Online reference ProCon.org and Numbers USA "The seven amnesties....")

I had to really think about the amnesty issue in deciding how I felt about it. Any country has the right to determine who comes within the country and why. In this case, it involved millions of people who were already here. That first amnesty was supposed to grant citizenship to millions, while increasing enforcement of immigration laws. It was supposed to have been a one-time-good-deal.

I decided it was good to grant the first amnesty. They were already here. They were hard working people. They just wanted a better life. Who could blame them for that? I was thinking as a Liberal.

I also remember a California proposition, which was coming up in a California election. It concerned allowing the children of illegal aliens to participate in the free school meal program. However, I cannot find an exact California proposition or legislation specifically dealing with the school meal program in such a manner.

I had to consider which way I would vote dealing with the school meal program, in reference to the children of illegal aliens. I did decide like others it was for the children and voted yes on the proposition. I was continuing to move in the direction of Socialism, although I did not realize it. I was just doing what seemed right.

California school children are given both breakfast and lunch. Breakfast was voted in on the basis that some children were not receiving that meal at home and the absence of that meal affected their learning. The lunch program has been in place for some time now.

One winter when Step Dad could not get work, when I was in my early schooling, I had oatmeal for breakfast, nothing for lunch and oatmeal for supper. We ate oatmeal for a couple of weeks before Dad found work.

By the time I had to make decisions concerning amnesty and school provided meals for children of illegal aliens, I had again become involved with Christianity even to the point of being involved with a church organization as part of its leadership.

In 1989, I was one of those Americans watching the television showing images of the Berlin Wall being torn down manually piece by piece as the Cold War was coming to an end, at least formally. I never thought of it being torn down, but it was. It came and it went twenty-eight years later.

The 1980s witnessed me obtaining an advanced education, married with children, obtaining a profession and the American Dream. I had returned to

I Could Have Been One

Christianity, but was thinking like a Liberal and moving toward Socialism. We had a recession and, at least in California, Socialism moved forward through the State Legislature as at least Liberal politicians were elected, if not some actual Socialists and maybe even a Communist or two. But I still did not know what actual Socialism was.

According to a historical documentary film on The Great Depression, which I do not remember who produced it or when, many people became interested in Socialism for the government to take care of them. There was a crisis. Was Socialism the answer? Did it prove itself to be the solution? At what cost? Besides local soup kitchens, there was the Works Progress Administration (WPA) established in 1935, by President Franklin D. Roosevelt, as part of his New Deal to get America back on its feet. The WPA was later renamed as Works Projects Administration. The Federal Government was spending its money in hard economic times. In good times, the government should save its money and in hard times spend it for recovery. Public projects such as highway construction gave men jobs. There were also jobs for women. Programs in which interviews were conducted, for historical research, were in place. I met one of those WPA workers. They made less money than Union jobs or non-government for that matter, but they did have jobs at a time when many did not. Those WPA workers shared their good fortune with others in works of charity. (Online reference History "WPA".)

I read that a man found in his grandfather's old trunk a Farm Labor Party membership card, 1918-1936. That Party was based on Socialism. A button of the Socialist Party, with the imprint of "Workers of the World Unit" on it, was also found.

One of my coworkers another lifetime ago told me his story. He was much older than I and about ready for retirement having been a young boy in the 1930s. He was the oldest sibling out of a handful. His family was traveling west, to California where orchards still bore fruit. That state received a lot of refugees, from the dust bowl and other places, at that time. His parents were trying to make do with what little money they had left and made the decision to leave the oldest son out on the road, in front of a farmhouse. They did and he was taken in temporarily and was given another place to live by some people, in town, who were in better financial shape. By the time our lives intersected he had recently received a high school diploma, which he had always wanted to achieve. His story was told at his graduation ceremony, as a testament to him and an example to others to fulfill their own dreams.

A family story I never heard when growing up, was told to me by the son of my Mother's cousin. Mama had two sisters both older than her. The cousin was the daughter of the oldest sister. When the Great Depression arrived, that sister had three children; two boys and a girl. Three! I knew of only two; one boy and a girl both much older than I. My Aunt and the children's father had divorced and my Aunt could not afford to keep the children. The father took in the oldest boy, but could not take on the others, who were placed in an orphanage. The boy was adopted and spent his life in another state. He was never spoken off. Once the Depression passed and my Aunt was better financially, she retrieved her daughter from the orphanage. The orphanage was never spoken of either. I received a phone call, from my second cousin one day. He had tracked me down, from the last letter I had written to his mother before she passed over.

1990s

It was in 1991 that Russian President Boris Yeltsin banned the Communist Party of the Soviet Union. Just as "Soviet Union" was short for the "Union of Soviet Socialist Republics" (U.S.S.R.) so is "Russian Federation" now short for the new formal name of "Commonwealth of Independent States". In 1993, the successor to the old Communist Party was reformed as the Communist

Party of the Russian Federation. So the Party is alive and well in Russia. It did not just go away. Online references Wikipedia "Communist Party of the Soviet Union" and "Communist Party of the Russian Federation". (Online reference The Free Dictionary "U.S.S.R.".)

What did change was that organizations like the Red Brigade, in Western Europe, seemed to just disappear and violent action ceased. Maybe the organization could no longer be financed, by the Russian government. There have been no more news reports concerning its activities of aggression, in Europe. So it is now most likely underground and taking orders from the new Communist Party of the Russian Federation. Perhaps they were told to turn their energies to political action, to be more of a Socialist than a Communist organization. But that is only my opinion.

And here is a good spot to explain that a Socialist takes control by politics, while a Communist takes control by force of armed uprising. I once heard it said that a Communist is a Socialist with a gun.

Then there was the news, in 1994, that Oregon had passed legislation legalizing euthanasia. I had to wrap my mind around how I felt about that. I knew my favorite uncle had cared for and watched my favorite aunt waste away from cancer, until her death and how hard it was on him. This was the Uncle who had stated to me, on the occasion of my Grandmother's heart attack, that he did not understand keeping an elderly person alive as their life was over and why not just let them go. I could see value in what he had said, for the sake of the individual as well as their family.

Decades later I would give authorization for the hospital not to resuscitate my Mother. She had a stroke. After a Code Blue, she told me to let her go. It was after that situation the doctor conferred with me concerning a Do Not Resuscitate Order, which I agreed to. Mama lived for many more years, but without any real quality of life.

However, while I did agree to natural death, I did not agree to euthanasia.

I had also seen my Father-In-Law die after some time fighting cancer. He was under Hospice care as my Aunt had been, at home, and being given morphine to the point of not being aware.

A person seeking physician assisted suicide would have to meet certain criteria, under Oregon's Death With Dignity Law. The person must:

1. be terminally ill
2. have six months or less to live
3. have made two oral requests for assistance in dying
4. have made one written request for assistance in dying
5. have convinced two physicians that he or she is sincere and not acting on a whim and that the decision is voluntary
6. be informed of "feasible alternatives" including, but not limited to, comfort care, Hospice care and pain control
7. not be influenced by depression
8. wait for 15 days

The physician may prescribe only a barbiturate sufficient to cause death and not include an injection or carbon monoxide. This actually is the way around the Hippocratic Oath that doctors take upon becoming a doctor, which states they will preserve life. They are only prescribing and not actually administering the barbiturate. They are not at the bedside of the person. The person has the option to take or not to take. But that is my opinion.

Now people in Oregon, who are fatally ill and will suffer physically, mentally and emotionally, may have an assisted death, at the time of their choosing. Would I want to do that under those conditions? Why not? Why suffer? Why just exist with no quality of life. Why exist without purpose? These were all thoughts that went through my mind, in deciding how I felt about the issue. Why not just die? We all die anyway. I guess maybe assisted suicide would be better. I moved further into the thinking pattern of Liberalism and Socialism. (Online reference "Euthanasia – Oregon's Euthanasia Law".)

California followed suit with their own version of such a law.

There is also the fact that more people now need welfare assistance than before and look to government programs. My parents and their generation used to talk about work houses and poor houses and old people's homes. Charles Dickens wrote *A Christmas Carol*, in 1843, twenty years before America's War Between the States, to put emphasis on caring for England's destitute. There is mention, in that book, of welfare institutions existing then. The poor and less fortunate have been a part of society as long as there have been societies and each society and generation decides how to deal with their own.

I have found material stating in this country, social programs go back to 1915, in some form of State program. The Social Security Act established in 1935, during the Great Depression, of the United States, had its beginnings as the Old Age, Survivors and Disability Insurance Federal Program. It was mandated to the States that they pay unemployment insurance. Therefore each State had to pass legislation to develop their own program. Out of that grew a form of an Unemployment Insurance Department, which grew to a partnership between employers and the Department, to assist those who would be collecting the insurance to find employment positions.

The Social Security Insurance (SSI) itself began as a voluntary deduction, from an employee's pay check, to only later become a mandatory deduction, by Congressional legislation. Both the SSI program and the unemployment benefits program have expanded to the point of having little resemblance to the original of the 1930s. My SSI number was assigned when I applied for the number, at the age of eighteen, which was required in order to be formally employed versa informally working for cash and no benefits,. Now the number may be assigned as soon as a child is born. However, it is voluntary. It is highly promoted to do so though. And the SSI number is now used by both government and private businesses for identification and filing systems. Online reference "Social Security for Children". (Online reference ERIC "A History of Unemployment Insurance…".)

We now have a wide variety of both adult and child food programs, at both Federal and State levels. There is the Food Stamp Program for those requiring assistance in obtaining a monthly supply and there is also the Women, Infant and Children (WIC) Program, which gives assistance in obtaining a food supply. And in some areas we have lots of food drives and give-a-ways.

For housing, there are "The Projects", which are apartments, as well as now low cost/low income actual houses; all provided by the government, at some level.

Even in small towns "The Projects" exist. My Stepdad and Mom ended up living in them. They were simple rows of small, ground level apartments, in long buildings.

Out of necessity we have been moving toward a social welfare lifestyle, in society and government. My parents did not have investments or any kind of a retirement savings plan. All they had was their respective Social Security Insurance. And that was not much as Stepdad did not pay into it when he was self-employed and Mama did not pay into it as a stay-at-home Mom.

Political Correctness seemed to rise out of nowhere. It was not put in place by legislation. What does it have to do with politics? It seemed to begin with the "not offending" black people as in not using the "N" word, which is a word I have heard one black person call another. As a white person I feel I do not have the right to use the "N" word even in casual conversation with a black person in the same manner as they would use it. By the way, I am not talking about the scientific word "Negro". And yes, I do know there are black people who do not like that word neither, since that is the word that the offensive "N" word stemmed from. To me, Political Correctness began as a positive action to become more sensitive to the history and feelings of others such as minorities, women, etc. Another move toward being Liberal/Socialist for me?

Another scientific word is "homosexual" just as "heterosexual" is. I say this because it seems homosexuals prefer the title "Gay" and do not like the title of "homosexual", which like "heterosexual" contains both male and female. I am now mentioning gay people because it was in the '90s that Gay Rights begin. At least it seemed to begin then, but it actually had begun back in 1924 in Chicago, as an organization named Society for Human Rights. When I was growing up, kids learned over time about male and female, but not about heterosexual and homosexual. Our parents knew, but that aspect of human life was never passed down to the kids. When kids grew up, sometime during their adult life, they learned about such matters. And as one can see, that early organization has nothing about gay or homosexual in its title. (Online reference InfoPease "The American Gay Rights Movement".)

So males used the term of "Gay" and females use the term of "Lesbian". And let's not forget every other identifying label concerning sexual behavior that our new society has adopted.

I had not really thought about gays or lesbians until California put same-sex couple domestic rights on the ballot. Having not thought about them, I had no idea about how I felt about domestic rights. What were domestic rights? The term was being used to indicate rights which a heterosexual couple has. The example that was used was that of a gay man in a hospital Intensive Care Unit (ICU). If the man was not gay, his spouse and family would be permitted to visit him. However, if the man was gay, his cohabitant partner would not be permitted to visit him as that person was not family. I figured everyone is human with feelings and emotions. I voted for Domestic Rights for Gays and Lesbians. I believe by then I was a Liberal. I had been accepting the thinking outside of the box. I was a Liberal Christian. (Online reference Wikipedia "LGBT rights in California".)

During this decade, I had upward mobility professionally and obtained management level. I began to observe the politics of the executive level involving competition and ambition. There is the saying that it does not matter what one knows, but who they know. In my case, this turned out to be true. My career was more than half over and I knew I really needed to change my situation, in order to obtain my financial retirement goal.

I had built a reputation for hard work and dedication. My resume was full of accomplishments and service, but I was being bypassed for upward positions, which would give promotion. I finally broke out of the going-nowhere cycle, when the opportunity presented itself to tell my plight to a manager, who I had once worked for and who was pleased with my performance. They, in turn, talked with another manager, who owned them a favor and who did not really know me and to whom I had applied for a position, which would give me the opportunity for upward mobility. I was accepted into that position. From there, I gained upward mobility success and my objectives toward my retirement goal. It was both. I worked hard, for what I obtained. However, due to circumstances I had to receive a little assistance in obtaining the desired opportunity.

I had become what my Stepdad called "a self-made man". With the exception of a cousin, who was much older than I, I was the only one of my Dad's family and my Mother's family and my Stepdad's family, of my generation and before, to receive advance education. My Mother's older brother was the only one of that generation or before to obtain professional success, without such an education. But that was when experience, hard work and stability counted for something. It was during that transition period between "starting at the bottom and working one's way up" and "having to have advance education to get anywhere".

Chapter Two

Twenty-first Century

Retirement Years

I am retired! I retired, with time for me. Or so I thought as I began to become busy with travel, for one reason or another, and paying attention to family and household issues, which I had not done much of before. I had planned for retirement, by building up home libraries, creating a Study out of my son's prior room, gathering up woodworking tools, establishing my garage man-cave, purchasing CDs of music I grew up with so I could rock-out in the man-cave, creating genealogy files and collecting hobby support supplies.

Little did I know the person who informed me I would be busier in retirement than when I was employed, had spoken true words. I became more interested in our country and world affairs. I had to educate myself. A decade plus ago I began to purchase more books and research the internet. I learned. I began to study history, which I had not done since college. I became familiar with the United Nations' Agenda for the 21st Century; commonly known as Agenda 21. I began to study the Socialist plan for bringing peace and equality to the world.

How do I know that it is a Socialist plan? The document does not state it is a Socialist plan. It comes from the United Nations and not a Socialist or Communist country. I had begun to research Socialism, Communism and Marxism. I am going to begin my report of such research with what is said to be "The most widely read political pamphlet in the history of the world" *The Communist Manifesto*, by Karl Marx, prefaced by Frederick Engels. It is not a large book.

I have heard over and over, from people who visited the Louvre, in Paris, France, that they expected the painting *Mona Lisa*, by Leonardo Da Vinci, to be very large. That is not the case. I suspect they had associated both the painting and the artist with the greatest of their respective reputations. I have personally seen the *Mona Lisa* and it is a small work of art.

So it is with *The Communist Manifesto*. I had expected to find a great novel sized book, but instead found only a small booklet; a small booklet the seeds of which are still feeding those who would change the whole world into the vision of Karl Marx.

Communist Manifesto and Related Research

In the first paragraph, of the Preface, Engels explains the work was first published as a platform plank, of the Communist League, which was a workingmen's organization began in Germany and later spread though the European Continent, before 1848, as a secret society. A few weeks before the French Revolution of 1848, the work was printed in London, England, for presentation for a Congress of the League. Later that same year, in Paris, a French translation was printed for distribution.

Please note this was before America's War Between the States. Also the French Revolution of 1848 is not THE French Revolution of 1789. The one in 1789 was the original French Revolution, which was followed by a period of continued unrest and bloodshed. More peaceful times did come to France and there was the rise of Napoleon Bonaparte followed by his march on Europe. France saw more unrest in the mid-1800s.

The previously mentioned paragraph is followed by the history of the Communist/Socialist movement, through early struggles, rebuilding and planning to involve both Europe and America. Some progress was made, in Europe, but by 1874 the International Working Men's Association as it was titled then dissolved. Note that America had been involved in its own struggles of the mid-1800s as in America's War Between the States.

Engels goes on to give the history of the translating and printing of *The Communist Manifesto* both across Europe, including Russia, and in America. It was also printed in various periodicals. It was translated, printed and read widely to influence the minds of men and thus affecting their attitudes toward their position in life and those in leadership affecting their lives. He follows up by stating in general, the movements in various countries were to no avail in changing life; basically, Socialism became held by the middleclass, who considered political changes, and Communism of the working class, who felt that they themselves would have to force the change and not wait on or expect support from the educated leaders; armed revolution. ***Therefore Socialism provoked thoughts of change within the political/economic systems, while the Communist looked to means of forcefully taking control and putting changes in place themselves.***

Engels further states, although the *Manifesto* was a joint production of himself and Marx, the fundamental proposition forming its nucleus was all Marx. The stated proposition is as follows:

> "...that in every historical epoch, the prevailing mode of economic production and exchange, and the social organization necessarily following from it, form the basis upon which

is built up, and from which alone can be explained, the political and intellectual history of the epoch; that consequently the whole history of mankind (since the dissolution of primitive tribal society, holding land in common ownership) has been a history of class struggles, contests between exploiting and exploited, ruling and oppressed classes; that the history of these class struggles forms a series of evolution in which, nowadays, a state has been reached where the exploited and oppressed class – the proletariat – cannot attain its emancipation from the sway of the exploiting and ruling class – the bourgeoisie – without, at the same time, and once and for all, emancipating society at large from all exploitation, oppression, class distinctions and class struggles."

That Preface was written in London, 30th January 1888; twelve years before the turn of the century.

Marx opens his *Manifesto* by stating, by that time, Communism had become a power as evidenced by the world powers of Europe themselves, including the Pope, Czar, French Radicals and German police-spies, acknowledging the existence of Communism and viewing it as a threat and counter-acting its movement. Therefore it was time for the Communists to publish their views, aims and tendencies of the Party itself. The last paragraph of the opening states that Communist of various nationalities had assembled in London and agreed for the following *Manifesto* to be published in the English, French, German, Flemish and Danish languages.

There are four chapters following: 1. Bourgeois and Proletarians, 2. Proletarians and Communists, 3. Socialist and Communist Literature, 4. Position of the Communists in Relation to the Various Existing Opposition Parties.

Using the 1932 New Popular Webster Dictionary the following definitions are given:

Bourgeois; a French citizen of the mercantile class.

Proletarian; pertaining to the common people, low.

Marx speaks out against the Bourgeois, but uses the term to refer to a people of any economic level class involved in the Capitalist system of production, goods and services. He also speaks out against the suffering of the Proletarian being used and downtrodden by such an economic system. *He further promoted the demise of the ruling class and the equalization of both the middle and the lower classes to be governed by their own selves, in the form of the "State", with any and all property being managed by the "State", for the common welfare of all people. Marx also promoted the abandonment of nations, in the wake of the working class of all nations uniting under the banner of Communism/Socialism to revote and forcibly or politically take over all governments and ruling class and replace them with the Communist "State".*

In Chapter Two, he not only denounces Capitalism, but also condemns private property as a product of Capitalism. He also goes so far as to make the following statements concerning elements of society through historical development:

> "Undoubtedly," it will be said, 'religious, moral, philosophical and juridical ideas have been modified in the course of historical development. But religion, morality, philosophy, political science, and law constantly survived this change.
>
> *'There are, besides, eternal truths, such as Freedom, Justice, etc., that are common to all states of society. But Communism abolishes eternal truths, it abolishes all religion, and all morality, instead of constituting them on a new basis; it therefore acts in contradiction to all past historical experience.'"*

He lays out ten measures to be taken in all countries stating that they will be different in different countries, but in the most advanced countries they will be pretty generally applicable. The measures are as follows:

1. Abolition of property in land and application of all rents of land to public purposes.
2. A heavy progressive or graduated income tax.
3. Abolition of all right of inheritance.
4. Confiscation of the property of all emigrants (one who leaves their country to settle in another) and rebels.
5. Centralization of credit in the hands of the State, by means of a national bank with State capital and an exclusive monopoly.
6. Centralization of the means of communication and transport in the hands of the State.
7. Extension of factories and instruments of production owned by the State, the bringing into cultivation of wastelands, and the improvement of the soil generally in accordance with a common plan.
8. Equal liability of all to labor. Establishment of industrial armies especially for agriculture.
9. Combination of agriculture with manufacturing industries; gradual abolition of the distinction between town and country by a more equable distribution of population over the country.
10. Free education for all children in public schools. Abolition of children's factory labor in its present form. Combination of education with industrial production, etc. etc.

In Chapter Three, he attacks Christianity and attempts to use it as a basis for his own beliefs.

> *"Nothing is easier than to give Christian asceticism (exceedingly rigid in the exercise of religious duties) a Socialist tinge. Has not Christianity declaimed against private property, against marriage, against the State? Has it not preached, in the place of these, charity and poverty, celibacy and mortification of the flesh, monastic life and Mother Church? Christian Socialism is but the Holy Water with which the priest consecrates the heartburnings of the aristocrat."*

Marx is speaking of the Catholic Church and the practice of religious groups of men and women known as priests, brothers and nuns who lived in communal life under strict rules of their respective group, including that of charity, poverty and celibacy while living an unmarried life. Mortification of the flesh such as whipping of one's self, was performed by the men of some groups during the Middle Ages. However, the Catholic Church was not against the ownership of private property or marriage or the State as its members were allowed to own private property and be married and be in positions of government or be of the ruling class. So Christianity such as Catholic Church, was not a Socialist organization.

However, **please note that the phrase of "Christian Socialism" was used in the early 1800s, by the person who gave foundation to Socialism itself.**

Marxism is both Socialism and Communism, which is forced Socialism. The difference is how the seeds of Karl Marx are brought into manifestation; politically/economically or armed physical revolution. Marx advocated physical revolution and what today is termed as "terrorism". That is what Communists believe in as evidenced by their past actions in Russia, Eastern Bloc countries also known as Russian Satellite Countries, China, Cuba and Viet Nam. Socialists, who are not Communists, believe in the taking over and control by political means. This is where the past and current times show variations of Socialism in various countries and where various social programs come into play.

Government Retirement benefits and national health care seem to be key elements in a country's socialist system. People like receiving what seems to be free government/national retirement/health care. Only it is not free. One way or another someone is paying for it. Marx did state heavy income tax. If a person pays a high tax rate consisting of the majority of their earnings, but at retirement receive full benefits for the rest of their lives to be totally taken care of, they paid the government for those benefits. The government is taking revenue from the citizen and redistributing it as it believes to be needed. The same with free health care. The government is taking revenue, in the form of taxes from the citizens and returning it in the form of a government benefit. There is no free lunch.

In addition, the government has control to determine what course of action to take in the redistribution of benefits. Countries have adopted such programs to some degree or another and their citizens seem to like that arrangement or they are just going along with it. That most likely depends on how efficient the government system of their respective country operates. That is just my opinion though.

The purer the Socialism, the more a Communist government must be in place to control the populace and manage the Socialist economic system of that country. The key is if a Socialist country is managed by force of arms, including police and/or military action.

Not wanting to leave the resources of the technology age untouched, I researched online as well. Since it is not my intent to give a deep study on political matters, but instead to put pieces of a historical puzzle together, I was not searching for an in depth study of the subject of Socialism. I wanted a condensed summary of Socialist history. I found one on Wikipedia. Since Wikipedia is a composition of individual submissions, I usually prefer to select other resources, if those resources meet my requirements. However, the summery I found is well written and inclusive and contains a list of 161 reference sources of research. And that was precisely what I was looking for. Thank you very much.

I have to quote exactly the first sentence under the heading of History of Socialism. *"The history of socialism has its origins in the French Revolution of 1789 and the changes brought about by the Industrial Revolution, although it has precedents in earlier movements and ideas."* And there is a French influence before the mid-1800s. The year 1789 was six years after the ending of the American Revolution of 1776 to 1783. This first paragraph makes reference to "…the Revolutions of 1848 swept Europe, expressing what they termed 'scientific socialism'. In the last third of the 19th century in Europe social democratic parties arose in Europe drawing mainly from Marxism. The Australian Labor Party was the world's first elected socialist party when the party won the 1899 Queensland state election."

As a personal note on the British colonization, of the island of Australia, and establishment of what became the Australian form of government, is that the people who were sent there to colonize were criminals, to one degree or another. They had been serving time in prison. Britain opened its prisons and literally shipped the unwanted off to the island. That was in 1788, which was eighteen years after the island was discovered, that the first convicts arrived. So it was four generations later that descendants of those unwanted decided they wanted Socialism. There was not a physical revolution, but an election of government officials. (Online reference Nations Online Project "History of Australia".)

Another personal note is during the French Revolution of 1789, not only did the populace rise up against those who oppressed them, but also they formed citizen committees for rule by the people themselves. Appointed citizen committees administering under the "State" administration is an aspect of Communism.

The next paragraph explains how different leaders of various Socialist groups had several ideas of supporting different ways of implementation of Socialist principals. All agreed on "Change". All agreed on the improvement of "Labor". The last sentence stated "Socialist governments established the 'mixed economy' with partial nationalizations and social welfare."

The third paragraph states the Viet Nam War, of both French and American, gave rise to a New Left the elements of which favored decentralized collective ownership in the form of cooperatives or workers' councils. An example is given of Venezuelan President Hugo Chavez championing what he termed "Socialism of the 21st Century", which included a policy of nationalization of national assets such as oil, anti-imperialism and termed himself a Trotskyist supporting "permanent revolution".

Under the heading of Origins of Socialism are Bible quotes of the New Testament, "...which inspired the communal arrangements of the Anabaptist Hutterites..." as follows:

Acts 2; 44-45: All the believers were together and had everything in common. Selling their possessions and goods, they gave to anyone as he had need.

Acts 4; 32: All the believers were one in heart and mind. No one claimed that any of his possessions were his own, but they shared everything they had.

Acts 4; 34-35: There was no needy person among them. For from time to time those who owned lands or houses sold them, brought the money from their sales and put it at the Apostles' feet, and it was distributed to anyone as he had need.

Note: The Anabaptist Hutterites were part of the Protestant Reformation, but chose to live apart from other Christians and society in general as the Christians did during the early days of persecution by the Roman Empire. The early Christians lived apart from society due to the persecution. The Anabaptist were persecuted by other Christians and society in general due to their separatist life style. What?! You're too good to live with us. You're secretive. You must have something to hide. Just my opinion of an aspect of human nature.

Following the above are who said what when to explain various thoughts of Socialistic means to an end; an end of the ruling ways of life, at that time, and an end to the downtrodden paths of life. "Associationism" became the term used in the early 1800s for utopian theories. Utopia...Heaven on Earth.

Englishman Robert Owen and Frenchmen Claude Henri de Saint-Simon and Charles Fourier were social critics of excesses of poverty and inequality of the Industrial Revolution and advocated reforms of distribution of wealth and the transformation of society into small communities in which private property was to be abolished.

The founders of French Socialism, Henri de Saint-Simon and Karly Roesling believed that a brotherhood of man must accompany the scientific organization of industry and society, that production and distribution must be carried out by the State, that allowing everyone to have equal opportunity to develop their talents would lead to social harmony, that the traditional State could be virtually eliminated or transformed and that rule over men would be replaced by the administration of things.

Charles Fourier (1772-1837) inspired the founding of the Communist communities of La Reunion near present day Dallas, Texas, North American Phalanx in New Jersey, Community Place and five others in New York State and elsewhere. This also occurred in Mexico, South America, Algeria, Yugoslavia and other countries.

Robert Owen also proposed utopian communities. He and his sons left England, immigrated to the United States and founded a Socialist community in New Harmony, Indiana. It failed in 1827.

"Marx believed that capitalism could only be overthrown by means of revolution carried out by the working class:...."

"The Social Democratic Workers' Party of Germany was found in 1869 under the influence of Marx and Engels." In 1875 it joined the General German Workers Association and later became the German Social Democratic Party, which is what it is known as today. However, this is a different name than Hitler's Socialist Party or the N.A.Z.I. Party, which is the abbreviated form for the National Socialist German Workers' Party.

In the early part of 1871, after France had been defeated in the Franco-Prussian War, there was a successful uprising in Paris. It established a government known as the Paris Commune, which ruled for three months, with a ninety-two member Communal Council. In 1891, Engels wrote a postscript to *The Civil War in France*, by Karl Marx:

> "From the outset the Commune was compelled to recognize that the working class, once come to power, could not manage with the old state machine, that in order not to lose again its only just conquered supremacy, this working class must, on the one hand, do away with all of old repressive machinery previously used against it itself, and, on the other, safeguard itself against its own deputies and officials, by declaring them all, without exception, subject to recall at any moment."

Marx and Engels united, in an international organization, 384 delegates from twenty countries representing approximately 300 labor and Socialist organizations, in 1889, known as the Second International.

> "In 1903, the Russian Social Democratic Labour Party began to split on ideological and organizational questions in Bolshevik ('Majority') and Menshevik ('Minority') factions,

with Russian revolutionary Vladimir Lenin leading the more radical Bolsheviks."

The Socialist Party of America was founded in 1897. This Party still exists today. In 1905, the Industrial Workers of the World (IWW) formed from several independent labor unions. The IWW opposed the political means of the Socialist Labor Party leadership and the craft unionism of Samuel Gompers. In 1910, the Sewer Socialist elected a Socialist Congressman and a Socialist Mayor of Milwaukee, Wisconsin. It is stated that most of Milwaukee's elected officials were also Socialist. After World War I, the Socialist Party declined in numbers having had a 1912 membership of 150,000. (Online reference of the name.)

Basically Marxism did not do well in the late 1800s and early 1900s, in France. However, the Federation of Socialist Workers of France advocated gradual reforms and was more accepted.

The nationalist action, of World War I, caused the Socialist to support their respective nations, for the most part. Some leaders denounced the War and would not support it. Lenin and Trotsky were among those leaders.

In the composition of this Wikipedia article, mention of anarchist has been given as to who, where, what and why. However, I am not concerned with anarchist, but I will give the writer credit for being all inclusive. By the way, there was mention of women leaders and feminist. So it was not just men involved in such movements. Oh…there are Anarcho Communist, who believe that the workers themselves must govern and not leave the leadership simply to the Socialist.

It is noted the anarchist movement assassinated numerous heads of state from 1881 to 1914, including the assassin of United States President McKinley claiming to have been influence by anarchist and feminist Emma Goldman.

Engels emphasized that Marxists must win over the great mass of the people before initiating a revolution. Both Marx and Engels believed later in their lives that a peaceful Socialist revolution was possible in England, America and the Netherlands. The two did disagree on France as Marx did not believe it was possible there, but Engels did.

October of 1917 brought with it the Bolshevik Revolution and the war between the Bolshevik Red Army and the traditionalist White Army to preserve the old Russia. The Bolshevik leader, Lenin, had also made enemies of Leftist of other groups including the Minority Party. The anti-Communist White Army was led by prior officers of the Romanov Russian Army and was composed of not only Russians, but also French and other elements supporting the cause. The Bolsheviks endured for six years and finally were victorious. Both the Revolution and Civil War was an example to many Socialists, confirming the validity of the ideas and strategy and tactics of both Lenin and Trotsky. (Online reference Encyclopedia Britannica "White Army Russian History")

The British Labour Party won seats in the House of Commons, in 1902, and had adopted a specifically Socialist constitution. The Labor Party, in Australia, had success and formed a national government in 1904.

> "In 1922, the fourth congress of the Communist International took up the policy of the United Front, urging Communist to work with rank and file Social Democrats while remaining critical of their leaders, who they criticized for 'betraying' the working class by supporting the war efforts of their respective capitalist classes. For their part, the social democrats pointed to the dislocation caused by revolution, and later, the growing authoritarianism of the Communist Parties. When the Communist Party of Great Britain applied to affiliate to the Labour Party in 1920 it was turned down."

"War efforts" refer to World War I.

From 1917 to '39, both revolutionary Socialism and the Soviet Union had its successes of progress and failures of difficulties throughout the Socialist movement worldwide. Since Joseph Stalin was the General Secretary of the Communist Party of the Soviet Union's Central Committee, during World War II, and the first Russian leader I remember hearing about, I will present this quote, from the article.

> "Within a few years a bureaucracy developed in Russia as a result of the Russian Civil War, foreign invasion, and Russia's historic poverty and backwardness. The bureaucracy undermined the democratic and socialist ideals of the Bolshevik Party and elevated Stalin to their leadership after Lenin's death. In order to consolidate power, the bureaucracy conducted a brutal campaign of lies and violence against the Left Opposition led by Trotsky."

This pitted followers of Trotsky worldwide against the U.S.S.R. and those who followed its policies and strategy.

During the late 1800s and early 1900s, in the United States, the Socialists gained both accomplishments and setbacks through involvement in various aspects of American life, including elections, trade unions, protests and riots. The Communist Party USA was formed in 1919 by former members of the Socialist Party of America.

Personal interjection: American trade unions, which were needed, quickly became the target for Communist/Socialist involvement. This was actually a natural occurrence since "labor and workers" are the bases of both labor unions and Communism/Socialism.

World War II had weakened the British Empire such as pulling out of India, and left the United States and Russia as the world leaders. Some saw this as a world with two irreconcilable and antagonistic political and economic systems. The Cold War had begun.

Personal interjection: I have heard people ask about the difference between Marxism and Fascism. Benito Mussolini as dictator of Italy ushered in so-called Fascism, during WWII. Marxism allows for a centralized government, which Fascism also allows for. However, Marxism also allows for ruling by committees and not by a dictatorship as such. In Soviet Russia, there was/is a central committee and other lower committees, which assist in the ruling. There is one person who heads the committee and is the representative of that country to other countries. Fascism does not allow for such government, but for a dictator as a ruler answerable to no one. Hitler was a dictator although his Party was Socialist. However, this goes along with the fact that there were various theories of implementation of Socialism and that he was the leader of a warring nation. So Mussolini and Hitler did have that in common. The Communists in Italy were active in the 1950s and still may be.

The democratic socialist parties of Eastern Europe ceased to exist, after WWII, due to Stalin imposing Communist regimes in those countries: the so-called Iron Curtain Countries or Eastern Bloc.

The Frankfort Declaration took a stand against both capitalism and the Communism of Stalin:

> Socialism aims to liberate the peoples from dependence on a minority which owns or controls the means of production (Capitalism). It aims to put economic power in the hands of the people as a whole and to create a community in which free men work together as equals... Socialism has become a major force in world affairs. It has passed from propaganda into practice. In some countries the foundation of a Socialist society have already been laid. Here the evils of capitalism are disappearing...
>
> Since the Bolshevik revolution in Russia, Communism has split the International Labour Movement and has set back the realization

of socialism in many countries for decades. Communism falsely claims a share in the Socialist tradition. In fact it has distorted that tradition beyond recognition. It has built up a rigid theology which is incompatible with the critical spirit of Marxism... Wherever it has gained power it has destroyed freedom or the chance of gaining freedom....

—The Frankfort Declaration, 1951

The first Socialist government in a North American country occurred, in 1944, in the Canadian Province of Saskatchewan, under The Co-operative Commonwealth Federation (CCF) of Thomas Douglas. Among other changes was the creation of the first system of Universal Health Care in Canada, which later was adopted nationally in 1965. A Bill of Rights was created as the first such charter in Canada, which led to a national Bill of Rights. In 1962, the CCF became the New Democratic Party.

Social Democracy in Government:
Post-WWII Britain saw the establishment of national control of resources, utilities, banking and health services. Post-war Europe had political and social changes as well as civil wars, in the late 1940s and '50s. Also the 1960s and '70s held changes of the working class, including those concerning women. The Berlin Wall destruction of 1989 occurred. In other words, the contest between the Left and the Right continued with both having gains and losses.

The last part of the article gives various Communist, Socialist, Conservative, counter-culture group actions around the world during the 20th Century, involving political and social reform as well as workforce changes, including women in the workforce. It also mentions the New Left, in the developed world and the adoption of Third Way policies.

The bottom -line is that Communism and Socialism marches on out of our past and into our present with goals for the future, while having various changes within its philosophy of means to an end. People want a better world not just for themselves, but for others as well. Is this not a good, positive goal?

And that is what Socialism is and the difference between Communism and Socialism.

Oh…I feel compelled to share the story of when my son came home, from a high school day. Okay…two stories.

First story: He informed me he had learned about how bad Capitalism was. I confirmed that Capitalism is not perfect, but it is the best we have because it encourages self-development, through hard work, and can also develop our personal growth in gaining knowledge and experience. It also can give goals to reach for and adjectives to obtain. I then asked what he would replace it with. He did not know. The teacher had only spoken against Capitalism, but had not given a replacement. Is there a replacement?

Second story: Another day he came home and announced he was studying about the Viet Nam War, in history. I felt old.

Agenda 21

I have heard it said that Agenda 21 goes back to the 1960s or '50s. That may be as far as the basic idea of establishing global improvement of people's lives through world Socialism, by way of agriculture and environmental improvements. For that matter, it may be said that the agricultural element is common to both Agenda 21 and the *Communist Manifesto*. Let's not forget that Communist China was founded on agriculture as the basis for its economy post WWII.

The earliest formal beginning I discovered was the 1972 United Nations (U.N.) Conference on the Environment, which identified "environmental protection" as the world's greatest problem and gave the world the United Nations program followed almost immediately by United States President Richard

Nixon's Executive Order that created the Environmental Protection Agency. At the time of this writing, that was almost fifty years ago; almost half of a century.

Four years later the U.N. Conference on Human Settlement, proclaimed "Public control of land use is…indispensable." In other words, government control of land; Socialism.

In 1983, the U.N. World Commission of Environment and Development began proceedings, and would issue a final report in 1987 called *Our Common Future*, which defined "Sustainable Development" as "Development that meets the needs of the present without compromising the ability of future generations to meet their own needs." I think of the Industrial Revolution, which began air pollution causing health and environmental problems. Then there was the destruction of rain forests, which destroyed the livelihood and erased the cultures of native people, for the sake of development without the consideration for the reality of what was being destroyed. If Sustainable Development can solve those problems, it seems like it might be a positive action.

The U.N. told the Commission to develop a plan, within five years, to implement the concept.

The result of that instruction was the 1992 U.N. Conference on Environment and Development, in Rio de Janeiro, Brazil, presenting what became Agenda 21. The reception of Agenda 21 was signed for by the 179 member nations, including the United States of America. President George H. W. Bush signed for the United States. It is my understanding that signing acceptance did not obligate a country to enforce the plan, but that it was for consideration. In fact, I have heard this point stated in defense of Agenda 21 being passed down to countries. In the case of this Country, passed down without the consent of the U.S. Congress. However, it is not a treaty, which Congress must approve.

However, when President Clinton signed Executive Order 12852 creating the President's Council on Sustainable Development, in 1993, to plan the implementation, then Agenda 21 became obligatory, under the United Nations terms of agreement. Such action constitutes a "treaty" and such action was not approved by the U.S. Congress. Following suite, in 2011, President Obama signed Executive Order 13575, which established the White House Rural Council, having the effect of taking control of almost all aspects of the lives of 16% of the American people.

Counteracting government implementation the Republican Party National Committee, in January 2012, wrote and approved a Resolution exposing United Nations Agenda 21. In the Resolution, it states that Agenda 21 is a destructive and insidious strategy viewed as a treaty and that, since the United States Senate did not endorse it, Agenda 21 is not legally binding on the United States. Some States, through their legislation process, have outlawed the Agenda 21 process. However, although I have heard that members of the United States Congress know about Agenda 21, I have not observed any mention of it from such politicians. Nor have I heard of it being mentioned by Socialists, but it is real all the same. I also dare say that the majority of the American populace do not have any idea of its existence either through not being aware of what is happening in their state and country or not having the opportunity to learn about it. I say this as an average American citizen, who pays some attention to political issues, but does not follow government proceedings all day every day.

I have also observed organizations or individuals involved in counteracting various aspects of Agenda 21 such as government land or water control, not wanting to actually relate their aspect of focus to Agenda 21. They say doing so only confuses people because it gives people too much to think about. They prefer to focus only on their respective piece of the puzzle of Agenda 21, without giving the whole picture of the reality of both the puzzle piece and the puzzle itself.

The basis of Agenda 21 is global environmental control involving land, water and air and all related industries and science, education and training, with improvement for women and children and work for everyone from low level manual labor to high level executives in contribution to the community and The State, from local to global level, with all aspects being sustainable for the whole world with all people and being equal materially. The results should be world peace; utopia through agriculture and world balanced markets. What is wrong with that?

In the language of the document itself:

> Providing an Effective Legal and Regulatory Framework through making laws and regulations more effective and establishing judicial and administrative procedures and providing legal reference and support services and establishing a cooperative training network for sustainable development law and developing effective national programs for reviewing and enforcing compliance with national, state, provincial and local laws on environment and development and national monitoring of legal follow-up to international instruments.

Promoting Integrated Watershed Development and Alternative Livelihood Opportunities.

All of the above is from various research and material I have collected over the years concerning the subject, including the document itself.

What Am I?

People are identified in a lot of ways. I have already mentioned by race and color. Another way of identifying a person is by numbers. I once knew a college student, whose class assignment was to write a paper concerning who she was. Her whole paper dealt with the personal identifying numbers she had accumulated, during her short life. And then there are labels. Some are good and some are not so good. Some are downright insulting. Our first labels are those we receive as a baby and the process continues all of the way up to our passing from this life. Labels are adjectives, which can describe our physical, mental and emotional aspects as well as our character and personality. A label can become a nickname. I knew a person named "Red". He had red hair. I once knew a person named "Tiny". He was large.

Political labels describe our position on the political spectrum; Communist, Socialist, Progressive, Far Left Liberal, Liberal, Moderate Liberal, Moderate Conservative, Conservative, Far Right Radical.

In the minds of some people, a Liberal is a Socialist. However, I have personally found there is a range of Liberals, which is why I place them between Socialist and Moderates. I did meet a person who actually identified herself as a moderate Liberal. Some people see no difference between a Progressive and a Socialist. Some say that the Socialists began calling themselves Progressives, in order to have a positive image attached to them. But what is a Socialist?

In the American Dictionary of the English Language, by Noah Webster, 1828, reprint the following is found:

> LIBERAL: free heart, generous, not selfish, embracing, open, candid, large amount, not low in birth or mind, improvement, bestowing

> CONSERVATIVE: preservative; having power to preserve in a safe or entire state, or from loss, waste or injury

> PROGRESSIVE: moving forward; proceeding onward; advancing

All of the above may be positive attributes and I dare say all may be good for humanity.

The pocket size 1932 New Popular Webster Dictionary has:

> LIBERAL: generous, munificent…plentiful

> CONSERVATIVE: having the tendency to preserve

> COMMUNISM: the doctrine of having property in common; socialism

> SOCIALISM: an economic theory or system of the reconstruction of society on the basis of co-operation of labor and community of property

> PROGRESSIVE PARTY: a political party in the United States

Random House College Dictionary, of 1973, has:

> LIBERAL: favorable to progress or reform, as in religious or political affairs; noting or pertaining to a political party advocating measures of progressive political reform' of or pertaining to representational forms of government rather than aristocracies and monarchies; of, pertaining to, based on, or advocating liberalism; favorable to or in accord with concepts of maximum individual freedom possible, esp. as guaranteed by law and secured by governmental protection of civil liberties; favoring or permitting freedom of action, esp. with respect to matters of personal belief or expression; free from prejudice or bigotry; tolerant; open-minded or tolerant, esp. free of or not bound by traditional or conventional ideas,

values, etc.; characterized by generosity and willingness to give in large amounts; given freely or abundantly; not strict or rigorous, free, not literal; of, pertaining to or befitting a freeman; a person of liberal principles or views; a member of a liberal party in politics, esp. of the Liberal party in Great Britain; of freedom, befitting the free.

CONSERVATIVE: disposed to preserve existing conditions, institutions, etc., and to resist change; cautious, moderate; traditional in style and manner, avoiding showiness; of or pertaining to the Conservative party; of or pertaining to political conservatism; having the power or tendency to conserve, preservative; a person who is conservative in principles, actions, habits, etc.; a member of a conservative political party.

COMMUNISM: a theory or system of social organization based on the holding of all property in common, actual ownership being ascribed to the community as a whole or to the state; a system of social organization in which all economical and social activity is control by a totalitarian state dominated by a single and self-perpetuating political party; the principles and practices of the Communist Party; communalism.

SOCIALISM: a theory or system of social organization that advocates the ownership and control or industry, capital, land, etc., by the community as a whole; procedure or practice in accordance with this theory; (in Marxist theory) the stage following capitalism in the transition of a society to communism; utopian socialism.

> PROGRESSIVE PARTY: a party formed in 1912 under the leadership of Theodore Roosevelt advocating popular control of government, direct primaries, women suffrage, etc.; a similar party formed in 1924 under the leadership of Robert M. La Follette; a left-wing political party formed in 1948 under the leadership of Henry A. Wallace.

I have used dictionries one hundred and four years apart, from 1828 to 1932, and forty-one years apart, from 1932 to 1973, to demonstrate how, over time, political labels developed. As one may observe, in 1828, the adjective was described by other adjectives, for the most part, and of course Communism and Socialism did not formally exist. By the 1930s reference to a political party is made, in reference to "progressive", and, by the 1970s, the adjective descriptions go more into the political environment. However, through it all, a person of liberal thinking holds less with tradition and custom as not observing or no longer viewing value in it and is more creative, while a conservative thinking person holds much more with tradition and custom as seeing value in what is to be preserved. From only the definitions, it is understandable how a liberal thinking person can move into being a progressive thinking person.

Question: If a liberal thinking person obtains an environment of their viewpoint and it is maintained over time becoming tradition and custom, does that liberal thinking person become a conservative thinking person if they what to preserve their tradition and custom against what was Conservatism and does the previous conservative thinking person then become a Liberal? Just wondering.

The term "liberal" has been in use for centuries and as one may observe it has become politicalized. Personally I like and even enjoy the definition of "liberal" of the 1828 dictionary. There was a phase being used not long ago. "Think outside of the box." In general, liberals as compared to conservatives do think outside of the box. A person may also be conservative in the political area, but liberal in other areas. A political liberal may be so on social issues, but conservative on other issues balancing that person out to a moderate. Thinking outside of the box is not just political though.

Inventors think outside of the box. They have to have a vision that not only sees what already is, but also what could be. They analyze and realize an idea. And inventors are involved in all human endeavors of improvement. An inventor is not only one who earns their living by inventing, but also anyone, in any profession, who brings an idea into manifestation. That idea is going to be what did not exist and therefore non-traditional.

So liberal thinking has been in existence ever since a human thought of handling fire, with respect, to use it for warmth and cooking and manufacturing such as metal work.

There is a key word, in the 1973 description of Socialism; utopian. Remember that word being used in earlier text? The word stems from ancient Greek and has been the subject of literature, science, philosophy, economics, ecology, religion and politics. Ecology embraces the preservation and protection of nature and therefore is the so-called Green Movement. Religion, of course, is the Garden of Eden and Heaven. Politics, of course, is Socialism.

Utopia equates to perfection between both humans and nature and humans in society. However, the two Greek syllables the word stems from mean "no" and "place". In other words, there is no place on earth utopia is to be found. And that is the goal of Socialism; to establish utopia on earth. Online reference Wikipedia "Utopia".

The key word in the description for Communism is "totalitarian". Socialism as an economic system and Communism as a form of government that promotes and supports and enforces Socialism. However, there is more to the two. Both also have in their description "social organization".

I Could Have Been One

Both believe in the holding of all property, in any form, for the common good and general community. The definition of Communism states the control of all property is by the government. The definition of Socialism includes "social organization", which in Socialist terms is Socialist government.

What the definitions do not state is that Communism believes in taking by force, while Socialism believes in taking by politics, by election and legislature. It has been said the only difference between a Communist and a Socialist is a Communist is a Socialist, but with a gun. That actually does seem to have been proven by history; armed revolution.

Ann Landers, who was a well-known advice newspaper syndicated columnist from the 1940s up to 2002, gave a simple definition, by example, in her column and it was recently reprinted, upon request. By the way, the name "Ann Landers" is a pseudonym used for the column itself. The column presented the following:

> **Ann Landers**
> SYNDICATED COLUMNIST
>
> **Dear Ann:** I am an inner city English teacher, and my students are reading George Orwell's *1984*. I am having a difficult time explaining communism, socialism and fascism without giving a full-blown, time-consuming history lesson. I recall you printed a humorous column some time ago explaining these concepts. Will you please print it again? I'm sure it will kick-start a lively class discussion. — **A Teacher in Mississippi**
>
> **Dear Mississippi Teacher:** Thank you for asking. It's an "oldie," but a "goldie." Here it is:
>
> Socialism: You have two cows. Give one cow to your neighbor.
>
> Communism: You have two cows. Give both cows to the government, and they might give you some of the milk.
>
> Fascism: You have two cows. You give all of the milk to the government, and the government sells it.
>
> Nazism: You have two cows. The government shoots you and takes both cows.
>
> Anarchism: You have two cows. Keep both of the cows, shoot the government agent and steal another cow.
>
> Capitalism: You have two cows. Sell one cow and buy a bull.
>
> Surrealism: You have two giraffes. The government makes you take harmonica lessons.

So what am I? It seems as though I, at the least, changed from Conservative to Liberal. Did I enter into Socialism? Socialism is an economic system.

I myself had benefited from such a system. I had collected unemployment benefits. Yes, I contributed to those benefits just as I contributed to Social Security, by being employed and, in the case of Social Security, by paycheck deduction. The government collected and redistributed. I had benefited from the Food Stamp program. And I had been in a government sponsored training program. Such social programs are provided by the taxpayers, which includes myself, via the government. Even if I did not believe in the Socialist economic system, I was part of it by practice and Liberal in my thinking of social issues. By my raising and what I had been taught in my glowing up years, I was at the Right of the political spectrum. However, during my adult years, of decision making once I began paying attention and voting, my thought process had relocated over into the Left.

The goal of developing utopia sounds good. Establishing global utopia. That sounds even better. If there is utopia, there is world peace. No more war. There would have to be a world government managing all nations. Well…we already have the United Nations. And they have Agenda 21. They have a plan of ecology. They are well educated intellectuals; people of worth and meaning. They have a global view of its problems. They have a solution. If highly educated people of worth and meaning can bring about global wellbeing and lasting peace, why not?

I stated I returned to Christianity, while holding Liberal views. I have discovered there are other Christians who are Liberal. What about Socialists? What about that term "Christian Socialism"? Are there Christians who are Socialists? Why would a Christian be a Socialist? Are there Christians who were Liberal and moved further over to the Left, to be Socialists? In my voting, in elections and on propositions, I had moved into the Left and toward Socialism. I need to examine the possibility of that and the reason why. I need to establish a foundation for why a Christian would be a Socialist. After all, I drifted away and fell away from Christianity and became, at least, a Liberal heading to Socialism and continued such thinking after my return to Christianity.

The Connection

In discussion, a friend told me it seemed some time ago he had read about early Socialism being based on early Christian communal life, which included assisting one another,; giving of one's resources for the sake of the community. This is not so much different from today. Church life is involvement in the activities of a church, which includes social activities, church community and aiding those church members who require assistance. Back in the persecution days of the early Christians, by the Roman Empire, community life would have also included banding together and protecting one another.

We now have the Interfaith Ministries or Interfaith Alliance. Besides assisting their own, they also assist those outside of their church community, including those who do not practice Christianity.

I researched and found a movement of Christian Socialism dating back to the **mid-1800s**. Apparently Capitalism was seen, by some Christians, as being idolatrous and rooted in greed. In other words, money/profit had become a god and Capitalism stemmed from greed.

Greed is the result of a mental process whereby something becomes dominant as the object of our thinking and actions. It becomes the vehicle driving towards a certain goal. It may be used for positive or negative. It may be combined with ambition to become a disciplined drive to achieve the goal. Greed is not always about money. If I want to achieve a goal such as writing this book, I use greed to drive my daily actions in researching and writing. I want to gather as much information of whatever subject matter is applicable and compose as much as I can concerning the relevance of that subject matter to the goal of the book. That is a positive use of greed. However, all good things in moderation. If I become so greedy that all I want to do day and night every day and night is research and composition, then I am creating a situation for bad effects to happen such as downhill health and isolation of self. I become a hermit. I will have gone to the extreme due to greed. I will not have time for anything else or anyone.

Did Capitalism stem from greed? Capitalism has been around since the days of bartering. I need those goods and you need the goods I have. Supply and demand and the equality of the goods determine if it is a good trade. We trade. It is a win win. Work was involved. Somewhere along the line, money was invented.

Instead of becoming Socialists, maybe those Christians should have become active in changing the business mindset from greed to fair labor practices and pricing for the good of all. This would have to be achieved over time, with some legislation and attitude change promotion such as thinking of the common good of competition, within limitations. Yeah…I know…more laws. But what can laws do? They can begin to change attitudes.

Money can be whatever is required by all for living; water, salt, seashells, precious metals, etc. Let's say seashells were first used. How might that have happened? By the trading of seashells for material goods. Let's say that seashells became a valuable and desirable item. People would trade just to obtain them and then they in turn could use them to trade for something else. And it became common practice, with seashells being the center of trading; like money.

We trade money for goods and services. Eventually coins of precious metals became money. Once the printing press came into common use, someone decided that money could be printed as a certificate based on precious metal. Banks developed for financial dealing and insurance companies developed for coverage of valuable goods such as aship's cargo being transported from one location to another. If the ship was lost a sea and the cargo never made it to the destination, the ship's owner was paid in money.

I agree money can become a god, for some people going to the extreme of greed. But I do not agree that Capitalism stemmed from greed. Capitalism developed naturally as a system by which people could trade goods for goods and work for money and trade money for goods and services, with services creating jobs for people to earn money by.

Capitalism itself did not become a god. Greed is within a person. If a person does not use greed in moderation and goes to the extreme of wanting more, more, more and "keeping up with the Jones", then there is a problem. "Keeping up with the Jones" was a saying for wanting what someone else had and having their lifestyle. In fact, too much greed can be the cause of one not having time for the one true God, of not following our Lord and Savior Jesus Christ.

It was not until the 1960s, in England, that a major movement developed and, in 2013, the Christian Socialist Movement became the Christians on the Left.

I found their web site stating the name change and declaring a membership of 1,500. The site is of those in the British United Kingdom and affiliated with the British Labour Party; Britain's Socialist political party. While 1,500 is not many, in comparison to the total population of the British United Kingdom, it is the matter that such people claiming to be Christians formed an organization, to further the goals of the Socialist.

There is also a website titled Christian Left, for Christian Liberals. They claim not to be Socialist, but they also promote such items as universal health care. I have also found other organizational websites concerning Christians and Left and Liberal and Socialism. There seems to be a combination to fit all Christians who lean to the left in either liberalism or socialism.

I found, on Amazon, books concerning Socialism and Christianity. I even found one with that title. Some promoting the combination and some countering it. I did not purchase any of those books because I did not want any of them to influence my own writing.

Not all Christians are traditionalist or conservative. Many are liberal, in that they think outside the box. Remember that is the basic definition of a liberal. An artist, writer, architect, administrator, designer, etc. may be a liberal simply because they think outside the traditional box, in the performance of their profession. In the case of Christians, I dare say they are thinking outside of the church box and finding ways to create heaven here on earth, through an economic, social, political movement. And now churches are splitting on social issues dividing conservatives and liberals, including the filing of law suits for church property.

During the 2008 Presidential campaigning, I came across a Christian supporting Obama. I asked them about Obama's abortion views and the Christian stated that such pro-abortion views were not important, since he was going to do great things.

Not long ago I came across an online news article concerning a protest rally. I do not remember exactly the who, when, where or why of it, but I do remember one of the photos presented with the article. In the photo was a young woman, who was holding up a sign that stated "Jesus was a Socialist". My thought was, "Where did that come from?" I had not thought about such an equation before. That photo is what started me on an exploratory journey.

Let us go back to my research of Socialism and the beginning of the Wikipedia article and the Bible verses:

Acts:

2: 44-45, All the believers were together and had everything in common. Selling their possessions and goods, they gave to anyone as he had need.

4: 32, All the believers were one in heart and mind. No one claimed that any of his possessions were his own, but they shared everything they had.

4: 34-35, There were no needy person among them. For from time to time those who owned lands or houses sold them, brought the money from their sales and put it at the Apostles' feet, and it was distributed to anyone as he had need.

And this is the connection between Christianity and Socialism. If this caring for others and giving to others aspect of Christianity was an inspiration for early Socialism, then it is easy to understand how some Christians would be drawn to Socialism.

The friend, who informed me there was a connection between Christianity and Socialism, told a story of how he first came to know that; a story of his father. Tom came home from his day of high school classes, and told his father about learning how Socialism was bad. His father stated Tom should not be so hard on Socialism, since it had part of its foundation in early Christian communal life. Tom was part of a devoted Christian family.

So what changed in that early Christian communal life, which was established in order to benefit the whole from the contributions of the individuals of the Christian community? Tom explained the change was in attitude. What caused the change? To put it in today's terms, the haves were supporting the have-nots. Human nature prevailed and the haves began to wonder why they had to support the have-nots. Those who had material goods had given them up, for the sake of those who could not fend for themselves; the widow, the orphan, the sick, the disabled. If new converts, of some means, were not available to follow in their footsteps, then who would support those who could not support themselves? The communal system broke down. I dare say once the Roman persecution was over there was not a reason for communal living per se, as banding together for protection was not necessary. Oh…have I mentioned the Romans worshiped many gods?

Let's continue, by viewing the parallel between Christianity and Socialism.

The Parallel

When I came to know what Socialism is, I came to realize there is a parallel to it. Just as I went to the seeds of Marxism, Communism and Socialism, in using the *Communist Manifesto*, I now go to the source of the other part of the parallel;

the teachings of Christ. I have already given Bible verses relating to what is supposed to be the foundation of Socialist beliefs, but what about other Bible verses? There are actually other Bible verses, of both the New and Old Testaments. Using the reprint of the 1599 Geneva Bible:

Matthew:

5:16. Let your light so shine before men, that they may see your good works, and glorify your father which is in heaven.

It is okay to do good works, in public. It is not okay to do so that the public may see and glorify the do-gooder or an organization represented, but that God is glorified. God may work through the do-gooder or organization as an instrument and the do-gooder or organization may receive recognition, but it is God who should receive the glory, for through Him the resources, including humans, are provided.

5:17. Think not that I am come to destroy the Law, or the Prophets. I am not come to destroy them, but to fulfill them.

Referring to the moral laws of the Old Testament. That is why the Old Testament is in the Christian Bible. Jesus was upholding the Ten Commandments given to Moses, by His Father.

In reference to the Ten Commandments, Christ said:

Mark 12:31. And the second is like, that is, Thou shall love thy neighbor as thyself. There is none other commandment greater than these.

Jesus had been asked which was the greatest Commandment of the Ten.

He summed up the first four, in "Love thy God". The first Commandment itself identifies God, with the following three giving instructions on how humans may show their love for God, in relation to Him. The following six give instructions on how humans may show their love for God, in relation to humans.

If one does not love God, there is not any use for the other nine. However, the last six may be used to maintain an orderly society.

So Jesus answered the question, but extended the answer to include a summary of the last six for loving thy neighbor.

Who is thy neighbor? All humankind.

Love thy neighbor. Do unto others as you would have them do unto you. The Golden Rule. Love equals charity, compassion, mercy and works of charity.

By the way, in following the teachings of Christ, we may have to love our neighbor, but that does not mean we have to like everything they do or say. However, forgiveness is part of loving our neighbor.

What else did Jesus say about works of charity?

Matthew 6:1-4. Paraphrasing – when one performs works of charity, do not do it in public so that men may know of your works and you gain acknowledgement for it, but do it in private and your Father in Heaven will give you acknowledgement for it.

The Apostles taught each in their own style, but each using the exact words of Jesus so as to maintain the truth, without variation, of Jesus' words and meaning. Therefore, in the New Testament writings, they teach as Jesus taught them. And there are many writings concerning charity.

James 1:27. Pure religion and undefiled before God, even the Father, is this, to visit the fatherless, and widows in their adversity, and to keep himself unspotted of the world.

Gives those we should assist as those who have lost their source of support. "…unspotted of the world." What has been placed in the world, through human action, which is not pleasing to God or for the glory of His name and disobedient of His laws, we should not make part of our own lives as a Christian.

II Thessalonians 3:10. For even when we were with you, this we warned you of, that if there were any, which would not work, that he should not eat.

The lazy should not be supported by charity or government welfare.

Now…since Christ upheld the moral laws, of the Old Testament, let's view something of what is in the Old Testament concerning who should receive charity.

Deuteronomy 10:18. Who doeth right unto the fatherless and widow and loveth the stranger, giving him food and raiment.

Children of single mothers. Wife of the deceased. Wife and children of the deceased. Unknown persons in need.

Psalm 82:3. Give justice to the weak and fatherless; maintain the right of the afflicted and destitute.

Defend those who cannot defend themselves against injustice.

Ruth 2:5-16. Paraphrasing – After destitute circumstances, in a foreign land, Ruth, of that foreign land, had traveled to Bethlehem, with her mother-in-law, Naomi, who was a Jew. Naomi instructed Ruth to go to a certain field and request to gather wheat, after the reapers. She was allowed by the foreman, after Ruth had told him her story and relationship to Naomi. When the landowner arrived and asked the foreman concerning her, he then personally instructed Ruth where to go in the field for the best gathering, protected her from any man and gave her water to drink.

Both the Jewish foreman and the landowner followed Jewish moral law and provided for the poor and a foreigner, with a relationship to a Jewish woman.

In summary, those who should receive charity are widows, orphans and strangers in need. Those who can work should work and not receive charity.

The bottom line is Christians should assist, with a hand-up, those who cannot fend for themselves. Sometimes a handout must be given before a hand-up, in order that the needy may gain stability and then, after the hand-up, may begin to support themselves.

Giving should be voluntarily, by the individual or church or organization, out of love for both God and humankind. Of course, a person does not have to even believe in God to have the inclination to assist those in need. They do it simply because of the goodness within them.

Now…with all of that being said, I am going to give as an example of the parallel, between Christianity and Socialism, a person who, to me, is an icon of that parallel; social activist Dorothy Day (1897–1980). To quote her, "We must talk about poverty, because people insulated by their own comfort lose sight of it."

Her autobiography *The Long Loneliness* was originally published in 1952, by HarperCollins Publishers, New York, New York.

"A Cleveland Communist said once, 'Dorothy was never a Communist. She was too religious.'" While growing up she had little Christian influences, through her family and friends, but did have Socialist influences through reading, while she observed the poor around her and felt that enough was not being done to assist them. However, having read the Bible she knew the Old Testament spoke of assisting widows and orphans and those who could not fend for themselves and Christ's words concerning the assisting of the poor. She also observed the different economic class levels; the haves and have-nots, the very wealthy through Capitalism and the conditions of those working for the very wealthy in mass production factories. This would have been shortly after the turn of the 1800s into the 1900s, when the working conditions of mass production had no restrictions concerning the welfare of workers, including child laborers in factories.

Having developed very strong idealistic thinking concerning social behavior toward the poor and downtrodden, including workers, she joined the Socialist Party when she attended the University of Illinois. Once again she had influences of both Christianity and Socialism, while at the university.

She was, however, ever mindful that while she had the opportunity to attend university others of her age did not and had to maintain gainful employment no matter how harsh. At the same time she was conflicted as to her rejection of Christianity, while holding to the Marxist slogan, "Workers of the world unite! You have nothing to lose but your chains." Dorothy finally did reject Christianity, to focus on the Socialist cause.

"Why was so much done in remedying social evils instead of avoiding them in the first place?" For example, both father and mother worked just to make a decent living, while their children were in day nursery, but why could not the father be paid a high enough wage so the mother would not have to work?

By 1915, restrictions on hours worked and low pay had been accomplished. She felt she was part of a movement moving forward for the social wellbeing of the common good. She was gratified with her part in the cause.

While at university, Dorothy meet a student by the name of Rayna and they became best friends.

Dorothy graduated, moved to New York leaving Rayna behind to finish her education. Dorothy obtained a reporter position with the *Call*, which "was politically a Socialist paper". "The term Socialist was a mild term for Communist then," Its leadership was having a conflict due to some favoring the American Federation of Labor (A.F. of L.), while others favored the Industrial Workers of the World (I.W.W.). The A.F. of L. opposed the Amalgamated Clothing Workers, who came out of the A. F. of L. The I.W.W. opposed the A. F. of L. Back then labor unions, which had formed for positive reasons, had quickly become the target of two elements; organized crime and Communism.

Her adventure into the political world of Communism, Socialism and anarchists had begun. She became acquainted not only with members of those groups, but also with their various leaders. The time period was just prior to the United States entering World War I. Many such organizations were against the U.S. becoming involved and held protests and peace meetings. University intellectuals were involved. There were also protests on social issues, for the betterment of living conditions for the poor. Her reporting threw her right into the midst of it all. So much so she "had no time for membership in any organization and never went to Socialist meetings."

Dorothy was employed, but poor. She lived among the poor noting differences between them and the middle class, of which she herself was from.

"I had bought a small phonograph for a dollar down and a dollar a week, plunging at once into installment buying, that plague of the poor, that dishonesty by which the poor are robbed of their meager earnings." Looking at the context in which this was written I believe that she is telling how she was thinking at that youthful time of her life. I consider this an example of not just her own misjudgment caused by her blinding zeal for the Socialist cause, her strong dislike for Capitalism and a lack of consideration for the opportunity of the poor to have and enjoy, by their own free will, but of that of young people in general. Yes, she was poor then, but she had not grown up poor. Yes, she was an intellectual, but she did not yet have the experience to temper her opinion. And that is my opinion, my two cents' worth.

The following were taken from various paragraphs:

"With all my radicalism, I was extremely conventional." "I was neither Christian nor a pacifist, and I certainly acted like neither." "I was not even acting like a good radical, lining myself up on the side of the 'capitalist-imperialist' press," She had become friends with journalist of conventional newspapers. "Often, in looking back on my past life I can see that I was not a good radical, not worthy of respect like those great figures in the movement who were fighting the issues of the day." "Our desire for justice for ourselves and for others often complicates the issue, builds up factions and quarrels. Worldly justice and unworldly justice are quite different things."

"So, I say, I do not really know myself as I was then. I do not know how sincere I was in my love of the poor and my desire to serve them. I know that I was in favor of the works of mercy as we know them, regarding the drives for food and clothing for strikers in the light of justice, and an aid in furthering the revolution. But I was bent on following the journalist's side of the work. I wanted the privileges of the woman and the work of the man, without following the work of the woman. I wanted to go on picket lines, to go to jail, to write, to influence others and so make my mark on the world. How much ambition and how much self-seeking there was in all this!"

It was April of 1917 and she was just nineteen. World War I had been existing since 1914 and the United States entered it in April of 1917, for the duration of it to 1919. During WWI, the Russian Revolution would occur March of 1917 and Communism/Socialism would capture its first country; its first national victory. It would continue to march through the world to this day and time. March 21st Dorothy Day would be at the celebration of the Russian Revolution in Madison Square Garden, New York City. She reveled in it.

1917 was a time of unrest among the people, of New York City, concerning the high cost of living and much unemployment. She also covered other protests concerning appeals for playgrounds and recreation centers and baby clinics and better schools. She wavered between her allegiance to Socialism and the syndicalism of the I.W.W. and anarchism. She continued to read the Socialistic literature of the day and continued to come to know various writers of such material and leaders in such causes. Finally deciding Socialism was too full of doctrine and not really understanding Karl Marx and, since the I.W.W. did have an immediate plan for the United States, she became a member of it.

Among her readings was an article published in the *Call* written by the vice-chairman of the Committee on Industrial Relations. The author had interviewed a Catholic priest. While reading the article, she discovered many quotes of Pope Leo XIII's *Rerum Novarum* on the social teachings of the Church based on the teachings of Jesus Christ. Pope Leo was elected in 1878 and served to his death in 1903.

She left the *Call* and moved over to a liberal newspaper called *The Masses*. That was six months before the paper shutdown due to the U.S. entering the War and such newspapers being suppressed. Toward the end of the shutdown, she was given the duties of editor. It was during that time period that her best friend, from university, entered back into her life.

Rayna visited from Chicago, but she and Dorothy would drift apart, after Rayna's return to Chicago. Long story short is Rayna married a Communist, relocated to Russia and died at a young age. Rayna Prohme was given a "Red" funeral, in which she was cremated and her ashes remained in Moscow.

After *The Masses* closed down, Dorothy joined a friend, who was a Suffragette, in picketing the White House. They were demanding rights for political prisoners, which they considered arrested members of their organization to be. Thirty-five of them, including Dorothy and her friend, were arrested and treated harshly. Their number included older ladies and those of well-to-do families. Their leader and spokesperson was one of those of influence. The ladies went on a hunger strike, which ended on the tenth day as the authorities, from President Wilson on down, had become very concerned. The demands of the ladies were met and they served the rest of their jail/workhouse time under favorable conditions.

Dorothy wrote it was an experience she would never forget, of men being capable of such treatment to each other; that it was one thing to write about and have a theoretical knowledge of sweatshops and injustice and hunger and a very different thing to experience it in one's own flesh.

While in the harsh isolation, with hardly any light to read by, during the first ten days, she requested a Bible and read the Psalms clinging to the comfort they gave. However, she gave no thought to religion during her last twenty days of confinement as she was in the world again. "I had seen myself too weak to stand alone, too weak to face the darkness of that punishment cell without crying out, and I was ashamed and again rejected religion that had helped me when I had been brought to my knees by my suffering."

This was during World War I, when many Communists and Socialist turned to Nationalism and fought for their respective countries, for which they were denounced by some Communist and Socialist leaders.

That is the time period and background in which Dorothy Day became a Communist and Socialist activist. Long story short is she would eventually became attracted to the Catholic Church, investigated it and converted to Christianity and Catholicism, to continue her passion concerning what is now termed social justice. She fought for fifty years for social justice by establishing the Catholic Worker Movement, which took political action and at the same time served the poor such as soup kitchens, etc. Her San Francisco home became the Workers' headquarters for organizing and ministering.

She had moved from formal Socialism to formal Christianity. She was the reverse of the movement by Socialist to gather Christians to their cause. Christians who started out being Christians and went to Socialism. It was the same principle of parallel in reverse.

For more information, go to the Catholic Worker Movement website.

The End

A friend told me that a person we were both acquainted with was a Socialist; that he had Socialist tendencies. Upon having the opportunity, I walked up to Matt and stated, "Someone told me that you are a Socialist." He kind of grinned and chuckled replying, "I am not a real Socialist. I just have some Socialist tendencies." I explained I was writing a book on Socialism and Christianity and requested an interview with him, which he granted. The following is the result of that interview.

Matt had some Christian influences, while growing up, and went to church as a child. Grandmother was Christian and influenced her daughter and grandson. The father had passed over when Matt was very young. Grandmother passed over when he was still growing up. It was just his mother and him. They stopped going to church. He began working as a teenager to help provide for them doing farm work during the summer and odd jobs during school time. Mother passed over, when he was twenty, from blood cancer. He saw her suffer and blamed God.

I Could Have Been One

He grew up during the 1980s having some Socialist influences. While in high school, he and a small group of friends, who came together because they liked to discuss current issues such as politics, could often be found together in deep discussion. Social Justice was an issue.

Both influences continued into adult life, but not so much Christianity. In college he read Socialist writings and history, including the *Communist Manifesto*. He found that Social Justice appealed to him, but not Communism, Marxism or Socialism.

He has not gone back to church, but continues to stay current on current events and politics deciding what is good or not good regardless of where it comes from. He does not belong to a political party or any formal movement. From conversation, I believe he is an annalistic and a moderate liberal. He himself does not like labels. He believes in finding the best solution no matter if it is from the Right or the Left or a common ground combination of the two or from elsewhere. Nor does he like to think about a child being hungry or a person suffering. Helping the child and the suffering is what is important to him and not who does it for what reason. He feels good when he helps someone.

He does believe Socialism and Christianity go hand in hand, to an extent, in that they both assist the poor. That extent being that their motivations are different. One is pragmatic and one is faith-based. One is not for God, but for assisting those in need because they are in need, while the other is for love of humanity in following the teachings of Christ.

Matt was not aware of the Socialist Christians movement until I brought it out during the interview.

He tries to use common sense in his thinking. If something makes sense to him, he accepts it. "It" may come from the Left or the Right, Socialism or Christianity or Conservatism. Therefore I believe he is somewhere in the middle politically, but a liberal thinking outside of any box. He believes

Communism is a form of government, which will take by armed conflict and is totalitarian. Socialism is an economic system. However, in complete Socialism, it must be supported by a Communist government. Many countries have a degree of Socialism, but not a Communist government, including this country.

He knows very little about Agenda 21.

His decision making on social issues is pragmatic and not done concerning God.

I find that Matt is a caring person, who asks the question, "Why does it happen?" Why does a child have to go hungry? Why does an elderly person have to suffer in death? Why do the poor have to go without, when there are so many different types of resources for a hand-up or could be? He is analytical and does not accept issues at face value. He examines an issue.

He does not like the United Nations. It was begun for a positive reason, but has now gone full Socialist, for global control.

Matt lives in a rural mainly Christian Conservative area in which many people believe that Communism and Socialism are the same and that Communism and Christianity have nothing in common. In an area where people have not thought about such issues or had the opportunity to examine them, it is easier to just lump Communism and Socialism together.

He is simply a good person who cares.

Christianity

Since I do not know how familiar a reader is with Christianity, I offer the following online resource for a basic familiarization. (Online reference allaboutreligion.org: History Of Christianity)

The Beginning of the Faith:

How did it all start? Christianity started about 2000 years ago in Judea (present-day Israel) with Jesus Christ and His faithful group of disciples. During this period, Judea was a cross-cultural mecca of bustling cities and farms. The emperor of Rome was the ruler. The Jews at that time hated Roman rule as it was but another reminder of the historical oppression they faced as a people. The polytheistic cultural beliefs of Rome were also pagan and intrusive to Jewish life. Some Jews saw that their only hope was to conform to this change. Others became religious zealots who formed pockets of guerilla resistance against Rome. Still others withdrew themselves into the Judean wilderness to study the Jewish law and wait for the eventual coming of their promised Messiah (savior).

The Arrival of Jesus Christ:
With this cultural and religious backdrop, the ministry of Jesus began. Jesus was a Jew. He observed the Jewish faith and was well acquainted with the Jewish Law. In His early thirties, Jesus traveled from village to village, teaching in the synagogues and healing those who were suffering. Jesus' teaching was revolutionary. He challenged the established religious authorities to repent from their self-righteousness and hypocrisy and realize that the Kingdom of God is rooted in service and love. Jesus' teachings stirred the hearts of people and created instability, something the Jewish religious authorities feared. Soon, a faithful group of men began to follow Jesus and call him teacher. These men became His disciples. Jesus taught His disciples about the will of God and about the "new covenant" God will bring to humanity through Him. Jesus helped them to see that mankind is bound to the pain and futility of life as a result of sin. Due to sin, mankind lost its relationship with God. The purpose of this "new covenant" is to restore those who accept it into a renewed fellowship of forgiveness and love with God. What is this new covenant? Jesus himself would pay for the sins of all humanity by being crucified unjustly on a

Roman cross. Three days later, He would rise to life, having conquered death, to give hope to a hopeless world. Well, it happened just as Jesus taught, and His disciples were witnesses to an amazing miracle. Their teacher, Jesus of Nazareth, died and three days later rose again to become their Messiah. Compelled by a great commission to share the love that the God of this universe had imparted upon them, the disciples began to proclaim this gospel of hope throughout the territory. Thus, from a small group of ordinary men that lived in a small province in Judea about 2000 years ago, the history of the Christian Church began, and the Christian Faith has since spread to the rest of the world. Their gospel message was simple: "For God so loved the world, that He gave His only begotten Son, that whosoever believeth in Him should not perish, but have everlasting life" (John 3:16).

Foretold by Prophecy:

Though most of the historical record for the start of the Christian faith is recorded in the New Testament accounts, the history of Christianity actually began with prophecy in the Old Testament. There are over 300 prophecies (predictions) that span over a period of 1000 years that are recorded in the Old Testament concerning the coming of a Jewish Messiah. A study of Jesus' life, death and background will show that He was undoubtedly the fulfillment of these Messianic prophecies. Thus, even long before Jesus walked the earth, His mission was made known to mankind through the Word of God.

A Faith Based on Historical Fact:

Did it all really happen? At first glance, the history of Christianity's origin may seem like nothing more than a fairy tale. Many feel that it's just too implausible, and even intellectually dishonest, for people living in the 21st century to believe that these events actually took place. However, the Christian faith, unlike any other religion, hinges on historical events, including one of pivotal importance.

If Jesus Christ died and never rose to life, then Christianity is a myth or a fraud. In 1 Corinthians 15:14, Paul exhorts his readers to grab hold of this central truth, that "And if Christ be not risen, then is our preaching vain, and your faith is also vain." The evidence for the resurrection is the key to establishing that Jesus is indeed who He claims to be. It is the historical validity of this central fact that gives Christians genuine and eternal hope amidst a hurting world.

The End.

There are major religions around the world. There are also minor ones followed by a native people or tribal people, who do not live in nature but with nature. It seems as though the more educated and scientific and technologically advanced a people are the more removed they are from religion. They replace religion with science. In the case of Communism and Socialism, they replace religion with their own design. However, even if a people denies a supreme being there is still the innate working within them; the innate knowledge of a supreme being. It is that the unspoken knowledge is not being allowed to rise to the surface. Those who live with nature know and listen to that innate knowledge of the Supreme Being; God. There is a quote by an American Southwest Comanche Chief named Quanah Parker, who stated that his people did not go into ceremony to talk about God, but they went into ceremony to talk with God.

Since the Bible gives the life events of Jesus Christ, maybe I should first begin this with some Bible history as a refresher reminder or something new for one who has not had the opportunity to learn about the Bible. It will also serve to put various aspects in proper perspective just as I examined the *Communist Manifesto*.

Both the Bible and the Catholic Church have been mentioned previously. Now I want to give some history concerning the Catholic Church and Christianity in general.

No matter what one thinks about the Catholic Church either past or present, historical documents do show that the Catholic Church can trace its linage back to Jesus and the Apostles, when Jesus stated, "...upon this Rock I will build My Church." That Rock being the Apostle Peter, whose name means "rock".

Almost exactly four hundred years, after the birth of Christ, a Catholic Council of Bishops convened to compile writings to be used as the standard of Catholicism; such a standard would state, "This is the life of Christ, what he taught and therefore what we believe". It would be used as the basis, of further writings by the Catholic Church, to expand on the teachings. Writings written by Christ's Apostles Matthew, Mark, and John as well as the Disciple Luke and the Jewish convert to Christianity, Paul, and the brothers James and Jude were believed to be of Divine Inspiration.

I am not asking anyone to accept this as fact. To begin with, one has to believe in God in order to believe in Divine Inspiration. In relation to Christianity, one has to believe in God in order to believe in His Son, Jesus Christ. I am simply presenting facts presented to me by research. It is up to the reader as to if they want to accept those facts or not. And to what degree they want to accept them; in part or in whole or reject them. That is why research references are given, to give foundation on what is written and for the reader's own research.

In reference to the Catholic Church, the term "catholic" began to be used in the 2nd century A.D. The word comes from the Greek language meaning "the whole of" or "universal". Therefore the universal church. It has been and is all over the world. At the time the term was first used, the Church existed throughout the world as known by the Mediterranean people, including countries to the east such as India. (Online reference "Got Questions – Your Questions. Biblical Answers. What is the meaning/definition of the word Catholic?")

I Could Have Been One

Some people believe that people in those days did not know how to read or write, at least not the general populace. Contracts were a verbal agreement. Therefore the saying, "A person's word is their bond." Don't know exactly when that saying came about, but the point is that it relates to verbal agreement. At some point, in time, the agreeing parties also began to shake hands on the verbal agreement, at least in some cultures. Consider the facts of history that Mediterranean cultures, at the time of Christ, did have elementary education. This was required for the sake of commerce, religious learning, government, etc. In the Jewish culture, boys as well as some girls did receive some form of elementary education. Of course the higher status a family had in the community, the more advance the education of their children would be. However, even the poor received some formal education, even if it was the original home schooling, of parents passing down what they themselves knew. There were also Scribes, who were dictated to in order for one's thoughts to be written down. So even a Jewish fisherman such as Peter, would have had some education, besides that of how to fish. (Online references American Bible Society "Education in Ancient Israel" and Barr Family "Questions on the Education of Jesus and the Apostles" and Ancient World History "Scribes".)

The New Testament holds letters, from Paul also known as Saul, to early Christian communities, which he as a prior Jewish military commander, who had been well educated, would have written with his own hand. In some cases, a written letter would be in the speaking style of a certain Apostle. When the Apostles taught, they did have their own personal style, but they always spoke the words Jesus said to them as a means of maintaining the validity of the words of Jesus. Therefore, if one was communicating either verbally or in a letter, one would use the same style and words to convey the same teaching. For formal use, such a letter would be titled as a letter from the Apostle whose style it contained such as First Letter of Peter to the....

While I have not researched if postal systems existed during the time of the early Christians, I am guessing that government or military written communications were delivered by courier, as was done during both the American colonies Revolutionary War and later the Civil War for military communication besides the use of the telegraph. After Christ and during the beginning of the Christian Faith, for personal communication, I am guessing it was hand carried, by a mutual acquaintance of both sender and receiver. There was intelligence and culture during the time of Christ. In any case, written communications did get delivered.

By the way, I make such injections as I do not know what a reader may or may not know. Many times a person does not have knowledge, on a certain subject, simply because they have not had a reason or opportunity to gain the knowledge. And I want to give a clearer picture of what occurred. Now back to the Bible History.

The Catholic Council wanted to select writings, which were of Divine Inspiration. Okay…faith is involved here. If one has faith, then one believes in Divine Inspiration. If one does not have faith, then there is only what is physical and mental and practical and rational. However, practical and rational can be subjective according to one's learning, experience and thought processing.

Writings were gathered and reviewed. They also had to be selected based on the requirements for the reason of the compilation and which were the best for that purpose. Added to the compilation would be the books of the Hebrews, which held their history and they based their teachings on, to compile the Old Testament. And please consider the meaning of the word "testament".

Why add the books of the Hebrews to the early Christian/Catholic writings? Jesus Christ was born, raised, grew up and lived his life as a Jew. He was of the linage of King David, whose linage was of Salmon and from him back to Jacob and Abraham. His parents, Joseph and Mary, were Jews, who obeyed Jewish law and Jesus Christ obeyed the same laws. Jesus attended the Synagogue, on the Sabbath, to pay homage to his Father; not his earthly father, but his Heavenly Father, God. The God of Jews and Christians. The history and culture of the Jews, to and during the time of Jesus Christ, is the history and culture that Christianity came out of and therefore, by extension, is the Faith History of Christians. The very early Christians were Jews as well as others and so were the Apostles. The great crowds of people who followed Jesus Christ, to listen to his teachings, were mostly Jews. Christians accept obedience to the same basic Faith Laws that the Jews do. They are called The Ten Commandments and were received by Moses, a Jew. Jesus Christ did not abolish that Law. He further expanded on it, such as no work on the Sabbath, except by necessity, such as saving of life be it human or animal. And, in reference to Christ, His performing a miracle on the Sabbath.

Laws come into existence due to a need to correct or establish a situation. That law may be either positive or negative. The traffic law stating that vehicles will stop at a red light is positive because it prevents accidents, by traffic control, thereby saving humans from harm and death. The United States Segregation Laws were established due to a society's need to control a body of people; a race. It came about because of the prejudicial selfishness of a White society; a negative. Every law contains both the letter of it and the spirit of it. Both the letter and the spirit coincide in the positive or negative of the law.

In the example of "no work on the Sabbath", the letter are those words whereas the spirit gives the exception coinciding with the teaching of Jesus Christ "love thy neighbor". That is also an expansion of The Ten Commandments stating that one shall not lie, cheat or steal. Jesus Christ defined what His Father had given to the Jewish people and, by extension, to Christians.

There are two types of law in Jewism; moral and ritual. Jesus emphasizes the moral law not the ritual.

Now…about those Gospel writers. Who were they? (Online references Amazing Bible Timeline, Learn Religions)

Research has been accomplished by going through historical records and writings. Sometimes pieces of a puzzle have to be put together. Sometimes historical records are conclusive and sometimes not. Sometimes the phrase "it is believed" has to be used meaning that the pieces seem to fit together, but without a direct connection from point to point.

Matthew: A Jew also called Levi in some Bible passages. His profession was that of tax collector; a dishonest tax collector collecting more than he should have and keeping the extra for himself. Therefore he may have been a person of wealth. Like the first four Apostles called to follow Jesus, he immediately did so upon Jesus calling him. He invited Jesus to his house for a feast with his friends such as other tax collectors. Jesus was challenged on His eating with known sinners. And Jesus said, "For I have come to call not those who think they are righteous, but those who know they are sinners." (Matthew 9: 9-13) After the Book of Acts written by Luke, there are no more verifiable records of Matthew's life.

Mark the Evangelist: While there are many Biblical people named Mark, this one is believed to have been a traveler with Peter, who recorded Peter's preaching in Rome and is identified in the Book of Acts as John Mark. He is also believed to have been a Jew or have a Jewish background due to his Jewish style of writing. In age, it is believed that he was most likely younger than Jesus and the Apostles. His travels may have taken him to Venice, Italy, where he may have been martyred. Since Peter himself was martyred in Rome and Mark may have travel to Italy with him, this may be true.

Luke the Evangelist: There is a lot of mystery about Luke. It is believed he did not actually know Jesus or even live in Palestine, but was a later believer and there is reference that he was born in Antioch and was an early convert to Christianity. He is known to have worked with Paul and believed to have worked with traditional writings concerning the life of Jesus and afterwards. If he worked with Paul, then he would have been taught the actions of the Apostles during their early days of forming the structure of the Church and local travels of Paul. It is believed he died close to one hundred years after Christ. His Gospels are important because of his detail in them and Acts tells of the early formation of Christianity.

Online reference: Cornerstone Bible Studies: *Gospel* means good news, in this case the good news of the birth, life, death and resurrection of Jesus Christ as recorded by Luke. W. Manson has noted that "Luke has cast his net wide, and produced a gospel the most voluminous and varied, the most vibrant and sympathetic, the most beautiful and sweetly reasonable of all that we possess." Contemporary author and theologian R. C. Sproul has said that of the four gospels of Matthew, Mark, Luke and John, Luke is his favorite. Well known and highly respected Biblical commentator Leon Morris has pointed out that Luke's grand theme throughout his gospel is the love of God for his people as shown in the life of Jesus. According to Morris, Luke's gospel "…is the longest of the four, and when Acts is added he has written more of the New Testament than any other single writer. Clearly a study of his writings is important for the student of the New Testament." Even more, it is important to study this gospel in order to gain a proper understanding of who God is, who we are, and who Jesus Christ is in God's perfect plan of redemption for the people of God.

John the Apostle: The brother of the Apostle James both among the first four called to follow Jesus. Both brothers seem to have a primary role to play in following Him. Paul described John as the pillar of the Jerusalem church. John did not suffer martyrdom, but was exiled to an island and wrote the Book of Revelations while in exile.

In the First Letter of Paul to the Corinthians, 1 Cor 2:6-10, he speaks of wisdom as given by the Holy Spirit. Using the Geneva Bible:

"And we speak wisdom among them that are perfect: not the wisdom of this world, neither of the princes of this world, which come to nought. But we speak the wisdom of God in a mystery even the hid wisdom, which God had determined before the world, unto our glory. Which none of the princes of this world hath known: for had they known it, they would not have crucified the Lord of glory. But as it is written, The things which eye hath not seen, neither ear hath heard, neither came into man's heart, are, which God hath prepared for them that love him. But God hath revealed them unto us by his Spirit: for the spirit searcheth all things, yea, the deep things of God. Paul is speaking of the same Holy Spirit which descended upon the Apostles, when they were in seclusion from the Jews. The same Holy Spirit which filled them and they got up and went outside and began to proclaim the Good News of the Lord. And it is that Holy Spirit with which the Apostles and Paul spoke to others of God and Jesus Christ.

On to Bible printing.

The first printing press, in 1456 Anno Domino (A.D.) (Latin for After Christ), was invented by Gutenberg, in Germany. The very first book printed on it was the Bible. Before then, the production of the Bible was by hand, produced by Catholic monks, and included beautifully accomplished art work as well as the hand printed word…literally. Of course, the mass production method, of the printing press, meant that the Bible, or any such printed book, could be sold to a greater number of people and at a much lower cost. By the way, Martin Luther was not even born until 1483 and the Lutheran Church was the first to be formed after the Catholic Church. So it was the Catholic Bible Gutenberg printed. And another "by the way" is that the Bible is the most printed and read book today, in all of its various versions.

The Old Testament had been translated from Hebrew to Greek, before Christ's birth. After Christ's death and the Apostles began to teach His Gospel, the books composed into the New Testament were written. From the reference I am using and from knowing that Alexander the Great spread the use of the Greek language, by way of his conquering army expanding his empire, I am actually assuming that all of those books were written in Greek.

Therefore both the Old and New Testament books would have been in Greek. Approximately three hundred years later, the Greek was translated into Latin, which was the language of the Roman Empire, and became part of the Latin Vulgate manuscript.

It was the Latin Vulgate Bible, which was first produced on the Gutenberg printing press.

In 1522, Martin Luther translated, into German, and published the New Testament.

A hundred and four years (1456 - 1560), after the Gutenberg Bible was printed, the Geneva Bible was printed in Geneva, Switzerland, by English Protestant refugees. It became the Bible of the Protestant Reformation and came to America, with early English settlers. There was a revision printed in 1576. The most popular King James Bible was printed in 1611. (Online reference *A Brief History of the King James Bible* by Dr. Laurence M. Vance.)

I have given this history since I have referred to the Geneva Bible previously and will again later, in order to use the language of the time most easily available, from as far back as possible.

The term "Protestant" comes from and is in reference to English protestors against the Church of England, which was established by King Henry VIII. Up until that establishment, Henry VIII had been Catholic. You may remember that he wanted to divorce his first wife, to marry another woman. The Catholic Church would not allowed it. The Pope said no. Henry broke from the Catholic Church and placed himself as the head of the Church of England, in 1534. This was seventeen years after Martin Luther founded his church as the original breaking from the Catholic Church.

Why does the Catholic Bible contain seven more Old Testament books than the Protestant Bibles, in variations of the King James Bible and in the Geneva Bible? Because when the Catholic Church combined both the Old and New Testaments, they used the same books the Jewish people themselves used, who also had selected which of their writings would be the official works, for teaching. When the King James was composed, the same occurrence happened. However, by then, the Jews had reselected and decided to remove the seven books. Although the seven books removed were still viewed as valid and important to their teachings, the books were also viewed as supporting material and not primary material. So....

The Acts of the Apostles tell of the events that took place after the Holy Spirit descended upon them. They began to teach, perform miracles, form Christian communities, determine what Jewish traditions and customs they should continue, etc. Their first administrative act was to appoint a disciple to fill the vacancy among the twelve left by Judas betraying Jesus and then hanging himself. Over time other organizational matters took place such as appointing Deacons and Bishops. Jesus had told them to go out to all parts of the world and tell of the "Good News." They did that too even as far away as India. And so it continued up into the Middle Ages.

Catholicism spread throughout the European continent. There were the Catholic Crusaders volunteering to stop the advancement of the Muslims and take back the Holy Land. Great cathedrals were built for the praise of and to the glory of God. Europe was Catholic. During the middle of the Middle Ages was the establishment of the Lutheran Church and the Church of England and Protestantism. Then during the original French Revolution, of 1789, the Catholic Church was deleted from that country.

The other major denominations either separated one way or another from the Church of England or from one that did separate or was founded by an individual or group mainly during the later 1500s to the 1700s or later into contemporary times, all of which was/is long after Christ.

The point is the only Christian Church in existence up to the time of Luther's separation from the Catholic Church was the Catholic Church, as historically proven.

Now, with all that being said, I did find the following concerning the Baptist Church, in general.

Baptist History.org: Our best historical evidence says that Baptists came into existence in England in the early seventeenth century. They apparently emerged out of the Puritan-Separatist movement in the Church of England. Some of these earnest people read the Bible in their own language, believed it, and sought to live by it. They formed separate congregations which accepted only believers into their membership, and they baptized converts upon their profession of faith. Their opponents nicknamed them "Baptists," and the name stuck.

Answers.com: There are a number of different religious denominations which have the name 'Baptist'. Although some doctrines differ between the various Baptist groups, they all base their beliefs on the Bible, and all give particular emphasis to the need for total water immersion on the part of adult converts as an essential part of induction into the faith. (Matthew 28:19, Acts2:41) Given that Jesus Christ was baptized in this way and that he taught his followers that they should go and make disciples and baptize them, it could be said that Jesus himself started the Baptist movement. Similarly it is also possible to take the view that John (John the Baptist) who started baptizing adult believers some six months before he baptized Jesus was really the founder of the Baptist church. Furthermore, as these individuals were carrying out God's will, then it could also be logically claimed that the actual founder of the Baptist church was God. Although the Bible record states that baptism is a fundamental part of Christianity, there is no record that the early believers called themselves "Baptists" or the "Baptist Church." Nor are there any records in the early centuries of Christianity that the special term "Baptist" was in any way ever applied to Christians. Many present-day Baptists trace their religious roots to various devout Christian groups who practiced adult baptism, such as the Waldenses (about 1177). However, the Waldenses were not called Baptists, nor did they call themselves Baptists. A more recent "predecessor" of the Baptist movement would be the Anabaptists, but again, they were not called "Baptists." One person many consider to be the person most responsible for the development of the modern Baptist Church was **John Smyth** (1570-1612), an English ordained Anglican minister who broke from Anglicanism and established his own "Baptist" church in the Netherlands in **1608/1609**. One member of that church, and baptized by John Smyth, was **Thomas Helwys**, who later returned to England and founded the first Baptist church there in **1612**, in Spitalfields, London. The congregation called themselves The General Baptists.

Okay…by using the same reasoning as stated above, any Church may say they were founded by God or John the Baptist, or Jesus. The above does state there are no records showing the Baptist Church, as named such, reaching back two thousand plus years ago. I could start my own church and say the same thing. Also there is the matter of Jesus Christ founding His Church upon the "Rock/Peter". And that is the true foundation. Therefore I consider John Smyth to be the actual founder of the Baptist Church having broken from Anglicanism.

Dorothy Day mentioned the Roman Catholic Church's Pope Leo XIII's writing, in 1891, which is relevant to the parallel. It is titled *On the Condition of the Working Classes* or *Rights and Duties of Capital and Labor*.

I have to quote the first paragraph:

> "That the spirit of revolutionary change, which has long been disturbing the nations of the world, should have passed beyond the sphere of politics and made its influence felt in the cognate sphere of practical economics is not surprising. The elements of the conflict now raging are unmistakable, in the vast expansion of industrial pursuits and the marvelous

discoveries of science; in the changed relations between masters and workman; in the enormous fortunes of some few individuals, and the utter poverty of the masses; the increased self-reliance and closer mutual combination of the working classes; as also, finally, in the prevailing moral degeneracy. The momentous gravity of the state of things now obtaining fills every mind with painful apprehension; wise men are discussing it; practical men are proposing schemes; popular meetings, legislatures, and rulers of nations are all busied with it – actually there is no question which has taken deeper hold on the public mind."

The writing states it is expedient to speak on the condition of the working classes so that the principles which truth and justice dictate for its settlement and that it is no easy matter to define the relative rights and mutual duties of the rich and poor, of capital and labor. The ancient workingmen's guilds (referring to the Medieval European trade guilds for the training, advancement and protection of the professional workers) were abolished in the last century, and no other protective organization took their place and it has come to pass that working men have been surrendered, isolated and helpless, to the hardheartedness of employers and the greed of unchecked competition. To this must be added that the hiring of labor and the conduct of trade are concentrated in the hands of comparatively few; so that a small number of very rich men have been able to lay upon the teeming masses of the laboring poor a yoke little better than that of slavery itself.

To remedy these wrongs the socialists, working on the poor man's envy of the rich, are striving to do away with private property, and contend that individual possessions should become the common property of all, to be administered by the State or by municipal bodies. They hold that by thus transferring property from private individuals to the community, the present mischievous state of things will be set to rights, inasmuch as each citizen will then get his fair share of whatever there is to enjoy. But their contentions are so clearly powerless to end the controversy that were they carried into effect the working man himself would be among the first to suffer. They are, moreover, emphatically unjust, for they would rob the lawful possessor, distort the functions of the State, and create utter confusion in the community.

It goes on to state a person hires himself out for labors so he may obtain property for his wellbeing and hold it as his own to do with as he pleases, for his benefit. If he is wise in his finances, he may obtain land or chattels. Socialists endeavoring to transfer the possessions of individuals to the community at large strike at the interests of every wage-earner, since they would deprive him of the liberty of disposing of his wages and of all hope and possibility of increasing his resources and of bettering his condition in life.

Both man and animal have the instincts of self-preservation and propagation of the species. However, man has intelligence and reason and may obtain material goods for both present and future use, for his welfare. Hence, man not only should possess the fruits of the earth, but also the very soil, inasmuch as from the produce of the earth he has to lay by provision for the future. Man precedes the State, and possesses, prior to the formation of any State, the right of providing for the substance of his body.

With this being written in 1891, it deals with the agriculture aspect of earning a living. A person owns land. People work the land. All for a living, for their wellbeing.

Now let's go into some basic Christian belief.

What is required to believe in God and Jesus? Faith is required and we are all given the same measure to grow.

Why is faith required? Because we cannot touch and feel, see or hear God or Jesus with our physical selves. And Jesus lived on this earth over two thousand years ago.

How do we know of God and Jesus? By having the opportunity in this life to do so.

Do all people know of God and Jesus? No, some have, but choose to not pay attention to such teachings as Christianity. Some have not due to their individual circumstances. Some do not know a reason why they should invest in such a thing as religion.

Of those who accept belief in God and Jesus, what are they known as? As Christians.

Who do Christians follow? They follow Jesus Christ?

Why do they follow Jesus Christ? Because they believe in life-after-death; Heaven and Hell.

For what purpose do they follow? To gain the reward of being in Heaven upon leaving this life and not having to suffer the punishment of Hell, for a misused life here on earth.

How do they know of Jesus Christ, Heaven and Hell and the reward or punishment? The Bible tells them.

Why believe the Bible? It tells of the historical background Jesus descended from and His life on this earth and is believed to be inspired by God by His knowing all things and therefore preparing for its composition, by inspiring the writings of both Testaments, and inspiring the selection of those writings during the process of gathering what would become the Bible.

Why did Jesus come into this earthly life? To teach and die for all people so they may be shown God's mercy and have the opportunity to be with Him in Heaven.

So being a Christian means following the teachings of Jesus Christ as told in the Bible, for our preparation for the next life of being with God in Heaven.

I am going to follow this up with a passage from the Geneva Bible.

Mark 4: 4 – 8, 14 - 20

Jesus said:

> "And it came to pass as he sowed, that some fell by the wayside, and the fowls of the heaven came, and devoured it up.
>
> And some fell on stony ground, where it had not much earth, and by and by sprang up, because it had not depth of earth.
>
> But as soon as the Sun was up, it was burnt up, and because it had not root, it withered away.
>
> And some fell among the thorns, and the thorns grew up, and choked it, so that it gave no fruit.
>
> Some again fell in good ground, and did yield fruit that sprung up, and grew, and it brought forth, some thirtyfold, some sixtyfold, and some a hundredfold."

When questioned by the Apostles concerning the meaning of the parable, Jesus explained:

> "The sower soweth the word.
>
> And these are they that receive the seed by the wayside, in whom the word is sown: but when they have heard it, Satan cometh immediately, and taketh away the word that was sown in their hearts.
>
> And likewise they that receive the seed in stony ground, are they, which when they have heard the word, straightway receive it with gladness.
>
> Yet have they no root in themselves, and endure but a time: for when trouble and persecution ariseth for the word, immediately they be offended.

Also they that receive the seed among the thorns, are such as hear the word:

> But the cares of this world, and the deceitfulness of riches, and the lusts of other things enter in, and choke the word, and it is unfruitful.
> But they that receive the seed in good ground, are they that hear the word, and receive it, and bring forth fruit: one corn thirty, another sixty, and some an hundred."

It is God, Jesus or a Christian who may sow the seed, which is the Word of God, of Jesus. If one believes in God and Jesus, then one must believe in Satan. Satan also known as Devil is he who rebelled against God, with followers, lost the rebellion and was cast out of Heaven. He had been in Heaven as an Angel and rebelled out of jealousy of other Angels and anger against God. He is as real as God and Jesus and wants to take us away from God. He wants us in Hell instead of Heaven, where he was cast out of. A person told me, "He hates us because we are made in God's image and just seeing us angers him."

Those who receive the Word of God for a short time are those who do not really love God and therefore are not willing to suffer for that love of Him. They heard the Word and believed, but did not actually study the meaning of that Word and did not practice the teachings of the Word. Therefore they did not get to know God and in knowing Him love and thrust Him. The same person stated, "They do not become sanctified or set apart."

Those who receive the Word in good ground are those who not only believe, but also study the Word and practice the Word and receive the graces of the Word, in knowing, loving and thrusting God. "They walk in Jesus's footsteps."

Now…in order to believe this, one must believe this earth is not the only plane of existence, there is life after death of our physical body. That we do have a spirit and a soul as both are spoken of in the Bible. Any living thing has a spirit. It is what gives all living creatures great and small life, it is the animation of things. If I am wrong in my Christian belief, so what? I won't even know if I am wrong when I die as I will be just…well…dead. Period. Nothing more. I will have lived a good responsible life though. So the question is, at death, what will be the measure of a person's life? Will it be material as in how much stuff and toys the person accumulated or will it be spiritual as in their closeness to God and Jesus in the next life?. What if I am right and there is life after death as Jesus Christ taught? Then the person who has not prepared for it will have a very big surprise. Oh My Goodness Gracious Sakes Alive!!!!!!!!!!!

Let's go to the Sermon on the Mount in Matthew 5: 3 – 12.

"Blessed are the poor in spirit: for theirs is the kingdom of heaven.

Blessed are they that mourn: for they shall be comforted.

Blessed are the meek: for they shall inherit the earth.

Blessed are they which hunger and thirst for righteousness: for they shall be filled.

Blessed are the merciful: for they shall obtain mercy.

Blessed are the pure of heart: for they shall see God.

Blessed are the peacemakers: for they shall be called children of God.

Blessed are they which suffer persecution for righteousness' sake; for theirs is the kingdom of heaven.

Blessed shall ye be when men revile you, and persecute you, and say all manner of evil against you for my sake, falsely.

Rejoice and be glad, for great is your reward in heaven: for so persecuted they the Prophets which were before you."

"Poor in spirit" footnoted as "Whose minds and spirits are brought under, and tamed, and obey God." This refers to the discipline of the mind and spirit, under the teachings of God and Jesus to love and therefore obey God. "Mind and spirit"; both combined to train one's self. Train as in forming a habit, which then becomes first nature of doing above all other things. Love God above all other things. Practice the teachings of God above all things; above grabbing onto worldly things.

All of these are of spiritual nature and the "kingdom of heaven" is included as a reward. Kingdom of Heaven; life after this worldly life; life after death.

Chapters 6 and 7, of Matthew, are also concerned with Jesus' teachings of what to do and not do to obtain the Kingdom of Heaven. A Christian should use both the Old Testament Psalms and the New Testament Gospels and writings for how to live.

Psalm 115 speaks of idols made of earthly material being worshiped as a god; a god which cannot see or hear or speak. Likewise, if the person lives only for the things of this world, which cannot see or hear or speak, such as a political-economic system they come to worship that and deny the living God.

Isaiah 58: 7-10

> Is it not to deal thy bread to the hungry, and that thou bring the poor that wander, unto thine house? When thou seest the naked, that thou cover him, and hide not thyself from thine own flesh? (Footnote: For in him thou seest thy self as in a glass.) Then shall thy light break forth as the morning, and thine health shall grow speedily: thy righteousness shall go before thee, and the glory of the Lord shall embrace three. (Footnote: That is the prosperous estate wherewith God will bless thee. The Testimony of thy goodness shall appear before God and man.) Then shalt thou call, and the Lord shall answer: Thou shalt cry, and he shall say, Here I am" if thou take away from the midst of thee the yoke, the putting forth of the finger, and wicked speaking: (Footnote: Whereby is meant all manner of injury.) If thou

> pour out thy soul to the hungry, and refresh the troubled soul: then shall thy light spring out in the darkness, and thy darkness shall be as the noon day. (Footnote: That is, have compassion on their miseries. Thine adversity shall be turned into prosperity.)

Some Christians believe one may achieve Heaven by faith alone while others believe it takes both faith and works. In researching online, including at a Lutheran site, I found a lot of material on the phase "by faith alone". Luther began it all, by adding the word "alone" to the Bible scripture and the Protestant Reformation continued with it and it is still being discussed today. I am not going to enter into such discussion as it will serve not my purpose, but I do want to bring the subject to attention as it is a Christian issue and an important issue of Christianity. The two Biblical passages are Romans 1:17, which speaks of God's righteousness, and James 2: 14–18 concerning both faith and works.

Other issues are prayer, alms and fasting as stated in Matthew Chapter 6. Prayer and fasting are Christian disciplines and alms involve works of charity. Works of charity are also performed by current day Social Justice or Socialism. However, what is the motivation for Socialists doing it?

There are two "works"; one, works of the law and two, works of love. Works of the law are performing obedience to the Ten Commandments such as keeping holy the Lord's Day, or to the church rituals such as going to services on Sunday. Works of love are those of assisting another, when done out of love for God and neighbor, in glorifying and praise of God.

There are also two conversions; one, of ourselves and two, of others caused by our love for them, including strangers. One can give a bit of Heaven to others. Early Christians said God is love. We should mature as Christians by not just following rules, but by taking opportunities to obtain grace blessings such as attending church services, "operate in our gifting" and mature through study.

Some interesting stories as an example of the love of Christianity, to be practiced, are as follows:

Jesus told the story of the shepherd, who after discovering a lamb was missing, left the other sheep to go in search of the lost lamb. Upon finding the lamb, he carried it back to the flock. And that is what our Lord does, when we have become lost in the world. He is there for us ready to give us His assistance, in getting back to where we belong, with Him. We only have to reach out through prayer and be open to Him. He wants only for us to ask for His help and He will provide.

Jesus took a known sinner as an Apostle. Matthew was a dishonest tax collector driven by greed until Jesus Christ chose him as a disciple. We first meet Matthew in Capernaum, in his tax booth on the main highway. He was collecting duties on imported goods brought by farmers, merchants, and caravans. He was also overcharging on the duty. Jesus came to accept and save sinners. He ate in the company of known sinners even at their homes. He accepted the ones who required the most attention, to believe in Him.

The Jews looked down on the Samarians. However, in traveling, Jesus took the alternate route that went into Samaria, where he met the Samarian woman at the well. She was another sinner having lived with men not her husband. He spoke of the living water that gives eternal life. She was open to His words and went into town to tell others who she had met and had received the living water of His teachings.

Another Samarian told of is that of the Good Samarian, who assisted a man who had been beaten and left for dead. The man had been previously past by supposed good men. The Samarian took the man to a place to be cared for and also paid for his care. The supposed sinner, as viewed by the Jews, behaved as a Christian.

One day Jesus interrupted men about to stone a woman to death, by Jewish law, for having an adulteress affair. He began to write on the ground and told the men that the one of them without sin should throw the first stone.

One by one the men left, after noticing what Jesus had written in the dirt. (Personally I believe that He wrote down each of their most grievous sins.) Once all of the men had left, He told the woman to go and sin no more. Jesus had mercy on her, as He has on us all. We commit no sin too great for Him not to forgive, if we ask and are sincere.

Some people believe Mary Magdalene was a prostitute. In any case, she was another sinner Jesus accepted, forgave in mercy and befriended. So much so she became a close disciple. Jesus is there for us, if we want Him.

Jesus also spoke of bread. John 6:35 & 51: Jesus said to them, "I am the bread of life; he who comes to Me will not hunger, and he who believes in Me will never thirst. I am the living bread that came down out of heaven; if anyone eats of this bread, he will live forever; and the bread also which I will give for the life of the world is My flesh."

There is also a warning about being an elitist and not being humble. Luke 18: 9-14, Jesus gave the parable of two men going into the temple; one being a Pharisee and one a Publican (tax collector). The Pharisee proudly raised his head looking upward and prayed to God telling of his own righteousness and his thankfulness in not being as other men, who disobeyed the Ten Commandments including the Publican. The Publican did not look up, but with humility and sincerity prayed that his own sins might be forgiven. Jesus said the Publican went to his home justified, in the eyes of God, and those who exalt themselves shall be brought low and those who humble themselves shall be exalted.

One of my favorite Christmas movies is *Miracle on 34th Street*." A single mom is raising her only child to be realistic and believe only in what is factual. Along comes a man who claims to be the actual Santa Claus. There is also the interaction of the mom and the single man in the apartment across the hall, who is an attorney. Mom works for Macy's, in New York City and one of her duties is to organize the Thanksgiving Day Parade, in which there has to be a Santa Claus, which is where the Santa Claus comes in.

Santa needs a place to stay and since he and the man across the hall from mom have become acquainted, Santa has the opportunity to introduce the girl to the children's play of pretending. At first the young girl does not believe in Santa, but begins to observe him interacting with children, at Macy's. Both she and the man across the hall begin to believe that Santa is who he says he is. Long story short is Santa ends up in court and the man across the hall becomes Santa's defense attorney. The case is if Santa actually is the one true Santa. The newspapers make the case a front page story day after day. The United States Post Office decides to deliver all of the letters from children down to the courthouse, where Santa is. Since an official government agency recognizes Santa as "the Santa", the defense wins and Santa does not have to go to the insane asylum. There's more. Santa gets the little girl the house she wants and the man across the hall becomes her new dad and mom begins to believe as well that Santa is the Santa. Of course the movie is done so those watching it also believe. Faith is believing what seems unbelievable.

Jesus told the Apostle known as "doubting Thomas" that because Thomas had actually seen Jesus, after the Resurrection, Thomas believed, but blessed are they that have not seen and have believed. They believe because of what has been passed down for over two thousand years first by word of mouth, then by the written word and then by the printed word; the Holy Bible.

Innate belief in a Supreme Being plus the Bible plus faith gives hope for eternal salvation and love for God, Jesus and our neighbor in charity. Our neighbor is everyone and we should see them all as children of God; every stranger, everyone we would rather not be around. This does not mean we have to associate with people we do not like, but we are to love them as children of God. Some people make us uncomfortable. They are not like us, for whatever reason, but again we are to see them as children of God. If those people are the homeless we encounter, we are to still love them and help them, if we can and if they want help. If our path crosses that of a known criminal, gang member or ex-convict, we do not have to associate with them, but we do have to love them as children of God. And all of them we can pray for. I believe it was Dorothy Day who said, "Most people would not care for them." She was speaking of those who need attention the most; the unwanted.

Jesus said the poor will always be with us. While the poor do not have to always stay poor, there are those who do not have the ambition and simply accept what they believe to be their position in life and exist instead of living. There are those who grew up poor or as a poor adult took advantage of opportunities available and used their abilities to reach out and up and grab onto the rung of the prosperity ladder to begin their climb pulling themselves up one rung at a time. When we encounter the poor, with an opportunity to assist them and we can, then we should. We should see the child of God in them and assist out of love. This may be accomplished as an individual or a service organization member or a church member.

Bible scripture frames social justice as in who to assist and that those who can work should work or go hungry. Charity can also be a form of evangelization, but it needs to be an example out of love, in order to show that Christian charity is love. Evangelization is simply advertisement through word and action. Socialists also perform this. However, evangelization is connected to Jesus Christ telling the Apostles to go throughout the world and teach the Good News of the Lord. So if a Socialist Christian or Christian on the Left does such are they doing it for the Socialist or are they doing it for love of God and Jesus? It cannot be for both.

I enjoy the Star Wars movies. May the Force be with you! The movie *The Last Jedi* describes the Force as that which holds everything in all of the universes together and connects everything with each other. Becoming one with the Force gives one abilities which those outside the Force do not have; those who have not opened themselves up to the Force. However, there is the dark side and the light side of the Force; both evil and good existing within the same cohesive power. And the side of light of the Republic continues to fight and survive against the dark side of the totalitarian government of the Order. Good and evil. Light and Dark. Republic and forced totalitarian Order. And life after physical death.

There have been many gods in many cultures. The predominate cultures of both the Greek and the Romans had many gods. The folk lore, of Northern Europe, tell of various gods. The Egyptians, of the Mediterranean Sea, had various gods. The Bible tells of various cultures having various gods. Some cultures have had major and minor gods; gods of both genders such as Hindu. Among it all, in that part of the world, the Jews and Christians had only one God; the one true God of all being and they still do to this day. It demonstrates the innate belief and the true belief.

This is from earlychristiandictionary.com.

Early Christian Dictionary, *The Doctrine and Practice of the Early Christians*

Poverty and Prosperity

Blessed be ye poor: for yours is the kingdom of God. Luke 6:20

But woe unto you that are rich! for ye have received your consolation. Luke 6:24

But the Lord said, No servant can serve two masters. If we desire to serve both God and mammon, it is unprofitable for us: For what advantage is it, if a man gain the whole world and forfeit his soul? Now this age and the future are two enemies. The one speaks of adultery and defilement and avarice and deceit, but the other bids farewell to these. We cannot therefore be friends of the two, but must bid farewell to the one and hold companionship with the other. Let us consider that it is better to hate the things which are here, because they are mean and for a short time and perishable, and to love the things which are there, for they are good and imperishable. For, if we do the will of Christ, we shall find rest; but if otherwise, then nothing shall deliver us from eternal punishment, if we should disobey His commandments. *Second Clement (A.D. 100) ch.6*

Therefore let not the godly be grieved, if he be miserable in the times that now are: a blessed time awaits him. He shall live again in heaven with the fathers, and shall have rejoicing throughout a sorrowless eternity. Neither suffer you this again to trouble your mind, that we see the unrighteous possessing wealth, and the servants of God straitened. Let us then have faith, brothers and sisters. We are contending in the lists of a living God; and we are trained by the present life, that we may be crowned with the future. *Second Clement (A.D. 100) ch.20*

"These are they that have faith, but have also riches of this world. When tribulation comes, they deny their Lord by reason of their riches and their business affairs." And I answered and said unto her, "When then, lady, will they be useful for the building?" "When," she replied, "their wealth, which leads their souls astray, shall be cut away, then will they be useful for God. For just as the round stone, unless it be cut away, and lose some portion of itself, cannot become square, so also they that are rich in this world, unless their riches be cut away, cannot become useful to the Lord. Learn first from yourself when you had riches, you were useless; but now you are useful and profitable unto life." *Hermas (A.D. 150) Ante-Nicene Fathers vol.2 pg. 14*

Have regard one to another, and assist one another, and do not partake of the creatures of God alone in abundance, but share them also with those that are in want. For some men through their much eating bring weakness on the flesh, and injure their flesh: whereas the flesh of those who have naught to eat is injured by their not having sufficient nourishment, and their body is ruined. This exclusiveness therefore is hurtful to you that have and do not share with them that are in want. *Hermas (A.D. 150) Ante-Nicene Fathers vol.2 pg.16*

Those who have never investigated concerning the truth, nor enquired concerning the deity, but have merely believed, and have been mixed up in business affairs and riches and heathen friendships, and many other affairs of this world - as many, I say, as devote themselves to these things, comprehend not the parables of the deity; for they are darkened by these actions, and are corrupted and become barren. *Hermas (A.D. 150) Ante-Nicene Fathers vol.2 pg. 26*

He said to me; "You know that you, who are the servants of God, are dwelling in a foreign land; for your city is far from this city. If then you know your city, in which you shall dwell, why do you here prepare fields and expensive displays and buildings and dwelling-chambers which are superfluous? He, therefore, that prepares these things for this city does not purpose to return to his own city.

O foolish and double-minded and miserable man, do you not perceive that all these things are foreign, and are under the power of another?" *Hermas (A.D. 150) Ante-Nicene Fathers vol.2 pg.30*

Therefore, instead of fields buy you souls that are in trouble, as each is able, and visit widows and orphans, and neglect them not; and spend your riches and all your displays, which you received from God, on fields and houses of this kind. For to this end the Master enriched you, that you might perform these ministrations for Him. It is much better to purchase fields [and possessions] and houses of this kind, which you will find in your own city, when you visit it. This lavish expenditure is beautiful and joyous, not bringing sadness or fear, but bringing joy. The expenditure of the heathen then practice not you; for it is not convenient for you the servants of God. *Hermas (A.D. 150) Ante-Nicene Fathers vol.2 pg. 30*

The rich man has much wealth, but in the things of the Lord he is poor, being distracted about his riches, and his confession and intercession with the Lord is very scanty; and even that which he gives is small and weak and has not power above... The rich man then supplies all things to the poor man without wavering. But the poor man being supplied by the rich makes intercession for him, thanking God for him that gave to him. And the other is still more zealous to assist the poor man, that he may be continuous in his life: for he knows that the intercession of the poor man is acceptable and rich before God. And this work great and acceptable with God, because (the rich man) has understanding concerning his riches, and works for the poor man from the bounties of the Lord, and accomplishes the ministration of the Lord rightly. *Hermas (A.D. 150) Ante-Nicene Fathers vol.2 pg.32*

These are men who have been believers, but grew rich and became renowned among the Gentiles. They clothed themselves with great pride and became high-minded, and abandoned the truth and did not cleave to the righteous, but lived together after the manner of the Gentiles. *Hermas (A.D. 150) Ante-Nicene Fathers vol.2 pg. 42*

Some of them are wealthy and others are entangled in many business affairs. The briars are the wealthy, and the thorns are they that are mixed up in various business affairs. These [then, that are mixed up in many and various business affairs,] cleave [not] to the servants of God, but go astray, being choked by their affairs, but the wealthy unwillingly cleave to the servants of God, fearing lest they may be asked for something by them. Such men therefore shall hardly enter into the kingdom of God. For as it is difficult to walk on briars with bare feet, so also it is difficult for such men to enter the kingdom of God. *Hermas (A.D. 150) Ante-Nicene Fathers vol.2 pg.50*

Now hear wherefore they have been found round. Their riches have darkened and obscured them a little from the truth. When therefore the Lord perceived their mind, that they could favor the truth, and likewise remain good, He commanded their possessions to be cut off from them, yet not to be taken away altogether, so that they might be able to do some good with that which has been left to them, and might live unto God for that they come of a good kind. *Hermas (A.D. 150) Ante-Nicene Fathers vol.2 pg. 53*

And when they see a stranger, they take him in to their homes and rejoice over him as a very brother; for they do not call them brethren after the flesh, but brethren after the spirit and in God. *Aristides (2nd century) Ante-Nicene Fathers vol.9 pg.277*

For God has given to us, I know well, the liberty of use, but only so far as necessary; and He has determined that the use should be common. And it is monstrous for one to live in luxury, while many are in want. How much more glorious is it to do good to many, than to live sumptuously! How much wiser to spend money on human being, than on jewels and gold! *Clement of Alexandria (A.D. 195) Ante-Nicene Fathers vol.2 pg.268*

Love of wealth displaces a man from the right mode of life, and induces him to cease from feeling shame at what is shameful... For what end, then, are such dainty dishes prepared, but to fill one belly? The filthiness of gluttony is proved by the sewers into which our bellies discharge the refuse of our food. *Clement of Alexandria (A.D. 195) Ante-Nicene Fathers vol.2 pg.280*

Accordingly he has not forbidden us to be rich in the right way, but only a wrongful and insatiable grasping of money... For he who sows and gathers more is the man who by giving away his earthly and temporal goods has obtained a heavenly and eternal prize; the other is he who gives to no one, but vainly "lays up treasure on earth where moth and rust corrupt"; of him it is written: "In gathering motley, he has gathered it into a condemned cell." Of his land the Lord says in the gospel that it produced plentifully; then wishing to store the fruits he built larger store-houses, saying to himself in the words dramatically put into his mouth "You have many good things laid up for many years to come, eat, drink, and be merry. You fool," says the Lord, "this night your soul shall be required of you. Whose then shall be the things you have prepared?" *Clement of Alexandria (A.D. 195) Miscellanies, book III ch.6*

So also let not the man that has been invested with worldly wealth proclaim himself excluded at the outset from the Savior's lists, provided he is a believer and one who contemplates the greatness of God's philanthropy; nor let him, on the other hand, expect to grasp the crowns of immortality without struggle and effort, continuing untrained, and without struggle and effort. *Clement of Alexandria (A.D. 195) Ante-Nicene Fathers vol.2 pg.592*

For if no one had anything, what room would be left among men for giving? ... He so praises the use of property as to command, along with this addition, the giving a share of it, to give drink to the thirsty, bread to the hungry, to take the houseless in, and clothe the naked... Riches, then, which benefit also our neighbors, are not to be thrown away... So let no man destroy wealth, rather than the passions of the soul, which are incompatible with the better use of wealth. So that, becoming virtuous and good, he may be able to make a good use of these riches. The renunciation, then, and selling of all possessions, is to be understood as spoken of the passions of the soul. *Clement of Alexandria (A.D. 195) Ante-Nicene Fathers vol.2 pg.594-595*

Abandon the alien possessions that are in your soul, that, becoming pure in heart, you may see God; which is another way of saying, Enter into the kingdom of heaven. And how may you abandon them? By selling them...It is thus that you dost rightly sell the possessions, many are superfluous, which shut the heavens against you by exchanging them for those which are able to save. Let the former be possessed by the carnal poor, who are destitute of the latter. But you, by receiving instead spiritual wealth, shall have now treasure in the heavens... For it was difficult for the soul not to be seduced and ruined by the luxuries and flowery enchantments that beset remarkable wealth. *Clement of Alexandria (A.D. 195) Ante-Nicene Fathers vol.2 pg.596*

But I think that our proposition has been demonstrated in no way inferior to what we promised, that the Savior by no means has excluded the rich on account of wealth itself, and the possession of property, nor fenced off salvation against them; if they are able and willing to submit their life to God's commandments. *Clement of Alexandria (A.D. 195) Ante-Nicene Fathers vol.2 pg.598*

A rich man is a difficult thing (to find) in the house of God; and if such an one is (found there), difficult (is it to find such) unmarried. What, then, are they to do?... To a Christian believer it is irksome to wed a believer inferior to herself in estate, destined as she will be to have her wealth augmented in the person of a poor husband! For if it is "the poor," not the rich, "whose are the kingdoms of the heavens," the rich will find more in the poor (than she brings him, or than she would in the rich). She will be dowered with an ampler dowry from the goods of him who is rich in God. *Tertullian (A.D. 198) Ante-Nicene Fathers vol.4 pg. 48*

John 10:1-18 tells of Jesus being the Good Shepherd and any other being a thief. (Online reference Bible Gateway.)

"Very truly I tell you Pharisees, anyone who does not enter the sheep pen by the gate, but climbs in by some other way, is a thief and a robber. The one who enters by the gate is the shepherd of the sheep. The gatekeeper opens the gate for him, and the sheep listen to his voice. He calls his own sheep by name and leads them out. When he has brought out all his own, he goes on ahead of them, and his sheep follow him because they know his voice. But they will never follow a stranger; in fact, they will run away from him because they do not recognize a stranger's voice." Jesus used this figure of speech, but the Pharisees did not understand what he was telling them.

    Therefore Jesus said again, "Very truly I tell you, I am the gate for the sheep. All who have come before me are thieves and robbers, but the sheep have not listened to them. I am the gate; whoever enters through me will be saved. They will come in and go out, and find pasture. The thief comes only to steal and kill and destroy; I have come that they may have life, and have it to the full.

"I am the good shepherd. The good shepherd lays down his life for the sheep. The hired hand is not the shepherd and does not own the sheep. So when he sees the wolf coming, he abandons the sheep and runs away. Then the wolf attacks the flock and scatters it. The man runs away because he is a hired hand and cares nothing for the sheep.

"I am the good shepherd; I know my sheep and my sheep know me— just as the Father knows me and I know the Father—and I lay down my life for the sheep. I have other sheep that are not of this sheep pen. I must bring them also. They too will listen to my voice, and there shall be one flock and one shepherd. The reason my Father loves me is that I lay down my life—only to take it up again. No one takes it from me, but I lay it down of my own accord. I have authority to lay it down and authority to take it up again. This command I received from my Father."

The End

This section is going to close with something I came across. Might have been an email sent to me or when I was research browsing. Anyway....

This is an absolutely incredible interview with Rick Warren, author of *Purpose Driven Life*. His wife now has cancer, and he now has "wealth" from the book sales. In the interview by Paul Bradshaw with Rick Warren, Rick said:

> "People ask me, 'What is the purpose of life?' And I respond: 'In a nutshell, life is preparation for eternity. We were made to last forever, and God wants us to be with Him in Heaven.'
>
> One day my heart is going to stop, and that will be the end of my body—but not the end of me. I may live to 100 years on earth, but I am going to spend trillions of years in eternity. This is the warm-up act - the dress rehearsal. God wants us to practice on earth what we will do forever in eternity. We were made by God and for God, and until you figure that out, life isn't going to make sense. Life is a series of problems: Either you are in one now, you're just coming out of one, or you're getting ready to go into another one. The reason for this is that God is more interested in your character than your comfort. God is more interested in making your life holy than He is in making your life happy. We can be reasonably happy here on earth, but that's not the goal of life. The goal is to grow in character, in Christ likeness.
>
> This past year has been the greatest year of my life but also the toughest, with my wife, Kay, getting cancer. I used to think that life was hills and valleys - you go through a dark-time, then you go to the mountaintop, back and forth. I don't believe that anymore.

Rather than life being hills and valleys, I believe that it's kind of like two rails on a railroad track, and at all times you have something good and something bad in your life.

No matter how good things are in your life, there is always something bad that needs to be worked on. And no matter how bad things are in your life, there is always something good you can thank God for.

You can focus on your purposes, or you can focus on your problems. If you focus on your problems, you're going into self-centeredness, which is 'my problem, my issues, my pain.' But one of the easiest ways to get rid of pain is to get your focus off yourself and onto God and others. We discovered quickly that in spite of the prayers of hundreds of thousands of people, God was not going to heal Kay or make it easy for her. It has been very difficult for her, and yet God has strengthened her character, given her a ministry of helping other people, given her a testimony, drawn her closer to Him and to people.

You have to learn to deal with both the good and the bad of life. Actually, sometimes learning to deal with the good is harder. For instance, this past year, all of a sudden, when the book sold 15 million copies, it made me instantly very wealthy. It also brought a lot of notoriety that I had never had to deal with before. I don't think God gives you money or notoriety for your own ego or for you to live a life of ease. So I began to ask God what He wanted me to do with this money, notoriety and influence. He gave me two different passages that helped me decide what to do, II Corinthians 9 and Psalm 72.

First, in spite of all the money coming in, we would not change our lifestyle one bit. We made no major purchases. Second, about midway through last year, I stopped taking a salary from the church. Third, we set up foundations to fund an initiative we call 'The Peace Plan' to plant churches, equip leaders, assist the poor, care for the sick, and educate the next generation. Fourth, I added up all that the church had paid me in the 24 years since I started the church, and I gave it all back. It was liberating to be able to serve God for free.

We need to ask ourselves: Am I going to live for possessions? Popularity? Am I going to be driven by pressures? Guilt? Bitterness? Materialism? Or am I going to be driven by God's purposes (for my life)?

When I get up in the morning, I sit on the side of my bed and say, 'God, if I don't get anything else done today, I want to know You more and love You better.' God didn't put me on earth just to fulfill a to-do list. He's more interested in what I am than what I do. That's why we're called human beings, not human doings.

Happy moments, PRAISE GOD. Difficult moments, SEEK GOD. Quiet moments, WORSHIP GOD. Painful moments, TRUST GOD. Every moment, THANK GOD."

The Differences

There are obvious differences of course.

Christianity was established over two thousand years ago. Communism/Socialism was manifested only one hundred years plus ago.

Christianity was founded on the basis of preparation for life after death following the spiritual teachings of a man being the Son of God. Communism/Socialism was founded on the teachings of a man wanting to usher in a new economic system and form of government.

Christianity would change the minds and hearts of humankind, through the use of our freewill to love one another and obtain a place with God in Heaven; for all eternity. Communism/Socialism denies such teachings and would control the actions of all humans for the earthly equality of utopia on earth.

Christianity is non-force by Jesus's teachings. Communism is by force of arms while Socialism is by force of politics by Marxist teachings.

Christianity has the document of the Bible to lead them. Communism/Socialism has the *Communist Manifesto* and the United Nations Agenda for the 21st Century also known as Agenda 21 and its follow-up document Agenda 2030. The American Communists/Socialists also have *Rules for Radicals*, by Saul Alinsky published in 1971, before his death in 1972.

I have not mentioned *Rules for Radicals* previously. It is a training manual for organizations and community activist on how to succeed in changing their own local communities, without force of arms. Upon obtaining the book, the first thing I did was to begin going through the first pages and there it was. "It" being what I had read about Alinsky doing. It is on the page with a quote from a Rabbi and one from Thomas Paine. It is the last entry and in Alinsky's own words.

I quote, "Lest we forget at least an over-the-shoulder acknowledgement to the very first radical: from all our legends, mythology, and history (and who is to know where mythology leaves off and history begins – or which is which), the first radical known to man who rebelled against the establishment and did it so effectively that he at least won his own kingdom – Lucifer."

He gave acknowledgement to Lucifer also known as Satan also known as the Devil. He must have admired the Devil.

Guess what I found on economicpolicyjournal.com: Hillary Clinton's 1969 Thesis on Saul Alinsky

"THERE IS ONLY THE FIGHT..." An Analysis of the Alinsky Model

A thesis submitted in partial fulfillment of the requirements for the Bachelor of Arts degree under the Special Honors Program, Wellesley College, Wellesley, Massachusetts.

Hillary D. Rodham, Political Science, 2 May, 1969

ACKNOWLEDGEMENTS

Although I have no "loving wife" to thank for keeping the children away while I wrote, I do have many friends and teachers who have contributed to the process of thesis-writing. And I thank them for their tireless help and encouragement. In regard to the paper itself, there are three people who deserve special appreciation: Mr. Alinsky for providing a topic, sharing his time and offering me a job; Miss Alona E. Evans for her thoughtful questioning and careful editing that clarified fuzzy thinking and tortured prose; and Jan Krigbaum for her spirited intellectual companionship and typewriter rescue work.

(Chapter I was on Alinsky's life.)

CHAPTER II

THE ALINSKY METHOD OF ORGANIZING: THREE CASE STUDIES

The Alinsky method of community organizing has two distinct elements. One, the "Alinsky-type protest" is "an explosive mixture of rigid discipline, brilliant showmanship, and a street fighter's instinct for ruthlessly exploiting his enemy's weakness."

The second, modeled after trade union organization methods, involves the hard work of recognizing interests, seeking out indigenous leaders, and building an organization whose power is viewed as legitimate by the larger community.

A small group of organizers including **Caesar Chavez**, of California grape strike fame, and Nicholas von Hoffman, now an editor of the Washington Post, were trained during the 1950s.

CHAPTER III: "A PRIZE PIECE OF POLITICAL PORNOGRAPHY"

CHAPTER IV: PERSPECTIVES ON ALINSKY AND HIS MODEL

CHAPTER V: REALIZING LIFE AFTER BIRTH

The previous chapter was a "perspective" rather than a "critique" because both Alinsky and his model are continuing to evolve. Although his basic premises, such as the primacy of power and the unavoidability of a relative morality are unchanged, his approach to the problem of redistributing power has shifted since his days as a labor organizer.

These shifts are not easily categorized, but they fall into two broad areas; his rethinking the meaning of community and the role of centralized national planning in social change. Central to Alinsky's evolving socio/political philosophy is his rethinking the idea of community:

PRIMARY SOURCES: Personal Interviews

Alinsky, Saul D. Mr. Alinsky and I met twice during October in Boston and during January at Wellesley. Both times he was generous with ideas and interest. His offer of a place in the new Institute was tempting but after spending a year trying to make sense out of his inconsistency, I need three years of legal rigor. Haffner, John. Reporter on the Back of the Yards Journal who represents the views of his neighbors regarding the community's future in conservatively chauvinistic terms. January, 1969, in Chicago. Hoffman, Nicholas von. One of the best of Alinsky's organizers and now a superb writer for the Washington Post. Talked with him by telephone in Washington in October. He was both helpful and provocative. Ryan, Phyllis. Social Worker on the staff of the Back of the Yards Neighborhood Council who left soon after I interviewed her in January, 1969. Her honesty about conditions in the area as well as her obvious distress over them contributed greatly to my understanding of the situation. Shimony, Annemarie. Professor in the Department of Sociology at Wellesley College. Mrs. Shimony criticized Alinsky's method during our conversation in March, 1969, helping me to focus my own opinions.

I have given only the chapter titles as what she wrote is not relative to this writing. I only want to show her connection to the men who acknowledge Lucifer and also show Alinsky's connection to Caesar Chavez.

I give this as background material; Hillary Clinton's 1971 letter to Saul Alinsky. By Dylan Stableford, Yahoo News, September 22, 2014, Yahoo News

I Could Have Been One

A letter from Hillary Clinton to the late community organizer Saul Alinsky in 1971 was published Sunday by the *Washington Free Beacon*.

In it, Clinton, then a 23-year-old law school graduate living in Berkeley, Calif., informs the Chicago activist she had "survived law school, slightly bruised, with my belief in and zest for organizing intact."

"The more I've seen of places like Yale Law School and the people who haunt them," Clinton wrote, "the more convinced I am that we have the serious business and joy of much work ahead, — if the commitment to a free and open society is ever going to mean more than eloquence and frustration."

Clinton first met Alinsky when she was at Wellesley working on her 1969 thesis on his controversial theories on community organizing, many of which were outlined in his 1946 handbook, *Reveille for Radicals*.

In the book, Alinsky encouraged community organizers to "fan the latent hostilities" of low-income, inner city residents and "search out controversy and issues, rather than avoid them." His 1971 book, *Rules for Radicals*, published a year before his death, expanded on that theme. "Pick the target, freeze it, personalize it, and polarize it," Alinsky wrote.

"Dear Saul," Clinton wrote in the 1971 letter. "When is that new book [Rules for Radicals] coming out — or has it come and I somehow missed the fulfillment of Revelation? I have just had my one-thousandth conversation about Reveille and need some new material to throw at people."

She thanked Alinsky for the advice he gave her about campus organizing.

"If I never thanked you for the encouraging words of last spring in the midst of the Yale-Cambodia madness, I do so now," Clinton wrote. She also asked if they could meet the next time he was in California.

"I am living in Berkeley and working in Oakland for the summer and would love to see you," Clinton wrote. "Let me know if there is any chance of our getting together."

She added: "Hopefully we can have a good argument sometime in the future."

Alinsky's longtime secretary, Georgia Harper, sent Clinton a letter in reply informing her he was away on a six-week trip to Southeast Asia, but that she had opened the letter anyway.

"Since I know his feelings about you I took the liberty of opening your letter because I didn't want something urgent to wait for two weeks," Harper wrote in the July 13, 1971, letter. "And I'm glad I did."

"Mr. Alinsky will be in San Francisco, staying at the Hilton Inn at the airport on Monday and Tuesday, July 26 and 27," Harper added. "I know he would like to have you call him so that if there is a chance in his schedule maybe you can get together."

The correspondence between Alinsky and Clinton was discovered in the archives for the Industrial Areas Foundation— a training center for community organizers founded by Alinsky — housed at the University of Texas at Austin.

According to Clinton's 2004 memoir *Living History*, Alinsky had offered her a job after her graduation from Wellesley, but she turned him down.

"He offered me the chance to work with him when I graduated from college, and he was disappointed that I decided instead to go to law school," she wrote. "[He] said I would be wasting my time, but my decision was an expression of my belief that the system could be changed from within."

July 13, 1971

Miss Hillary Rodham
2667 Derby #2
Berkeley, California 94705

Dear Miss Rodham:

Your July 8 letter to Mr. Alinsky arrived while he was away. He is not expected back in this office for about ten days, and when he returns, he will be coming from a six-week Asian trip.

Since I know his feelings about you I took the liberty of opening your letter because I didn't want something urgent to wait for two weeks. And I'm glad I did.

Rules for Radicals is out - published officially on May 14, 1971 by Random House.

I am enclosing several copies of reviews of Rules in which you may be interested.

Mr. Alinsky will be on the Dick Cavett Show on July 22 (if they it the same night they tape it).

You will hear from him on his return.

Sincerely yours,

(Mrs.) Georgia Harper
Secretary to Mr. Alinsky

gh

P.S. - Late item - Mr. Alinsky will be in San Francisco, staying at the Hilton Inn at the airport on Monday and Tuesday, July 26 and 27. I know he would like to have you call him so that if there is a chance in his schedule maybe you can get together. I would suggest your calling around 9 a.m. on either that Monday or Tuesday.

> When is that new book coming out—or has
> missed the fulfillment of Revelation? I have
> thousandth conversation about Reveille and nee
> to throw at people. You are being rediscovered
> Left-type politicos are finally beginning to
> the hard work and mechanics of organizing. I
> law school, slightly bruised, with my belief
> organizing intact. If I never thanked you for
> of last spring in the midst of the Yale-Cambo
> now. The more I've seen of places like Yale L
> people who haunt them, the more convinced I a
> serious business and joy of much work ahead,—
> a free and open society is ever going to mea

```
Hillary Rodham
2667 Derby #2
Berkeley, Calif. 94705


                          MR. SAUL ALINSKY
                          c/o The Industrial Areas Foundation
                          8 South Michigan Ave,
                          Chicago, Illinois


Personal
```

This is from online Encyclopedia Britannia.

A student leader in public schools, she was active in youth programs at the First United Methodist Church. Although she later became associated with liberal causes, during this time she adhered to the Republican Party of her parents. She campaigned for Republican presidential candidate Barry Goldwater in 1964 and chaired the local chapter of the Young

Republicans. A year later, after she enrolled at Wellesley College, her political views began to change. Influenced by the assassinations of Malcolm X, Robert F. Kennedy, and Martin Luther King, Jr., she joined the Democratic Party and volunteered in the presidential campaign of antiwar candidate Eugene McCarthy. So she grew up having a Christian influence, but at least drifted away in college, if not knowingly left. She was a Republican, but then became a Democrat. College seems to have a way of doing that to students.

This I found online and copied.

Liberals in this case range from Far Left to maybe Moderate. Do not forget Liberals are used by the Communist/Socialist, for their own bidding.

Source: The Week, Wednesday, 8 October 2014, Why do so many liberals despise Christianity?

Liberals increasingly want to enforce a comprehensive, uniformly secular vision of the human good. And they see alternative visions of the good as increasingly intolerable.

By Damon Linker | 6:06am ET

Many of the health care workers assisting Ebola patients are missionaries. So what? (REUTERS/Jo Dunlop/UNICEF/Handout via Reuters)

Liberalism seems to have an irrational animus against Christianity. Consider these two stories highlighted in the last week by conservative Christian blogger Rod Dreher.

Item 1: In a widely discussed essay in Slate, author Brian Palmer writes about the prevalence of missionary doctors and nurses in Africa and their crucial role in treating those suffering from Ebola. Palmer tries to be fair-minded, but he nonetheless expresses "ambivalence," "suspicion," and "visceral discomfort" about the fact that these men and women are motivated to make "long-term commitments to address the health problems of poor Africans," to "risk their lives," and to accept poor compensation (and sometimes none at all) because of their Christian faith.

The question is why he considers this a problem.

Palmer mentions a lack of data and an absence of regulatory oversight. But he's honest enough to admit that these aren't the real reasons for his concern. The real reason is that he doesn't believe that missionaries are capable "of separating their religious work from their medical work," even when they vow not to proselytize their patients. And that, in his view, is unacceptable — apparently because he's an atheist and religion creeps him out. As he puts it, rather wanly, "It's great that these people are doing God's work, but do they have to talk about Him so much?"

That overriding distaste for religion leads Palmer to propose a radical corollary to the classical liberal ideal of a separation between church and state — one that goes far beyond politics, narrowly construed. Palmer thinks it's necessary to uphold a separation of "religion and health care."

Item 2: Gordon College, a small Christian school north of Boston, is facing the possibility of having its accreditation revoked by the higher education commission of the New England Association of Schools and Colleges, according to an article in the Boston Business Journal. Since accreditation determines a school's eligibility to participate in federal and state financial aid programs, and the eligibility of its students to be accepted into graduate programs and to meet requirements for professional licensure, revoking a school's accreditation is a big deal — and can even be a death sentence.

What has Gordon College done to jeopardize its accreditation? It has chosen to enforce a "life and conduct statement" that forbids "homosexual practice" on campus.

Now, one could imagine a situation in which such a statement might legitimately run afoul of an accreditation board or even anti-discrimination statutes and regulations — if, for example, it stated that being gay is a sign of innate depravity and that students who feel same-sex attraction should be subject to punishment for having such desires.

But that isn't the case here. At all. In accordance with traditional Christian teaching, Gordon College bans all sexual relationships outside of marriage, gay or straight, and it goes out of its way to say that its structures against homosexual acts apply only to behavior and not to same-sex desires or orientation.

The accreditation board is not so much objecting to the college's treatment of gays as it is rejecting the legitimacy of its devoutly Christian sexual beliefs.

The anti-missionary article and the story of Gordon College's troubles are both examples (among many others) of contemporary liberalism's irrational animus against religion in general and traditional forms of Christianity in particular.

My use of the term "irrational animus" isn't arbitrary. The Supreme Court has made "irrational animus" a cornerstone of its jurisprudence on gay rights. A law cannot stand if it can be shown to be motivated by rationally unjustifiable hostility to homosexuals, and on several occasions the court has declared that traditional religious objections to homosexuality are reducible to just such a motive.

But the urge to eliminate Christianity's influence on and legacy within our world can be its own form of irrational animus. The problem is not just the cavalier dismissal of people's long-established beliefs and the ways of life and traditions based on them. The problem is also the dogmatic denial of the beauty and wisdom contained within those beliefs, ways of life, and traditions. (You know, the kind of thing that leads a doctor to risk his life and forego a comfortable stateside livelihood in favor of treating deadly illness in dangerous, impoverished African cities and villages, all out of a love for Jesus Christ.)

Contemporary liberals increasingly think and talk like a class of self-satisfied commissars enforcing a comprehensive, uniformly secular vision of the human good. The idea that someone, somewhere might devote her life to an alternative vision of the good — one that clashes in some respects with liberalism's moral creed — is increasingly intolerable.

That is a betrayal of what's best in the liberal tradition.

Liberals should be pleased and express gratitude when people do good deeds, whether or not those deeds are motivated by faith. They should also be content to give voluntary associations (like religious colleges) wide latitude to orient themselves to visions of the human good rooted in traditions and experiences that transcend liberal modernity — provided they don't clash in a fundamental way with liberal ideals and institutions.

In the end, what we're seeing is an effort to greatly expand the list of beliefs, traditions, and ways of life that fundamentally clash with liberalism. That is an effort that no genuine liberal should want to succeed.

What happened to a liberalism of skepticism, modesty, humility, and openness to conflicting notions of the highest good? What happened to a liberalism of pluralism that recognizes that when people are allowed to search for truth in freedom, they are liable to seek and find it in a multitude of values, beliefs, and traditions? What happened to a liberalism that sees this diversity as one of the finest flowers of a free society rather than a threat to the liberal democratic order?

I don't have answers to these questions — and frankly, not a lot hinges on figuring out how we got here. What matters is that we acknowledge that something in the liberal mind has changed, and that we act to recover what has been lost.

Damon Linker is a senior correspondent at TheWeek.com. He is also a consulting editor at the University of Pennsylvania Press, a contributing editor at The New Republic, and the author of The Theocons and The Religious Test.

Communism Manifested
Bella Visono Dodd

I purchased her autobiography *School of Darkness*, after learning of her and her life. The original publication was by P. J. Kenedy & Sons, New York, 1954. What I have is a 2017 reprint edition, by Angelico Press as a republication.

She begins the book with a quote, from John Banister Tabb. "And in the School of Darkness learn what mean 'The things unseen.'" John Tabb was an American poet, who was also a Catholic Priest. His life spanned from 1845 to 1909. There is meaningful reason why such a quote is given.

The following is a summary of Bella's life and importance. It is a long summary, but I feel her course of life deserves the attention to details, which explains her development into what she became and her transitions. There are many historical references. If the reader does not recognize a reference, research it. Everything is online.

Part way through the book I decided to be briefer in my summary as each paragraph has important information and therefore changed my method of writing to key subject matter.

In writing the summary, I use a mixture of her words and my own. In presenting the facts, I use her's. Sometimes I paraphrase and I give commentary, at times. Sometimes Bella does not fully explain a statement. Therefore I link passages together from this and that page, but I work not to assume what she had left out. For example, the name of "Visono" I would assume is her maiden name, but that is not said by her. Therefore I did not know if it was Rocco's surname until I read other resources.

Her mother, Teresa, owned her family's generational farm, in southern Italy, and had been widowed, after having nine children. The youngest was a baby at the time of the father's death. Teresa and the children followed the future husband, Rocco Visono, to America, to the Italian community in East Harlem. In

I COULD HAVE BEEN ONE

early 1904, Teresa and Rocco were married. Later that same year Teresa had to return to Italy and deal with matters of the farm. While there, Teresa gave birth to Maria Assunta Isabella; hence Bella was an Italian American.

Teresa left the baby in the care of a shepherd couple, for almost six years. They cared for, loved her and raised her Catholic. After an early 1900s depression, her mother had the money to go back to Italy and bring Bella to America, where she finally met her older brothers and a sister and her father.

Four months later Bella was able to speak enough English to attend school; a public school, which had been a "charity school" also known as "soup school". The school day always began with prayer and song.

The family moved from one section of New York to another as their financial situation improved. It was in the last neighborhood that Teresa found work caring for two, elderly, maiden sisters, who lived in a large colonial house. When the last sister passed, Teresa discovered the house and land, which was large enough for decent size farming, had been left to her. It became a home of activity and of cousins as the older children married and had their own families.

Due to their neighbors being Scotch, Irish and German, Teresa and Rocco stopped attending the two Catholic, neighborhood churches. They felt they did not fit in. Their home continued to be Catholic though and the children were encouraged to go to church, but they followed their parents example. However, the neighborhood public school had Bible reading. Bella enjoyed the Psalms and Proverbs.

She also learned American history and visited church graveyards, often placing flowers on this and that grave in respect for Americans who had lived before her. The local librarian, who took an interest in Bella's learning interests, introduced her to the granddaughter of Horace Greeley; a famous editor and patriotic American. The granddaughter was the wife of a church minister and held a children's sewing circle once a week. Bella became one of the children. They sang Christian songs and sometimes there would be an outing. Her small community held respect for one another and showed kindness to all.

World War I (WW I) began; the war to end all wars. Bella became a reader of newspaper war reports and commentary. In 1916, Bella was about to enter high school, when a trolley accident occurred. ("Trolley" A trolley was a long, open, passenger car powered by electricity via overhead powerlines and moved on rails like a railroad car throughout a city.) The trolley stopped and Bella was getting off, when apparently the trolley started moving again and she was thrown from the car and her foot ran over by the moving trolley.

For almost a year, she was in the hospital having treatments and operations, after her left foot had been amputated. She was saddened by not being able to enter high school and learn Latin. Latin was taught in Catholic high schools even into the 1950s. In the early 1900s, public schools taught the subject as Latin was used in the sciences and was part of a good education. A doctor brought her his Latin grammar, college text book and began teaching her. One of her prior school teachers as well as the sewing circle lady would visit. The teacher brought her a book of Christian poems. She suffered pain and saw death during her time in the hospital.

After treatments and operations were not healing her wound, Teresa took her home, where she used crutches. She spent time reading and writing poetry. Books had been left in the house by the previous owners, who had been Methodist. They included hymnbooks, old Bibles, Christian commentary, the sermons of John Wesley and a book titled *In His Steps*. The old Bible illustrations, sermons and the book made a lifetime impression. She composed a prayer, "Dear God, save my soul and forgive my sins, for Jesus Christ's sake. Amen." Her sister had a miscarriage and later passed during an influenza epidemic. By then all of the brothers had married and left home. She and her mother grew closer and her father, in her words, treated her like his pet.

The following year she entered high school and by winter received her first apparatus for walking. She became active in school, including outdoor activities such as hiking. It was a thriving school of children of various European decent, of different religious faiths and all of middle class families. During that time, an East Bronx girl introduced her to a paper called *The Call*. It was a Socialist publication. Bella began reading that paper and feeling as though she had a calling, for "Social Justice". So the term we use today is not new, as this was back during WW I.

Since she could not participate in physical education classes, the gym teacher would give her courses in anatomy and hygiene. The teacher was Irish Catholic. Upon learning that Bella was also Catholic, she invited her to join the girls club at a Catholic church on Saturday afternoons. The girls sewed simple garments, for the poor, and a Nun read to the girls. There were also weekend retreats, which she enjoyed. However, when on a private retreat, she was so untaught concerning the Catholic faith she could not understand the spiritual readings. Though she was emotionally moved by the Catholic Church services, she rejected her feelings and stirrings as unscientific as that was the prevalent thought, in educational circles at the time, concerning science and religion as being in opposition.

Upon graduation from high school, she won a state scholarship, was awarded copies of Shelly and Keats as prizes for excellence in English and had been selected as the most popular girl in her class.

The following school year saw her at Hunter, which was the New York college for women, with the goal of becoming a teacher. Bella found it in transition from a female academy to an actual college. The faculty were older, refined, academic ladies, who still behaved in the old-fashioned manners. The exception was the younger, freshman English teacher, Sarah. Most were Protestant, with some Catholics and a few Jews.

There was another English teacher; a Jewish lady, Dr. Adele. She taught her students something about the Jewish holidays, in both practice and writings. Dr. Elizabeth taught Middle Ages history, in a way that gave an understanding of the time period; not just dates and names of places, people and events. It gave Bella a realization of the important role of the Catholic Church during that time.

Bella joined the Newman Club, which is a Catholic students' organization. It still exists today. However, she found it to be only social and seemingly anti-intellectual. The faculty advisor was one of the elderly, Catholic ladies who found it difficult to change with the times. It was not what Bella was looking for.

Therefore she found other girls, with a strong intellectual drive and sense of social reform responsibility. Her best friend was a like-minded Jewish girl named Ruth. Ruth was from a practicing Jewish religious family; not just cultural non-practicing. Bella became close to the family and spent Jewish holidays with them. She learned not only from Dr. Adele, but also from Ruth's family something about Judaism. She saw the family bound together by their religion, which her own family was not.

Bella also had friends whose parents had been in the Russian Revolution of 1905. Those friends had grown up hearing about Socialist and Marxist theories. They talked of the future, of a "new world", they were going to be part of building. Some of the group did not believe in God, while some believed that maybe He existed…or not.

Sarah most affected Bella's thinking. She would read books on Communism, which Sarah would bring to class and loan to students. In class, Sarah had compared the Russian Revolution to the original French Revolution saying it had a great liberalizing effect on European culture.

Bella wrote a term theme paper for Sarah's class on monasticism. Monasticism began in Middle Ages Europe, with both Catholic men and women becoming monks and nuns. Monks lived in monasteries, while Nuns lived in convents with each living a community lifestyle of prayer, work and meditation. Some lived in silence, not going outside their monastery or convent, while others did. While Bella received a good grade, as the work was done well, she was scorned by Sarah for choosing such a subject. Bella explained she was impressed by the selfless men and women who served mankind by putting self aside. Sarah must have been scornful because it was about the Catholic Church and she supported what Karl Marx had written against the Church and monastic life. I believe Sarah to have been a Communist.

By the time Bella returned to school the following autumn, she would be skeptical of religious concepts. She had drifted into acceptance that those who believed in God were anti-intellectual and that belief in an afterlife was unscientific. As she and others consulted with Sarah, outside of class, Sarah was able to program them toward the Socialist-Communist philosophy of Karl Marx, by questioning existing patterns of moral behavior and promoting pragmatic approaches to moral problems.

In her junior year, Bella was elected president of her class. She and her friends fostered experimental and new proposals and condemned Capitalism. While attending an intercollegiate conference, at Vassar College, with the Hunter Student Council president, the subject of sororities came into discussion. The conference considered sororities a social problem. Bella does not give a reason for such consideration. My guess is that such organizations were viewed as belonging to the wealthy as a network for the advancement of Capitalism. The conference also discussed the importance of a student honor system and the enforcement of punishment.

In her senior year, she was the President of the Student Council. She led the movement to establish the honor system at Hunter. Bella adopted a creed of "Write me as one who loves my fellow man." She took it as her creed of fellowship as it "…kept some of the significance of the Cross even while it denied the divinity of the Crucified…willingly accepted pain and self-immolation; but it was skeptical of a promised redemption." She felt that she did not need an old-fashioned religious creed any more as she was a modern follower of science and was going to spend her life serving her fellow men.

She graduated in 1925, took the exams for teaching in both elementary and high school, in New York. Ruth and she enrolled at Columbia University, for their summer session, with the goal of obtaining master's degrees. Bella decided it was time for another foot operation and entered Saint Francis Hospital, where a competent surgery was performed and six weeks later she was walking with ease. Soon she had obtained a position as a substitute teacher, for the History Department, at a high school, teaching six classes in Medieval and European history. This she did, while trying to promote an interest in politics.

In 1926, she was offered a position, in the Political Science Department at Hunter College, which she accepted. She had a full program of fifteen hours a week teaching freshman. Dr. Dawson, who was a man and the Department Chairman, had taught at Princeton, when Woodrow Wilson was president there. He had supported Woodrow Wilson as President of the United States. He still supported him as well as the League of Nations and believed the International Court at The Hague would bring international stability. He also believed in such reforms as a city manager system, direct primaries and executive budgets. She had been one of his favorite students due to her passion for study. While his student reading at the library, she gained an interest in American government and the fundamentals of the U.S. Constitution. Ruth was also employed at Hunter, in the same department. She and Bella both became Dr. Dawson's assistances. And both attended graduate school at Columbia, in political science. Another high school friend, of both Ruth and Bella named Margaret, was in the exact same positions and circumstances as they.

The three of them encountered professors whose views were that WW I had not been fought to make the world safe for democracy and that Germany had been shamefully treated by the Versailles Treaty. Some young professors were discovering the importance of current activity in political parties and practical politics. To teach the students the democratic process, they sent their students all over the city on related research projects. The students learned of political bosses and clubhouses. Bella took a course on the United States Senate, which included its treaty-making powers. There were also other new courses such as newspaper media and public opinion. The young students were learning the possibilities of participation in government control and various means of achieving it.

This new knowledge the three passed on to their own students, at Hunter, using the same type of field research work. When a Hunter Socialism student asked to visit Socialist clubs as well, permission was given as all political clubs were to be visited. The three taught the radicals of that day and were the conservatives of the future and there could be no progress if there are no radicals. In her own future, Bella would believe that statement to be meaningless. Is the first part of the statement meaningless?

Apparently the field research involved surveying people. Bella states they cataloged people into either "right" or "left". Placing the Communist on the "Left" as advanced Liberals and therefore giving them the importance of being necessary for progress. Remember the simple definition of a liberal is one who thinks outside the box.

It is at this point, in her writing, that Bella gives her hindsight belief. "Communists usurp the position of the left, but when one examines them in the light of what they really stand for, one sees them as the rankest kind of reactionaries and communism as the most reactionary backward leap in the long history of social movements. It is one which seeks to obliterate in one revolutionary wave two thousand years of man's progress."

She taught at Hunter for thirteen years later regretting what she taught, how she taught and why she taught it. She learned the truth that people are not born "right" or "left", but they only become so through education based on philosophy, which is as carefully organized and as all-inclusive as Communism. She states she was among the first of a new kind of teacher, who was to come in great numbers to the city colleges. Indeed, in the future, to junior colleges, four year colleges and universities. Even high schools.

In her graduate work, she studied American history, national politics, the rise of nationalism, the two hundred corporations controlling America at the end of WW I, imperialism, the John Dewey Society promotion of social needs and progressive education, the Progressive Education Association, the social frontier and in the near future a collective society in our world and especially in our country and, in teaching, one must prepare the student for that day.

By the way, John Dewey dates from the late 1800s to the mid-1900s. He founded the movement of pragmatism philosophy applied to society and politics, which gives foundation to Marxism, Communism and Socialism. Remember that the *Communist Manifesto* was written by Karl Marx before America's War Between the States. Dewey was an American prominent in his field. Online reference used.

Consequently her own learning led her to teach against respected public groups such as charities, churches and other organizations, because they tried to better social conditions with old- fashioned ways. She states such teaching had a destructive effect on her, when she realized she had tried to wreck the students' former way of thinking without giving them a new path to follow because she herself had no new path to follow. I see it as her only learning and teaching, but not thinking about what she was learning due to accepting blindly, along with others, and therefore teaching with the purpose of trying to set right the things wrong with the world. She was not yet a Communist.

By the way, knowledge is not always truth. If I learn something I believe is fact and I pass that knowledge on to someone else, then it also becomes knowledge to that person. However, if it is indeed not a true fact, then I have passed on a falsehood, which that person accepts as true. Or, if the person who told me had an agenda in doing so and intentionally lied, then I accepted that lie as a true fact and passed it on. Many people, for one reason or another, pass on what they believe to be a true fact, when it is not. Executives, who have an agenda and twist the truth or outright lie to their managers, who in turn pass the information on to their personnel, who in turn pass the information on to the public, have created a web of intentional falsehood being circulated unintentionally. Knowledge may be true or false.

Now…back to Bella.

She was angry with those who had money without working for it and who did nothing to relieve the increasing misery of the working class. By the early 1900s, those children and grandchildren of the 1800s Industrial Revolution leaders, land barons and financial tycoons inherited their parent's wealth, after being educated and trained for the purpose of carrying on the family business empire. They were the "upper class" of society.

Through her association with the Teachers College of Columbia, which contained teacher students from all over the United States, she realized the possible effect the college could have on the country, with thousands of teachers to influence national policy and social thinking.

She learned George Counts, who was an associate of John Dewey, had gone to Russia and set up the education system of the revolutionary period of the Russian Government; the new Russian government. He had translated the Russian Primer into English and was eager to have American teachers study it carefully. I do believe Russian Communism/Socialism was going to come to America, in the form of children's public elementary education.

Through her Columbia classes and such places as the International House, she met foreign students as young and eager as herself to learn and change the world. None were aware of the tight web of power which set the stage for molding their opinions. She desired to be "a citizen of the world", which made it easy and natural for her to accept communism and its emphasis on internationalism. She "...began to seek my spiritual home among the dispossessed of the earth."

During her learning/teaching days, she began to wonder about the significance of the practical elements of life. She viewed such elements such as obtaining academic degrees, higher profession status, goals and objectives for advancement, as not being worthy of a life of service to others. Only later did she realize the significance is all around us and comes from order, from purpose.

After receiving her Masters of Arts, in 1927, she, Ruth and another friend, Beatrice, vacationed the summer away at a resort lake. She began to wonder about family and found herself feeling that family stability was mostly due to the cherishing of traditions, to the renewing of memories of the past including friendship with God and boundless loyalty to each other.

New York University Law School saw both she and Ruth enter its classrooms. While Ruth earnestly studied law, Bella was preoccupied with the need to change the status quo. However, she continued her studies, while still teaching at Hunter. At Hunter, she became a student advisor.

Bella's mentor Sarah committed suicide, in 1928. She had been trying to change the salary scale to coincide with positions, at Hunter, but could not break through the old-fashioned system. Those who were close to her went into an emotional tailspin. Two years before, the class sizes at Hunter had begun to increase and were still doing so, but this year there was an attitude transition of students. Instead of being there because they wanted to earnestly study, most were there because their parents wanted them there. Their parents wanted something better for their children than they themselves had had. The children entered free municipal college as though they were entering public, free elementary or high school, because they were supposed to.

Bella took the bar exam, to practice law in New York, in 1930. However, she took a leave of absence from Hunter and she and Beatrice set off for Europe.

She was tired, restless and wanted to leave responsibility and just be young and enjoy life.

They flew to Germany, to Hamburg. She found it to be an exciting old city. Communists were marching, singing and meeting everywhere. There were fine old churches, homes and restaurants. They visited with the middle class, who had strained faces telling of their bewilderment not knowing how they were in a predicament or where they were going. In Berlin, more of the same was evident along with sexual and moral degradation. They found friends, from Hunter College, at the University of Berlin and talked to students in general. Socialists, Communists and National Socialists were fighting each other and undermining Conservatives attached to their own country by national love of one's homeland. Violence was common in the city, including around the university.

Bella states she did not realize, at the time, that for close to a century the educational world of Germany had been subjected to systematic despiritualization, which would result in dehumanization. That made it possible for despiritualized men to serve both the Nazis and the Communists with loyalty. It was believed Fascism would not go to Germany the way it did in Italy because in Italy there was a lack of general education. Plus Germany had its Civil Service. Well…Hitler would use both the universities and the Civil Service. Later Bella would view education itself as not being a deterrent to the destruction of a nation. She would discover the real question was what was the kind of education for what purpose and goal and under what standards? That question still holds true today and will continue to do so!

The two traveled on to Vienna, then Venice on to Florence and Rome, where the presence of Fascism was everywhere in an array of government officials and soldiers. It was not the Italy Bella had known as a young child.

In Paris, she picked up two cables at the American Express office. Ruth had sent one announcing Bella passing the bar exams. Her parents asked her to come home as they were lonely without her.

The pair of tourists took a ship back to America. During the cruise, they met a group of New York school teachers, who invited them to join the Teachers Union. Upon attending the Union meetings, she found strife between groups wanting control of the small organization. She did not understand the why of it, in an intelligential group. Later she would realize Left-Wing politics wanted control of each and every organization.

The 1930s arrived and the stock market crashed. Bella resigned her position at Hunter College and began a clerkship, for admission to the New York Bar, at a lawyer's office. On her European tour, she had met a man named John Dodd, who lived in New York. The two began seeing each other. He was ten years older than Bella, from a Georgia family, with ancestors dating back to the early settlers and loved his country, state and the South. He had worked in industrial centers, enlisted in the Canadian Royal Air Force and then the United States Army Air Corp during WW I. Due to an aircraft crash he obtained a spinal injury that left him a highly nervous person. The two married at the County Clerk's Office as John was anti-clerical.

Two years later the Great Depression was affecting more people and soup kitchens were set up to feed the hungry; those who had employment and then did not. Bella began to see the same facial expressions as she had in Europe. She returned to Hunter College, where many instructors were unpaid and had no security of tenure or promotion.

An Instructors Association was formed and she was in leadership. The Association won concessions and Bella was elected as one of two representatives to the Faculty Council, with the authority to vote as the Association wished. This process was new to the academia environment. However, even some of the older professors were happy to see the process give the school's President a hard time. The President was a young Irish Catholic, from the public school system, who the trustees wanted as the man had friends in City

Hall. He started making changes and ran into a brick wall composed of both the older professors and the students.

The next year saw the country of Russia transform into the Union of Soviet Socialist Republics; Communist Russia. In the U.S., such organizations as Friends of the Soviet Union sprang up. It was led by engineers and social workers and soon went into the arts, sciences and education worlds. Communist students had influence on their young teachers. Young Communist League and League for Industrial Democracy, which originated in England among the Fabians, which was an organization formed to change the world into their Socialist image. There were school protests both on and off campus.

Remember I mentioned the depression of the very early 1900s? These students were born and raised then. In Communism, they saw something that was supposed to make all people equal to have prosperity. They had "hope" in their future through which they were given purpose; cause and reason to be alive. Remember the Communist slogan "Power to the Worker"? Those student organizations began to unconsciously ally themselves with the working class of blue collar, manual laborers, to add the element of education and project planning to future action. They became the backbone of hundreds of Communist organizations, to provide active men and women for mass movements of the next two decades.

Bella wrote her book in the 1950s. The twenty-year period she was referring to was the 1930s and '40s. In the early '30s, the Communists/Socialists of New York colleges both public and private started meeting together for effective organization of the movement. These were young people. Some of whom would rise through the ranks of their profession to positions of influence, with some in the United States and others in Europe.

At first, the American Association of University Teachers (AAUT) was formed to fight for the bread-and-butter issues of the lower ranks of college personnel. It was short-lived. Margaret Schlauch, of New York University, had organized the meetings of both public and private colleges. It was she who invited those of Hunter College to attend. It was also she who arranged small meetings, at her house, to form another organization after the AAUT ended. Bella was about to discover how wheels within wheels operated. Non-collegiate people showed up to enlist the other attendees in the struggle against Fascism.

At that time, a woman named Harriet Silverman and her husband Engdahl were international agents of the World Communist Movement. Harriet was one of the non-collegiate people, who spoke at Margaret's meetings. She invited Bella to her home. Like herself, Harriet's home was poor, although bookshelves lined the walls and were filled with Communist related material. On the wall hung a picture of Vladimir Lenin draped with two Communist red flags containing the laborer's hammer and the farmer's sickle. It was he who stated the goal of Socialism is Communism.

Note: Both Fascism and Communism are totalitarian dictatorships. Fascism is by an individual and Communism is by a government collective of people.

Due to Harriet's poverty Bella felt guilty for having a good job and a comfortable apartment. Bella gave what money she had on her to Harriet. Harriet then suggested the involved college teachers should organize an anti-Fascist literature committee, for the purpose of doing research, writing pamphlets and raising funds. At that point Harriet informed Bella she was indeed a Communist. Bella was fine with that and wanted to fight Fascism and asked how funds collected would be distributed. Harriet replied, "Through the Party and its contacts." She then asked Bella if she would like to meet Earl Browder. An appointment was made with him for the following week, at the New York Communist Headquarters.

The whole building was shabby and looked worse than Harriet and her apartment. Bella found the director of the Communist Party, at least in New York, looking like a Midwest college professor; an older gray haired man. It was a friendly meeting during which Earl listened to Bella's information about her activities and he talked to her of the Party goals against Fascism. Harriet, her apartment and building were examples of how most Communist were poor either out of life events or out of giving financially all to the Communist cause. Even their business offices and buildings were the same. Of course that did not bring attention to them either.

At the meetings of the Anti-Fascist Literature Committee, the original school activists knew of the Communists among them, but it was impolite to ask questions of why. They raised thousands of dollars and spread the Communist propaganda among lively activity. Bella stated it was a call to action of the innocents, although she never really knew how many were innocent. I believe, by innocent, she means a person who was not a Communist having been recruited for a cause to help the world's oppressed. Good hearted people not truly knowing who they were working for.

Bella worked the fund raising under the direction of Harriet, who would bring well-dressed, sophisticated Communists consisting of doctors, lawyers and businessmen, to the fund raisers. And there were those who were threadbare like Harriet giving the look of having given all for the cause; more than those like Bella; the petty bourgeoisie. There were also those of the performing arts, who would visit between acts at nightclubs or theaters. Other Communist were the blue collar workers. The common ground of this mixture was that the past society was bad, the present corrupt and the future would be worthwhile only if it became collective.

Unemployed Councils were established all across America. In preparation for a revolution, the Communist enlisted the masses as instructed by Karl Marx, in the *Communist Manifesto*. In some cases, Rent Parties were formed to raise the rent money due by some comrade. It was seen as doing good for the people; for the unemployed worker.

Bella continued teaching and her involvement with the Instructors Association, at Hunter College, to better the economic conditions. She was invited by Communist teachers to attend meetings where she met top executives of the Class Room Teachers Association, which was a grass roots movement. They were being taught techniques of mass action and carefully organized on the basis of class-struggle philosophy. And they were secretly associated with the Trade Union Unity League. They had two missions; one, to convert a considerable number of teachers to a revolutionary approach to problems and two, to recruit as many as possible for the Communist Party. Some of the teachers were members of a Teachers Union Local, of the American Federation of Teachers and formed an organized minority opposition to non-Communist leadership.

All Red unions of the early 1930s helped give publicity to problems of human survival during the Great Depression. The Red organizations capitalized on them while the conservative organizations were too inept to act. Red delegations, to the Board of Education, issued attacks against city officials and the Teachers Union. Teacher leaders, of the Red minority within the American Federation of Labor (AF of L) Teachers Union, organized unemployed teachers to fight for having them in the Teachers Union itself so that later on that Union could gain control of the AF of L Teachers Union. There were two Unions involved in the situation.

Bella did not become a Communist overnight, but over time. She was grateful for their support of the Instructors Association and admired many of them. They had taken her into their circle and made her feel comfortable. She was not interested, at the time, in their long range objectives, but welcomed assistance on immediate issues and admired them for their courage and respected their fight for the common worker. She did not discuss their dictatorship of the common worker.

Ruth tried to warn her that eventually she would get hurt by the Communist. Bella countered that she was only interested in present problems and not future takeover, for the sanity of the American people would prevail. Bella was not the only naïve person caught up in the unseen insanity. She came to see the Party's use of the young people, which is still going on by Socialists/ Communists. She saw them burnout before they reached maturity. And she saw the inexhaustible supply of people willing to be sacrificed, for the cause. To her, much of the strength of the Party was/is derived from this very ruthlessness in exploiting people.

When Bella was invited to join, Harriet stopped it. Bella was to remain her contact, but not be seen at secret Party meetings. At that time, the Communist Party itself was underground. The Center was contacted concerning the matter and it was decided Bella was not to be enlisted. Harriet gave her Marxist literature and instructions. Bella accepted the discipline even though it was double dealing. She was willing for the sake of organization of the labor movement in America. Only later would she learn only non-important Party members were exposed to the public. Harriet comforted and mentored her saying she was to be saved for more important tasks. She became a tool of a secret, well-organized world power.

One day Bella came across an acquaintance from her childhood. They visited and she learned he was Chairman of the Education Committee of the New York City Assembly. She informed him of the lack of teacher tenure and wanting to change that. They met the next day and drafted a bill. In those days, teachers knew little, if anything, concerning the legislative process. The Communist representatives, from the three city colleges, met with Bella and they examined each and every word until they felt they had perfected it. Bella learned that was the procedure in Communist life, for committees to perfect everything. The tenure bill was passed and Bella became regarded as a legislative expert and was placed in the position of legislative representative of the Teachers Union Local as an officer of the AF of L Union and became more important to the Communist Party.

In 1936, she obtained a six month leave of absence from Hunter College, to serve as the legislative representative of the Teachers Union spending most of her time in Albany, New York, and Washington D.C. and at New

York's City Hall. She succeeded in getting two bills passed and the Union was very pleased. She came to represent the growing educational pressure group the Communists controlled. The New York Teachers Union increased its membership by recruiting unemployed and substitute and Works Progress Administration (WPA) teachers. The Union also worked with the Communist section of the Parents Teachers Association (PTA) as well as several student organizations. Bella soon organized a block of Teacher-Union Captains based on New York Assembly Districts. If legislation was pending, she ordered her Captains to put pressure on Assembly District Representatives.

The Communist Party filled important positions of the American Labor Party, which it controlled, with teachers of practical politics experience. At that time, Bella became one of the Teachers Union delegates to the AF of L Central Trades and Labor Council of New York. Being young and idealistic and eager to serve the workers, Bella was proud of her position. And she became a member of Communist Party "faction" in the AF of L, which meant that she met regularly with the Communist Party members of the AF of L and the leaders of the Party to push AF of L policy to the Communist line. The Communists were doing the same within other labor groups.

That same year she met, through the Party, committees of striking seamen. Under the leadership of the Communist Party, they were fighting both ship owners and corrupt leadership of the old International Seamen's Union, which was an affiliate of the AF of L. The seamen wanted support from the Central Trade and Labor Council, to present their grievances before delegates of New York's organized labor body. Bella was to present a petition of demands for reorganization of their union along democratic lines. She did and pandemonium broke loose. Bella was escorted home by the group of Communist delegates fearing for her safety. She had learned acts of daring supported by appearances of moral justification have a terrific impact in building a movement regardless of whether or not one wins and the Communists know how to use this tactic. She also learned that serving the Communist cause always came first above serving any other organization.

Bella learned many lessons, from her Communist tutors. Lenin held in contempt any Union wanting only to increase the worker's economic condition as he believed the liberation of the working class would not come through reforms. Such Unions were guilty of the Marxist crime of "economism". Trade Unions were useful only for political purposes to win worker acceptance of the theory of class struggle and to convince them their only hope of improving their conditions was in revolution.

Communist leaders believed the worker was too complacent with what they had and had to be politicalized with action to accept class struggle. Bella saw workers striking just for the sake of striking for any reason. They were being trained without knowing it. It did not matter if they won or lost.

By now, one may see a pattern of guided, individual training by placing a person in various positions with each position holding more responsibility, at a higher level and at a more in-depth involvement. The person still representing their original organization, but becoming involved with other organizations and moving deeper into the Communist activity and even the Party itself. Bella continued to learn Communist tactics.

Communist Party factions prepared for organizational meetings and government meetings by reviewing what was to be done by whom and when and what objectives were to be achieved. By meeting time, they were prepared, organized, trained and disciplined with a detailed program. Before others had a chance to think, they were already winning advantages. In non-Communist controlled organizations, there were "sleeper cells" of active members to disrupt and destroy the power of the opposition. This tactic is still used today by the Socialists. New unknown people, of the Communist Party, were pushed forward against an established political machine; people who had not the experience of such positions and levels of responsibility. However, the

Communist Party could mold and control them. Nobodies became somebodies and somebodies became nobodies as required to meet the objectives of the Party.

In 1936, Washington D.C. forces planned to establish the American Labor Party (ALP), to solidify the labor vote in New York, for President Roosevelt. The Communists pledged their support and used the AF of L, to move as a block within the ALP. During the State Teachers Federation Convention, the idea was to politicalize labor Unions creating a Party of their own like the British Labor Party. By 1936, the Communist control of the AF of L had lessened. However, they still had their own people in key positions, in the AF of L and in vital industries, for long-range planning. It was easier to control a small organization than it was to control a large one. The Party also liked educated people as they were current on Party writings and had more ability than the common worker.

Why would the Communist want Roosevelt in the White House? President Herbert Hoover was in office when the Stock Market crashed and the Great Depression began. He tried to counter the Depression, but failed. People wanted a new person in office and Roosevelt, who believed in social programs and was a Democrat, was the best choice to back, for the Communist to gain political ground for control. And that is my opinion.

Bella was well educated and accomplished, passionate for the worker, ready to obey and willing to learn. She was the perfect target for useful control. Therefore she was placed higher and higher until she obtained national status, within the Communist Party and also won a seat in the New York City Assembly. Her activities became so numerous and involved she resigned her position at Hunter College.

During the Spanish Civil War (1936-'39), the Party gave continuous support of the Spanish Leftist government, in money, fighters and propaganda. The American Communist military unit Abraham Lincoln Brigade was formed as an American Division, of the Communist International Brigade, using Lincoln's name as they had that of other patriots to stir men's spirits, for their own purpose. The Soviet Union was funneling funds to the American Communist Party for support of the cause.

Also in 1936, the leadership of the Teachers' Union resigned due to Communist control. The Party saw to it that the new office manager was who they wanted in place. No one knew she was a Communist, including Bella who had dealings with her and found it hard to deal with her. Only later did Bella discover the office manager was not only Communist, but also the sister of a high up official. The office manager was there to control the Union, which is why she halted Bella's special interest needs of the Instructors Association of Hunter College.

Earl Browder, who was a high up Communist leader and would later become the head of the New York Communist Party, was warning Union leaders not to regard Marxism as Dogmatic, but flexible in meeting new situations. Party literature was composed of double talk used purposely by Marx and Lenin. Browder also emphasized the importance of relying on Stalin, who was the Russian leader at the time, due to his shrewdness in dealing with all, including English and American capitalist. His slogan was that Communism was Twentieth Century Americanism.

The Old Guard, of the Communist Party, who had worked hard from the beginning of the cause, was very controlling and allowed for no opposition. They were stern and never smiled. The Party had been and continued to be their life as the Party always came first and foremost.

The Party had an espionage system working within not only other left-wing groups, but also in the Unions. That network of spies gave intelligence on all that was happening anywhere, at any time and was under the direct supervision of the office manager's brother, who reported directly to the chief of the Party's intelligence service.

The affiliating teachers with labor began in 1902, in San Antonio, Texas. A charter was issued by the AF of L. The same year the Chicago Teachers Federation, which was organized in 1897, affiliated with the Chicago Federation of Labor. By 1916, twenty teachers' organizations in ten states had affiliated with labor. The American Federation of Teachers was sparked by Socialists in the beginning. However, over time the Communists used the Federation's own rules for a takeover. The Socialists maintained splinter groups. Political innocents were those who believed that American politics was ruled by the Republican and Democratic Parties.

The Rapp-Coudert Committee was established by the New York State Legislation, to investigate Communist and other subversive activities throughout the State in its education system in 1940 to 1942. By the conclusion of its investigations, almost 700 people had been interviewed as well as some 500 witnesses as to the extent of subversive activities in New York City education. Teachers, professors and college administrators were removed from their positions. From the City College of New York, over fifty faculty and staff were terminated. Three organizations were found to have been penetrated by the Communist Party; Teachers Union, College Teachers Union and American Student Union. No Nazi or Fascist conspiracy was found. Source: New York State Archives.

Of course the Communists tried to counteract the investigations. Bella herself burned membership lists. Money was raised and a team of lawyers formed, committees with positive names such as Friends of the Free Public Schools were formed along with attractive, positive literature printed and distributed to organizations and public officials. The Party intelligence system was also in play as its officers, in splinter groups, trade unions, major divisions of the body politic, police department and intelligence divisions of government were used to supply information concerning the investigations such as who was to be interviewed. The Union members to be called were warned and instructed ranging from stalling by saying they were sick or enter a hospital or even move. Most teachers were told not to answer questions and take contempt citations or to resign from their employment. A lawyer or Union representative would be assigned to them.

And Bella's father passed over.

In reviewing her past, Bella realized how important to the American Communist movement the teachers had been. They were not only used as free-of-charge teachers in Party education, but they traveled and visited Party figures outside of the United States. Most were idealistic, selfless frontline people in committees and were the backbone of the Party's strength in both the Labor Party and later in the Progressive Party. Yes, at one time, there was an actual Progressive Party. Those within the inner Party functions provided thousands of contacts among young people, women's organizations and professional groups. Some financed Party activities, supported husbands who were Party organizers or on special assignment.

The Party would attack the opposition with smearing, name-calling, frame-ups, carefully combing through a person's history and background. If there was nothing to use in an attack, then some innuendo was started in a smear campaign so the public would believe there had to be some truth to the lie. This tactic is still done today.

And Bella and her husband divorced. He was disturbed by her increasing activity with the Communists, for he loved America and was pro-British. He did not believe in the Communist phony peace campaigns, which Bella was part of. Bella still did not see Communism as a conspiracy, but as a philosophy of life for the common people; the worker.

Members of the Furriers Union had been imprisoned for industrial sabotage. Animal fur was used for clothing during the early and mid-1900s. That was before the appearance of People for the Ethical Treatment of Animals (PETA). Bella was assigned to work with a committee of women, including wives of the imprisoned, to visit Congressmen (Women were not in Congress yet.) and the Department of Justice. Bella and wives of the imprisoned men talked to Mrs. Eleanor Roosevelt, at her New York apartment. This was before she moved to the White House. Mrs. Roosevelt was sympathetic and stated she would do all to get their memoranda into the hands of appropriate officials. She also stated she believed Communists should be permitted as members, but not leaders, of trade unions.

I read somewhere some time ago that Mrs. Eleanor Roosevelt was approached and befriended by two Socialist women, after her husband was elected President. I am not saying that Bella was one of them. The women guided her into Socialist thinking. Franklin D. Roosevelt increased the authority of the Presidency and of the Federal Government to support public interest in conflicts between big business and labor and moved the United States forward as a world power. He also took measures against big business mistreating their employees and became involved in world politics and situations. His New Deal expanded the authority of the Federal Government.

And Bella's mother passed over, she felt her personal life had ended and she belonged only to the Communist cause.

Attached to the Party, for some time, was a Workers School, at Party Headquarters. Its faculty was old-time Communists teaching both Party members and sympathizers mostly courses in Marxism-Leninism, trade union history and in popularizing the current line of the Party. It was for indoctrination and had a foreign atmosphere about it. A new location for a new school was purchased, by Earl Browder. It was to have a patriotic look referencing the American Revolution and America's War Between the States, but in a Marxist status. The new school was named the Jefferson School of Social Research. Chicago had the Abraham Lincoln School, while Boston had the John Adams School and New Rochelle had the Thomas Paine School. These schools were to play a part in what was termed "The Third Revolution" that was to destroy the Great American Republic. One Communist told Bella that Communism would come to America under the label of Progressive Democracy and in labels acceptable to the American people.

Bella had maintained a small area of her mind free of all things so she might escape there for freedom from all else. She taught at the Jefferson School, but refused relocation to California as director of its Labor School. She came to realize the schools were for indoctrination and did not like it. She was in everything except officially named a Communist.

The Party announced that whole sections of the capitalist class had joined the "democratic front" also known as "Roosevelt camp of progress". To what extent of being a major event, I have no idea. It was most likely propaganda based on a small degree of fact. But that is just my opinion.

War causes estranged bed-follows. The government consulted and utilized the Communist leadership to pull together divergent groups in a win-the-war effort of unity. There was also the Russian war relief movement. Families of wealth such as Vanderbilt and Morgan, gave generously. The Communist decided to take advantage of this, by creating the Russian Institution, in New York City, with an imposing headquarters on Park Avenue. It was so respectable it was allowed to give in-service courses to school teachers for credit. It was a propaganda agency.

The Party would establish such authority over its members it could sway their emotions both for and then against the same person or issue. In 1943, Bella noticed a lack of file material on social questions such as housing and welfare. She asked another Party leader, of her same high status, why that was. He replied they were a revolutionary Party and not a reform group to patch up the bourgeois structure. That was when she realized the Party had no long-range programs for welfare, hospitals, schools or child care. They had plagiarized programs from the various civil-service unions. She established a law office, with the approval of the Party and for the Party's reasons.

1943 saw Franklin D. Roosevelt technically dissolve the Communist International. It was done not by his authority, but by his insistence. This means the United States President knew of the Communist organization and had influence with the Communist Party, who had supported him through his Progressive Party.

In 1944, Earl Browder, as leader of the American Communist Party, dissolved it. However, it was re-established under the name of the Communist Political Association, with the same leaders, organization and friends. In 1991, Russian leader, Boris Yeltsin, disbanded the Russian Communist Party. However, it reestablished under a different name. Same tactic forty-seven years later; almost five decades and the same tactic is used. Bella was told the reason for Browder's action was that the current line in world Communism was based on the Roosevelt pledge to the Soviet Union of mutual co-existence and continued postwar Soviet-American unity. Later that year the Communist Party planned a Progressive Farmers Committee for the re-election of Roosevelt.

Every time a situation came into existence or an event was upcoming the Communists would form a committee to target the requirements involved. This included Party participation in government elections.

It was postwar 1945 and again the Communist Party was planning for universal military training, action against the no-strike postwar pledge and the labor-management charter. Bella felt that all three elements were simply straws blowing in the wind and pointed to ultimate State control of the people. The Communists were in favor of a United Nations Charter, to be adopted in San Francisco, California. The move toward a lasting peace via the United Nations was contradictory with universal military training. The three were aimed at two different purposes. One, the need to control people and two, the need to build a worldwide organization. The post-World War II Cold War, between Russian and the U.S., had begun.

I Could Have Been One

Also that year Browder was condemned and removed from his high position. He remained a Party member, but was no longer in good graces. He was expelled the next year. This happened due to his establishment of the Communist Political Association. A national Emergency Convention voted to dissolve that organization and re-establish the old Communist Party. It also voted to intensify Marxist-Leninist education throughout the whole Party and to return to the use of the term "comrade".

From 1945 to '47, several thousands of members were expelled based on the rationale that they were either too much on the Left or the Right. Bella was caught up in the purge, but escaped expulsion. However, she was still under surveillance and investigation.

The Party began strife tactics to separate and control the American people. One possibility considered, but not started, was that the Party assist the Negros, of the South, to form their own nation and secede from the United States.

And Bella was ill in body and spirit. She began to draw back on her activities and also voice opposition to recommendations of action from Party leaders, when she had legal ground to stand on.

In 1948, the Communists took control of the small Progressive Party. This was done in case the Communist Party itself became illegal. The limited and controlled Progressive Party would be a cover organization and a substitute for the Communist Party. The Party was becoming illegal in Europe and was going underground.

Bella was called before a Discipline Committee. As a National Committee member, she was not obliged to obey the call. However, she did. The Committee did not have solid ground to purge her. It dismissed her and began a smear campaign. Later she was pressed with charges and ordered to appear before the local Section Commission. She did and they expelled her, without opportunity to defend herself in any way. The *Associated Press* phoned her and asked for a statement regarding her expulsion from the Communist

Party. She stated, "No comment." The following day New York newspapers printed the story giving all the unfounded and undefended charges. Three days later the Communist paper *Daily Worker* did the same. Afterward a campaign of hate by personal phone calls and letters began along with being blackballed as an attorney. Supposed friends denied her comfort. The warning words of Ruth so long ago had come true. The Communists had used her and tossed her away.

She continued to read the New Testament, which she had always done even in her starkest Party delusion days. In her feeling of security and affection she had felt in the Party, she failed to realize it was not personal emotion, but group acceptance depending on what the Party wanted. She, however, operated on real emotions.

The *New York Post* asked her to write a series of articles concerning her break up with the Party, for which she would be generously paid. At first she accepted and wrote, but as she read them over she decided she did not want them published and refused the offer. A weekly magazine made a more lucrative offer, but it was refused. She did not want to hurt Party people she still felt affection for and realized they too were entrapped as she had been.

Everything that had meant something to her in her life was gone. She was lost.

Because she had been on the Communist National Committee, she was approached by an old acquaintance, who was not a Party member as far as she knew, but was a Liberal and friend of the Party. He had associated with the Party. After catching up on old times, he asked if she knew a certain professor that Bella had heard of vaguely as a British Communist agent in the Far East. The acquaintance came back again, with the professor's attorney. Bella gave an affidavit that she had not heard of the professor while a leader in the Communist Party. Thinking that was the end of the matter, she was surprised upon receiving a subpoena to appear before the United

States Senate Foreign Relations Committee hearing. Before the Committee, she answered questions by truthfully telling of what she did or did not know.

She began to see how ignorant she had become, by reading only Party literature. Bookshelves contained only Party approved material. If a writer was expelled from the Party, his books were removed. There had been systematic rewriting of Soviet history, the Revolution and in some cases the blotting out of any mention of certain unwanted people. She thought of successive purges. Suddenly she too wanted answers to the questions she was being asked by the Committee and she wanted the truth. She found herself targeting the duplicity of the Communist Party and her interest in political events was renewed. The spell which had come over her, after being expelled, was broken.

Riding the train from Washington D.C. back to New York City she thought of the Episcopalian cemetery, where as a child she had put flowers on this and that grave of American patriots. Suddenly she became aware of the reality of what was facing the Country and a fear of what was being planned by Communist forces against the American way of life. That same passion she had in the Communist Party, while thinking she was helping the "worker", came back as an overwhelming desire to help keep safe from all danger the people of smalltown America.

With such understanding, Bella came alive again. She had purpose. In reading the Congressional Report on the hearings on the Institute of Pacific Affairs, she found she was again able to interpret events. During her time with the Party, she had accumulated a large store of information about people and events. Often the information did not fit into the picture presented by the Party to its members. Now her store of odd pieces was beginning to develop into a recognizable picture.

She had regarded the Communist Party as a poor man's Party and thought the presence of certain men of wealth within it as accidental. Now she regarded the Party as a monolithic organization with the leadership in the National Committee and the National Board. But that was only a façade for the illusion of the poor man's Party, which was in reality a device to control the "common man".

Many parts of the puzzle did not fit into the Party structure. Parallel organizations, which she had known of but not examined, became clear and their connections with the Party organization apparent. Party members were told, in 1945, that America had a different role to play and would be the last taken by the Communist as they would often find themselves in opposition not only to the interest of the government, but also of the "worker". She realized she and others had been poised on the side of those who sought the destruction of their own Country; her own country.

During the peace campaign, Bella had asked a question concerning if the Party would oppose their young men entering the United States Army. Her higher up answered that if the Party did, then how would their young men learn to use weapons with which to seize power? Now she thought of all the men who had been thought expendable and prayed, "God help them all!"

As the year wore on, Bella came across others who had been purged. They too were struggling to find their way back to reality by seeing psychologists or drinking themselves into numbed hopelessness. She even wondered why she was alive. She tried connecting with her brothers and their families, but too much time had passed and their world did not really hold a place for her.

She was back in Washington, in the fall of 1950, as a lawyer on an immigration appeal. Running into an old friend, who was now a Congressional Representative. He greeted her warmly and invited her to his office. Upon arriving, they visited and Bella gave her grateful appreciation of their visit a year ago, when they had lunch and talked of Bella's mother, whom he had known. He had reverently talked of God, in the busy and noisy Manhattan restaurant.

Upon learning of her purging and difficulties, he asked if she wanted FBI protection. She was afraid of the FBI. He then commented he could only pray for her safety and asked, "Bella, would you like to see a priest?" She found herself answering, "Yes, I would." He had his secretary contact Monsignor Sheen at Catholic University, in Washington. That priest knew well of Communism/Socialism and had a television program for the education of Catholics and those who were interested in Catholicism.

He drove Bella over for her appointment as all kinds of thoughts of the unknown ran through her mind. She entered the Monsignor's office and was ready to run out, when he entered and greeted her warmly with, "Doctor, I'm glad you've come." His welcome caught her off guard. She tried to speak, but broke into tears as her emotions came to the surface. He led her to a small chapel, where they knelt and he prayed. A calmness came over her as she was conscious of stillness and peace. He stated he would be in New York next winter and invited her to visit him for instructions in the Faith.

Bella continues the book, by saying her rejection of the wisdom and truth the Catholic Church has preserved and has used to establish the harmony and order set forth by Christ, she had set herself adrift on an uncharted sea with no compass. She and others grasped with relief the fake certitude offered by materialists and accepted a program which had been made even more attractive because they appealed for "sacrifice for our brothers", but such phrases are empty unless they have the solid foundation of belief in God's Fatherhood.

That Christmas Eve Bella attended Catholic services. During the new year, Bella came across Catholics she had known before and Catholic books were given to her. She was introduced to the author of one, who in turn introduced her to a Catholic organization in which she became involved. She was discovering a new world of sincerity and warmth to counteract the effects of the hateful, insincere world she had spent her life in. She deepened herself in the Catholic Faith just as she had done so in Communism through practice, reading and being mentored by the Monsignor. She examined her life and the twist and turns it had given her and was ready to be formally accepted back into the Church of her raising and was.

It was after her new found lasting peace she was able to face the questions in her mind, concerning the difficult ordeal of appearing before government agencies and investigating committees. She still did not want to hurt those as blind as she had been and dreaded the campaign of personal abuse that would be renewed against her. She came up with three questions. Does her Country need the information she would be called upon to give? Would she be scrupulous in telling the truth? Would she be acting without malice?

She decided her Country did need the information to educate people with. As for the abuse, most of it came in the form of using Bible verses to condemn her. Today Bible verses are used to recruit Christians to serve the Socialist cause. And malice? She was at peace and malice belongs to the hateful. The book is ended with the following:

"…I am keenly conscious that only a generation of men so devoted to God that they will heed his command, 'Love one another as I have loved you.' can bring peace and order to our world."

She does not say, in the book, if she did indeed give information to her Country through the U.S. Government. However, on Wednesday, June 17 and on Monday the 16th of November of 1953, she gave testimony before the United States House of Representatives Subcommittee of the Committee on Un-American Activities. I found those testimonies at archive.org and Scribd.

I also found, in the National Archives, a letter to a Congressman concerning Communist textbooks infiltration of American schools. The sender had asked Bella how the Party was able to get them into schools nationwide. Bella replied it was done through the individual Boards of Education and the Party trained certain people, with proper qualifications, to write to the Boards. The sender asked the Representative what chance a good American teacher had to properly teach when books concerning Red (Communist) history and teachings had to be used by the teacher as mandated and what chance had the student to become a good, loyal citizen, for the past twenty years. Twenty years; two decades. The letter was written 24 July 1953. The decades of the 1930s and '40s.

In reference to the archive.org document concerning the Investigation of Communist Activities in the Columbus, Ohio, Area, Wednesday, June 17, 1953, United States House of Representatives, Subcommittee of the Committee on Un-American Activities, the Committee Chairman stated,

> "The Communist conspiracy provides for the infiltration of every phase and field of American life. Communist objectives are to create strife between labor and management and within the labor group itself, to cause people to be suspicious and distrustful of the Government and the law enforcement agencies thereof, to make them dissatisfied with the American way of life, particularly its economic system, to create doubts concerning their religious teachings, to set class against class, minorities against majorities, and even minorities against minorities when it suits their purpose.
>
> It is a process of attempting to soften and weaken the American people and its institutions so when the time comes to move in, the task will be so much easier to accomplish. This is not theory. The Soviet Union has brought behind the Iron Curtain 600 million people since 1933 by the use of these methods. Of course, such a conspiracy can act only through individuals. These individuals must promote the Communist program in the various American institutions with which they are identified since they cannot act in a vacuum. We find them active in the labor movement, in industry, in Government, in

our educational institutions, in the entertainment field, and I am sorry to say, in some instances in the field of religion."

During the preliminary questioning of Bella Dodd as to her background, she testified that not all Communists carried Communist Party identification cards and those who did would use only first names or pseudonyms.

Later she stated, "...letter sent from France to the United States which said we American Communists had better stop playing the democracy game, stop working so closely with the **liberals and democrats** (as in those who believe in democracy) **and get back to the job of preparing for revolution....**"

When asked about people who are not Communist getting involved in and supporting what the Communists were, she stated, "Yes; the Communist support seems to be large because people are sucked into things which seem to be good in themselves. They don't recognize that the Communist Party uses these slogans, these generalizations, in order to break down their resistance, and ultimately they are tied in with the Communist movement."

In relation to leaving the Communist Party, she stated, "Unfortunately, unless one has a religious background and a tremendous devotion and understanding of American history and the American system of Government, one is left floundering because one doesn't know where to go."

In further testimony on the subject, she stated, "Yes, they (Communist) forget to tell you that as far as they are concerned, before they are through taking power, they will kill off large sections of the working class if it doesn't go along with their program."

In response to questioning about the Communist Party's use of minorities, she answered, "There is no more depressing problem than the way the Party uses the minority groups for the purpose of creating chaos and division among the people, creating fear and hatred among themselves in order that the many Communist organizations may promote the things in which they are interested."

Concerning the dictatorship of the Communist Party, she stated if a member of the Party wrote a book, on any subject, it had to be submitted for review by the Party Cultural Committee, for conforming to whatever the Party line was at any given time.

In reference to the influence of the Communist on education, she testified that, from 1925 to about 1949, various colleges of America dropped all courses on ethics and religion; law schools dropped courses on constitutional law. It was part of despiritualizing the American people.

In discussion of the use of nursey rhymes giving Communist rhetoric, Bella said, "…if you are going to seize the minds of children, you seize them as early as possible."

On the question of Communists destroying belief in God, she answered, "There is no doubt about the fact that for the first enemy of the Communist is a belief in the fact that you are created by a Divine Creator. That they have to get rid of before anything else. If they can wipe that out, then it is easy, because if you don't believe in a God, all you believe in is better material advancement, and the Communists promise greater material advancement for all."

Mention was made of "…millions of people in concentration camps under the heel of the Russian Government."

She stated,

> "The Communist have a way of changing names and labels. When the old names become discredited, they change these names. They change the name of the Communist Party. In some South American countries, you have any number of parties that do not go under the name of Communist Party.
>
> How shall we recognize them, then? We can only recognize them by the fact that they believe that there is no

God; that a person is just born, grows, dies, decays, and that is the end. They believe that the individual doesn't matter; that the collective matters. They believe that certain people should have the power to run a country."

In reference to the Scribd Eighty-Third Congress, First Session, Committee on Un-American Activities, United States House of Representatives, Investigation of Communist Activities in the Philadelphia Area, Monday, November 16, 1953, the following is presented.

This hearing was a continuation of one the previous year dealing with the Communists' efforts and their success in infiltrating into the vital defense industries in the Philadelphia area and based on investigations conducted by House Committee on Un-American Activities staff over the past year.

The hearing began as the other had done, with Bella stating her background and Party activities.

The question was asked why Communist leadership of a Union remains in authority even if it is known by the Union members that they have such leadership. The example of the United Electrical Workers Union was given. I, myself, remember hearing of that Union being the largest and most powerful, when I was in my twenties. That was in the 1960s.

To summarize Bella's response, the Moscow trained, financed, tightly knit Communist leadership works around the clock, while the Union member is busy working, raising a family, even working a second job. The leadership decides who will be a Union member. No membership equals no job. The worker wants to keep his job and will vote in the same leadership to do so. Also the industrialists were willing to work with the Communists leadership due to maintaining stability. The Communists would fight hard to begin with, in order to obtain control of the Union and improving working conditions. Once they had control they spent their time getting the workers into Union welfare and educational plans; taking more money out of the workers pocket to use for the Communists' own objectives.

It was brought out, by Bella, that manufacturing contracts of American war materials were being given to Communist led unions in Italy. It was being done through the action of Communists both here and there and the Italian Communists could gain favor with their workers since they supplied work for them.

Therefore the U.S. Government needed to do something about the Communist leadership, the cooperating industrialists as well as international Communist Union action. The question was how to do it. Bella suggested the American Federation of Labor, Congress of Industrial Organizations and the Railroad Brotherhoods of America could assist Congress in formulating a course of action as everyone in the industries knew which were the Communist dominated Unions, but no one wanted to point the figure at them. One of the Representatives was planning to introduce a bill to outlaw the Communist Party.

Communist Control Act of 1954: The Communist Control Act is United States legislation signed into law by President Dwight Eisenhower, on 24 August 1954, which outlaws the Communist Party of the United States and criminalizes membership in or support for the Party or "Communist-action" organizations and defines evidence to be considered by a jury in determining participation in the activities, planning, actions, objectives or purposes of such organizations. The Act has since been ruled unconstitutional in federal court but has not been ruled on in the Supreme Court and has never been enforced. In other words, the Communists found a way to make it ineffective.

It was brought forth, by Bella, that Lenin's theory of trade unionism is that a union is important not for its economic force, but for its political force and political power. Therefore Communist Party members affiliated with a union would push the union into the position of putting forth and supporting the Communist political objectives.

She also stated that as far as the teaching of children was concerned, there would have to be a certain ideology. The children would have to be taught in accordance with the directives of the Communist Party. If the Party directives were to eliminate the private ownership of property, children would have to be taught in that directive.

The Communist Party believes in eliminating all religion and all belief in God and Communist teachers would have to promote the Communist Party program as far as they possibly dare to do so without losing their position as a teacher.

Further questioning noted that Lenin stated he would agree to kill two-thirds of the people in order to have the one-third saved for Communism. Bella followed that up with giving an idea of how much danger the people of the world are in spiritually, mentally and physically; that the American people are not aware of how deep Communism goes by it being all-pervasive permeating the very marrow of the nation's bones to the point of Americans not recognizing what Communism is. Americans have to stop thinking about the immediate issues of Communism and go to the fundamentals of it. It is a movement for the destruction of the life of the human individual.

When Lenin was in Saint Petersburg, in the Soviet Union, there were only 23,000 members of the Communist Party, but by being highly organized, centralized and well financed they were able to take control over 180 million Russians.

Bella made the statement that she believed the American Communist movement would have been smashed a long time ago if people in our economic and political positions and cultural society did not give any support including financial to the movement. The American people, in general need to be aware.

The Communists had a long-range program and were looking to take hold of the minds of the youth of the time, in hopes that when they grew to adulthood they would be in a position to take over. They were not training the youth for that day, but for a future of the Soviet world.

Population control was addressed with the question of how the Communist would solve the problem of population in nations, with example of the population of China, India and the United States, at that time. In a Communist approved book, by William Z. Foster, he stated the process of natural selection of the human species could not be allowed, but had to be done artificially. In other words, the killing of millions of people would be a good thing as the reorganizing and rebuilding of the human race.

As in her first hearing, there was questioning concerning her knowledge of the Teachers Union and how the Communists used it.

I had read that during her testimony on November 16th, she gave information concerning the Communist infiltration of the Catholic Church, by recruiting over a thousand men, who were atheist and homosexuals, to enter the Church's seminaries, with the purpose of becoming priests and moving up into the administrative levels of the Church so they could change and damage the Church from within over time to something not resembling the original Church.

However, such testimony was not listed in the Government hearing transcripts I obtained on Bella Dodd. I have also read such testimony was off-record, for fear of assassination by the Party. Therefore I am referring to another online source of LifeSiteNews article "Catholic abuse crisis is likely no accident, but a strategy to 'destroy Church from within'", September 17, 2018.

The article states a process called "ideological subversion" or "active measures" was being used in America to corrupt the young, get them interested in sex, take them away from religion, make them superficial and enfeebled, destroy people's faith in their national leaders by holding the latter up for contempt, ridicule and disgrace, cause breakdown of the old moral virtues of honesty, sobriety, self-restraint and faith in the pledged word. This came from a 1983 video, of a former Soviet KGB (Russian Secret Police), who defected in 1970, claiming the West was slowly being subverted into Marxism by the methods previously stated.

The main targets were and are institutions of religious faith, education, media and culture. For all appearances America firmly rejected Soviet Communism during the Cold War. However, there was a massive undercurrent of Marxist-Leninist indoctrination at many, if not most, universities and institutions of learning, in media and artistic communities in the West throughout the 1960s and '70s. Such indoctrination was never challenged by fundamental American patriotic values. The demoralization process in the U.S. had already been completed to a degree beyond the wildest dreams of the top leadership in the Russian Kremlin, by the time the video was produced in 1983.

The next part of the article goes into Bella Dodd's testimony, in a public affidavit, concerning the Communist infiltration of the Catholic Church.

The Communist infiltration was so extensive that in the future "you will not recognize the Catholic Church." In the 1930s, eleven hundred men were placed in the priesthood in order to destroy the Church from within, with the idea for those men to be ordained and move up in authority to influence as Monsignors and Bishops. A Catholic philosopher and professor Alice von Hildebrand, who was a friend of Bella, stated Bella had dealt with no fewer than four Cardinals within the Vatican who were working for the Communist Party and confirmed Bella's statements of testimony.

In the late 1920s and 1930s, directives were sent from Moscow to all Communist Party organizations. In order to destroy the Catholic Church from within, party members were to be planted in seminaries and within diocesan organizations. Bella, herself, put some 1,200 men in Catholic seminaries. She had followed an order, of Stalin, to recruit men distinguished by their complete lack of faith and moral virtue and engage them to infiltrate.

When she informed Monsignor Sheen of what she had done as a Communist and received instruction from him on the Catholic Faith, he instructed her, as a penitential mission to pay for her crushing debt, to work in opening the eyes of blind American citizens to the horror of Communism. She did so from the 1950s to her death in 1969, by traveling across America giving talks to shake her fellow citizens awake to atheistic Communism.

The Communist infiltrators would have gained influence and authority, by which they would have admitted more men devoid of morals and Christian faith into the seminaries for decades. Some infiltrators may have become the administrators of those seminaries. This continued for decades and by now would be into the fourth generation of such men. The abuse which has rocked the Catholic Church going back into the 1960s may not have been a matter of priests giving in to temptation, although some may have been, but the majority by a comprehensive and pervasive attack, of a Trojan horse tactic, on Christian morality and faith by a cunning and profoundly evil enemy.

The article continues on, saying that sexual abuse and the practice of homosexuality is a perfect way to demoralize the Church and cause it to lose its moral authority in the eyes of the public and among believers and cause people to abandon the faith.

Manning R. Johnson

Using archieve.org I found the testimony of another prior Communist named Manning R. Johnson, of the New York City area, who testified on July 8, 1953, before the United States House of Representatives, Subcommittee of the Committee on Un-American Activities, New York, N. Y.

Some of the same people, who had questioned Bella Dodd, were present at this hearing.

Mr. Johnson was a black man, who had joined the Communist Party in 1930. By the mid-1930s, he had achieved national status within the Party. He remained so until 1940, when he left the Party having discovered it was not what it seemed and he would turn against it and fight.

It was stated the Committee before him was studying the activities of certain individuals in the field of clergy, with special attention to their alleged Communist and subversive activities.

In giving the Party's position on religion, Mr. Johnson stated the Communist program is for ceaseless struggle or war to complete extermination and extinction of religion from the face of the earth. That Communist education will root out belief in the super-national and remove religious prejudices, which stand in the way of organizing the masses for **Socialism.**

Mr. Johnson had been instructed in atheism when he joined the Party, and now religion was false and there was no God as men created God. He produced a sample of the Party literature used for such purposes throughout the United States. The material had been written by prior Episcopalian Bishop William Montgomery Brown, who had been expelled from the Church for heresy and began to attack the Christian religion. He also wrote children's book to indoctrinate them. A book titled *Science and History for Boys and Girls* was shown. It was anti-God and Christianity and pro-Communism.

By another Communist author and artist, was a children's cartoon book depicting the evils of Capitalism and Republican Government. And there was also a reader for older children. Some material targeted the Catholic Church.

In all, there were seventeen exhibits shown of Communist material, throughout the hearing process.

In later testimony, Mr. Johnson stated he had hidden his own religious beliefs, while a Communist. Since leaving the Party, he joined the Baptist Church and attends church services.

The old policy of the Party was to convince the worker and farmer to atheist beliefs, before he became active in the Party movement. In 1932, Earl Browder reversed the policy. A person could come into the movement and then be indoctrinated to atheism. In the case of religion, a Church was to be infiltrated and then destroyed. Church members were to be brought into the movement by breaking down any resistance to Communism, so that an actual Christian element would appear within the Party, in appearance to the general public. Christians becoming involved with the movement were then indoctrinated to be anti-religion.

Mr. Johnson brought forth documentation having in it the following:

"The Communists are Marxists, Leninists, Stallinists."

"That is why the (Communist) seventh world congress formulated the new tactical orientation which seized the final and irrevocable victory of **socialism**. The inability of the bourgeoisie to overcome the collapse of the capitalist stabilization and the growing urge of the struggle for **socialism**."

As may be observed, there is a connection between Communism and Socialism, although the two American organizations struggled against each other, at least for a while.

"It is the tactic to draw wide masses into revolutionary class struggle where the working people, both Christians and Jews, will be welded into a millionfold strong revolutionary army, led by the Communist International under the leadership of Stalin at that time." Remember this was in the 1950s, when Stalin was the leader of Russian. The Communist believed the revolution was not that far away and would be under the current leader.

Mr. Johnson stated the Party realized that without subverting the millions of persons in the churches revolution in the United States was unthinkable. Marx stated the masses must support a revolution. Therefore the masses had to believe in Communism even by subversion. Mr. Johnson also stated the chairman, of the American League against War and Fascism (ALWF), which was a Communist front organization to fundraise as part of its so-called peace movement, was a Communist Party member, who was Reverend Harry F. Ward, and called him the Red dean of the Communist Party in the religious field.

In respect to the great number of ministers who were involved one way or another in the ALWF or other Communist front groups were loyal citizens and fine, good, religious men who were completely duped. However, the Communist clergymen and fellow travelers (their supporters) and those under Communist Party discipline were not duped. They were fully conscious and fully aware of what they were doing and utilized their position to infiltrate and seek to subvert the majority of clergy in the interests of the aims and objectives of the Party of the United States.

The Reverend Ward was connected with the Methodist Federation for Social Action, the People's Institute of Applied Religion and other Communist front groups. The Methodist Federation for Social Action had been the Methodist Federation for Social Service. This is only an example of how the Party used churches and its members. An issue of the Party's ALWF *Fight* magazine was submitted having in it both national and international news of Communist action and commentary.

It was pointed out, through documentation, that large groups of young people were involved in the Communist movement, including members of the American military, including officers.

An issue of *Fight* contained an article by Al Hamilton titled "What's My Choice." Hamilton was chairman of Social Action, National Council of Methodist Youth. In the article, it is stated

"For some time certain true spiritual forces of the church and the economic forces in the present-day society have been moving in opposite directions,…. Sincere and intelligent Christians are faced with a choice, support of the church's struggle for social justice and peace or military state, speaking for the dominant economic group in a capitalist society. "or" …the Christian must begin to aid in the organization of workers, students, and intellectuals for fundamental economic change and for effective action to stop the functioning of the totalitarian state." In this case, the word "Republican" is referring to our form of government and not the political Republican Party. Hamilton further states, "Thus the Christian today must choose between the conscientious loyalty to the best in society, loyalty to those who will pay the price of another war, the workers, the students and professionals or subjection to the will of the state that has become merely the expression of the profit system, unable to maintain itself except by war."

Communists use the word "state", in general, as a government body. In this case, Hamilton is referring not to the Communist State totalitarian government of Russia, but to the United States government. He was accusing the U.S. government of being what the Russian government was and is or any Communist government of any country. Accuse the opposition to be or doing what oneself is or is doing. He was writing Communist propaganda to obtain Christian support of the Communist objective. Notice his use of the phrase "social justice", which has permeated our society today. The phrase is not new. It is only being used again by the Socialist.

Back to Mr. Johnson.

In answering the question of what the methods were of infiltration and subversion in the religious organizations used by the Communist, Mr. Johnson informed the Committee of Gilbert Green, who had become a fugitive Communist and fled to Russia, for violation of the Smith Act. He had been a member of the Party's Political Bureau, central committee or national committee, Young Communist International Executive Committee and national committee of the Young Communist League of the United States as well as an official of the American Youth Congress.

He had written a magazine article, in 1935, for International Youth, the official organ of the executive committee of the Young Communist International, with headquarters in Moscow.

The Smith Act of 1940, made it a crime to advocate the violate overthrow of the United States Government.

The summary of the article is that the major plot to take over religious organizations was planned during the mid-1930s.

Later headlines in the February 17, 1953 *Daily Worker* boasted of 2,300 Protestant ministers supporting the Communist. The ministers had signed letters of petition asking for talks, with President Eisenhower, for clemency for the Rosenbergs. The President had already denied such an appeal for clemency in the form of commuting the death sentence. I vaguely remember the Rosenbergs. There was much controversy concerning their case of being Communists spies, who were convicted in 1951 of passing U.S. nuclear secrets to the Soviet Union. They were executed in 1953. The controversy continued.

A Doctor of Divinity, Bernard M. Loonier, who was dean of the University of Chicago Divinity School, forwarded the new appeal to the President asking for commutation of the death sentence due to the controversy surrounding the case and the situation of American society at the time "…the death sentence in this instance is an indication of our national weakness rather than our national strength. It is a reflection of our own growing hysteria, fear and insecurity."

Mr. Johnson was questioned on the process of such letter writing. He explained the Communists composed lists of people who have in any way supported a Communist cause, be it a real or a front cause. They categorize the lists according to subject matter. At the least, they have the person's name, contact information and profession. When the Party requires counteraction of another's cause, event or organization, a letter campaign is put in place. People of various places and professions, are contacted to write and the information as to where to send the letter, for either collection or straight to a person or organization, is given.

Committees were established for everything; committees, sub-committees, committees for a Party-line program, committees for various Party organizations and organizational levels, committees for front organizations, etc.

This Party network tactic was the same as described by Bella Dodd. When a new front organization was formed, the lists of people were gone through and people on the lists were picked out to be contacted by a sub-committee, of the formed committee, to obtain sponsors of whatever that committee was for. Such people would not even know they were supporting a Communist function, but they had become involved to be approached later on to be recruited deeper into the Party activities. These people were used to give a respectable front to such activities.

So the ministers were not necessarily Communist, but people being used. Questions were asked whether Dr. Loonier was a Communist and Mr. Johnson replied Loonier was not, to his knowledge.

At that time, most Americans believed in God and attended church. If a church leader had his name associated with a non-church organization, to support a social service or justice cause, then the church membership would feel such an organization was worthwhile.

Continuing the inquiries concerning religious infiltration and subversion, Gilbert Green's report to a Party national committee was referred to. According to Mr. Johnson, Green said young men had to be reached through trade unions, unemployed organizations and cultural workers organizations. For youth, organizations such as YMCAs and YWCAs, community houses, church organizations, amateur athletic unions and others had to be infiltrated. In the South, more than 300 Party members were also members of church youth organizations and especially the Baptist Young People's Union. Organizational structure, of such organizations, needed to be changed, to fit the Party structure. In the South, especially for the Negro youth, the church was the center of all cultural and social activity. It was predicted in Alabama, that in a short time the church youth organizations could be taken over, with secret cells existing within them. Mr. Johnson stated in the South, there was success, which was due to using the church as a cover to carry out the program of national liberation for the Negro. He further explained that by "national liberation" was meant the Party program of revolt by the Negros in the South and the establishment of an independent Negro republic separate and apart from the rest of the United States. This of course has not happened.

The actual document of Green's report was submitted as record. He had spoken of the conditions in the North relating to the young men and the youth. He felt it would be necessary to train those who would be **miseducating** the youth, by skilled and trained Party leaders. Teachers? The term "youth settlement" or "settlement house" is used. Apparently these were community youth centers having activities for children up to teens, with the leadership being young adults who had grown up in that youth center. Therefore the idea was to recruit the leadership to the Party and indoctrinate them to be Party teachers of the youth. This is but an example of tactics; an example of Mr. Johnson's testimony.

The Communist article "Problems of National Groups in United States" by Irene Browcler, May 1939:

> It is the greatest mistake to deal with the Church, whether Catholic or Protestant, as one reactionary mass. The same political divisions run through it as through society in general, determined by much the same considerations. Class divisions are, of course, the basic ones, and we can always rouse the democratic instincts and sympathies of working-class members of the church, and can often reach them effectively through their church, provided we do not offend their religious susceptibilities and thereby throw them back under the influence of reactionary religious leaders.

Daily Worker, New York, May 7, 1953, Dr. Harry F. Ward's Achievements Recounted at Dinner, in His Honor, by David Platt, sponsored by *Now World*

Review, a **progressive** monthly devoted to circulating the truth about the **Socialist and People's Democracies** abroad: A student of Dr. Ward, Rev. Jack McMichael, of the Methodist Federation for Social Action and one of his students at Union Theological Seminary stated, "His influence on the churches of this country is incalculable. When you see ministers taking a courageous stand on civil liberties and peace, it is because of the inspiration of Dr. Ward's work."

There is nothing wrong in and of civil liberties or peace, but to the Communist they are only labels to be used for the Party's programs.

Dr. Ward would soon be 80 years of age. He had taught at a Christian seminary and had influenced countless students according to the Communist infiltration program. And one of his students was a Communist involved with a church.

He was British and was involved with the British labor movement since 1889, knowing the leader Tom Mann. He came to America at the age of seventeen, to become a rancher, teamster and was involved in the organization of the Amalgamated Clothing Workers' Union, with Sidney Hillman. He authored fifteen books starting in 1913, was for years chairman of the American League against War and Fascism and the American League for Peace and Democracy as well as being general secretary of the Methodist Federation of Social Service from 1911 to 1944, while also being a professor of Christian Ethics for twenty-five years and chairman of the American Civil Liberties Union from 1920 to 1940. For many years, he had been the chief architect for Communist infiltration and subversion in the religious field.

All of those labels sound really meaningful and worthwhile and, if I looked only at labels and not at what was behind them, I would think he was a great man too, but he was a Communist acting on behalf of the Party in their front organizations while writing Communist Party approved material. He was indeed an enemy of the United States.

He had been in the Soviet Union in 1924 and 1931 spending a year there to study the incentives of **socialism**.

Socialism – What's in It for You?, by A.B. Magil, New Century Publishers: Magil had for years been a national leader of the Communist Party, in the United States. He wrote there are religious people who, far from considering **socialism** a menace, see in it the fulfillment of the ethical principles of their faith. It is this that has attracted to **socialism** distinguished clergymen like the Dean of Canterbury, Dr. Harry F. Ward, professor emeritus of Christian Ethics at Union Theological Seminary and Reverend Eliot White, formerly of the Grace Episcopal Church of New York.

Protestant Digest, April 1939, published by Protestant Digest Council for Democracy, article "United Christian Council for Democracy": The magazine was published up to the 1950s. It was a Communist publication. The purpose of the organization was to bring together, for education and united action, members in all Christian churches, who are intent upon expressing the social imperatives inherent in the Christian religion. It was a Communist front publication full of well-meaning words meant to relate to Christian thinking, but relating to the goals of Communism/**Socialism**. Mr. Johnson testified the publications aim and purpose was to use the infiltration of the Protestant denominations to carry the Materialist, anti-religious policy of the Communist Party into the denominations under the guise of religion and to provide ministers with material for sermons to be delivered to the congregations at regular services. The publisher was under Communist Party discipline and would be depended upon to carry out the Party-line.

Issue after issue of the *Protestant Digest* and its article were submitted as exhibits showing subject matter distributed to ministers giving commentary on various social issues of current events all as mandated by Party-line.

The People's Institute of Applied Religion, which was a Communist front organization involving churches, including in the South, was discussed as well as the use of the Bible, by the organization to twist its passages into the Party's own meanings to indoctrinate.

When asked if the Party used only Negros, in the South, Mr. Johnson replied that race did not matter; Negroes, Whites, Mexicans.

One of the magazine articles was on 161 church leaders who asked President Truman to grant amnesty to eleven convicted Communists who violated the Smith Act. Rev. Eldward D. McGowan, minister of the Epworth Methodist Church, Bronx, New York, presented the letter, with its signers, to the President. A statement of condition was also presented that if President Truman did not grant amnesty, then the matter would be taken to newly elected President Eisenhower. Among the 161 were seven Bishops of the Episcopal Church, including one of the initiators Right Rev. Normand B. Nash of Massachusetts, Bishop Arthur W. Womack of the Colored Methodist Episcopal Church, Bishop G.W. Taylor of the Reformed Zion Union Apostolic Church, twelve clerics professors in theological schools or universities and a number of national officers, state and district superintendents in several denominations together with the executives of local church federations. The majority were parish ministers of 15 denominations in 33 states. At the time, there were only 48 states.

Infiltration of the Christian churches began in the early 1930s. Fifty years later would have been enough time for clergy affected by Soviet propaganda to rise to the position of Bishop becoming Communist along the way or for a Communist man to become a minister in the 1930s and rise to Bishop. All 161 had to know the eleven convicted were Communist; Communist enemies of the United States. Why would they want amnesty for Communists? Unless they themselves were Communists.

Following are some of the others involved and their positions, for examination:

Right Rev. Reginald Mallett, Bishop of Northern Indiana Episcopal

Rev. Albert W. Palmer, former Moderator of the Congregational Christian Churches

Dr. Wilbur E. Saunders, President of Colgate-Rochester Divinity School

Rev. Forrest C. Weir, Executive Director of the Church Federation of Los Angels

Rev. Abbott Book, Executive Director of the Northern California-Nevada Council of Churches

Rev. C.C. Adams, Secretary of the Foreign Mission Board of the National Baptist Convention Inc.

Rev. Albert Buckner Coe, Superintendent of Massachusetts Conference of Congregational-Christian Churches

Rev. Lewis H. Davis, District Superintendent of the New York East Conference of the Methodist Church

Rev. Prof. Nels F.S. Ferre of Vanderbilt University, Nashville

Rev. Prof. Kolland E. Wolfe of Western Reserve University, Cleveland

Dean J.H. Satterwhite of Hood Theological Seminary (African Methodist Episcopal Zion), Salisbury, North Carolina

Rev. Prof. John Oliver Nelson of Yale University Divinity School

Rev. John Haynes Holms, Minister-emeritus, Community Church of New York

Rev. Guy Emery Shipler, Editor of The Churchman

Rev. William B. Spofford, Editor of The Witness

Rev. Harold A. Bosley, First Methodist Church, Evanston Illinois

Rev. J. Raymond Cope, First Unitarian Church, Berkeley, California

Rev. John Howard Melish, Church of the Holy Trinity, Brooklyn

Dr. Henry Neumann, Ethical Culture Society, Brooklyn

Rev. Calvin C. Ellis, Louisville, North Carolina and Rev. James A. Jones, Durham, North Carolina, both ministers of the African Methodist Episcopal Zion Church

Rev. William B. Cemmer, Board of Publications, Disciples of Christ, Saint Louis, Missouri

Very Rev. Paul Roberts, Dean of Saint John's Cathedral Episcopal, Denver, Colorado

Very Rev. Louis M. Hirshon, Dean of Christ Church Cathedral Episcopal, Harford, Connecticut

Rev. Raymond Calkins, nationally prominent Congregational minister

Rev. Prof. Massey H. Shepherd Jr. of the Episcopal Theological School, Cambridge

Rev. John Paul Jones of the Union Church of Bay Ridge Presbyterian, Brooklyn

Rev. Dana McLean Greeley, Arlington Street Unitarian Church, Boston

Rev. Charles A. Hill, Hartford Avenue Baptist Church, Detroit

Rev. Kenneth de P. Hughes and Rev. George L. Paine, Episcopal ministers of Cambridge and Boston

Rev. Shelton Hale, Bishop of Saint Philip's Church, New York

Why have I taken the time and made the effort to copy this list? So that the level of church administration and organization, university and seminary involvement, in the wide span of national location may be seen in black and white. And this is not even the whole list! Further testimony by Mr. Johnson:

The Communists had some small forces in the seminaries and under the leadership of Harry F. Ward. These were quickly augmented by additional recruits and siphoned into the divinity institutions by manipulations of Communists cells in the seminaries. This infiltration was expedited by the use of considerable forces the Communists had in educational institutions, which were eligible for hire by divinity organizations.

The plan was to make the seminaries the neck of a funnel through which thousands of potential clergymen would issue forth carrying with them, in varying degrees, an ideology and slant which would aid in neutralizing the anti-Communist character of the church and also to use the clergy to spearhead important Communist projects.

This policy was successful beyond even Communist expectations. The combination of Communist clergymen, clergymen with a pro-Communist ideology, plus thousands of clergymen who were sold the principle of considering Communist causes as progressive, within 20 years, furnished the Soviet apparatus with a machine which was used as a religious cover for the overall Communist operation ranging from immediate demands to actually furnishing aid in espionage and outright treason. Communists in churches and other religious organizations were instructed to utilize the age-old tradition of the sanctity of the church as a cover for their own dastardly deeds. Through Reds in religion, we have a true living example of the old saying: "The Devil doth quote the Scripture."

The Communists also infiltrated religious publishing and slanted it toward the Communist programs giving their own clergy printed material from which to speak from the pulpit.

With only ten percent infiltration, the Communists could control the other ninety percent of church members and organizations, through their planned action of subversion.

Such infiltration was not only accomplished in the United States, but also in other parts of the world. There is a lot of online material on the subject as well as other books published by former Communists. Now I know why my Stepdad asked, "Are you sure it is not a Communist front?"

During the Viet Nam War, an American Army patrol came across a large stream of blood, which had flowed downhill, on the road they were traveling. They followed the blood uphill until they found the source inside the gates of a Vietnamese Catholic orphanage. The priest and nuns had been stripped of their clothing, cut so they would bleed to death, tied and hung on poles. All of the children had been slaughtered. They had been killed by the Communist even though they were not a threat. Killed because they were Christian. I was told this by one of the soldiers who saw the sight.

More reality of Communism/Socialism is as follows:

I Could Have Been One

On Jan. 10, 1963, Congressman Albert S. Herlong Jr. of Florida read a list of 45 Communist goals into the Congressional Record. The list was derived from researcher Cleon Skousen's book *The Naked Communist*. These principles are well worth revisiting today in order to gain insights into the thinking and strategies of much of our so-called liberal elite.

> Thursday, January 10, 1963 website- http://disruptthe-narrative.com/2013/01/08/45-communist-goals-by-dr-cleon-skousen-1958/
>
> Mr. Herlong. Mr. Speaker, Mrs. Patricia Nordman of De Land, Fla., is an ardent and articulate opponent of communism, and until recently published the De Land Courier, which she dedicated to the purpose of alerting the public to the dangers of communism in America.
>
> At Mrs. Nordman's request, I include in the RECORD, under unanimous consent, the following "Current Communist Goals," which she identifies as an excerpt from "The Naked Communist," by Cleon Skousen:
>
> [From *The Naked Communist*, by Cleon Skousen]

45 Communist goals and how far they have been completed into this Century:
The comments are not that of this writer.

1. U.S. acceptance of coexistence as the only alternative to atomic war. (CHECK. Presidents (both parties) have routinely supported U.N. measures that subject our sovereign power to the U.N.)
2. U.S. willingness to capitulate in preference to engaging in atomic war. (CHECK. 44 has made a systematic effort to decrease the U.S. number of nuclear warheads while our enemies continue to grow theirs.)

3. Develop the illusion that total disarmament [by] the United States would be a demonstration of moral strength. (CHECK. 44 not only apologizes for our strengths, but works to undermine them in the name of moral strength.)
4. Permit free trade between all nations regardless of Communist affiliation and regardless of whether or not items could be used for war. (CHECK.)
5. Extension of long-term loans to Russia and Soviet satellites. (CHECK. Let's understand this does not refer to satellites in the sky, but to governments supportive of Communist Russia's agenda. Currently, these would be the governments who embrace totalitarian regimes.)
6. Provide American aid to all nations regardless of Communist domination. (CHECK. Currently this refers not only to Communist domination, but also to Radical Islamic domination such as Al Qaeda, Taliban, Hamas, etc.)
7. Grant recognition of Red China. Admission of Red China to the U.N. (CHECK. 1971)
8. Set up East and West Germany as separate states in spite of Khrushchev's promise in 1955 to settle the German question by free elections under supervision of the U.N. (CHECK. 1961 – remember, this list was written in 1958.)
9. Prolong the conferences to ban atomic tests because the United States has agreed to suspend tests as long as negotiations are in progress. (CHECK. Even in 2013 the conference is still going on.)
10. Allow all Soviet satellites individual representation in the U.N. (CHECK, what are now Belarus and Ukraine were Soviet satellites until gaining their independence in 1991.)
11. Promote the U.N. as the only hope for mankind. If its charter is re-written, demand that it be set up as a one-world government with its

I Could Have Been One

own independent armed forces. (Some Communist leaders believe the world can be taken over as easily by the U.N. as by Moscow. Sometimes these two centers compete with each other as they are now doing in the Congo.) (CHECK. Agenda 21.)

12. Resist any attempt to outlaw the Communist Party. (CHECK – is it illegal? Nope, these days we are surrounded by mindless twits who think "Socialism is Cool".)
13. Do away with all loyalty oaths. (CHECK. Note the continued degradation of The Pledge of Allegiance and the systematic removal from schools and community government events.)
14. Continue giving Russia access to the U.S. Patent Office. (CHECK. Not only does Russia have access, the entire world has access via the USPTO website.)
15. Capture one or both of the political parties in the United States. (CHECK. The Democratic Party ideals are largely communistic in nature. Whether or not they want to recognize or admit it.)
16. Use technical decisions of the courts to weaken basic American institutions by claiming their activities violate civil rights. (CHECK, CHECK, CHECK. Too many examples to list.)
17. Get control of the schools. Use them as transmission belts for socialism and current Communist propaganda. Soften the curriculum. Get control of teachers' associations. Put the party line in textbooks. (CHECK, and none are so insidious as the NEA.)
18. Gain control of all student newspapers. (CHECK. Control the schools, control their media.)
19. Use student riots to foment public protests against programs or organizations which are under Communist attack.
20. Infiltrate the press. Get control of book-review assignments, editorial writing, policymaking positions. (CHECK, CHECK, CHECK. Too

many to list, but the December 30, 2012 Op-Ed favoring dumping The Constitution is a good example.)

21. Gain control of key positions in radio, TV, and motion pictures. (CHECK, CHECK, CHECK.)

22. Continue discrediting American culture by degrading all forms of artistic expression. An American Communist cell was told to "eliminate all good sculpture from parks and buildings, substitute shapeless, awkward and meaningless forms." (CHECK. Look around. How many sculptures do you look at and ask, what the heck is that supposed to be?)

23. Control art critics and directors of art museums. "Our plan is to promote ugliness, repulsive, meaningless art." (CHECK. Jesus on the Cross in urine, Mary surrounded by multiple buttocks with elephant dung, etc. all praised as "art". I won't give the artists the dignity of mentioning their names.)

24. Eliminate all laws governing obscenity by calling them "censorship" and a violation of free speech and free press. (CHECK. Many of us remember George Carlin's Seven Forbidden Words. While all of them can now be heard on cable channels, most of them can be heard on even network television.)

25. Break down cultural standards of morality by promoting pornography and obscenity in books, magazines, motion pictures, radio, and TV. (CHECK. In 1953, the word "pregnant" could not be said on the I Love Lucy Show. We can all name shows where married couples had twin beds. Now, anything goes and what is on even network television used to be referred to as pornography.)

26. Present homosexuality, degeneracy and promiscuity as "normal, natural, healthy." (CHECK, CHECK, CHECK. The point here? Undermine the family unit and weaken the community by creating single parent homes and non-reproductive couples. However, as

many same-sex couples do have the desire to have children, this aspect of the mission has failed to a degree. The irony is that most "isms" consider homosexuality as offensive, however, as with anything else, it provides a means to their ends and the homosexual population are too eager to join the cause without knowing the history behind the "acceptance".)

27. Infiltrate the churches and replace revealed religion with "social" religion. Discredit the Bible and emphasize the need for intellectual maturity which does not need a "religious crutch." (CHECK, CHECK, CHECK.)

28. Eliminate prayer or any phase of religious expression in the schools on the ground that it violates the principal of "separation of church and state." (CHECK. The ACLU and atheist groups have made this their primary mission. And the ignorance of the American people and the courts have allowed it to continue. THERE IS NO SEPARATION OF CHURCH AND STATE CLAUSE IN THE CONSTITUTION.)

29. Discredit the American Constitution by calling it inadequate, old-fashioned, out of step with modern needs, a hindrance to cooperation between nations on a worldwide basis. (CHECK. See 20. Even sadder, a few years ago, a dear friend of mine referred to The Constitution as "just a 200-year-old piece of paper".)

30. Discredit the American Founding Fathers. Present them as selfish aristocrats who had no concern for the "common man." (CHECK.)

31. Belittle all forms of American culture and discourage the teaching of American history on the ground that it was only a minor part of the "big picture." Give more emphasis to Russian history since the Communists took over. (CHECK.)

32. Support any socialist movement to give centralized control over any part of the culture–education, social agencies, welfare programs,

mental health clinics, etc. (CHECK. Wilson, FDR, LBJ, and the hits keep coming under 44's regime.)

33. Eliminate all laws or procedures which interfere with the operation of the Communist apparatus. (In progress. The EPA and onslaught of Executive Orders are two of the strongest examples of completely bypassing the checks and balances created in the Constitution.)
34. Eliminate the House Committee on Un-American Activities. (CHECK. Renamed to Internal Security Committee in 1969 and eliminated in 1975. In 1959 Truman called it "the most un-American thing in the country today.")
35. Discredit and eventually dismantle the FBI.
36. Infiltrate and gain control of more unions. (CHECK. We all remember SEIU President Andy Stearn's Marxist tribute when he announced Workers of The World Unite." Here's 44 saying his presidency will be for the SEIU.)
37. Infiltrate and gain control of big business. (CHECK. If you can't infiltrate, create your own. Think "Global Warming" and Green Energy.)
38. Transfer some of the powers of arrest from the police to social agencies. Treat all behavioral problems as psychiatric disorders which no one but psychiatrists can understand [or treat]. (CHECK to the 2nd statement. We all remember when it was widely accepted that some people are just plain mean. Now, the blame has to be shifted to some ethereal psychiatric disorder so that the person can be held harmless for their deeds.)
39. Dominate the psychiatric profession and use mental health laws as a means of gaining coercive control over those who oppose Communist goals.
40. Discredit the family as an institution. Encourage promiscuity and easy divorce. (CHECK. See 22-28. In 1950 there were 385,144 divorces. By 2009 that number has jumped to 2,318,615.)

41. Emphasize the need to raise children away from the negative influence of parents. Attribute prejudices, mental blocks and retarding of children to suppressive influence of parents. (CHECK. Rather than raising children away from parents, this was accomplished through removing parental guidance in the home and the promotion of ideas like freedom of expression, being your child's best friend, removal of rules in the home by "training" parents that discipline was bad for their child's self-esteem, etc.)
42. Create the impression that violence and insurrection are legitimate aspects of the American tradition; that students and special-interest groups should rise up and use ["]united force["] to solve economic, political or social problems. (CHECK. Three words – Occupy Wall Street.)
43. Overthrow all colonial governments before native populations are ready for self-government. (CHECK. If not all, certainly several. Mau Mau Uprising anyone? Hmmm, what rings about the Mau Mau Uprising? Oh yes, it took place in Kenya, home of 44's "father".)
44. Internationalize the Panama Canal. (CHECK. In 1999 the U.S. handed the Panama Canal over to the corrupt government of Panama. Panama subsequently signed a 50-year lease for two ports at each end of the Canal with Hong Kong's Hutchison Whampoa Company, run by Li Ka-shing, who is closely associated with the Beijing regime. This gave China's Communist Party de facto control over the most strategic waterway in the West.)
45. Repeal the Connally reservation so the United States cannot prevent the World Court from seizing jurisdiction [over domestic problems. Give the World Court jurisdiction] over nations and individuals alike. (IN PROGRESS. In the following year, 1959, Hubert Humphrey introduced into the Senate S. Res. 94 to repeal the Connally Reservation. This was followed by H. Res. 267 was introduced in

favor of Humphrey's bill. While no official repeal is found in the Congressional records it is widely known that 44 and his supporters favor acquiescing to international law in U.S. cases.)

Communism/Socialism Today

We have covered the first half of the Twentieth Century, but today is in the beginning of the 2020s. Today we hear not about Communism, but about Socialism. President Trump has openly spoken against Socialists and Socialism. Why the switch? The Communist Party did not just go away and there are the Democratic Socialists of America very active in political support, including financing. Bernie Sanders' Party of young people; college students buying into a materialistic cause having been instructed by Socialist university teachers, who may have had such teachers themselves. And the trade unions… are they still Communist or are they now Socialist?

Remember trade unions became not about the welfare of the workers, but about political activity. Such unions now send money to politicians, who will propose and pass legislation favorable to the Socialist agenda. And that is why unions are against "Right to Work" laws, in the States. If there are such laws, then workers do not have to belong to a union and have union dues taken out of their paycheck. If there is a problem with management, they can go to the bargaining table themselves. If workers do not have to be union members, that decreases the amount of union dues collected as well as the amount of people under Socialist control, to further their agenda. Less dues means less money going to politicians, from that source. "Right to Work" is about worker's rights. Not unions.

An example of what some unions have become came about in Wisconsin, when the governor went against the unions. Some union members/thugs, under the cover of darkness, went to the State Capital and trashed the grounds, broke out windows and did other damage. Once it was all cleaned up and repaired and replaced, they did it again. This is part of the current Communist/Socialist criminal action that goes on in America. While there was violence back in the early days of union activity, it was in times that were rough. Today is not rough. My gosh...there is the Civility movement.

I had heard the Communists made a deal with the Socialists. The Communist would back off and give the Socialists the chance to take the United States by political measures. If that did not happen, then the Communists would rise up in arms. Don't know if that is true though. In researching for such an agreement, I came across an article, from the online source BBC News, New York, 1 May 2014, "The curious survival of the US Communist Party":

In 1991, with the collapse of the Soviet Union, the Communist Party United States of America suffered a crippling blow, but about two to three thousand members nationwide were figured at the time of this article six years ago. Although the headquarters are now in an elegant New York building, which is still a blend-in with the neighborhood, and the offices are modern, there are still present the writings of Marx, Engels and Lenin on the bookshelves. Rent from the building's other office spaces pay for the *People's World*, which descended from the Party's prior *Daily Worker*. Yes, rent... Capitalism.

There are only two paid staff members, with others assisting as volunteers. The ultimate aim is for **Socialism** to usher in a new era in the country, with the great wealth of the United State to benefit all of the people and the long term goal of the Communist community ending all class divisions, with a society of equality and the withering away of the state; the government as it exists today. Or so they say of the aim.

The 1930s and '40s are declared as the Party's heyday having a strong network across the country and scoring several local election successes. Three Democratic congressmen were secretly Communist Party members. Membership was above 100,000 at the time, with a wide influence.

The Cold War brought investigation of U.S. Communists and allies mostly at the hands of the House Un-American Activities Committee and Senator Joe McCarthy. During that time, it was felt, by the Party, that the Communist revolution was going to happen and such investigations were just part of the first wave of repression. There was a Party parallel underground structure, including some spies for Moscow, from which a substantial amount of funding came.

When the Hungarian revolt occurred and was repressed, in 1956, as well as in Czechoslovakia, in 1968, the Party maintained an orthodox, pro-Moscow line. A split came when Gus Hall, leader of the Party from 1959-2000, supported the coup by Soviet hardliners against Mikhail Gorbachev, in 1991. It was core members, who refused to give up regardless of how bleak things appeared. Members who have extremely strong beliefs and invest an incredible amount of themselves into the Communist Party. So said Vernon L. Pederson, who was speaking for the Party. He was of the Communist Party of Maryland.

He also stated the immediate task was to defeat America's extreme right, by contributing to a broader coalition of left-wing groups. So there is a broad coalition of leftist groups. Socialist and not Communist groups?

The Party Chairman, Sam Webb, pointed out events as successes of the Occupy movement, election of Socialist Ksharna Sawant, to Seattle's City Council, Bill de Blasio becoming the Mayor of New York and that even Republicans are talking about poverty. A **Socialist** society is the goal in the "foreseeable future" with Communism "probably much more distant." Webb admitted that first the economic system of **Socialism**, is stalled and then comes the government system of Communism, to enforce it.

Tony Pecinovsky, who was a thirty-six year old district organizer for the Party in Kansas and Missouri and Tennessee, said the fading memories of the Cold War and the CPUSA's pragmatic, grass-roots activism have lessened the stigma around Communism, but prejudice endures on the ground.

Anti-Communism and all that is still very real, in terms of the far right wing in our nation still exists. The nationwide TEA Party elements that existed during the Obama presidency was proof of that. So the Communist Party tries let their work speak for them and not make it so much about the "C" word. So they are trying to hide the fact that the work is indeed Communist work, which is a tactic that was used in its heyday.

The Party had a convention the following June, of 1919, and Webb wanted to have a conversation about changing the Party's name of Communist. And there it is; a name change to sound more acceptable and positive.

The Communist Party USA was formed by a split of the existing Socialist Party of America, in 1919. Due to the leaders of the CPUSA opposing certain Russian Party leaders, major funding from Russia ended in 1989, which was three years before the collapse in Russia.

Since the *Washington Times* website coverage of the Communist Party USA 2019 Convention, in Chicago, states that the Party's goal is to act with the left-wing, of the Democrat Party, in ousting President Trump, apparently the Party did not change its name at the 2014 Convention and is still in motion.

I decided to go onto the Socialist Party of America website and I found the following. It begins in the late 1950s, but goes only to early 1970s. However, the 1960s was a turbulent decade of American history, with the country having gone from Rock & Roll into the Civil Rights movement. I have summarized the article in order to make it an easier read.

Socialist Party of America History
Civil Rights & the War on Poverty

In 1958 the party took in the members of the recently dissolved Independent Socialist League, which had been led by Max Shachtman, who had developed a Marxist critique of **So-**

viet Communism as "bureaucratic collectivism", a new form of class society that was more oppressive than any form of capitalism. Shachtman's theory was similar to that of many dissidents and refugees from Communism. His intelligent analysis attracted young socialists and his denunciations of the Soviet 1956 invasion of Hungary attracted younger activists.

Shachtman's youthful followers were able to bring new vigor to the Party, and he encouraged them to take positions of responsibility and leadership. A young leader sent others to help Bayard Rustin with the civil-rights movement. Rustin had helped to spread pacificism and non-violence to leaders of the civil rights movement. The civil rights movement benefited from the analysis of Shachtman. Rustin and his young aides organized many protest activities. The young socialists helped Rustin and A. Philip Randolph organize the 1963 March on Washington, where Martin Luther King delivered his I Have A Dream speech.

Michael Harrington soon became the most visible socialist in the United States when his book *The Other America* became a best seller. Harrington and other socialists were called to Washington, D.C., to assist the Kennedy Administration and then the Johnson Administration's War on Poverty and Great Society.

The young socialists' role in the civil rights movement made the Socialist Party more attractive. Harrington was an officer and staff-persons of the League for Industrial Democracy (LID), which helped to start the New Left Students for a Democratic Society (SDS). The three LID officers clashed with the less experienced activists of SDS, like Tom

Hayden, (Comment: Tom Hayden was married to the American traitor Jane Fonda, who caused the death of American POWs in North Viet Nam.) when the latter's Port Huron Statement criticized Socialist and Liberal opposition to Communism and criticized the labor movement, while promoting students as agents of social change. LID and SDS split in 1965, when SDS voted to remove from its constitution the "exclusion clause" that prohibited membership by communists: The SDS exclusion clause had barred "advocates of or apologists for" "totalitarianism". The clause's removal effectively invited "disciplined cadre" to attempt to "take over or paralyze" SDS, as had occurred to mass organizations in the thirties.

The experience of the civil rights movement, and the coalition of labor unions and other **progressive** forces, suggested America was changing and that a mass movement of the democratic left was possible. In terms of electoral politics, Shachtman, and Harrington argued it was a waste of effort to run electoral campaigns as "Socialist Party" candidates, against Democratic Party candidates. Instead, they advocated a political strategy called "realignment," that prioritized strengthening labor unions and other **progressive** organizations that were already active in the **Democratic Party**. Contributing to the day-to-day struggles of the civil-rights movement and labor unions had gained socialists credibility and influence and had helped to push politicians in the **Democratic Party** towards social-democratic positions, on civil rights and the War on Poverty.

Socialist Party of America History

Transition From Labor Socialist to Social Capitalist

In its 1972 Convention, the Socialist Party had two Co-Chairmen, Bayard Rustin and Charles S. Zimmerman (of the International Ladies Garment Workers' Union, ILGWU) and a First National Vice Chairman, James S. Glaser, who were re-elected by acclamation. In his opening speech to the Convention, Co-Chairman Bayard Rustin called for the group to organize against the "reactionary policies of the Nixon Administration"; Rustin also criticized the "irresponsibility and elitism of the 'New Politics' liberals".

The Party **changed its name to** "*Social Democrats, USA*" by a vote of 73 to 34. Renaming the Party as SDUSA was meant to be "realistic". The New York Times observed that the Socialist Party had last sponsored a candidate for President in 1956, who received only 2,121 votes, which were cast in only 6 states. Because the Party no longer sponsored candidates in Presidential Elections, the name "Party" had been "misleading"; "Party" had hindered the recruiting of activists who participated in the Democratic Party, according to the majority report. The **name "Socialist" was replaced by "Social Democrats" because many Americans associated the word "socialism" with Soviet communism.** Also, the Party wished to distinguish itself from two small Marxist parties, the Socialist Workers Party and the Socialist Labor Party. (Comment: Again we have a connection between Communism and Socialism.)

The Unity Caucus had a supermajority of votes and its position carried on every issue, by a ratio of two to one. The Convention elected a national committee of 33 members, with 22 seats for the majority caucus, 8 seats for Harrington's "coalition caucus", 2 for "a Debs caucus", and one for the "independent" Samuel H. Friedman. Friedman and the minority caucuses had opposed the name change. (Comment: I recognized the name of "Friedman" and looked him up. He ran for Vice President twice as a Socialist.)

The convention voted on and adopted proposals for its program by a two-one vote. On foreign policy, the program called for "firmness toward Communist aggression". However, on the Vietnam War, the program opposed "any efforts to bomb Hanoi into submission"; instead, it endorsed negotiating a peace agreement, which should protect Communist political cadres in South Vietnam from further military or police reprisals. Harrington's proposal for an immediate withdrawal of U.S. forces was defeated. Harrington complained that, after its March 1972 convention, the Socialist Party had endorsed George McGovern with a statement loaded with "constructive criticism"; Harrington complained also that the Party had not mobilized enough support for McGovern. The majority caucus's Arch Puddington replied that the California branch had been especially active in supporting McGovern, while the New York branch had instead focused on a congressional race.

Rise of the Social Capitalist

Late in October 1972, before the SP's December convention, Michael Harrington resigned as National Co-Chairman of the Socialist Party. Although little remarked upon at the time despite Harrington's status as "possibly the most widely known of the Socialist leaders since the death of Norman Thomas," it soon became clear this was the precursor of a decisive split in the organization.

Harrington had written extensively about the **progressive** potential of the **so-called "New Politics" in the Democratic Party** and had come to advocate unilateral withdrawal from the Vietnam war and to advocate positions regarded by more conservative party members as "avant-garde" on the questions of abortion and gay rights. This put Harrington and his co-thinkers at odds with the party's younger generation of leaders, who espoused a strongly labor-oriented direction for the party and who were broadly supportive of AFL-CIO leader George Meany.

In the early spring of **1973**, Harrington resigned his membership in SDUSA. That same year, Harrington and his supporters formed the **Democratic Socialist** Organizing Committee (DSOC). At its start, DSOC had 840 members, of which 2 percent served on its national board; approximately 200 had been members of Social Democrats, USA or its predecessors whose membership was then 1,800, according to a 1973 profile of Harrington. Its high-profile members included Congressman Ron Dellums and William Winpisinger, President of the International Association of Machinists. In **1982 DSOC established the Democratic Socialists of America (DSA)** upon merging with the **New American Movement, an organization of democratic socialists mostly from the New Left.**

The Union for Democratic Socialism was another organization, which was formed by former members of the Socialist Party. David McReynolds, who had resigned from the Socialist Party between 1970 and 1971, and many from the Dems Caucus, were the core members. In **1973, the UDS declared itself the Socialist Party USA, which quickly in recent years declined into a capitalist clique that preys on the disenfranchised.**

And I decided to find the following website for some more history.

A History of Democratic Socialists of America 1971-2017
Bringing Socialism from the Margins to the Mainstream
by Joseph M. Schwartz,
DSA National Political Committee, July 2017

Democratic Socialists of America (DSA)—and its two predecessor organizations, the Democratic Socialist Organizing Committee (DSOC) and the New American Movement (NAM)—had their origins in the early 1970s, at the beginning of a long-term rightward shift of U.S. and global politics. This shift to the right—symbolized by the triumph in the 1980s of Ronald Reagan and Margaret Thatcher—somewhat overshadowed the central role these organizations played in the movements of resistance to corporate domination, as well as in today's ongoing project: organizing an ideological and organizational socialist presence among trade union, community, feminist and people of color and other activists. (Comment: "People of Color" While it is all inclusive and in some cultures the term "black" is used for any dark completion person, it seems that "people of color" is just another way of saying "Colored".)

DSA made an ethical contribution to the broader American Left by being one of the few radical organizations born out of a merger rather than a split. DSA also helped popularize the vision of an ecumenical, multi-tendency socialist organization, an ethos that enabled it to recently incorporate recently many thousands of new members, mostly out of the Bernie Sanders presidential campaign.

The Founding of DSA Through the Merger of the Democratic Socialist Organizing Committee (DSOC) and the New American Movement (NAM)

We were 6,000 strong at the time of the merger in the spring of **1982**. Before the merger, both DSOC and NAM had made modest but significant contributions to the trade union, community organizing and feminist movements, as well as to rebuilding a left-labor coalition within and without the **Democratic Party**. Though shaped by distinct cultural and historical experiences, most members of both organizations had come to the same political conclusions: an American socialist movement must be committed to democracy as an end in itself and work as an open, independent socialist organization in anti-corporate, racial justice and feminist coalitions **with non-socialist progressives.** (Comment: Does this mean Liberals?)

DSOC, founded in 1973, when a defeated anti-Vietnam War wing split from the remnants of the Debsian Socialist Party, grew in less than a decade from a small cadre of a few hundred to an organization of nearly 5,000. It had a significant network among trade union and **left Democratic Party activists** as well as a rapidly growing, predominantly **campus-based Youth Section**.

Unlike DSOC, the **New American Movement, founded in 1971, had its origins not in a wing of the Old Left but in Students for a Democratic Society (SDS) and the socialist-feminist women's unions of the late 1960s and early 1970s.** Founded by a talented core of **New Left** veterans fleeing the sectarian excesses of late

SDS and graduating from campus to community politics, **NAM focused on building a grassroots "revolutionary democratic socialist-feminist" presence in local struggles around issues such as affordable housing, reproductive freedom and utility rate reform. NAM not only played an important role in the reproductive rights movement, but also helped the Left reconceptualize the relationship between race, gender and class.** (Comment: "Reproductive Rights" Just a nice, fancy Liberal way of saying "abortion".

DSOC's greatest political contribution undoubtedly lay in making real Harrington's vision of **building a strong coalition among progressive trade unionists, civil rights and feminist activists and the "new politics" left-liberals in the McGovern wing of the Democrats.**

The history of the 1960s and early 1970s had made the concept suspect: how could a labor movement led by prowar, socially conservative George Meany, which had implicitly supported Richard Nixon over George McGovern in the 1972 presidential race, unite with middle-class, anti-war and "new politics" activists who often dismissed the entire labor movement as bureaucratic, anti-democratic, sexist and racist? And how could activists of color and feminists trust labor leaders or mainstream Democrats who urged these social movements not to rock the boat by militantly demanding an equal voice at the table? Harrington envisioned uniting the constituencies of the three Georges (Meany, McGovern and Wallace) and getting feminists, trade unionists and black, Latino and Socialist activists in the same room talking politics.

It seemed utopian, if not naive, in 1973. But by the late 1970s, partly because of the success of the DSOC-inspired Democratic Agenda, coalition politics had become a mantra among trade unionists, activists in communities of color, feminists and the **LGBTQ** community. (Comment: Thus we have blacks, Hispanics, women and alterative sex groups pulled into political action, where they were not before.)

Democratic Agenda began as the Democracy '76 project. DSOC put together a labor-left coalition to fight for a real commitment to full employment at the 1976 Democratic Convention. The project, which gave headaches to Carter operatives at the nominating convention, foreshadowed the political divisions of Carter's presidency. After the election of 1976, Democracy '76 evolved into Democratic Agenda, which picked up active support from the leadership of such unions as the American Federation of State, County and Municipal Employees, the United Auto Workers and the Machinists, as well as from feminists, activists in communities of color and left activists in and around the Democratic Party.

The height of Democratic Agenda's influence came in the spring of 1978 when, at the Democratic Party mid-term convention, it got 40 percent of the conference vote for resolutions rejecting the Carter administration's abandonment of the fight for full employment and for efforts to curtail the power of Big Oil. In the spring of 1979, Machinists Union President (and DSOC Vice-Chair) William Winpisinger announced a "Draft [Senator Ted] Kennedy" movement. The coalition brought together by Democratic Agenda reached its fullest political expression in that campaign, although it was ultimately unsuccessful. (Comment: Rumor had it that Ted Kennedy did not accept the nomination for the Presidency because he was gotten to and told if he did, he would end up like his brothers or he thought that himself and decided to stay alive. As it is, he filled the Senate seat far too long.)

The founding leaders of NAM and DSOC could not have constructed a merger on their own. NAM's New Left veterans, nurtured by the Communist politics, of the anti-Vietnam War movement, could not accept the left-wing anti-Communism of DSOC's founding leadership (an anti-communism formed in anti-Stalinist struggles). Conversely, many of DSOC's leaders could not understand the refusal of some NAM leaders to recognize opposition to authoritarian communism as a central moral obligation of Democratic Socialists. Not surprisingly, the two stickiest issues in the merger talks focused on the organization's ideological positions on communism and the Middle East. Interestingly enough, few members have since questioned the organization's principled opposition to authoritarian regimes of all stripes nor the need for a viable, independent Palestinian state and a cutoff of U.S. military aid to Israel to promote complete and unilateral Israeli withdrawal from the occupied territories. (Comment: Now we have the international aspect of the Middle East.)

The infusion of newer members in both camps spurred the merger process. DSOC's younger activists, many of them students, some veterans of the Gene McCarthy and McGovern campaigns, found NAM's emphasis on grassroots activism and socialist-feminism inspiring. In NAM, former communists, many of whom had joined in the mid-1970s, agreed with DSOC's emphasis on coalition work with non-socialists and valued DSOC's greater national visibility.

Joint work on Democratic Agenda and on mobilizing for an Anti-Draft march in Washington, D.C. (where 40,000 people called for an end to both the military draft and the economic draft based on mass inner-city unemployment) led to a decrease in mutual suspicions. In December of 1980, DSOC put the accomplishments of European social democracy on display in Washington, D.C., at a 3,000-person conference on "Eurosocialism and America: An International Exchange" The conference's emphasis on the struggle for greater worker control over investment and production decisions convinced many in NAM that the distance between themselves and DSOC had dwindled. (Comment: I remember the saying, "We have to be more like Europe." I wondered why, since this is America. We are our own people, with our own way of doing things due to being "the melting pot". It may be different, but that does not mean it is wrong. It is just different. We do not need to follow suit with other world areas.)

DSA in the 1980s: Linking Struggles for Social Justice Abroad and at Home

When delegates from DSOC and NAM met in Detroit in March 1982 to form Democratic Socialists of America, they shared Harrington's perpetual optimism that corporate irresponsibility would give rise to popular demands for democratic control over the economy. Reagan's "evil empire" rhetoric and his assaults on the women's, civil rights and labor movements temporarily served to coalesce the American Left.

Across the globe, a new spirit of unity and optimism pervaded the Left, centering upon a rejection of statist and authoritarian conceptions of Socialism. In Europe, the French Left gained the presidency for the first time. Numerous socialist parties adopted workers' control as a programmatic focus and developed relations with Eurocommunist parties whose members concurred that democracy and civil liberties must be central to the socialist project. In the Third World, revolutionary movements in Nicaragua, El Salvador, Zimbabwe and elsewhere searched for a third way between egalitarian (social equality) capitalist development and authoritarian communist modernization.

Keynesian economics begun in early 1983 and would provide the material basis for the following decade of right-wing dominance across the world.

It was on this terrain—the most conservative decade in Western politics since the 1950s—that DSA would be built. At its founding, DSA consisted of almost 5,000 members from DSOC and 1,000 members from NAM. By 1983 DSA reached 8,000 members, which it would not surpass till the early 1990s. The 1980s were not easy on DSA or on the broader Left; there were many defensive battles. As the Liberal coalition decomposed, DSA continued to argue that only democratic industrial, labor and trade and investment policy could restore **global growth** with equity.

They managed to help build an alternative, affirmative, democratic left program and vision. Although DSA's refusal to endorse a Democratic Party candidate in the 1984 primary reflected the electoral Left's split among presidential primary candidates Alan Cranston (nuclear freeze), Walter Mondale (the AFL-CIO and the National Organization for Women) and Jesse Jackson (African-Americans, some left trade unionists and independent Leftists), our work in the 1984 Democratic presidential primary built ties among labor, feminist and anti-militarist **Progressives** that made a modest, but real, contribution to broader left unity four years later behind the stronger, second "Rainbow Coalition" Democratic primary bid in 1988 by Rev. Jesse Jackson, whom DSA endorsed early, in November 1987. **Many of DSA's policy goals—progressive taxation, cuts to wasteful "defense" spending and the need for universal social provision of quality health care, child care, education and housing**—found a more powerful expression in this primary campaign, the first truly multiracial, (implicitly) social democratic one in U.S. history.

Jackson lost the nomination to Walter Mondale and Michael Dukakis. Following their defeat by Reagan in 1988, the mass media pronounced the "L" word— liberalism— dead. It was left to Socialists to speak up against the gutting of public provision through Liberal social welfare programs, despite our criticisms that the Liberal welfare state failed to democratize power relations and treated its beneficiaries more as "clients" than as citizens.

The Youth Section, in part thanks to the speaking schedule of Harrington, its staff and the visibility of then Co-Chair Barbara Ehrenreich and many others, showed the most "counter-cyclical" growth in the organization through much of the **1980**s. The Youth Section played a significant role in both the Anti-Apartheid and anti-intervention in Central America revolutionary movements, linking the struggles for **social justice** abroad with the struggle for social justice at home. It helped introduce scores of student activists to trade union struggles, with the campus-labor institutes enabling many of the Youth Section alums to go on to become labor organizers and union staffers.

DSA's presence among **progressive** trade unionists and the movements for a democratic U.S. foreign policy allowed us to play an initiating role in the large labor-led, Anti-Apartheid/anti-intervention marches held in Washington, D.C., and San Francisco in 1987. By linking these struggles with the fight for democratic trade union rights at home and abroad, DSA contributed to the growth in awareness on the Left of the importance of **international labor solidarity**. Globalism.

In the fall of 1987, in commemoration of the 25th anniversary of the publication of Michael Harrington's *The Other America*, a DSA-inspired coalition, Justice for All, held rallies, teach-ins and press conferences in more than a hundred cities across the nation. Protesting cuts in Medicaid, food stamps, welfare and federal aid to housing, the events also reminded the public of many of the successes of the Great Society (for example, Head Start, Medicaid, public health centers and a radical decrease in poverty among the elderly because of the expansion of Social Security). The DSA office hummed with the sound of organizing.

Comment: It is the government's work to provide an environment for prosperity and not an environment of welfare; an environment providing American jobs so those on welfare can get off. Not an environment of expending welfare.

DSA in the 1990s: Support for Medicare for All; Opposition to Austerity, Welfare "Reform," and Neoliberal Globalization

The argument that democratic public provision increases social justice and efficiency took on a new level of public visibility in the early 1990s when DSA made the struggle for a universal health care system (modeled on the Canadian "single-payer" system) its major national priority. They helped build the "single-payer" or "Medicare for All" movement as an alternative to the Clintons' failed plan to expand coverage by the private insurance system. The high moment of the campaign was a multi-city tour by Canadian health care providers, trade unionists and health care advocates who explained the Canadian system to U.S. audiences.

The collapse of communism in 1989 proved less of an immediate boon to Democratic Socialists than many of us had hoped. Those who had suffered in Eastern Europe and the Soviet Union did not embrace Socialism, but rushed headlong into the embrace of free market capitalism.

Our direct mail campaigns in the early to mid-1990s boosted membership from 7,000 to 10,000. Thousands responded to DSA's argument that the collapse of Communism (a critical gain for democracy) in no way justifies the injustices of capitalism nor ends the struggle against them. And perhaps more would have joined if Harrington had lived beyond the collapse of the Berlin Wall to be able to articulate why the collapse of an authoritarian system that Democratic Socialists had always opposed did not refute the Socialist project.

Comment: "A critical gain for democracy" I believe is being used in relation to Democratic Socialism and not to the true meaning of the word.

Harrington never wanted DSA to be overly reliant on him, but we all understand our debt to him as his generation's most effective voice for Socialism in the United States. DSA continued to grow without him, but a new nationally recognized spokesperson for Democratic Socialism would later appear—Bernie Sanders.

The Clinton administration's commitment to balanced-budget austerity, plus its support for the North American Free Trade Agreement and for the gutting of Aid to Families with Dependent Children (AFDC) foreshadowed the move of center-left governments to what British Prime Minister Tony Blair would term "third way" social democracy. This neoliberal program of economic deregulation (particularly of finance), decrease in taxes on the rich and corporations, decimation of union power and defunding of public goods (particularly means-tested anti-poverty programs), became the dominant policy of Social Democratic parties in the United Kingdom, France and Germany.

While many liberal organizations opposed Clinton's welfare reform, which yielded a radical increase in child poverty over the next 20 years, DSA organized strongly against it. In addition, the Youth Section, which changed its name to **Young Democratic Socialists** in 1997, founded the "Prison

Moratorium Project" as one of the earliest anti-mass incarceration efforts in the age of the New Jim Crow. **In the late 1990s many YDS and DSA chapters participated actively in the "global justice" movement to build transnational solidarity, as well as institutions that would democratize the benefits of a global economy.**

Comment: "New Jim Crow" are not laws, but the use of a negative reference to stir up action against the number of blacks in the prison system. If any person, no matter the so-called color of their skin, including those of pale complexion are found guilty of a crime and prison time is the punishment for that crime, they go to prison. Period. If there are a mass number of the same race in the prison system, then that situation is due to those committing crime and there is the appeal process. Instead of working to get criminals out of prison, why not look if there is a social reason why so many are committing crime and try to correct that such as lack of morals, hunger?

DSA turned much of its attention in the late 1990s to working closely with the Congressional Progressive Caucus and local **global justice groups** to oppose the Multilateral Agreement on Investment (MAI). This proposed international treaty, which would have stripped national governments of the right to legislate **democratic** controls over the behavior of foreign investment capital, foreshadowed President Obama's proposed Trans-Pacific Partnership. By 1999 a new global Left appeared to be forming, with **progressive** unions and Socialists joining with younger **more anarchist-oriented** protesters to take on the International Monetary Fund and the World Trade Organization.

DSA 2000-2015: Opposition to War; Support for the Economic Justice Agenda, Occupy and Racial and Gender Justice

But 9/11/2001 would change all that, as the Bush administration deployed the "war on terror" as a means to quash any forms protests. DSA actively participated in the anti-Iraq and Afghanistan war movement, with Young Democratic Socialists playing a significant role within it. But once ground troops were committed to Afghanistan and Iraq, the movement found it hard to convince the public that you cannot fight decentralized terrorist threats by massive military means.

Comment: "Decentralized" does not fit the situation. There was a terrorist leader and a military style structure of command, for his terrorist non-conventional army. Its headquarters was wherever the leader was. The head of the snake was cut off. "Massive Military Means" Massive would have been the draft being instituted to have a massive buildup of the American military as during World War II. That did not happen. Military forces as it was were used.

DSA can take some solace from the role it played, in the Bush II era, in building **opposition to the bipartisan efforts** of the Bush administration and the Wall Street wing of the Democrats to forge a compromise. The compromise aimed to use long-term cuts in Social Security and Medicare to secure lower taxes on corporations and to achieve "fiscally responsible" budget deficit reduction. DSA brought into this work an alternative vision of an "Economic Justice Agenda"

(EJA), which chapters popularized through local Congressional and State legislative hearings. In retrospect, the EJA prefigured the program of the 2016 Bernie Sanders campaign. The agenda called for creating a truly **progressive** tax system so as to redistribute from the **1% to the 99%, expanding** universal social welfare programs and engaging in large-scale public investment in **alternative energy** and **mass transit**. But the Bush II era saw the left and DSA playing defense to prevent attacks on existing universal social welfare programs. **Bipartisan** people dominated the mainstream media with calls for "fiscal discipline" and public spending cuts.

Comment: I do remember something about cuts to Social Security and Medicare. As for lower taxes on corporations, that could have given those corporations money to expand their businesses and provide more America jobs, which would also mean more tax revenue from those corporations would have been going to the government, which in turn would have made up for the initial loss of tax revenue. The so-called progressive tax system would have taken much from the very people who have investments in corporations that provide American jobs. Such taxing would have caused consolidation of businesses and or closure of businesses, thereby destroying job availability. It was an attack on Capitalism itself. America needs jobs, not more social welfare to create more generational welfare with. Those who can work, should be provided work opportunities, and those who cannot for whatever reason should receive government assistance.

DSA After the Great Recession

The bipartisan consensus around budgetary austerity crashed and burned with the Great Recession of 2008, a direct product of the neoliberal model of growth through financial and real estate speculation. Just as DSA grew through its opposition to the neoliberal Democratic Clinton agenda in the 1990s, by 2010, frustration with the Obama administration's moderate program gave rise to the first significant growth in DSA chapter activity in over a decade. This growth was in part aided by a revival in YDS activity from 2006 onwards and the graduation of some of this cohort into DSA chapter leadership. Many DSA and YDS chapters joined Occupy from Day One. In a few major cities, the predominant "horizontalist" and "anti-statist" youthful leadership of the encampments meant DSAers (young and old) had to operate with considerable skill to appeal to the newly politicized participants (as DSA does take the question of who holds state power seriously). But DSA grew among activists who realized that the occupation itself was a tactic, while building a mass movement for economic democracy involved long-term movement and institution building. At the same time, DSA groups became heavily involved in movements for a living wage and for a path to citizenship for undocumented peoples.

Comment: "Great Recession" Really? Is that like the Great Depression? The Occupy movement was first endorsed by the likes of Nancy Pelosi, but then was unendorsed once protest against the movement began. The movement was seen as an opportunity, by Socialist multi billionaire George Soros to once again attack America. He began to organize, train, supply and finance protestors. Training classes were held for those responding to newspaper advertisements like a job opportunity. Once trained, the person was supplied with camping gear, good, water, etc. When contacted for a protest assignment, the person would gather with others, protest and earn their pay. I believe that it was law enforcement who proved that non-resident protestors were the ones causing property damage; paid protestors. Soros is now 89 and still wants to destroy America. He pours money into any person or movement he feels will be a move toward that goal.

"Living Wage" So the Democratic Socialist of America are the ones who are responsible for trying to raise the minimum wage to that of a person of professional experience; trying to make all workers equal regardless of position and qualifications.

"Path to Citizenship for Undocumented Peoples" In other words, amnesty for illegal aliens, which has already been done seven times, with some amnesties being modified to include those not originally included.

But while DSA and YDS did increase their ranks among this renewed **radical cohort**, the organization still stood at 6,500 members in 2012, with DSA having ten or so moderately strong locals and a similar number of campus groups. The New Left veterans who had built DSA were now aging into their 60s, and often DSA gatherings would have very few people present between the ages of 25 and 60. But they were able to mount a national student debt campaign that helped bring the issue into mainstream electoral politics. At the 2013 and 2015 conventions the organization also reiterated the centrality of racial justice struggles to Socialist organizing, with a good number of chapters supporting Black Lives

Matter and fighting against mass incarceration and for equitable urban public education. In addition, our **Socialist-Feminist Working Group** helped numerous locals raise tens of thousands of dollars for the **National Network of Abortion Funds**.

DSA: Bernie and Beyond

But the levelling off of organizational growth in the 2000s would all change with DSA's decision in late **2014** to make its number one priority the movement to support Bernie Sanders running for president. DSA took the position that for maximum exposure and effectiveness Sanders should not only run, but should run in the **Democratic** primaries—and that advice proved to be spot-on. It started out with a coordinated "We Need Bernie" campaign that had DSA urging Bernie to run, and then shifted to **"People's Revolution 101" DSA**-sponsored teach-ins that introduced Bernie activists to basic Democratic Socialist principles. As a result, DSA grew healthily through the Sanders campaign, going from 6,500 members in fall 2014 to 8,500 by Election Day 2016.

DSA made clear that Bernie's New Deal or Social Democratic Program did not fulfill the Socialist aim of establishing worker and social ownership of the economy. Sanders' program proved sufficiently radical and inspiring. Sanders made clear that he opposed state ownership of corporations, but no mainstream reporter was astute enough to know that the particular socialist tradition that Sanders came out of favored worker, not state ownership, of most firms. DSA also worked in the campaign to reach out to organizations rooted in communities of color and to feminists, as those were the two constituencies most needed to broaden out Bernie's base among **millennials** and white working-class **Democratic** primary voters.

Bernie's refusal to abandon his Democratic Socialist identity and his clear position that only by building mass social movements could you change power relations gave his campaign a clear **class-struggle character**. Polls indicated that the majority of people under 40 had a more favorable view of Socialism than of Capitalism. DSA's visibility grew, amid the press noting the increasingly favorable attitude towards "Socialism", for some a vague desire for a more egalitarian society akin to Sanders' Denmark examples. Curious Sanders supporters Googling "democratic socialism" found DSA's web page coming up first. Many in DSA had hoped that a Hillary Clinton victory would allow DSA to help lead an anti-neoliberal Democrat opposition pushing for Medicare for All, progressive taxation, stricter regulation of the financial sector, etc.

DSA veterans and national staff were shocked to see that on the day after Trump's victory one thousand people joined DSA. In our best past year maybe 1,200 new members joined over 12 months. From November 9, 2016, to July 1, 2017, over 13,000 people, mostly between the ages of 18 and 35, joined DSA. The creative use of social media and Twitter by DSA volunteers drove much of this growth. In addition, through a strong chapter mentoring program, our national leadership, volunteers and staff helped people in 48 states and

D.C. create over 100 new DSA chapters and scores of new YDS chapters. In many red states, brand new DSA chapters have led the opposition to the Trump administration's attempts to gut Medicaid, organizing an open Socialist presence in March 2017 at the House of Representatives and local town hall meetings and sitting in at local Senate offices during the July 4th recess. In blue states such as New York, New Jersey, New Mexico and California, DSAers are at the forefront of the fight for state-level Medicare.

DSA at 24,000 members in **July 2017** is the largest Socialist organization in the United States since the Communist Party before its implosion in 1956 after the Khrushchev revelations about Stalin. Most young people joining the organization want to be active, and our new chapters across the country have already incorporated thousands of members into activist projects. These include working to elect open Socialists to local city and county councils as well as to state legislatures.

As Democratic Socialists, we enter coalition efforts with no preconditions that our allies embrace our Socialist politics. But we engage in these politics as open Socialists—we will be called Socialists whether we choose the name or not. Anti-Socialism remains the most profound anti-democratic ideology in the United States.

Our 2017 convention will determine a realistic set of national priorities and work to strengthen relations among our national staff, a new elected leadership (the National Political Committee) and the most crucial element of the organization—our local chapters and campus groups. DSA works to build its own organizational capacity and to legitimate Socialism as a mainstream part of U.S. politics. We also are committed to working in coalition with forces that **oppose both right-wing rule and the dominant national corporate wing of the Democrats.** We want to continue Sanders' "political revolution" by broadening out that political trend to include a stronger base within the labor movement and, most importantly, among **progressive organizations** rooted in communities of color. If we take up those challenges, DSA may be able to sustain the most important Socialist presence in U.S. politics since the Debsian Socialist era of 1900 to 1920. That's a huge responsibility, but one that the influx of talented organizers into DSA enables us to take on.

And that ends that.

The mainstream organization may have switched from the Communist to the Socialist, but the same tactics and goals and objectives are the same; infiltrate, divide, and conquer, front organizations, etc. Older generation Democrats say the Party is not theirs anymore. It has been highjacked. The Republican Party is in the process of being infiltrated.

By the way, if Socialism/Communism is so good and brings utopia, why are there so many human rights violations in Communist countries?

Socialism Manifested

Due to how Socialism has been presented, for example as "social justice" meaning everyone in society is entitled to the same, I believe some people, especially those of the younger generations, have no idea what real Socialism is.

Using online sources some definitions of the phase "social justice" are as follows:

From businessdictionary.com: The fair and proper administration of laws conforming to the natural law that all persons, irrespective of ethnic origin, gender, **possessions**, race, religion, etc., are to be treated equally and without prejudice. See also civil rights.

From Wikipedia:

> Is a concept of fair and just relations between the individual and society, as measured by the **distribution of wealth**, opportunities for personal activity, and **social privileges**. In Western as well as in older Asian cultures, the concept of social justice has often referred to the process of ensuring that **individuals fulfill their societal roles and receive what was their due from society**. In the current global grassroots movements for social justice, the emphasis has been on the breaking of barriers for social mobility, the creation of safety nets and economic justice.
> The End

Social justice assigns rights and duties in the institutions of society, which enables people to receive the basic benefits and burdens of cooperation. The relevant institutions often include taxation, social insurance, public health, public school, public services, labor law and **regulation of markets, to ensure fair distribution of wealth, and equal opportunity.**

Irrespective of possessions: Well that is interesting, as I had not seen "possessions" involved before. I have observed those with a lot of possessions also known as property should share with others. In fact they should not even have property. Property should be held by the "State" or be distributed as wealth so all may be equal.

Socialism as measured by the distribution of wealth. Take from the rich and give to the poor. Are the RICH Socialist elitist of this country giving to the poor? My guess is they are giving the money they make under the Capitalist system to themselves and to the Socialist cause; Clintons, Pelosi, Soros, Sanders, etc., etc., etc. Oh...wait, Soros is financing the professional protestors. Does that count? I suspect that Soros is also financing Antifa.

Opportunities for personal activity and social privileges? Sounds like code for...I don't know...maybe opportunities to serve the State and obtain from the government a standard of living depending on the value of that service; maybe ranging from having to share a house that was once private property, and have one bedroom for the whole family, with common areas such as the living room and kitchen, to having one's own apartment. That is what was enforced as Socialism under Communism. How is it that children adopted from a Communist country, have to be taught now they do not have to lie, cheat, steal and fight to survive? These are actual circumstances I know about from a Russian who was able to leave their country and make their way to America and from an American couple who adopted a Russian child. Then there was the Russian foreign exchange student who came to America and continued to cheat his way through school to obtain higher grades and therefore better opportunities later, as if he was still in Russia where he had learned to do so to survive. I learned from a German student situation the government decides how a student's education shall progress, by the test scores achieved and potential shown; advance education or trade school. The students do not have the freedom to decide for themselves as American students do.

Process of ensuring that individuals fulfill their role in society and receive the proper due from society. Okay, just what is the role of the individual in society and society's role to the individual? How about this? The individual is, by society, to be in a safe home environment supplied with proper food, shelter, clothing and requirements of life as necessary such as school supplies, from childhood to adult. Thus the government shall provide an environment of prosperity so parents may provide the previously mentioned items. The child shall be given the opportunity for a proper education from childhood to adulthood, of both academic and trade studies. With the government providing the environment for prosperity, then the adult shall have the opportunity to obtain gainful employment in their profession so that they too may have the same opportunities as their parents. In taking advantage of their lifetime opportunities, a person will be a contributor to their society during their working life and may therefore be able to enjoy retirement life as afforded by society and government.

Those who require assistance either in childhood or adult life, for reasons of physical or mental, shall be given the opportunity for such assistance. They shall also be given the opportunity for learning in both academic or trade, as applicable. They shall have whatever opportunity for independence that their abilities may afford, with assistance from family or government so they may live their life in dignity contributing to society as they can and then they too may enjoy retirement or continue life as they had been.

So, those who can work will and those who are not fully able or cannot work at all will be taken care of. Conditions for the environment of prosperity shall be caused and provided by the government. Citizens shall contribute to their community and society as they are able in whatever fashion they have the opportunity to do so. And that is what I think the relationship between government and society and society and individual should be.

Regulation of markets, to ensure fair distribution of wealth, and equal opportunity: In other words, no free markets, but controlled by the State or world government. This applies directly to Agenda 21.

Between this section and previous ones, I believe one can observe what Socialism actually is; an economic system as determined by a totalitarian government to provide utopia on earth.

Again, Lenin said the goal of Socialism is Communism.

Speaking of Lenin, I came across an online reference of this blueprint as follows:

LENIN'S QUOTES REVEAL SOCIALIST/ COMMUNIST BLUEPRINT

In his quotes, Vladimir Ilich Lenin, the builder of the Soviet Communist State, left guidelines on destroying a free country. Pay careful attention as you read because you will notice these guidelines have been carefully followed by the radical leftists in our country. Even the last one on the list has now been accomplished!

"Corrupt the young, get them away from religion. Get them interested in sex. Make them superficial, destroy their ruggedness."

"Get Control of all means of publicity and thereby: Get the people's minds off their government by focusing their attention on athletics, sexy books and plays, and other trivialities."

"Divine the people into hostile groups by constantly harping on controversial matters of no importance."

"Destroy the people's faith in their natural leaders by holding up the latter to ridicule, contempt and obloquy."

"*Always preach true democracy but seize power as fast and as ruthlessly as possible.*"

"*Encourage government extravagance, destroy its credit, produce fear with rising prices, inflation and general discontent.*"

"*Foment unnecessary strikes in vital industries, encourage civil disorders and foster a soft and lenient attitude on the part of government towards such disorders.*"

"*By specious argument cause the breakdown of the old moral virtues: honesty, sobriety, continence, faith in the pledged work, ruggedness.*"

"*Cause the registration of all firearms on some pretext, with the view of confiscating them and leaving the population defenseless.*"

"*The key to a successful Communist takeover of a free society is for the State to get control of the health care system. Lenin called socialized medicine "the keystone to the arch of the Socialist state."*"

Research statue of Lenin in Seattle.

I think here is a good placement for a quote from Franklin D. Roosevelt, "Those who seek to establish systems of government based on the regimentation of all human beings by a handful of individual rulers...call this a new order. It is not new and it is not order." From an article I found some time ago. I do not know what or where it was from.

Our Nation was founded on the principles of a Republic containing elements of democracy in government by representation of the people. We do not live under a dictator or rule by committee of appointed officials. So of what was Roosevelt speaking of? He was speaking of government regulation of all human beings. However, he seemed to have at least had Socialist leanings. Was he a political Socialist speaking against revolutionary Communism? Or was he speaking against the Socialist N.A.Z.I.s and Fascist Hitler, who was acting like a Communist, in trying to physically take over the world? Roosevelt died in the Presidency, during World War II.

After him John F. Kennedy stated, "There's a plot in this country to enslave every man, woman and child. Before I leave this high and noble office, I intend to expose this plot." It was seven days before his assassination. From an article I found some time ago. I do not know what or where it was from.

Another aspect of Socialism is the Fabian Society of Great Britain. An organization called The Fellowship of the New Life was formed by an English visionary elitist during the Victorian Era, in 1883. The following year, in January, the Fabian Society was established off the previous organization as a semi-secret society. I have previously mentioned this Society and that their goal was/is to mold the world into their Socialist image. They still exist today and serve as an affiliate to the British Labour Party, which grew from the Fabians. One of their images depicts the two founding leaders with raised hammers ready to strike blows against a floor model of a plant earth globe, to reshape the whole wide world. Above it is their moto of "Remould It Nearer to the Hearts Desire". Their coat-of-arms is a wolf, wrapped in sheep's skin as in "a wolf in sheep's clothing" depicting the "deceit through secrecy" element of the Society. It was designed by George Bernard Shaw and later it was removed as one of its public symbols. They are also an affiliate of the Foundation for European Progressive Studies. Subsidiaries are the Young Fabians, Fabian Women's Network and Scottish Fabians. I also saw, on a different website, the Welsh Fabians.

Back in the early 1900s, the Fabian elitist were considering eugenics, which is defined as the study or practice of attempting to improve the human gene pool by encouraging the reproduction of people considered to have desirable traits and discouraging or preventing the reproduction of people considered to have undesirable traits. The science of generative or procreative development; the doctrine of progress or evolution, especially in the human race, through improved conditions in the relations of the sexes. The science of improving stock, whether human or animal. Their consideration was that of birth control, of the unwanted, by sterilization. There was such a backlash against the Society, they dropped the consideration. Their current membership is seven thousand plus, at last count, and always headquartered in London, England. All of this is online. (modernhistoryproject.org Fabian Society A wolf in sheep's clothing) (theguardian.com/eugenics)

I have a book titled *The Creature from Jekyll Island, A Second Look at the Federal Reserve*, by G. Edward Griffin, 5th edition 2010, copyright 1994, American Media. The Fabians are in it as having played a part in world financing. The book concerns how the Federal Reserve Bank (FRB) was conceived, by whom, when, where, why and how. And its effects on this Country. There is a whole chapter concerning The London Connection. The secret meeting was held in 1910, on a recently purchased privately owned island, by J.P. Morgan, named Jekyll Island, which was among the Sea Islands off the Atlantic coastline from South Carolina to Florida. Jekyll Island was off the coast at the location of a small fishing village of Brunswick, Georgia. Its attendees were high power men in both government and finance, including those representing European interests. The cover story was the party was there for duck hunting. A great many banks had been established, over twenty thousand, within the United States. In 1913, when the Federal Reserve Act was passed, by Congress, 71% of banks unchartered by the Federal Government was holding 57% of nationwide deposits. This gave competition to large banks holding Federal Government charters, with the largest being the National City Bank of New York.

Competition was also developing from companies using profits to expand their businesses, instead of using bank loans. There was also the danger of bank closure, if they cashed checks worth more than they had taken in deposits as cash reserve in the vault. Due to the gold standard being used, if a customer demanded all of the money in their bank account be paid to them as "payments-on-demand", the bank had to do so. If most customers did this, it was called a "bank run". There was also "currency drain", when one bank demanded debt payment from another bank, as in one bank cashing a check written on another bank's account, by one of its account owners. Banks make money by loaning money and charging interest. The more money loaned the more interest collected. Some banks would loan more than they actually had in their vault, which meant if their account owners demanded money in their accounts, there might not be enough to cover the amount demanded. The bank would go bankrupt and close. Another factor was that banks, at that time, could issue their own bank notes also known as paper money, as long as they had the gold to back the value of the notes up. All of this competition and unstable banking had to be fixed. The FRB was supposed to do just that, but over decades under various financial conditions, it has failed to meet its objectives and therefore its goal.

One of the models used in the construction of the FRB was the *Reichsbank* of Germany, which is a government-central bank. A few years later, that bank created a massive hyperinflation in Germany and wiped out the middle class and the entire economy.

The FRB brought nationalized home loaning, through regulation of the industry. That is called Socialism.Read the book. It is only approximately six hundred pages.

Now...back to the Socialist Fabians and their part in it all. Under the chapter Nearer to the Heart's Desire speaking of the International Monetary Fund and the World Bank, which were created at a global financiers and politicians meeting, at Bretton Woods, New Hampshire, in 1944, The dominant thinkers were the Fabian Society and John Maynard Keynes from England and the U.S. Assistant Secretary of the Treasury, Harry Dexter White. White was later discovered to be a Communist. He and the Fabians were there for their common goal of world Socialism. By the way, the next chapter is Building the New World Order.

John F. Kennedy applied to the Fabian London School of Economics in 1935, in his late teens, for one year to study political economy. However, he fell ill during that year and did not finish. Apparently it was not unusual for the young adults of wealthy families to attend there, to fill out their academic resume.

The Council on Foreign Relations (CFR) is the think tank of the Fabian's plan to implement their Socialism in America. It was a spinoff from the failure of the world's leaders, at the end of World War I, to embrace the **League of Nations as a true world government**. Fabian members met and formed two closely related opinion-making bodies. The English was the Royal Institute of International Affairs and the American was first known as the Institute of International Affairs, but was reorganized in 1921 as the CFR.

The CFR is a small group, but many of America's influential leaders, including those who became President, have been through the group as in membership. By the way, I am quoting from the book, which was well researched. However, my own thought is did every person who went through the organization realize what it was and how much did it mean to each person? Sometimes a person will become involved in something simply as an opportunity to gain experience and expand their resume, in order to obtain a higher position later on; career building.

The author comments that phrases such as "monetary coordination mechanisms, modern world economic order, convergence of political values and new world order may not mean much to the average reader, as they sound pleasant and harmless, but they are code phases with specific meaning to those who know. Sounds like Agenda 21 language.

There is an organization called Club of Rome, which was formed in 1968, of intellectuals of various academic and professional fields, who discuss end-of-world scenarios based on predictions of over population and famine. In its

1991 book, they wrote "In searching for a new enemy to unite us (the human race), we came up with the idea that pollution, the threat of global warming, water shortages, famine and the like would fit the bill…. All these dangers are caused by human intervention…. The real enemy, then, is humanity itself."

A member of the Club, who is a Fabian, said, "I do not pretend that birth control is the only way in which population can be kept from increasing… War, as I remarked a moment ago, has hitherto been disappointing in this respect, but perhaps bacteriological war may prove more effective. If a Black Death could be spread throughout the world once in every generation, survivors could procreate freely without making the world too full…. He went on to say, that under a world government, food could be distributed based on population control. If a nation's population continued to grow above the set limit, then that nation would receive less food as a punishment and incentive to maintain the set limit population.

Really!? These people are supposed to be intellectuals? The real enemy is humanity. Therefore target humanity, by pragmatic reasoning. Another online source stated the Club wants to divide the world into ten regions. Regions…sounds like Agenda 21.

As a finishing touch on Fabianism and the Federal Reserve Bank, I came across a couple of names I recognized; William Jennings Bryan and Alan Greenspan. Bryan was familiar as he was one of the most powerful Congressional Democrats. At first he opposed the Federal Reserve Act because it would privately issue money rather than through the government. Compromises were made to give the appearance of public control and Government Issue, but in fact did neither. Due to the appearance of the compromises he voted for the Act. He was appointed as Secretary of State, but became disillusioned by the duplicity of his own Government and resigned. Greenspan was a supporter of the gold standard, on which U.S. money was based on, between 1879 and 1933, and was against the Government being subservience to a banking cartel such as the FRB. That was in 1966. After he become the Director of J.P. Morgan & Company, which was a financial institution going back to the Industrial Revolution, and also was appointed Chairman of the FRB in 1987, he became quiet on his opposition. By the way, the Federal Reserve Bank is not Federal and not a bank and not a financial reserve. The FRB is chartered by Congress. And again... the U.S. Government now owes more money to it due to loans from it, than the Government owes to China. And we are no longer on the gold standard.

Norman Mattoon Thomas, 1884 – 1968, was a leading American Socialist, pacifist and six-time Presidential candidate for the Socialist Party of America. In a 1944 speech, he stated that the American people would never knowingly adopt Socialism, but, under the name of Liberalism, they would adopt every fragment of the Socialist program until one day America would be a Socialist nation, without even knowing how it happened. He also stated that he no longer needed to run as a Presidential candidate for the Socialist Party as the Democrat Party had adopted their platform.

From article I found some time ago. I do not know what or where it was from.

Remember my pointing out when I wrote of something in the past that people seem to think it is a new thing or how something was called by one name in the past, but is now called by another name? I even have a book titled *Old Errors and New Labels*. It addresses the issue of people, in the present, thinking that because something is modern and in the present, with them, that the something is new and therefore the best. In fact, the something may just be under a different label than it was before and actually existed before the present. And it may have been in error when it existed before. A new name does not make something better.

I have heard talk of "modified Socialism", to update the old Socialism and make it better according to today's society of modern thinking and technology. Is the modified version in existence in Agenda 21? Let's examine that.

Previously I give the history of the development of the U.N. document and something of what it is about. I obtained that knowledge from the document itself, from the U.N. website, before one had to register to receive their "release to public" book. I printed it directly from the website. There is also a book titled *Behind the Green Mask: U.N. Agenda 21*, by Rosa Koire, copyright 2011, published by her organization The Post Sustainability Institute Press, Santa Rosa CA.

The author is a Democrat, who began an organization known as Democrats Against UN Agenda 21. There is a website. At the time she wrote the book, she had been a commercial real estate appraiser specializing in eminent domain valuation, for thirty years, analyzing land use and property value. It was this expertise which caused her to begin investigation and discovery of the planning revolution that is sweeping the nation. She found corporate, political and financial interests behind it and UN. Agenda 21 as it relates to real estate property. She is also a public speaker on the subject. At times I will use "Me" or "Rosa" in order to interject my own comments and then continue with the paraphrasing of Rosa's book.

"Eminent Domain" A process by a level of government used to obtain required privately owned land, to use for the "common good" of the public. This involves some kind of a development project. The phrase itself has gained a negative connotation due to its misuse by government not acting for the "common good", but for the good of its own self. It was put in place for a positive reason, but is not always used for that reason. In California, cities were declaring an area as blight, obtaining the land not at fair market value, but for the least amount of money possible or for nothing, if possible, in order to turn the area into a "sustainable development" land use project per Agenda 21. This is from news articles I read some time ago. I do not know what or where they were from.

Okay...let's see what Rosa has to say. Since I will be using other related material as well and interjecting my own comments, I have decided to designate which is which at the beginning of each using the titles of Rosa, Other, Me. For my short comments, within a paragraph, I shall enclose them with parentheses.

Rosa: In 2005, (6 years before the book's copyright) she was elected to a citizens' oversight committee, to review a proposed 1,300 acre redevelopment project in which 10,000 people lived and worked. Her research into the documents justifying the plans led her and her business partner to challenge the fraudulent basis for the project. The city removed the neighborhood, which involved Rosa's business property, in an attempt to halt her taking any action. Rosa and her partner formed a business and property owners association and a non-profit organization to raise donation money and *pro bono* legal work. They sued the city to stop the project. They lost in both the Supreme Court, which gave permission to continue the case. They took the case to a court of appeals, where they lost again. During that three year fight, the project was delayed and the Country's economy collapsed. The city had failed to implement its plan, but had until 2018 to use eminent domain over the area. It was during the course of the legal challenge that she became aware of the source of the planning revolution that she had observed for the past ten years. It was the United Nations Agenda for the 21st Century also known as Agenda 21 and its Sustainable Development land use programs through the diversion of property taxes to redevelopment agencies.

She opens the Preface saying the arm of UN Agenda 21 (called the Plan henceforth, in my paraphrasing) is long and reaches into every area of the world. (Its goal is one world government totalitarian control; Communism.) The philosophy of Communitarianism pervades the Plan in balancing the rights of the individual with the so-called rights of the community; the "State". The rights of the community are not defined in a constitution and therefore can change without warning or notice. The slogan of the Plan is to protect the rights of future generations and all species against the potential crimes of the present. ("Species" refers to animals, fish, birds and humans.) It is both a smokescreen and a declaration of entitlement. (Guess what caused the "entitlement movement") By merely living and exhaling we pose a direct danger to the earth that is self-destructive and damaging to those lands that we steward. Under the banner of saving the planet, we are drowning Liberty and under the mask of green our civil liberties are being restricted, constricted and suffocated everywhere. The Plan is now being imposed locally. (This is not only happening in America, but also throughout the world as a global movement.)

The United States Constitution guarantees its citizens that we are born with the rights of life, liberty and the opportunity to pursue happiness, with happiness equaling the right to own real estate property for both business and residential use. Part of the American dream is owning one's own house. How are individual rights balanced with community rights? Example: Two glasses, with one containing water and the other containing milk. Water represents individuals within a Constitutional Republic, which we are, and milk represents the Communitarian State. Pour both glasses into a pitcher. The result is watery milk. "The Third Way" "Rights of the Community" is now known as "Global Community" and we are told it is the enlightened form of political discourse. If one wants individual rights and freedoms, that person is labeled as "selfish".

History of Socialism, Wilipedia: Under "The emergence of a 'New Left' in the developed world":

> In many developed nations the adoption of The Third Way policies by social democratic parties has led to the rise of many new socialist parties running on solid left-wing agendas.

Many of the reasons used to justify this such as for the good of the planet and everyone's security and for health and to protect children and stop bullying (Civility) and violence and to protect the "rights" of those in the future are worthwhile ideas. However, they result in restrictive laws and

Simulated Reserve and Corridor System to Protect Biodiversity

As Required by the UN Covention on Biological Diversity, Wildlands Project, UN and US Man and Biosphere Programs and World Heritage Program as a Vital Step in Attaining Sustainable Development

This map was used in the United States Senate to stop the ratification of the United Nations Convention on Biological Diversity

- Core Reserves & Corridors Little to no human use
- Buffer Zones—Highly Regulated Use
- Border 21/La Paz Sidebar Agreement of NAFTA-200 Mile Wide International Zone of Cooperation
- Normal Use
- Indian Reservations
- Military Reservations

ordinances that criminalize people. The Plan involves education, energy market, transportation, government, health care, food production, stock market, large corporations, financing, housing, retail business, etc., etc., etc. It is to inventory and control all natural resources, means of production and human beings of the world, by means of global domination. (Socialism/Communism) Related buzz words and phrases have impregnated our language within a single generation. People have been using them, in some cases, without even knowing where they come from. Such terms as "sustainability", "sustainable development", "smart growth" and "high density urban mixed use development" all come from the Agenda 21 document as well as a lot of other wordy phrases.

Another program called the Wildlands Project sets aside land for non-human habitat; (wild animals). In anticipation of our objections to such plans, our civil rights will be dissolved.

Maps are from online The Wildlands Project and UN Convention on Biological Diversity Plan to Restore Biodiversity in the United States, with text from website Sovereignty International, Inc., 1981:

The map, on the previous page, was prepared by Michael Coffman, for Senator Kay Bailey Hutchison's objections to the Convention on Biodiversity Treaty (CBT), on the Senate floor, during the 103rd Congress.

Rosa: The Treaty was first proposed by the International Union for the Conservation of Nature, in 1981. The land use policies required by the Treaty were also expressed in dozens of other United Nations documents and at other United Nations conferences and incorporated into the agendas of None Government Organization (NGO), for implementation through programs and legislation at the local, state and federal level long before the Treaty was ever presented to the world. Many U.S. land use policies have been implemented through such means.

Me: NGOs have appointed personnel; not elected by the citizens and not associated with any level of government. However, they may be made up of government personnel such as City Council Members within a county or counties forming a "Region". "Region" is another buzz word.

Rosa: In 1994, the Senate Foreign Relations Committee approved the ratification of the CBT, with a 16 to 3 vote. Later that year the Senate Majority Leader, George Mitchell, for the second and final time, withdrew the CBT from the Senate calendar, after it was not even voted on due to Senator Hutchison's visual aid.

Me: To begin with, all the Senators had to see was the text of the Treaty, without any graphics. THIS ACTUALLY HAPPENED!!!

Rosa: As one may observe, only the light green areas are for "human habitat". The red areas are for wildlife, some of which are dangerous. Notice that most of the map is in red especially in the Western United States. That is because the Federal Government already has control of most of the land in the Western U.S., by means of ownership as the ratio of Federal land to State land is shown in the following percentages:

Nevada 87.6, Utah 67.9, Alaska 67.0, Idaho 65.2, Oregon 55.5, California 49.9, Wyoming 49.7, Arizona 44.3, New Mexico 36.2, Colorado 35.9, Washington State, 32.8, Montana 31.9. Notice that Nevada is almost all federally owned, with Utah and Alaska and Idaho and Oregon being over half and California and Wyoming being close to half. The rest are over 25%. Some of these Federal lands are various National Parks.

After the red, the color yellow is the most used as buffer zones between and around human habitat areas, which are really small. That orange strip at the bottom left is the NAFTA zone between the U.S. and Mexico.

Another map shows the major Corridor zones. These corridors coincide with the areas that have the most red, of the previous map, which mean that they are not for humans, but animals. Starting with the top corridor named Arctic Corridor it runs between Alaska, in the Northwest, and the Labrador Sea, of Canada, in the Northeast. Running off the Arctic Corridor are the Pacific

Corridor down through Washington State, Oregon, California and into Baja, Mexico; the Spine of the Continent down to the Panama Canal Zone; the northern loop running off of and down into the Minnesota/Wisconsin area and swinging back up to the Arctic Corridor; the Atlantic Corridor running between New Brunswick, of Canada, which is above our State of Maine, and the tip of Florida and connected with the Arctic Corridor by means of another, small corridor.

This means the Treaty was only for the U.S. part of the Plan. The Plan takes in the whole world, including the Americas of North America, Central America and South America, which is why this map includes Canada and the Central America.

Another point is that eventually there will be no States and therefore no United States. There will be only Regions; North America Region, with smaller regions within it. Or maybe it will be titled North American Union. There is already a European Union. Maybe "Union" will be the larger region.

Let's examine those North America Corridors starting with the Arctic Corridor. It cuts through mainland Canada, which has thirteen Provinces and Territories. Since these corridors are all about human control, let's conduct the examination from that viewpoint. The top part of the Spine of the Continent Corridor takes up most of the far west part of Canada leaving a land strip between it and the Artic Corridor above the United States. That strip joins with the U.S. land mass east of the Rocky Mountains, which is the natural barrier of the Spine of the Continent Corridor. Do not forget that roads and highways in the Corridor areas will not be maintained and will be taken over through time by wild plant life.

On the north side of the Arctic Corridor is a land mass going north into islands that enter the Arctic Circle; islands which are Canadian Territories. Both the Arctic Circle and Hudson Bay to the east are natural barriers. The east part of the Arctic Corridor cuts through Canada leaving small land masses here and there. The Labrador Sea and the North Atlantic Ocean are natural barriers on the east, with Hudson Bay closing in to the west of the land mass north of the Arctic Corridor. Canada will become mainly a land of wilderness filled with wild animals and bordered by water masses.

Down in the U.S., the Pacific Corridor uses the Sierra Nevedas' as its natural barrier leaving only a small strip along the Pacific coastline. Between that Corridor and the Spine of the Continent are mountains and dessert. Most of the Continental land mass is within the U.S. from the western Great Plains to the Midwest and to the Appalachian Mountains, which is the natural barrier within the Atlantic Corridor. In the Midwest, the Mississippi River is the natural barrier, except at its top. The Spine of the Continent cuts through Mexico taking most of its land mass.

In respect to illegal migration, Mexicans have come over or under the Southern U.S. border and people from Central America have gone into Mexico and maybe some of them have followed the Mexicans over or under our Southern border. Over time both the U.S. government and the Mexican government have encouraged such migration. In the State of Tennessee, Spanish is like the second language and there are now illegal aliens in States where there were none before such as Missouri. Or so I am told. The Socialists have fought the building of a wall on our Southern border. Is all of this part of moving those south of us into our Country for the end Plan?

With so much population being herded into many small areas, seems like there would have to be population control such as abortion, euthanasia. Just saying. **SUSTAINABLE *development*.**

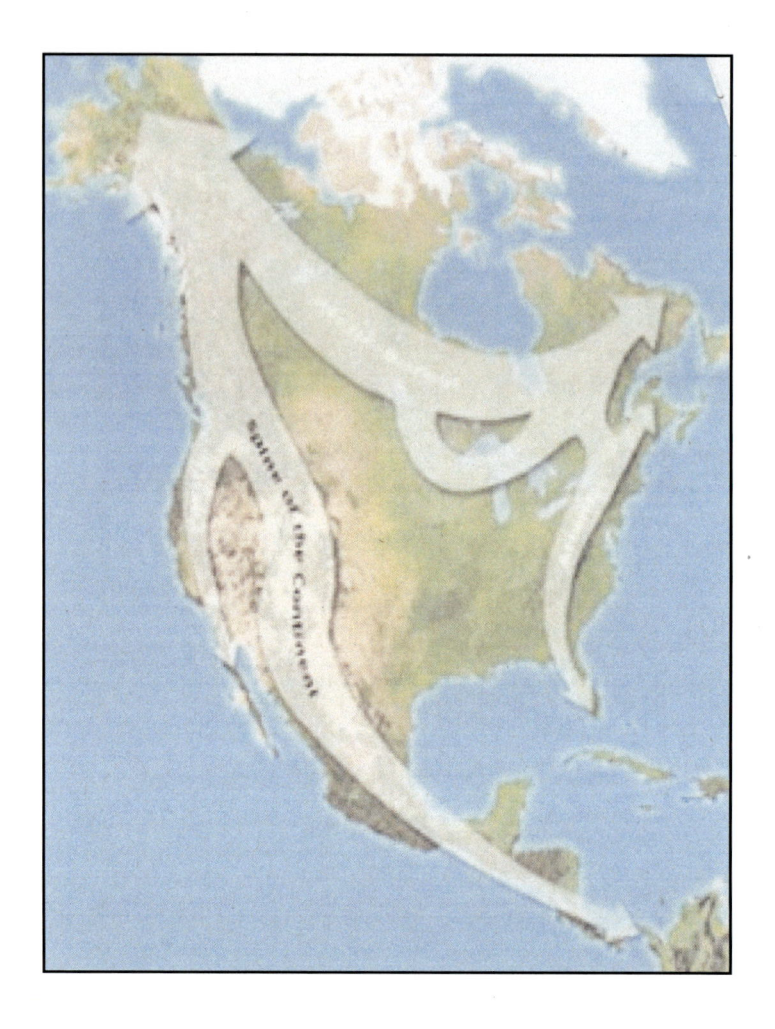

Why are there small "human habitat" areas surrounded by buffer zones, surrounded by animals zones, with wide and long corridors of no-man's land? Control of the human species! Small communities are easier to control. Areas of wild animals mean less enforcement personnel required to control a mass population. How are all of today's populace going to fit into those small areas? There will be no privately owned houses because there will be no houses, at least not for the common folk. Apartment buildings, condos, projects, residential above retail stores. Packed in!

There is another issue involved. NO MAJOR HIGHWAYS North, South, East or West. With the existence of small, human habitat areas surrounded by buffer zones surrounded by animal zones, there will be no need for such highways. Any roads from one human habitat area to another will have to be through the buffer zone. If there are roads going through wildlife zones, there would have to be high walls along each side of such roads. Only government personnel would be allowed to use the roads. If a common person wanted to visit family or friends in another human habitat area, they would have to apply for authorization and be issued a temporary passport, for a certain amount of days. Or maybe that would not even happen!

Individual rights are to give way to the needs of the communities as determined by a globalist governing body. People are to be herded into human settlements or "islands of human habitation" close to employment centers and transportation.

Communication: Would the common people be able to communicate with each other, if they live in different human habitat areas? Would email be allowed?

Another aspect is that each human habitat area would have to begin with and continue with common people having the education and skills to provide any and all required services for a smooth existence in the community. That means planning and figuring for the control of who receives what education and how many when. Perhaps that future society will expand on the structure of today's trade industry, from apprenticeship to master craftsman, into all service areas required, from birth to death. After all, it is all about control by regulation.

Wildlife has already been introduced by Federal Agencies, under the Obama Administration. Rosa tells of billionaire media owner Ted Turner owning thousands of acres of Montana land and is apparently releasing wolves and bears onto his land to repopulate it. I once met a Montana resident, who told a wild story. J.D. King was a young film maker exposing the fraud and corruption behind the introduction of wolves to Yellowstone that affected his father's livestock on his ranch in Montana. The film was produced in 2011 under the title of *Crying Wolf*. A bigger, better, faster hybrid wolf was released onto Montana land, by a Federal agency, under the Obama Administration. Natural wolfs are beautiful and already big; a sight to behold. But these hybrid wolfs are even much bigger and faster. They are, by nature, pack animals. They live and hunt in packs. They bred and increased the size of their packs. They attacked both wild game and hunters. They destroyed not only hunting in the area, but also the whole hunting supporting industry. AND they began to travel out of the State of Montana and into neighboring states. These packs cannot be hunted on the ground. They have to be hunted by aircraft. The news media does not give such stories because the populace is not supposed to know about such events. I found out only because that Montana man was traveling across America letting people know what was happening. Letting us know of an Agenda 21 project. THIS ACTUALLY HAPPENED!!!

Individual rights are to give away to the needs of the communities as determined by a globalist governing body. People are to be herded into human settlements or "islands of human habitation" close to employment centers and transportation.

If one knows only of this one and that event, there may not be much thought of it. However, put this and that event together with other events here and there all over the country and one has a planned end goal, with the events being the objectives to that goal.

Here is a way to picture it. Have you ever seen an "ant farm"? For those of you who have no idea what I am talking about here is the description. In nature, ants will establish their colony wherever there is suitable soil. They dig tunnels as long and as deep and as many as they want. They may leave the tunnels and go out and about looking for food, to take back to the colony. Or some may leave and begin a new colony. They are free to move around and go and do as they please. Back when I was growing up one of the teaching and entertainment tools was what was called an ant farm. It consisted of a plastic base, to stand on, and a plastic frame, on the stand, holding two pieces of clear plastic approximately twelve inches by twelve inches, with just enough space in between the clear plastic for an ant to dig though, but be seen. One could watch the ants as they dug the tunnels for their new colony. However, they could dig only so far and so deep and only so many. They could not go out and about. They were confined to the limitations of the plastic environment. Not an environment of nature, but an environment constructed for them to live and work in. There was no food source and after a time, of living and working, they died and the ant farm was tossed away. They served their purpose, while famine destroyed them.

Rosa: Under the United Nations Agenda 21 Sustainable Development Plan, its policies are woven into all of the General Plans of cities and counties in the United States and to be woven into States and the Nation, with the bases of Communitarianism.

Most people know the United Nations to be a peace-making, community serving organization, through relief services of food and medicine. However, it has underlying motives. National governments are to take control of all land use, including private property. (Remember that Socialist believe that there should be no private property, but only public communal property.) This is on the supposed reasoning that private owners cannot take care of their own land and that the government can do a better job. Individual rights will give way to the need of the community as determined by a globalist governing body; United Nations.

The Agenda 21 Plan cites the affluence of America as being a major problem, which needs to be corrected by lowering the standard of living in America so that people in poorer counties will have more, through the redistribution of wealth. Only then will there be "Social Justice", which is another cornerstone of Agenda 21.

Rosa: President Clinton's President's Council on Sustainable Development (PCSD) was made up of Cabinet level government officials, captains of industry including Ken Lay of Enron and non-profit groups such as the Sierra Club. It gave a multi-million dollar grant to the American Planning Association to design a legislative guidebook to be used as a blueprint for every city, county and state. Its purpose was to implement the Agenda 21 Sustainable Development Plan. The guidebook is titled *Growing Smart Legislative Guidebook: Model Statutes for Planning and the Management of Change*. It was not a guidebook, but a blueprint of how to construct. By 2002, every planning department, at every government level everywhere, had a copy and was implementing its practices. Every university, college, junior college, private school and teaching institution in our Nation was using *Growing Smart* in its curriculum. *Growing Smart* is Smart Growth.

Me: I remember seeing the promotion of the Green Movement at an elementary school. Led by teachers, the children had taken green plastic cups and placed them into the chain-link fence of the school. When the placement was completed, the cups spelled out the letters of words supporting the Green Movement.

Rosa continued: Evidence of this is that many developments in metropolitan areas all look the same, including in smaller cities. Commercial, industrial and multi-residential land was rezoned to "mixed use" and built the same way of ground floor retail, with two or three stories of residential above. Condo construction is another Smart Growth project. For such development, Redevelopment Agency funds were used. In most places, most money in a city's General Fund is not as much as it once was and what there is goes to support Fire and Police Departments. The other funds are diverted into the Redevelopment Agency, as it is the only agency in government that can fund a bond without a vote by the people. Private property taxes pay for those bonds. A city or county infrastructure may not be funded, left to go into bad condition due to such diversion of funds. With the diversion causing less and less services to the public, the standard of living for the public is lowered.

Me: The description of "mixed use" is what I heard a person, who had traveled in the Iron Curtain countries also known as Soviet Satellite countries, say he observed during his travels in those countries. Nothing new.

I remember Redevelopment Funds being used for the funding of the sale of municipal bonds to finance city low-cost housing development. It did not go on a public ballot. I also remember that due to California legislation the City had to use up current Redevelopment Funds by a deadline. There was some kind of restriction and condition going into place.

After 9-11, there was an increase of people applying for acceptance to both Fire and Police academies. Cities increased their emergency personnel by hiring those graduates, offering them very good packages of salary and benefits. I am not saying emergency services do not deserve such hiring packages. I am saying in California, some cities over extended and ended up going bankrupt due to such packages.

Taxation without Representation. Sound familiar? That was part of why the American Colonies rebelled against the English King and we had our American Revolution. And that is why it is actually illegal!

Rosa continued: With redevelopment, cities have the right to take property, by eminent domain, even without the permission of the property owner and give or sell to a private developer. A property area is declared as "blight" and the property taxes, of that property, are diverted away from the General Fund and into the Redevelopment Agency. (Condos or low-income housing may also be built.)

"Human Habitation" is restricted to lands within the Urban Growth Boundaries of the city, where only certain building designs are permitted. Rural property is more and more restricted as to what uses it can be for. Regulations increase as to land and water use, while roads and services decrease. This forces people off the land and into becoming more dependent on life in the city.

Me: I remember some time ago California legislators were thinking of passing a law for taxing both range and dairy cattle owners, for each head of cattle based on the rationale that cows pass gas and therefore pollute the air. Rosa uses the Green Mask analogy because the world's environmental condition is used as a basis for the Plan. It is the Green Movement. Remember Al Gore's *An Inconvenient Truth* concerning global warming supposedly caused by humans?

Environmentalists play a large part in the implementation of the Plan, since the Plan uses the environment as an excuse to put control measures in place. California Central Valley has been the world's breadbasket. However, the Plan is to equalize markets. One way of achieving that is to begin the destruction of such a breadbasket, in the affluent country of America. A small, two inch fish was introduced to a section of the northern Central Valley and the environmentalists began legislative action to have crop field irrigation pumps shut off saying the fish could not survive otherwise. The federal government, via an agency, shut off the pumps. The crops began to die. The County Sheriff, who is obligated only to the residents of their county except for county budget reasons, turned the water pumps back on by cutting the locks the feds had put on the pumps. The feds returned and put more locks on. The Sheriff cut them again. The feds put more on. In the meantime, the crops have died and there is no harvest; no money for the generational farmers affected by the environmental action. Finally the Sheriff stopped cutting the locks, but legislative action was begun on behalf of the farmers, many of whom had left the area. The farmland was lost. The farmers could not even sell their property as it was good for nothing. If I remember correctly, the federal government did decide to pay the farmers some money for their land. Seems like it was for fair market value at the time, it was not worth anything.

Even before Agenda 21 came about, environmentalists were in play. Remember the Sierra Club, in California, and their filing a law suit to stop the

I Could Have Been One

lumber industry due to owls prominent in the lumber area, which involved a very wide and long area of northern California? The owls' homes were being destroyed. The Sierra Club won the law suit and the California lumber industry disappeared. Therefore the cost of lumber in that State increased due to transportation cost, including the cost of Christmas trees. Then not long ago, California added on a fee, for lumber coming into the State. That was adding insult to injury.

Remember the Environmental Protection Agency (EPA) wanting to take control of all water in America, including future rain puddles? The Federal (EPA) down to local EPAs have developed regulations concerning the misuse of land, water and air and levy fines for violations of such regulations. The local EPA is supposed to be under the oversight of County Commissioners, but at least in some cases the EPA gets to do whatever it wants. And where does all of that fine money go? One's rights have been balanced.

The California State Water Board developed a plan to divine the State into water regions titled Phase One, Phase Two, etc. One Phase after another was to be taken control of until all water in the State was controlled. The plan was called Substitute Environmental Document (SED). Article Ten, Section 2, of the California Constitution declares water within the borders of the State belong to the people. What the Water Board was wanting to do was illegal. However, in California, their Constitution is not referred to as it is not cared about. What the Californios signed has been discarded, to ease the way for Communist/Socialist use. The makeup of the Board, at that time, was all Liberal, with maybe a Socialist, and one Conservative. The Conservative ended up resigning. For Phase One, the reason for control was for the protection of fish. Dam control of the water flow was to be increased, to get the fish safely through the course of the rivers. However, this would have the effect of rushing the water through both fishing and agricultural areas and destroying the livelihood of families, who depended on the fishing and its supporting industries and the farming and its supporting industries. Agenda 21. Irrigation districts along the way would have to use existing or potential stored water from the reservoir to satisfy the Board's demands. The SED also had a new annual requirement for those irrigation districts to store a large amount of water in the reservoir for fish, which would limit the storage flexibility and delivery capabilities. The stated losses would have been $1.6 billion in economic output, $167 million in farming revenue, $330 million in labor income, and 6,576 jobs.

Rosa continued: Advocacy has become the nice-sounding word for lobbying and influencing. National organizations such as Complete Streets, Thunderhead Alliance and others conduct training programs, for their members, on how to pressure for redevelopment, and also for candidate training for public office, in order to infiltrate and have influence. It can start with wanting a bike path and go on to other development.

A term of "Transit Villages" is used for towns to be demolished and rebuilt in the image of Sustainable Development. (Whole towns!)

By bringing down the standard of living of middle class Americans or of any industrial nation, it is not bringing up those of Third World countries. It is bringing others down to their level. (Seems to be the reverse of what it should be.)

The "Delphi Technique" is used to manufacture consensus. The Council on Sustainable Development incorporated the Delphi Technique into its recommendations so that "more rapid change" could be imposed through clever manipulation. It was developed by the RAND Corporation as a mind control technique, to be used during the Cold War. The idea is to channel a group of people to accept a point of view that is imposed on them, while convincing them it was their idea. It can be used on a single person or a massive group. People are trained in how to operate the technique for the desired results. They present a range of choices to a group. However, the choices have been tailored to the desire outcome. Most often conducted at public meetings called "visioning meetings" it may be hosted by a government body or utility group or an organization. Funding may come from Sustainable Development grants. It is the way of obtaining public input, when it is required by regulation, policy or legislation, but at the same time obtain what is wanted to further that part of the Agenda 21 arm down into the local community.

The only input allowed will be that which supports what is desired. Any other comments or questions will be counteracted by trained operatives called "shills" sitting close to the person with the comment or question. An attendee is to sign in the meeting at the door and receive a name tag. They may be seated at a table or in an auditorium. Once the meeting is started a brief overview will be given. No questions will be allowed. The facilitator may ask questions to try and establish the demographics of the attendees such as age range, race, gender, etc. Speakers will be professional, creditable people. A tight schedule is adhered to and allows little time for questions. If any questions are allowed, they are briefly answered or tabled until later. Various types of information media will be used, all very attractive and colorful depicting what will induce the attendee to be favorable to the presentation. The shills, who will be at each table or spread throughout the room even standing on the side, will be observing attendees' behavior. Any people noticed showing leadership ability will be approached later to become involved, if they were supportive. Any objections will be met with shaming or points of guilt or embarrassing remarks. People who are followers might join in. There may also be a splitting of the attendees into two groups; those who offer no objection and those who have. The "haves" will be left in place, while the others are taken into another room, to finalize the meeting with the desired outcome. The group that is left in the original room will soon be dismissed, with a, "Thank you for your input."

The Delphi Technique serves the Green Mask by deceit to the public so as to not cause any opposition to the reality of what is occurring. There are no news-making events allowed. Those who participate in such deceit should have charges of subversion brought against them.

The International Council on Local Environmental Initiatives (ICLEI), under the United Nations as an implementation element of the Plan, was created in 1990 as a non-governmental organization to implement Agenda 21 locally around the world. ICLEI (pronounced ick-ly) brings the international to your town. It serves as a lobbying and policy consultant designed to influence and change local governmental policies related to all aspects of human life. Founded two years before the Rio Earth Summit, where the formal precepts of Agenda 21 were introduced to the world, it sells trainings to governments, sets up climate adaptation programs, measures and monitors community greenhouse gas emissions and more, for a fee. ICLEI changed its name so it would not be recognized as an international organization. It is now Local Governments for Sustainability (LGS). (This occurred after conservatives began to figure out who they were, what they were supporting and how they were doing it. Name change. Nothing new.)

Here is a surprise. Or is it? ICLEI/LGS has been receiving funding from our own government, by way of federal agencies; Commerce, Environmental Protection, International Development and Agriculture. Up in the millions.

LGS is involved in local general planning all over the world, including the United States. The Agenda 21 Plan requires certain elements of all localities of the world to have in their own General Plan; transportation, biological resources, community development, energy and socioeconomic. Socioeconomic generally includes Community Participation using Delphi meetings, Public Safety or Community-Oriented Policing, Environmental Justice of curbing or eliminating industry, or child endangerment/family law, Education of indoctrination, Economy of picking winners and losers and Parks and Recreation for bike lanes. (These are not unusual departments within a city/town administrative structure. It is that components of Agenda 21 is incorporated into them that is important or that such components NOT be incorporated into them is important.)

A city/town's general plan may even have the U.N. Agenda 21 logo on it composed of three circles interlocking at the middle. The circles are Ecology, Economy and Social Equity. The intersection is Sustainable Development. The Sustainable Development logo is similar having three circles, with each circle intersecting with the other two causing both a three section design, off of the middle and also a common section design, in the middle. The circles are Social, Environment and Economic. The three section design is composed of Bearable, at the intersection of Social and Environment, Viable, at the intersection of Environment and Economic and Equitable, at the intersection of Economic and Social. The common section is Sustainable.

Me: ICLEI/LGS are operatives of the United Nations. In this country, they are committing un-American activities, in trying to support Agenda 21 in changing this country to a non-Republic. They are trying to change our elements of democracy within our Republic. They are trying to destroy our way of life, under Capitalism. Therefore they are enemies of our country, both foreign and domestic, and should be arrested, tried and convicted on charges relating to if they are an American citizen or not. If an American citizen, they should be tried for treason. If a foreign agent, they should be charged for subversion. Just because the United Nations are headquartered in New York, New York, does not give them the right to destroy our way of life, through subversion. In fact, charges against the United Nations should be brought against them in an international court, by the United States Government.

Rosa's book is very detailed and based on what occurred/is occurring in California for decades as well as in other metropolitan areas, in other states. The degree of implementation varies most likely as to how much influence Socialists have in a given county, city or town. California is trying to lead the nation in Socialism.

I attended a City Council meeting. The newspaper had stated before the meeting there would be a presentation made by a development agency which had been hired by the City. I sat there observing the presentation and realized the agency representative was presenting Agenda 21 planning.

It did not have single family dwellings included, but started with duplexes. It also had the typical "stack and pack" of downtown retail stores on the ground floor, with two or three residential floors above. A bypass highway was going around the small city of 70,000, off of the major highway that ran on one side of town. Normally one could get through town in only ten minutes. At the end of the presentation, the presenter threw in a bike path as though it was a side novelty. This was all based on the population of the town increasing greatly.

During the recess between the presentation and the meeting itself, I listed myself as one who wanted to address the City Council. I had not planned to do so, but after that observation I had to.

When called to address the Council, I stated I was wondering just where all the increase in population was going to come from. Due to consideration of destroying dams north of us, by their local government and an agency, I said maybe the people whose homes and land would be flooded might come south to us. Then I stated that recently, at a previous Council meeting, I had warned of Agenda 21 and it was making its way to local cities. I continued by saying it had arrived, in the form of the presentation we had just observed. I could feel the glares I received from the agency people. When finished, I turned in their direction to go back to my seat. I looked directly at them and met their hateful glares. I had hit the nail on the head.

I witnessed other Plan occasions, at City Council meetings.

It was called the Smart Valley Places Community Leadership Institute Graduation. Fourteen community members had gone through classes on the working of their city government. Two Hispanic women were introduced.

They explained the classes involved one city's Partnership for Healthy Children and various department managers of another city. Each graduate was called forward to receive their graduation document. Both English and Spanish were used as graduates expressed their appreciation for the opportunity to learn. Then it happened. One of the graduates stated she had been "invited" to participate. So it was not a course of study to be applied for, at least not for everyone. "Smart" Valley"…Community Leadership. After the meeting, I checked for a website with such a title of the Institute and I found it and verified its location. I had the right organization. It used the phrase "Sustainable Communities" and off to the side had a link for "Myths and Facts About Agenda 21". It was Socialism! It was after that I informed the City Council of Agenda 21. Anyone or any organization who supports Agenda 21, in any way or shape or form, should be prosecuted on charges of treason and subversion.

"Choose Civility": While attending a City Council meeting, a representative from the town's school district north of us was introduced. He gave a presentation on "Choose Civility" using the counteraction of bullying as the foundation of the new movement and gave the City Council six, large, yellow, Choose Civility flags; one for each of the City government buildings. I wondered about it as something just did not seem right. I knew it was related to Agenda 21, but the foundation he used could not be gone against, at least not without further information. In researching Choose Civility, I found it to have begun in Canada. Canadian Civility movement teachers came to the United States and found people to become such teachers here and trained them. It is an indoctrination method for control of people. It is Agenda 21. It is Socialism.

Back before ICLEI changed its name, but after becoming aware of that organization, I began to notice different types of organizations appearing. They were all NGO. One was a three county organization formed to have influence over the environmental planning of the Tri-County Region. Its title included the name of the county it was formed in, but its goals included both my own county and the one south of mine. Upon investigating, I found it had "partnered" with various agencies, including ones which had been in existence for a long time and had reputable status such as health organizations. It obtained those organizations due to the health issues relating to clean air.

I have already mentioned the State university regional outreach, at the migrant camp, which was operating out of its own city and county, but region wise reached into my county.

I cannot currently find any information of the organization, California law or regulation concerning cities having to have a City Council member as a member of the organization, but it did have to do with city government within maybe the county or region. I believe it was an association maybe? It was a newly organized NGO. In any case I do remember a lady, from another City Council north of our town, attending our City Council meeting and requesting our Council become involved and send a Council member to the organization. Shortly after the State itself made it mandatory that all City Councils have a representative at their local organization. Our Council did abide by the State law and one Council member was assigned the task of attending and reporting.

Another incident occurred, when I was attending a Meet and Great of four candidates for the City Council, in the upcoming election. There had been word of a Hispanic women's organization going from place to place denouncing lack of diversity in candidates. They wanted to force diversity. After each candidate had introduced themselves and said something about themselves, it was Question and Answer time. A man stood and began saying there needed to be diversity among office candidates and the community should find those people to run for office. The candidates looked at each other and one stated he was Mexican following by another declaring he was Assyrian. It was stated that our Mayor was Portuguese. The man was a lawyer affiliated with the women's group, who had sent him in and he did not do any preparation and only followed their orders of agenda. How is this related to Agenda 21? I do not know that it directly is. What I do know is Agenda 21 uses women and minorities, at least here in the United States.

There is something else I need to say about Agenda 21 and that is the Socialists want to destroy Capitalism. Part of Capitalism is free markets. The Stock Market deals with the finances of production and manufacturing companies ranging from food to transportation to entertainment to any human need or requirement. Guess what will be deleted under Agenda 21. Yup, the Stock Market. Why? Because the United Nations will decide what will be grown by who and who will manufacture what and how much of whatever. THIS IS THE PLAN!

I am going to finish off this section with the following:

Americanpolicy.org, Agenda 21 in one easy lesson, United Nations Biodiversity Assessment Report, What is not sustainable? Ski runs, grazing of livestock, plowing of soil, building fences, industry, single family homes, paved and tarred roads, logging activities, dams and reservoirs, power line construction and economic systems that fail to set proper value on the environment.

I am assuming "not sustainable" means the item cannot be allowed to exist. Also the idea is to take the land and water back to the days before humans. Even American Indians/Native Americans had a form of single family homes, including of logs and they did set proper value on the environment.

Aaaah…No more ski runs. Does that extend to any recreation facility that has to be constructed in nature? What about golf courses? No more beef, lamb, goat? That leaves chicken, fowl, fish and plant food sources. Horses can be fed with grains. No more preparing the ground for planting? Does that include gardens; flower and food? Hothouse grown vegetables and grains only, in planters? No more fences? Because fences indicate private property? What about government property, with fences. Is that an exception or will the fences be taken down. Does that include the fence around the White House? What about walls for protection, from those wild animals? Is that allowed? No more industry? Really?! No industry of any kind? Well there goes peanut butter. Not even non-polluting? Oh…waste. What about waste? Industries have waste matter that have to be disposed of. It does not have to be hazardous material. Now I ask you. How is anything ever going to be produced? Maybe it means no more machine industry? Maybe it means everything will be produced by hand the old fashioned way, as in the days of the cottage industry? Oh…single family homes! There it is. No more paved and tarred roads? Maybe dirt and rock? Concrete? No more logging activities? Okay…no industry, no mass production of materials and now no lumber to build with. Metal has been used to construct buildings, but that requires an industry. Will buildings be built only of stone? But those stones have to be taken from somewhere and change the ecology of that place. What about furniture? What is all of that going to be made of? Simulated wood, plastic, metal…it all requires industry. Dams provide electrical power besides holding water. No more power line construction? Is electrical power going to be by local, single building generator only or will it be only by underground cables? Does any of this seem contradictory to reality? Is this actually going to be followed in full measure? Are they nuts?

This stuff is real. It is documented. It is official. IT ACTUALLY HAPPENED JUST LIKE THE PLANNING OF THE WILDLANDS!

There is a lot of material on the web concerning Agenda 21. It is real and it is Socialism and it is insidious. The United Nations is a Socialist organization. This is not a political party or race or gender issue. It is a human issue. This is what Conservatives are fighting. This is what all people should be fighting. Those who are not are either unaware, are the ones who believe that their life will be better when Agenda 21 is fully manifested into reality or those who believe they will have a high status, while living in Communitarianism of

The Third Way. I believe if that reality does occur, a lot of people will be in for a big surprise. Including Socialist Christians. Some minorities will rise to some level of committee placement, but it will be the elite who will be in control. The rich elite. Not all people will be equal.

Question. What happens when the Socialist take control? Will all of those "social justice" welfare programs still exists to provide assistance to whoever wants it? Even generational welfare people, who are able to work? Free health care. Free education. Free food. Free housing. Free this and free that. Free, free, free. And just who is going to provide the funding for all of this free stuff? The government? Guess where the government get their funding from? Federal Reserve Bank printing more and more money to "loan" to the government? China? NO. It will highly tax those who will work. And who will work? All those able to work. There will no longer be a free ride, no free lunch. Well, maybe in public schools. Will all schools be public so only the totalitarian government can indoctrinate students? Remember that was being done right here right now by the Communist. Remember the goal of Socialism is Communism. The government will either own the industries and businesses or have so many regulations on them they will in effect own them. When the American car industry went under and the government bailed them out, the government began to control them and say who the industry leaders would be. And that was under a Communist President. What! We had a Communist President!? When did that happen? Obama was trained by a Communist, with the aid of his maternal grandparents, who were at least Socialist, if not Communist. His mother was a Socialist. His trainer had ties with Communist Russia. Obama became a Communist puppet and still is. He did not just go away. He is still active.

It is not my intention to present a study on Agenda 21, as that is not the purpose of this book. It is my intention to show how insidious the Socialist Plan for the future is. However, before I move on to writing another chapter,

I do want to present the following as what various States have done or have tried to do in legislative action against Agenda 21. This is the earliest report I found and it is only a sample of what is online concerning the subject of "state legislation against Agenda 21".

More States and Counties Now Opposing Agenda 21 - August 30, 2012

Also see this link for the National Republican Committee wording on Resolution Opposing Agenda 21 and for the state of Alabama who through their legislature banned Agenda 21 from their state at this link:

http://www.wpaag.org/agenda_21__rnc_resolution_opposing%20Agenda%2021.htm

Wyoming, Montana, Minnesota, Washington, Oklahoma, Iowa, Texas, South Dakota, Wisconsin, and Arkansas have all passed Resolutions Opposing Agenda 21 (Sustainable Development, and Smart Growth). More counties are also passing such resolutions. Some of these have exact or almost exact language as the Republican National Committee Resolution. That resolution can be found at this link, but is almost identical to the Wyoming Resolution below:

http://www.wpaag.org/agenda_21__rnc_resolution_opposing%20Agenda%2021.htm Iowa calls Agenda 21 a "diabolical collusion."

Agenda 21 is the United Nations agenda behind bike trails (for recreation now but for transportation in the future) and the control of private property in order to build high density housing (managed land use). Environmentalists' view is that cars produce more greenhouse gases than any other activity in our country, and high density housing will reduce the use of cars and push people into using public transit instead of cars.

I received an email from a Floridian yesterday saying "I found your anti-Agenda 21 list on the internet. You may find this info helpful. Also there is anti-Agenda 21 language in the 2012 GOP Platform that was just approved at the Tampa Convention. He sent me an up- to-date list of states and counties. I looked up all these links and have included the language (or at least most of it) found in these platforms listed below. (This is not an email I received, but was included in the referenced material.)

Wyoming: http://wygop.org/wp content/uploads/2012/05/2012.platform.and_.resolutions. Pdf see page 29 of this document.

34. Resolution Opposing United Nations Agenda 21 (Wyoming GOP Platform)

Whereas the United Nations Agenda 21 is a comprehensive plan of extreme environmentalism, social engineering, and global political control that was initiated at the United Nations Conference on Environment and Development (UNCED) held in Rio de Janeiro, Brazil, in 1992; and

Whereas the United Nations Agenda 21 is being covertly pushed into local communities throughout the United States of America through the International Council of Local Environmental Initiatives (ICLEI) through local "sustainable development" policies such as Smart Growth, Wildlands Project, Resilient Cities, Regional Visioning Projects, and other "Green" or "Alternative" projects; and

Whereas this United Nations Agenda 21 plan of radical so-called "sustainable development" views the American way of life of private property ownership, single family homes, private car ownership and individual travel choices, and privately owned farms; all as destructive to the environment; and

Whereas according to the United Nations Agenda 21 policy, social justice is described as the right and opportunity of all people to benefit equally from the resources afforded us by society and the environment which would be accomplished by socialist/communist redistribution of wealth; and

Whereas according to the United Nations Agenda 21 policy National sovereignty is deemed a social injustice; now therefore be

RESOLVED, the Wyoming Republican Party recognizes the destructive and insidious nature of United Nations Agenda 21 and hereby exposes to the public and public policy makers the dangerous intent of the plan; and therefore be it further

RESOLVED , that the U.S. government and no state or local government is legally bound by the United Nations Agenda 21 treaty in that it has never been endorsed by the (U.S.) Senate, and therefore be it further

RESOLVED, that the federal and state and local governments across the country be well informed of the underlying harmful implications of implementation of United Nations Agenda 21 destructive strategies for "sustainable development" and we hereby endorse rejection of its radical policies and rejection of any grant monies attached to it.

Montana: http://www.mtgop.org/index.php/about/party-platform.html - just use find tool a search for the word agenda

United Nations Agenda 21 and Land Use

We recognize the destructive and insidious nature of the United Nations Agenda 21 and hereby expose to the public and public policy makers the dangerous intent of the Agenda 21 plan.

Minnesota: http://www.mngop.com/pdfs/platform.pdf - This can be found under Section 10 and under Support our Troops and Allies.

Not only should the United States abstain from surrendering its national sovereignty to the United Nations or any other international organization, but we believe the United States should end its participation in the United Nations, Agenda 21, the World Bank, and the International Monetary Fund altogether.

Washington: http://www.wsrp.org/resources/party-documents Use the find tool and search for Agenda or just follow the section numbers in the document.

Section 16: We believe the preservation of LIBERTY is dependent upon the sanctity of our NATIONAL SOVEREIGNTY. The US Constitution is our supreme law of the land. The President shall not negotiate and the Senate shall not ratify any treaties, U.N. resolutions, agendas or foreign law, religious or otherwise, that are contrary to the US Constitution. Agenda 21, the Kyoto Protocol, Sharia Law, and others threaten our sovereignty. Therefore, judges, state and local authorities must be barred from using foreign agendas, laws, and resolutions for the purposes of interpreting United States law.

Oklahoma: http://gallery.mailchimp.com/512354e730a88fee4fcc330f7/files/2011_State_Platform_as_Adopted_5_7_2011.pdf - see pages 25 and 29.

28. We support strengthening protections for homeowners against arbitrary zoning change, which damage property values and oppose "Sustainable Development".

5. We support a free market-based public transportation system as opposed to government funding.

6. We oppose public-private partnerships and the use of eminent domain to build and operate toll roads and bridges.

6. We oppose the adoption of any United Nations sustainable development "Agenda 21"initiatives into the governmental planning authorities, policies, or body of law of the United States of America.

Iowa: http://www.iowagop.org/about (Could not find original link but found here: (Use find and type in Agenda or look for the sections by the numbers)

2.13 We demand that the term "sustainable development" be defined, vetted, and controlled by county and state agricultural agencies whose private property it impacts rather than the UN, other international or Agenda 21 agencies, or any federal organization.

9.6 We strongly oppose the diabolical collusion of the United Nations in establishing the unconstitutional "sustainable development agenda 21" in our local communities, our state and our nation.

11.6 We oppose any treaty that would regulate the use of Iowa lands and waters such as the UN Agenda 21 plan, which is being implemented throughout the United States and which restricts or destroys the property rights of Americans under the guise of environmentalist initiatives such as Sustainable Development, Smart Growth, Wildlands Project, Resilient Cities, Regional Visioning Projects, and others with similarly "Green" sounding names. United Nations Agenda 21 policy deems America's national sovereignty a social injustice and Agenda 21 concludes "the only way to make the future sustainable is to reduce America's living standards and transfer their wealth to developing nations".

16.9 We call for the Iowa legislature to repeal SF2389 that mandates regional planning for central Iowa through the "Tomorrow Plan", which is a by-product of Agenda 21.

3.14 We strongly oppose government monies being given to private organizations such as Planned Parenthood, AARP, ACORN, ACLU, and other groups which lobby for policies contrary to the views expressed in this platform. [Note: AARP has received grants for EPA training and sponsored training featuring radical transportation environmentalists speakers like Dan Burden.]

Texas – Using find tool doesn't work on this one.

http://www.tfn.org/site/DocServer/2012-Platform

Final.pdf?docID=3201 page 21 Using find tool doesn't work on this one.

United Nations Agenda 21 -The Republican Party of Texas should expose all United Nations Agenda 21 treaty policies and its supporting organizations, agreements and contracts. We oppose implementation of the UN Agenda 21 Program which was adopted at the Earth Summit Conference in 1992 purporting to promote a comprehensive program of sustainable development projects, nationally, regionally and locally. We oppose the influence, promotion and implementation of nongovernmental organizations, metropolitan and/or regional planning organizations, Councils of Government, and International Council for Local Environmental initiatives and the use of American (Texas) citizen's taxes to promote these programs.

I COULD HAVE BEEN ONE

<u>South Dakota</u> http://southdakotagop.com/about-the-party/our-platform/

1.14 The South Dakota Republican Party supports efforts to prohibit the adoption or implementation of policy recommendations that deliberately or inadvertently infringe or restrict private property rights without due process, as may be required by policy recommendations originating in, or traceable to "Agenda 21," adopted by the United Nations.

Also See Following South Dakota Resolution 8 at this link: http://southdakotagop.com/about-the-party/resolutions/resolution-8/

WHEREAS, the South Dakota Republican Party recognizes that we are called to be good stewards of the land and its resources, and

WHEREAS, the South Dakota Republican Party views United Nations Agenda 21 as a comprehensive plan of extreme environmentalism, social engineering and global political control, that was initiated at the United Nations Conference on Environment and Development (UNCED) held in Rio de Janeiro, Brazil, in 1992; and

WHEREAS, United Nations Agenda 21 is being covertly pushed into local communities throughout South Dakota and the United States of America through the International Council of Local Environmental Initiatives (ICLEI) through local "sustainable development" policies such as Smart Growth, Wildlands Project, Resilient Cities, Regional Visioning Projects, and other "Green" or "Alternative" projects; and

WHEREAS, United Nations Agenda 21 plan of "sustainable development" views private property ownership, single family homes, private vehicle ownership; individual travel choices, and privately owned farms as destructive to the environment; and

WHEREAS, according to United Nations Agenda 21, social justice is described as the right and opportunity of all people to benefit equally from the resources afforded us by society and the environment which United Nations Agenda 21 would accomplish by socialist/communist redistribution of wealth; and

WHEREAS, according to United Nations Agenda 21 national sovereignty is deemed a social injustice; now therefore be it

RESOLVED, that the South Dakota Republican Party recognizes the destructive and insidious nature of United Nations Agenda 21 and hereby exposes the dangerous intent of United Nations Agenda 21; and therefore be it further

RESOLVED, that the South Dakota Republican Party views United Nations Agenda 21 as an infringement on the inalienable rights of citizens of the United States.

RESOLVED that South Dakota, its local governments, and school districts be well informed of the harmful implications of implementation of United Nations Agenda 21 and we hereby reject its destructive strategies for sustainable development.

<u>Wisconsin - 2012 – 3: Agenda 21 -</u> http://www.wisgop.org/platform-res-olutions <u>Use find tool and type in Agenda</u>

WHEREAS United Nations (UN) Agenda 21 is a comprehensive plan of extreme environmentalism, social engineering, and global political control initiated at the 1992 UN Conference on Environment and Development (UNCED); and

WHEREAS Agenda 21 is being covertly pushed into local communities throughout the United States by the International Council of Local Environmental Initiatives (ICLEI) via local "sustainable development" policies such as Smart Growth, Wildlands Project, Resilient Cities, Regional Visioning Projects, and other "green" or "alternative" projects; and

WHEREAS Agenda 21 views the American way of life, including private property ownership, privately owned farms, single family homes, personal automobiles, and individual travel choices all as destructive to the environment; and

WHEREAS one of Agenda 21's stated goals is "sustainable development," which in fact equates to no development; and

WHEREAS another of Agenda 21's stated goals of "social justice," which, in fact amounts to a collectivist redistribution of wealth; and

WHEREAS, according to Agenda 21 policy, national sovereignty is deemed a social injustice; and

WHEREAS the Republican National Committee did on January 24th adopt a resolution to expose the destructive intent and insidiousness of Agenda 21;

THEREFORE BE IT RESOLVED that the Republican Party of Wisconsin, in convention assembled, fully recognizes and rejects Agenda 21's destructive and insidious nature; and

BE IT FURTHER RESOLVED that the Republican Party of Wisconsin, convention assembled, holds that the UN Agenda 21 treaty has no legally binding authority over the U.S. government or any state or local governments in that it has never been endorsed by the U.S. Senate; and

BE IT FURTHER RESOLVED that the Republican Party of Wisconsin, in convention assembled, endorses the rejection of any Agenda 21-related grant monies by federal, state, or local governmental entities; and

BE IT FURTHER RESOLVED that the Republican Party of Wisconsin, in convention assembled, hereby exposes to both the public and to public policy makers Agenda 21's true nature and intent; and

BE IT FURTHER RESOLVED that the Republican Party of Wisconsin, in convention assembled, should, in those ways that it is able, work to prevent or reverse the entrenchment of Agenda 21 and its initiatives in the State of Wisconsin by ensuring that the public and those elected officials within its sphere become informed as to the great danger to national sovereignty, states' rights, local control, and individual liberty that exist in implementing Agenda 21 "sustainable development" strategies.

Nevada - Nevada Republican Party Condemns Agenda 21 http://libertarianreview.us/2012/11/29/towards-integrity-then-unity/ - was passed unanimously.

Therefore be it resolved, that the Nevada Republican Central Committee recognizes the destructive and insidious nature of United Nations Agenda 21 and hereby exposes to the public the public policy makers to the dangerous intent of the plan; and,

Therefore be it further resolved, that we recognize that neither the U.S. government nor any state or local government is legally bound by the United Nations Agenda 21 "Soft Law" in that it has never been formally ratified by the United States Senate; and,

Therefore be it further resolved, the federal, state, and local governments across the United States need to be well informed of the underlying dangerous implications of the implementation of the United Nations Agenda 21's destructive strategies for so-called "sustainable development" and we hereby endorse the rejection of Agenda 21 and its radical policies, and the rejection of any grant funds attached to it; and,

Therefore be it further resolved, that the Nevada Republican Party and every Nevada Republican County Central Committee work with their public officials to identify and eradicate all legislation, ordinances, policies, procedures, et al, that are in accordance to the goals of Agenda 21; and,

Therefore be it further resolved, that the Nevada Republican Party and all Nevada Republican County Central Committees work vigilantly to actively oppose all proposed legislation, ordinances, policies, procedures, et al, in their respective political areas, which are in accordance to the goals of Agenda 21; and,

Therefore be it further resolved, that any Nevada Republican who actively works to assist in for the implementation of Agenda 21 goals be immediately censured by the appropriate County Central Committee and/or the Nevada Republican Central Committee; and,

Therefore be it further resolved, that upon the approval of this resolution the Secretary of the Nevada Republican Central Committee shall deliver a copy of this Adoptive Resolution to:

-The President of the United States
-Each member of Nevada's delegation to the U.S. Congress
-The leadership of the Nevada State Legislature
-The Chair of the Nevada Republican Party
-The Chair of each Nevada republican County Central Committee

Arkansas - Unanimously passed at GOP state convention in 2012. http://www.arkansasgop.org/?a=Files.Serve&File_id=eadacc83-3f31-44c4-a39a-87ebbba644ca

WHEREAS, the United Nations Agenda 21 is a comprehensive plan of extreme environmentalism, social engineering, and global political control that was initiated at the United Nations Conference on Environment and Development (UNCED) held in Rio de Janeiro, Brazil, in 1992; and,

WHEREAS, the United Nations Agenda 21 is being covertly pushed into local communities throughout the United States of America through the International Council of Local Environmental Initiatives (ICLEI) through local "sustainable development" policies such as Smart Growth,

Wildlands Project, Resilient Cities, Regional Visioning Projects, and other "Green" or "Alternative" projects; and,

WHEREAS, this United Nations Agenda 21 plan of radical so-called "sustainable development" views the American way of life of private property ownership, single family homes, private car ownership and individual travel choices, and privately owned farms; all as destructive to the environment; and,

WHEREAS, according to the United Nations Agenda 21 policy, social justice is described as the right and opportunity of all people to benefit equally from the resources afforded us by society and the environment which would be accomplished by socialist/communist redistribution of wealth; and,

WHEREAS, according to the United Nations Agenda 21 policy National sovereignty is deemed a social injustice; now therefore be

RESOLVED, the Republican Party of Arkansas recognizes the destructive and insidious nature of United Nations Agenda 21 and hereby exposes to the public and public policy makers the dangerous intent of the plan; and therefore be it further

RESOLVED , that the U.S. government and no state or local government is legally bound by the United Nations Agenda 21 treaty in that it has never been endorsed by the (U.S.) Senate, and therefore be it further

RESOLVED, that the federal and state and local governments be well informed of the underlying harmful implications of implementation of United Nations Agenda 21 destructive strategies for "sustainable development" and we hereby endorse rejection of its radical policies and rejection of any grant monies attached to it, and therefore be it further

RESOLVED, that upon the approval of this resolution the Republican Party of Arkansas shall deliver a copy of this resolution to each of the Republican members of our State Legislature, all Republican candidates, and to our Arkansas Republican Delegates to the National Republican Convention with instruction to recommend for adoption into the Republican Party Platform at the 2012 Convention.

Link to Arkansas Resolution Opposing Agenda 21 http://www.arkansasgop.org/?a=Files.Serve&File_id=eadacc83-3f31-44c4-a39a-87ebbba644ca

Following is a list of various counties that oppose Agenda 21, Sustainable Development, and Smart Growth.

Natrona Wy. 2012 GOP Platform www.natronagop.com/PDF/Platform-ResolutionsBylaws2012/2012_PRB.pdf — A-21...pg.4 sect.B line 8

Tulsa County Oklahoma 2011 GOP Platform http://docs.google.com/viewer?a=v&pid=sites&srcid=dHVsc2Fnb3Aub3JnfGhvbWV8Z3g6NmM1MjNiMjFmZWNhYzhiYw —-A-21...pg. 2-3

Spokane County Washington 2010 GOP Platform www.spokanegop.com/about-us/party-platform —-A-21...section 8-g

Martin County Florida 2011 GOP Platform http://martingop.org/download/newsletters/MCREC%20Platform.pdf —-A-21...pg. 14 and 15 (MOST COMPREHENSIVE)

Laramie County Wyoming 2012 GOP Platform www.laramiecountyrepublicanparty.com/images/2012_Platforms_Resolutions.docx —-A-21...pg. 4 to 6

Washoe County Nevada 2012 GOP Platform www.washoecountygop.org/about-us/2012-washoe-county-republican-party-platform/ —-A-21...scroll to SOVEREIGNTY section

Clallam County Washington 2012 GOP Platform http://clallamrepublicans.org/wp-content/uploads/2012/05/CCRP_County_Platform_2012.pdf —-A-21...pg. 3

Snohomish County Washington 2012 GOP Platform (adopted April 2012) www.snocogop.com/Platform/2012platform.pdf —-A-21...pg. 4

Washington County Nebraska 2012 GOP

Platform www.thewcrp.com/about/platform/ —A-21...scroll to Environment And Natural Resources
Lubbock County, Texas 2012 GOP Platform www.lubbockgop.org/documents/LCRP/-2012%Platform%20Final.pdf —A-21...pg.27
Bandera County Texas 2012 GOP
Platform www.banderagop.org/wp/?page_id=259
Jefferson County Washington 2012 GOP Platform http://youra.net/images/gop/platform12.pdf A-21...pg.3 Posted August 30, 2012 by Women Action Group - Updated January 10, 2013

Clarification: Although current social justice appears to be for the assistance of those who require it and some people involved in the forward movement of Socialism believe only that, not all people helping those in need are Socialists. They are just people helping people. They may or may not be Christian. They do not belong to any organization or group. They act only as an individual person, who observes a need and is pro-active in fulfilling that need simply because they are a warm-hearted, kind person. They are a positive person taking positive action. Their community is a better place because of them.

The following article is a demonstration of how the Socialist United Nations operates covertly.

Global Research Editor's Note

In October 2014, the conference of Catholic bishops in Kenya released a statement regarding the tetanus vaccine programme implemented under UN auspices.

The issue was subsequently addressed by Kenya's Catholic Doctors Association. (see article below).

Published below are the following texts:

- a recent review article pertaining to the 2014 findings of Kenya's

Catholic Doctors Association concerning the tetanus vaccine. No update is provided in this article with regard to Kenya.
- the original 2014 statement by the Conference of Catholic Bishops.
- the 2014 response by UNICEF and the WHO with regard to the tetanus vaccine.

May 23, 2019

*** The End

According to LifeSiteNews, [November 2014] a Catholic publication, the Kenya Catholic Doctors Association is charging UNICEF and WHO with sterilizing millions of girls and women under cover of an anti-tetanus vaccination program sponsored by the Kenyan government.

The Kenyan government denies there is anything wrong with the vaccine, and says it is perfectly safe.

The Kenya Catholic Doctors Association, however, saw evidence to the contrary, and had six different samples of the tetanus vaccine from various locations around Kenya sent to an independent laboratory in South Africa for testing.

The results confirmed their worst fears: all six samples tested positive for the HCG antigen. The HCG antigen is used in anti-fertility vaccines, but was found present in tetanus vaccines targeted to young girls and women of childbearing age. Dr. Ngare, spokesman for the Kenya Catholic Doctors Association, stated in a bulletin released November 4:

"This proved right our worst fears; that this WHO campaign is not about eradicating neonatal tetanus but a well-coordinated forceful population control mass sterilization exercise using a proven fertility regulating vaccine. This evidence was presented to the Ministry of Health before the third round of immunization but was ignored." (Source.)

Dr. Ngare brought up several points about the mass tetanus vaccination program in Kenya that caused the Catholic doctors to become suspicious:

Dr. Ngare told LifeSiteNews that several things alerted doctors in the Church's far-flung medical system of 54 hospitals, 83 health centres, and 17 medical and nursing schools to the possibility the anti-tetanus campaign was secretly an anti-fertility campaign.

Why, they ask does it involve an unprecedented five shots (or "jabs" as they are known, in Kenya) over more than two years and why is it applied only to women of childbearing years, and why is it being conducted without the usual fanfare of government publicity?

"Usually we give a series three shots over two to three years, we give it anyone who comes into the clinic with an open wound, men, women or children." said Dr. Ngare.

But it is the five vaccination regime that is most alarming. "The only time tetanus vaccine has been given in five doses is when it is used as a carrier in fertility regulating vaccines laced with the pregnancy hormone, Human Chorionic Gonadotropin (HCG) developed by WHO in 1992." (Source.)

UNICEF: A History of Taking Advantage of Disasters to Mass Vaccinate
It should be noted that UNICEF and WHO distribute these vaccines for free, and that there are financial incentives for the Kenyan government to participate in these programs. When funds from the UN are not enough to purchase yearly allotments of vaccines, an organization started and funded by the Bill and Melinda Gates Foundation, GAVI, provides extra funding for many of these vaccination programs in poor countries. (See: Bill & Melinda Gates Foundation Vaccine Empire on Trial in India.)

Also, there was no outbreak of tetanus in Kenya, only the perceived "threat" of tetanus due to local flood conditions.

These local disasters are a common reason UNICEF goes into poorer countries with free vaccines to begin mass vaccination programs.

Health Impact News reported last year that UNICEF began a similar mass vaccination program with 500,000 doses of live oral polio vaccine in the Philippines after a Super Typhoon devastated Tacloban and surrounding areas. This was in spite of the fact there were no reported cases of polio in the Philippines since 1993, and people who have had the live polio vaccine can "shed" the virus into sewage systems, thereby causing the actual disease it is supposed to be preventing. (See: No Polio in the Philippines Since 1993, But Mass Polio Vaccination Program Targeted for 500,000 Typhoon Victims Under Age 5.)

A very similar mass vaccination with the live oral polio vaccine occurred among Syrian refugees in 2013, when 1.7 million doses of polio vaccine were purchased by UNICEF, in spite of the fact that no cases of polio had been seen since 1999. After the mass vaccination program started, cases of polio began to reappear in Syria. (See: Are UNICEF Live Polio Vaccines Causing Polio Among Syrians? 1.7 Billion Polio Vaccines Purchased by UNICEF.)

It seems quite apparent that UNICEF and WHO use these local disasters to mass vaccinate people, mainly children and young women. Massive education and propaganda efforts are also necessary to convince the local populations that they need these vaccines. Here is a video UNICEF produced for the tetanus vaccine in Kenya. Notice how they use school teachers and local doctors to do the educating, even though the vaccines are produced by western countries.

Online reference: WND EXCLUSIVE, Obama affirmed radical U.N. agenda in lesser-known speech. Addressed General Assembly day before high-profile appearance. By Jerome R. Corsi Published September 29, 2015 at 7:02pm.

President Obama addresses United Nationals General Assembly in New York Sept. 28. UNITED NATIONS – President Obama's speech to the opening session of the United Nations' 70th General Assembly on Monday drew considerable attention, but most Americans likely were unaware of a speech he gave the previous day to the same world body in which he affirmed America's commitment to a controversial, **utopian** plan to **"transform" the world**.

As many focused on week three of the National Football League season Sunday, Obama spoke with little fanfare to the closing session of the **United Nations Sustainable Development Summit** that was convened Sept. 25-27 as a high-level plenary meeting of the General Assembly.

The U.S. and the 192 other U.N. members unanimously adopted the **"2030 Agenda for Sustainable Development,"** a plan to "end poverty, fight inequality and injustice, and tackle climate change by 2030."

It's a plan some critics call a **"blueprint for global governance."** As WND reported, Agenda 2030 is seen as a "reboot" of the controversial Agenda 21 plan, adopted in 1992, which the U.N. has described as a "comprehensive plan of action to be taken globally, nationally and locally by organizations of the United Nations system, governments and major groups, in every area in which human impacts on the environment."

"And so, today, we commit ourselves to new **Sustainable Development Goals**, including our goal of ending extreme poverty in our world," Obama told the U.N. meeting Sunday, **committing** the **United States** to Agenda 2030. "We do so understanding how difficult the task may be. We suffer no illusions of the challenges ahead. But we understand this is something that we must commit ourselves to."

Not only did that president tell a Muslim king that the United States is not a Christian country, but also he sold the United States to the United Nations. But there has been no treaty ratified by the United States Congress.

Note: Remember that the verbiage sounds all well and good. However, it is how it will be implemented and what is not openly said and what the reality of the results will be that matters.

Obama was no sooner elected and messed up the taking of the oath of office, for the Presidency, then three programs were announced; one, a youth corps from elementary school to college level and two, a mandatory senior citizens community service and three, a private army equal to the regular Federal Army. All three were seen as Communist/Socialist/NAZI programs. A youth corps to train and indoctrinate America's future generations. A senior citizen program to put retired people to work for the "State". And an army trained and indoctrinated and supplied for the overthrow of the American Republic and the establishment of The Third Way New World Order, under the United Nations enforcement of Agenda 21 and Agenda 2030. An army loyal only to the Communist/Socialist leadership and then their government once they have taken over America.

Those three programs did not come about due to the backlash the Obama administration received. However, that does not mean that the programs are not just on the backburner for right now.

Let's not forget the National Security Agency collecting, without proper legal procedure of court issued warrants, electronic information on all American citizens. And the discovery that they were constructing an underground storage center for it all.

And then there was the discovery of the Homeland Security Agency (HSA) taking over unused prison camps, throughout the country, placing them under armed guard. For what? The HSA was also purchasing firearms and ammunition in very large volumes. Why? There was also the story going around about the HSA purchasing shackles and coffins. However, I am not sure of the validity of that one.

The rest of it was made public through various news media.

Was He or Wasn't He?

Another lifetime ago, when I was into attending presentations, I attended one on The Principals of Biblical Government and another on Jesus being in politics.

Offhand I would have said Jesus was not. However, I am finally going to actually go through Neil Mammen's book titled *Jesus Was/Is Involved In Politics, The only way to a happier, healthier, safer, and mutually prosperous America*, published by Rational Free Press, in association with the American Family Association, copyright 2007. A person may obtain the book at www.JesusisinvolvedinPolitics.com website. The book is very well researched. For Bible verse quotations, he used the New International Version, by the International Bible Society. Since I do not have that Bible, I will continue to use the Geneva Bible, for any interjections I might make.

I will be mostly paraphrasing what Neil has to say, as I go along, and will put in parentheses my own comments. If I am going to give paragraph(s) input, I will identify as "Me:".

Please join me on this investigation.

Oh My Goodness Gracious Sakes Alive! One of the Chapters is "Was Jesus a Socialist?" Neil states he saw a photo of a young woman, at a protest, with a sign saying Jesus was a Socialist; the same photo I saw. Neil also states such belief is a complete misunderstanding of what our Lord told us to do. (I went online and looked for the photo using "images" There is only one such photo, but apparently the idea of Jesus being a Socialist is well used on the Left as I found a whole lot of other similar images. Some of which related to Communism. They do not like Christianity, but they sure do want Christians on their side and try to recruit them in order to use them.)

So, what else has Neil said?

He gives examples of government agencies, office holders, and judges making decisions based on legislation, regulations, and policies that are legal but are restrictive of a person's rights, such as homeschooling, a private organization's or business's right to determine service based on moral beliefs, as in a church's right to not marry a gay couple, a Christian baker's right not to provide a gay couple with a wedding cake. (Christians are to love the sinner but hate the sin.) Thus he brings in moral and legal issues.

People vote lawmakers into office. Lawmakers make laws. People have to live under those laws. Lawmakers made the laws through pragmatic thinking, without consideration for moral issues. Christians are people living under the law. Christians should exercise their right as a citizen of the United States of America and vote for those who will be lawmakers willing to consider all aspects of a situation and not use just pragmatic reasoning. Moral justice equals TRUE social justice. His book has questions and answers from conversations he had with people, who questioned and commented.

California Senate Bill 777 passed allowing boys and girls to enter the school restroom, of the opposite sex, depending on if they felt like a girl or a boy THAT DAY. A Los Angeles school actually tried to implement this. (California also passed a similar Bill stating a place of business did not have to have one restroom for women and one for men. A general restroom could be had for both, as in the type that has multiple stalls and open urinals and the entrance/exit door has NO lock. Both genders could use the same restroom at the same time. Both Bills received an uproar of a backlash, especially from many protective fathers and husbands not to mention mothers and wives.)

Laws violating American freedom of speech and worship have cost people and churches thousands of dollars in fines as well as prison time. There are over 600 such well documented cases of injustice. (There is in this country as well as others persecution of Christians. Why? Because of the Socialism/Communism movement and their belief that Christians are the enemy and the competition. It is not just the fanatical Muslim movement.) Such laws originated with Senators and Representatives and could have been stopped by involved Christians. Those Senators and Representatives and Assembly persons represent Christians as their constituents just like they do anyone else. So Christians need to make their voices heard.

The author began his journey, toward what and who he is today, as a young, Christian, college student, in the 1980s, who was a pro-choice Liberal not interested in politics. He was not thinking for himself or conducting his own research, but accepted Liberal doctrine. He states he was a "Left Wing Christian". When he did begin thinking, he did not want to admit he was wrong and had been all that time because that would have implied he had been fooled and fighting the wrong battle. (He was not by himself and good people still get fooled by wolves in sheep's clothing.)

Neil states that when he uses the term "Bible believer" he is including Orthodox, Protestants, Catholics, Jews (The Old Testament is theirs.), Evangelicals, Coptics and such.

(I found the following very interesting, as I have previously posed a question concerning such an issue) And I quote: "...200 years ago we Conservatives would have been considered Liberals. Classical Liberalists believed the government should not provide social services or regulate industry and banks and held to strict constructionist views of the law."

Just because Jesus did not do something does not mean it is a bad or unwise thing to do. Jesus did not stop the Romans from massacring His own people, the Jews, nor did he ever fight for the freedom of slaves. (However, his kingdom was not of this world. He was here but for a short time and was on a mission as given to Him, by His Father in Heaven. He was not to be an earthly leader, but the Savior of us all. We, on the other hand, are here until our Father calls us and can and should help others out of love for our neighbor, in our preparation for entering the next life. No, I have not just said that a Christian should be a Socialist!) Jesus never married. Does that mean that we should not marry? No, we should in accordance with the Bible.

If Jesus did do something, we should follow His example as a teaching moment for us.

The Romans did not manage Israel or make all of the Jews' laws. A big misconception that most people have is that the Romans ran Judea as an extension of Rome. While it is true the Romans did conquer and rename Judah to Judea, they did not run or legislate or create all of its civil laws. People seem to think the Romans were a civil police force, the army of Judea and lawmakers and judges in territories they controlled. Just as America did not manage Japan or the American Sector of Germany, after World War II, but allowed those countries to have their own local governments, so it was with the Roman occupation.

Similarly Judeans, in 33 A.D., at the time of the crucifixion of Jesus, had a fully functioning political system that included their own executive, legislative and judicial authorities, with the legislative and judicial being combined. They were self-governing in many respects, but the Romans gave them a level of self-governance above what they gave most other conquered nations. The Jews had control over their laws and were allowed to pass their own sentences on most crimes, with the only punishment the Jews could not exact being the death sentence. The Jews also had their law enforcement, jails and Temple guards and King Herod, the Jewish political leader, had his own army. When King Herod had all babies of approximately two years old killed, in Bethlehem, the soldiers were most likely Jews or hired mercenaries. (Neil states "...in Bethlehem,...." Others think the event occurred in Nazareth due to the passing of approximately a two year time period, from the birth of Jesus. But the point is that Roman soldiers were not involved.)

The Sanhedrin were the lawmakers, in Judea, based on their form of a constitution; the Torah. They were not only in charge of religious law, but also civil. Any matter not claimed by Roman authority, was claimed by the Sanhedrin, which was made up of the scribes, Pharisees and Sadducees. The ones that Jesus advised, admonished, condemned and chastised concerning corrupt laws and incorrect or twisted interpretations of the original Hebraic Law.

Me: The process of Jesus' Passion and Crucifixion is a good example of how both Roman and Jewish laws differed.

John 18:3 Judas then, after he had received a band of men and officers of the high Priests, and of the Pharisees, came thither with lanterns and torches, and weapons.

It was the Jewish leadership that Judas had gone to and contracted the betrayal of Jesus and it was them that arrested Jesus, in the darkness of night.

18:15 Now Simon Peter followed Jesus, and another disciple, and that disciple was known of the high Priest: Therefore he went in with Jesus into the hall of the high Priest.

It was the Jewish High Priest Caiaphas that Jesus was taken before for preliminary processing of questioning to determine charges to place against Jesus.

18:29-31 Pilate then went out unto them, and said, What accusation bring ye against this man? They answered, and said unto him, If he were not an evil doer, we would not have delivered him unto thee. Then said Pilate unto them, Take ye him, and judge him after your own Law. Then the Jews said unto him, It is not lawful for us to put any man to death.

Caiaphas could not find fault to document as official charges, which is why they gave no direct response to what the charges were to Pilate, the Roman administrator. The Jews wanted Jesus put to death and only Pilate could give that sentence.

18:38-40 Pilate said unto him, What is truth? And when he had said that, he went out again unto the Jews, and said unto them, I find in him no cause at all. But you have a custom that I should deliver you one loose at the Passover: will ye then that I loose unto you the King of the Jews? Then cried they all again, saying, Not him, but Barabbas: now this Barabbas was a murderer.

Pilate could not find a charge to press against Jesus and tried to use Jewish law to free Him, which the Jews denied His freedom, by their own law. So Pilate continued the Roman process and had Jesus punished, by scourging and mockery by the Roman soldiers, in order to present Jesus again to the Jews, as punished, and try to obtain freedom for Him again saying he could find no fault in Jesus. However, the Jews cried out for crucifixion. Again Pilate questioned Jesus, who in response stated: John 19:11 Jesus answered, Thou couldest have no power at all against me, except it were given thee from above: Therefore he that delivered me unto thee, hath the greater sin.

Two more times Pilate tried to free Jesus, but the Jews continued to argue saying since Jesus claimed to be a king, then He spoke against Caesar, the Roman Emperor, and that the Jews had no king except Caesar. At that point, Pilate ordered Jesus to be crucified, under Roman law, as Jesus setting Himself against Caesar.

Neil continued: Since the Sanhedrin determined legislative, executive, judicial, civil and criminal law, they were like modern day politicians. Since Jesus was always talking to various members of the Sanhedrin trying to influence them, calling them to account, showing them that many of their laws both civil and religious were wrong and overly numerous, then **Jesus was involved in Politics!**

Not all Pharisees were bad. There were those that were God-fearing and Jesus approved and bless them. His admonitions were targeted at just those particular ones who were hypocrites and into power and publicity and looking not at the intent (spirit) of the law, but only at the letter of the law and manipulated it to oppress people. Jesus was chastising bad politicians and working with the good ones.

Jesus even insulted Herod, in Luke 13:31, by calling him a fox, which in that culture meant Herod was a varmint. Foxes live in the ground and were pests raiding chickens for food. It was like calling Herod a slinking, slimy, cowardly, wicked, thieving, dirty rat. In Matthew 23:27, Jesus called the teachers of the law and Pharisees hypocrites likened to whitewashed tombs looking beautiful on the outside, but full of dead men's bones and everything unclean.... And in Matthew 23:33 He call them snakes and a brood of vipers.

Jesus would call an evil man an evil man and a hypocrite a hypocrite. What Would Jesus Do? He would speak out against evil politicians and correct them. So must Christians!

Jesus did speak out on both moral and civil issues as in the woman caught in adultery, the moral and legal basis of divorce and even the ethics of paying taxes to Caesar.

America is great because of our Christian heritage. That heritage gave us our Constitution, but it is up to us, as Christians, to maintain our Christian heritage or it will slouch towards oppression and corruption because, if we do not, our Constitution will fall meaningless and fade away little by little under Socialist restrictions. If not in the lifetime of our generation, then our children's. Christians must read and understand the United States Constitution.

For example, the First Amendment states "Congress shall make no law respecting an establishment of religion, or prohibiting the free exercise thereof; or abridging the freedom of speech, or the press; or the right of the people peacefully to assemble, and to petition the Government for a redress of grievances." "…shall make no law respecting an establishment of religion…." From that, the phrase "separation of church and state" came about. Some people believe that means there cannot be the Ten Commandments on the front of a courthouse or the Christian cross on the graves of American military personnel at National Cemeteries or prayer in school or prayer on government property or prayer or singing Christian songs in public, etc. etc. etc. It does not mean that! "…establishment of religion…." is the wording, as in the government cannot establish any religion as the Nation's religion. That and only that! Nothing else! Period!

Neil gives the example of Romans expecting to have free stuff and free entertainment in the Colosseum, as in observing the death of gladiators (slaves) and later Christians' deaths. Rome became a socialist society. It became weak through the attitude of entitlement. (A life of entitlement within itself is a form of slavery; of dependency.)

Me: Americans have become conditioned to free stuff. Buy a box of laundry detergent and get a free piece of dishware. Commercialism uses buy one and get one free. I am not saying such practice and advertisement within itself is bad or wrong. I am saying over a long period of time people here come to expect the free stuff. It is human nature. It is conditioning without conditioning having been the goal. The businesses only wanted to sell their product, but it has had a side effect. So when something is free, we automatically want it just because it is…well…free.

Speaking of who gives us things; what about our rights? A right is not earned or it would be what is due to us such as pay for work done. A right is not a privilege, as a privilege is something that does not have to be given and can be taken away, as in being able to do something that others may not. Does the government give rights? No, they give what is earned by contract or a privilege by law; voting, although it is termed as a right of citizenship, it is a privilege of citizenship. Rights come from an authority. Rights come from the highest authority and they are unalienable rights, which cannot be taken away, as they come from God. Life, liberty and the pursuit of happiness.

Okay I got my two cents in. Now back to Neil.

Rights cannot be self-assigned. Self-assigning has no real foundation for demanding a right. Rights are not a social contract. A slave is held in bondage, although they have the right of liberty and the pursuit of happiness. A slave is taken and may be sold and dealt with as the so-called master pleases. The slave did not sign a contract. Being a slave is not a right. If government gave us our rights, then the government could justly take them away; like a privilege. If they did come from the government, then there would be no inherent moral value saying that everyone must get the same rights. So rights have to come from God, Himself. (By the way, one does not have to even believe in God to have unalienable rights.)

One of the major concerns of politics is rights, which is directly tied to "true social justice". But rights come from God; therefore politics must be concerned with God.

What if there is no God? Then morality is merely the preference of those in authority as in might makes right. If Hitler had won World War II, then the murder of Jews would have been okay. If the Confederate States of America had won America's Civil War, then slavery would have continued and been okay. (Just a historical point. Nineteen other nations ended slavery, without war.)

If God is taken out of the Declaration of Independence, the Bill of Rights and the United States Constitution, then that foundation for those *Unalienable Rights* is taken away. And if those Rights are taken away, our freedoms are taken away. So-called rights/privileges would be granted by the popular opinion of the government, at any given time and only for as long as that opinion was in favor.

Another point is the difference between "rights" and "goods". If a right depends on someone else's service, work or money, it is not a "right", but "goods" and not God given or a Constitutional Right. Nor is the right to own a house or business, as granted under "the pursuit of happiness" Right, entitle one to a free residence or business. The Right is only the opportunity to earn a living by using one's mental and physical capacity under the circumstances in which one is living and be able to afford a residence or business. If one believes they are entitled, by right, to government provided goods such as healthcare, subsidized housing, medicine, food or welfare or even a guaranteed minimum wage, under so-called "social justice", they are wrong because they are not talking about a "right", but about "goods" being provided by someone else's mental and physical capacity providing tax revenue to the government to provide such "goods". Such goods may be given or not given depending on the popular opinion of the government at any given time. *True Social Justice* starts with respecting and protecting people's Unalienable Rights.

Now that the difference between "rights" and "goods" has been established there is another issue; the Right to Bear Arms. Under the Unalienable

Rights of Life, Liberty and the Pursuit of Happiness, this Second Amendment to the United States Constitution holds within it that a person can protect and defend not only their self, but also their families and property and even other people. Why? Life may be protected from harm or being taken. Liberty is the freedom to protect and defend, with just cause, without being arrested and prosecuted and punished. Pursuit of Happiness includes such protection and defense in order to maintain what one has obtained, through their mental and physical capacity. Therefore equipment and supplies must be obtained in order to protect and defend meaning that guns may be owned and ammunition may be obtained and owned without infringement on that Right. Neil also states the protection and defense is about being against governments that would take our freedoms away. The Second Amendment is in place to protect the First Amendment.

The Founding Fathers of our Country did not develop or come up with these concepts. Of course they included them in the formation of our government, of our Country. If one researches church sermon archives of the two centuries before 1776, one finds God as the source of Unalienable Rights including freedom for slaves and freedom of worship and freedom from tyranny and other freedoms were preached from the church pulpit. It is well documented that many of the concepts of the Declaration of Independence came from John Locke, who was an Enlightenment Era Christian. While the document was composed during the Enlightenment Era, concepts came from the Bible.

The Declaration of Independence and the U.S. Constitution are directly connected through the wording of both giving the Constitution its moral foundation. This Country was founded on Christian principals and God-given morality and rights.

Some governments take away rights including by restrictive laws. The Declaration of Independence was based on the fact that the British Government had taken away some rights of the American colonist and restricted others. (When Fidel Castro and his Communist forces took over Cuba, the new Communist government put restrictions on privately owned businesses to the point that for all practical purposes the government owned the businesses and the owners were simply caretakers.)

There is objective right and wrong and relativistic thinking leads to immorality and injustice. A liberal Rabbi was on a talk show and he claimed there is no objective right or wrong. The talk show host gave him a situation of being in 1943 and in front of a Nazi Gestapo officer who has his pistol drawn. The officer asks, "Rabbi, I am about to shoot you. Is there any reason why I shouldn't?" The Rabbi was then asked, by the talk show host, what he would say to the officer. Would he say, "…because it is what? Wrong? Then the Rabbi was asked, "What do you say to him if there is not right or wrong?" To the relativistic thinking Gestapo officer there was no right or wrong. Therefore he could do as he pleased. By relativistic thinking, the killing of the Jews was okay. It was not morally wrong. It was simply what needed to be done to achieve the goal. Such logic denies God and morality.

Since the U.S. Constitution is based on morality, then it stands to reason that Constitutional Law should be based on morality and not just pragmatic thinking. The principles that the Constitution were founded on applies just as much today and as it will tomorrow as it did when it was composed. It is founded on unchanging principles and on unchanging Natural Law. It is because the Constitution is founded on objective God-given morality that it will be in danger of becoming non-existent, if more and more Americans abandon objective morality and stop believing that God exists and therefore stop believing in moral behavior.

Me: Natural Law is defined as a body of principles that are considered to be inherent in nature and have universal application in determining whether human conduct is right or wrong, often contrasted with positive law. An ethical theory that gives the position of the existence of a law whose content is

I Could Have Been One

set by nature and therefore has validity everywhere. A rule or body of rules of conduct inherent in human nature and essential to or binding upon human society.

It is the reasoning of relativistic thinking that Communism/Socialism does not believe in God and wants Christians to turn away from God so they may use them and take control. If God does not exist and there is no moral right or wrong existing, then they may lie, cheat, steal and kill without any guilt or regret.

Neil: Some people say morality cannot be legislated or that only social issues are legislated. So what are the politicians legislating? Some legislated issues are sex crimes, murder, theft, forgery, fraud, child abuse, elder abuse, etc. All of these are moral issues. Therefore the politicians are legislating moral behavior! Maybe they don't think so, but they are. (These crimes are all against the Ten Commandments.) Although some issues may seem to be only cultural or social issues, they are indeed moral as well. It could be said that slavery was a cultural and or social issue, however it was and is a moral issue. As for as the equality of all humans, Christianity is the only major religion to teach it. (American slavery actually was ended after the War Between the States, by Congress, with the 13th Amendment to the U.S. Constitution. That was moral legislation by Congress.)

Can laws based on morality be enforced? Let's take murder; thou shall not kill. The law outlaws murder. Can it be enforced? No and yes. No, because the law itself does not stop one person from murdering another. Yes, because the punishment can be a deterrent to one who is thinking about committing murder, as society observes the enforcement of the law by investigation, arrest, trial, conviction and punishment.

The Bible, which claims all people are equal, with equal rights, was used in freeing the American slave, also declares homosexual acts as immoral and damaging to the body. So when human rights, which comes from the Bible, are used to justify same-sex marriage how can a person validate what is not validated by the Bible, by claiming equal rights or human rights, when the source (the Bible) was just invalidated by trying to justify homosexuality?

What about trying to change the situations that create the immoral behavior? Legislation can make it a crime to murder, but it cannot force a person to love another. That has to happen over time, by changing attitudes from hate, to understanding, to love. ("Love one another as I have loved you.")

Was Jesus a Socialist? In reference to the Sermon on the Mount, as in Matthew 5-7, it cannot be applied to governments; only to individuals. Some people think loving one's neighbor means the government should collect taxes and feed the poor and then raise more taxes and give to the needy in the form of free healthcare and housing and that it would be the most loving thing to do and Jesus would want us to do it. Jesus did say to give to the poor, take care of others, sacrifice for our neighbors who are not even related to us and provide medical assistance to the stranger and give food to the hungry and shelter the homeless and visit the prisoners.

But He said you and I should do it. James 1:27 says, "Religion" that our God our Father accepts…is this: to look after orphans and widows." Note it clearly says "Religion" not Government. Jesus never said the government should do it, but that you and I should do it. (Faith Based Charity! Churches know their communities and the needs of that community down to who requires what.)

Paul in Romans 13 says that the authorities are the minister of Justice, not a provider of charity. In Mark, 10:21 Jesus tells the rich young ruler to give his money to the poor; not to the government. Jesus did not say to take money away from the selfish and give it to the poor, nor did He say to take money from the rich and give it to the struggling. He never even said to take money from the extremely rich. By the way, let us not forget the words of Paul in II Thessalonians 3:10 "If a man will not work, he shall not eat."

Bottom line is the government, through threat of punishment, takes money, in the form of taxes, and it is that money that is used for welfare programs.

(Even if the government borrows money from China or has the Federal Reserve Bank print more money and loan that to the government, the tax payer is still the one who feels the effects of such loans, which has to be repaid someday.)

Bottom line is Jesus never promoted socialism and therefore *Jesus was not a Socialist*.

Socialism is not good for the persistence of faith. The more socialist a country is the less Christian it is, as proven by how Christian Holland and Sweden used to be and how, with the increase of Socialism, those countries are very less Christian. For Christians to crave Socialism seems like a self-extinguishing death wish. (Of course that is just what a Socialist infiltrator of a church wants.)

God designed work and responsibility to be satisfying and compelling goals to be hard to achieve and fulfilling and work to be worth the effort. Healthy competition should be an incentive and discipline to build character. (The Socialists do not want strong character. They want obedient followers, who do not think for themselves, as demonstrated in the Bella Dodd writings.)

How does a socialistic government ensure that people work as much as they can and not instead take as much as they can without the government becoming a totalitarian regime? It cannot. Socialism leads to a dependency of people on handouts and a form of totalitarianism or go into inflation and bankruptcy. For the former, think China, Russia and North Korea. For the latter, think Greece and Europe. Socialism is the dependency of the fooled masses engineered by the elite to control the masses.

If Christians themselves are feeding the poor, administering to the sick, clothing the needy and sheltering the homeless, then the government would not have to do it. Some people believe Capitalist are greedy and selfish. However, it is the Capitalist countries that provide the most to charities, while the Socialist countries give the least. If one took up a collection in America, for a charitable cause, one would discover that liberals and progressive give up to 30% less than conservatives.

If one wanted to take control of or destroy a culture (American), one would break down the family by relaxing sexual laws and degrading the culture through entertainment. Then for compassionate reasons, the government would establish itself as the provider of welfare, in replacing the responsibility of fathers. (The economy going into a recession and the housing market going upside down would also take place.)

A morally and legally constrained free market system is the only one that has ever worked reliably. "Morally constrained" means the government ensures that contracts are kept and ensures that no man is given an unfair advantage. A free market is based on honoring of contracts and rights and not a forced equality of results, as in force sharing of the fruits of another's labor.

Information from data accumulated by the Heritage Foundation:

> "The simple fact is that children are suffering because the U.S. welfare system has failed. Designed as a system to help children, it has ended up damaging and abusing the very children it was intended to save. The welfare system has failed because the ideas upon which it was founded are flawed. The current system is based on the assumption that higher welfare benefits and expanded welfare eligibility are good for children. According to this theory, welfare reduces poverty, and so will increase children's lifetime well-being and attainment. This is untrue. Higher welfare payments do not help children; they increase dependence and illegitimacy, which have a devastating effect on children's development." Onlinewww.heritage.org/Research/Welfare/BG 1084.cfm

> "The data showed that welfare plays a powerful role in promoting illegitimacy, triples the level of teen sexual activity, doubles the probability that a women will have children out of wedlock, triples the level of behavioral and emotional problems amongst kids and doubles the probability that a boy will engage in criminal activity. Instead of solving economic problems, government welfare socialism created monstrous moral and spiritual problems. The kind of problems that are inevitable when individuals turn responsibility for their lives over to other. The legacy of American socialism is our blighted inter cities, dysfunctional inner city schools and broken Black families."

Quoted from *Uncle Sam's Plantation*, by Star Parker. She wrote of her own life observing two Americas; one of the poor on socialism and one of the wealthy in capitalism.

The fix for this is for people to obey God's moral laws concerning personal responsibility, marriage, divorce, sex and for the Church and not the government to be the solution provider. True social justice is not trying to put people on welfare, but trying to get them off it because it is not good for them or their children. Yet the Church cannot be the solution provider to sufficient people if it is over taxed, over restricted, repressed or oppressed. Anyone who cares about the poor and the oppressed has to first care about the laws of this nation in order to delete the over taxation and restriction and repression and oppression.

Me: *So…Jesus did not teach socialism and was not a Socialist! It is Leftist propaganda! And Jesus did get involved in politics and through Christians has been and is and will continue to be.*

As for the issue of claiming Socialism goes back to the early Christians and their communal practice, a person close to me, who has studied theology and the early days of Christianity, stated that socialism was not the reason for their communal life style. As stated in the Acts of the Apostles 2:41-46 He gives accounts of about three thousand being baptized that day, with many wonders and signs performed by the Apostles in the following days. This was after the descent of the Holy Spirit upon the Apostles, in Jerusalem. There was communal living by all giving of their possessions to be distributed according to the need of each person. Most of such communal living was in Jerusalem, where the Christians were persecuted by some Jews. Also with thousands coming into Christianity, they would have been from every walk of life including those in need. Also living communally gave the opportunity for new believers to observe and learn in a community setting; a faith community setting. They were practicing being Christian. **Not Socialist!**

Also in Matthew: 6:24 No man can serve two masters: for either he shall hate the one, and love the other, or else he shall lean to the one, and despise the other.

7:17 So every good tree bringerth forth good fruit, and a corrupt tree bringerth forth evil fruit.

7:21-27 Not everyone that saith unto me, Lord, Lord, shall enter into the kingdom of heaven, but he that doeth my Father's will which is in heaven. Many will say to me that day, Lord, Lord, have we not by thy Name prophesied, and by thy name cast out devils? And by thy name done many great works. And then will I profess to them, I never knew you, depart from me ye that work iniquity. Whosoever then heareth of me these words, and doeth the same, I will liken him to a wise man, which hath builded his house on a rock: and the rain fell, and the floods came, and the winds blew, and beat upon that house, and it fell not: for it was grounded on a rock. But whosoever heareth these my words, and doeth them not, shall be likened unto a foolish man, which hath builded his house upon the sand: and the rain fell, and the floods, and the winds blew, and beat upon that house, and it fell, and the fall thereof was great.

Just because a person thinks they are working in the Lord's name does not mean they actually are. If they are working in the name of Socialism, they are not working in the name of the Lord. One may serve either the Lord or Socialism, but not both. As demonstrated, TRUE Social Justice is not Socialism.

Actually the fact that some people believe socialism began during the early days of Christianity demonstrates the parallel between Christianity and Socialism and the difference. Socialism is for control of people on this earth, while Christianity is for gaining Heaven, in the next life. Socialism is the earthly god, while Christianity has our Heavenly Father; the one true God. These days the Socialists are using such belief as propaganda.

America and Israel

Besides the parallel between Socialism and Christianity, I have noticed a parallel between America and Israel. Long story short is God took his chosen people out of the land of Egypt. After saving them from the Egyptians, the Israelites first praised God for His deliverance. Later they complained of the desert hardships, although God give them food and drink. A governing system was established among the twelve tribes and laws were composed for the order and behavior of the people and articles for the formal worship of God were constructed. However, while Moses was receiving the Ten Commandments, from God on the Mount of Sinari, the Israelites constructed a golden calf to worship instead of God. Forty years the Israelites traveled lost through the desert.

The older generations died in the desert without entering the Land of Canaan, including Moses. Israelite slaves did not enter Canaan, but a people who knew of slavery, but had not suffered slavery. The various people of Canaan worshiped false gods, and were delivered into the hands of God's chosen people so that they might establish themselves in Canaan.

Part of the laws composed, in the desert, dealt with not practicing the worship of false gods of Egypt or Canaan, where they would be going into. So they were not to worship the gods of either the land they had left or of the land they would enter. See Judges 2:11-14 and Kings 17:1-7. However, some of the Israelites would worship the false gods of other nations and an Israelite king set up the worship of such a god. God set other nations against the Israelites and punished them by death, destruction and slavery; both of the faithful and of those who had betrayed God. Time after time this happened, but each time the descendants, of those who had betrayed God, did not learn from their own history and committed the same, which again God punished them. He punished over and over.

Exodus 34:7 Yet he does not leave the guilty unpunished; he punishes the children and their children for the sin of the fathers to the third and fourth generation.

Psalms 9:17 The wicked shall be turned into hell, and all the nations that forget God.

God may punish the people of a nation by various means including allowing us to suffer the natural consequences of our anti-God choices including trying to serve both God and men, which cannot be done. God punished the United States for its slavery. We are now well past the fourth generation of those involved in the War Between the States, but have we learned from the past? Are we to be judged and punished again, by way of a totalitarian, communitarianism lifestyle of Communism/Socialism?

In Neil's words,

> "If you care about the weak and the oppressed and bad political policies that create more suffering, notice that God has placed you in a country where you can glorify Him by doing something about it. Take advantage of that. When God judges our nation because of others or because of our

leaders, you and I, the followers of Christ, and our children and the poor will also suffer the physical consequences!"

Speaking of Europeans, when this continent came to the attention of European nations and began to be settled in masse, it was due to the discovery of the natural resources of the continent, by Spain and France, and also for wanting to leave the oppression of England behind as well as wanting a new way of life, from Europe.

Like the Israelites the Europeans had to deal with the natives of the new Americas and vice versa. There was bloodshed, treaties and prejudice on both sides. Over time the Europeans traveled further and further into the continent just as the Israelites had done in Canaan. Just as slavery existed during the time period of the establishment of Judah and Israel, slavery came to America. Just as Israel saw war between the two sons of Solomon, in brother against brother, for the rule of the nation and that war ending in the nation of Israel being split in two, with the establishment of the nation of Judah; America saw war, of brother against brother, as the United Sates was split in two, with the establishment of the Confederate States of America. The difference, of course, is that the War Between the States occurred after the split, the Confederate States lost the War and the United States was as before the War. America was punished for its evil, by bloodshed, of both North and South.

Just as Israel fought many wars, the United States has also fought many wars. After World War II, European Jews went back home to Israel and established their nation. During different time periods, America has had a great flow of peoples, from all over the world, to the extent of being titled "The Melting Pot" and a Statue of Liberty being gifted and placed in New York City harbor having an inscription welcoming the huddled masses. It was those huddled masses that have built America just as the refugee Jews built their own nation.

Israel has survived her neighbors just as America has survived attacks both from without and within. Israel is still surviving her neighbors just as America is still fighting Socialism/Communism. But America's enemy is within and needs assistance from its conservative, patriotic and also Christian citizens. For the fight is against Socialist, un-American and anti-God citizens.

Israel was punished. Will America again be punished?

Jeramiah 4 tells of Jeramiah's foretelling of Israel's destruction, if Israel did not return to God in worship and praise and glorification and obedience to the Ten Commandments and the Jewish laws. Such a foretelling holds for Christians, including those claiming to be Christians, but are Socialists. And those non-practicing Christians.

God chose a people to be the ones He would care for generation after generation and they were to worship only Him. However, time after time they drew away from Him and time after time He punished even to destruction and slavery. And time after time He showed them mercy and forgave them and gave them a prosperous life.

By extension, all people are His children and we are to worship only Him. Will we give Him reason to forgive us, to have mercy on us? If this nation is brought to destruction and we are enslaved, from within or without, how long will our children and grandchildren for generation after generation suffer, before He has mercy on them?

I do not want that for my grandchildren. Do you?

World Upside Down

Since the younger generations have not lived the history of the older generations, they do not have anything to compare the "here and now" with the "good old days" of the past. The "here and now" will someday be their "good old days" and then they will have something to compare with.

To my generation and older, the world is upside down. Our present is 180 degrees out from our past. The polarity has reversed from positive going on to negative. Remember the world I grew up in? A post-World War, Christian, conservative, patriotic, earn one's way, be of value, contribute to the community, anti-Communist environment. Times were simpler, less confusing and straight forwardly uncomplicated. One knew about cause and effect, taking responsibility for one's actions and not being entitled except to what was earned. There were sayings such as "Buyer beware.", "There is no such thing as a free lunch.", "For God and Country." and "As American as apple pie".

One by one:

Post-World War: There was the Viet Nam War and has been the Iraq Wars and Afghanistan War, under the War-On-Terror. Viet Nam was the first war America actually lost. Before that was the stalemate of North Korea. With Nam, there were American anti-protests and expatriates. The circumstances were not traditional as America was involved in a civil war, with nothing about it being civil. One did not know who might be the enemy including women. An attack could be by a single person. Congress was actually calling the shots. Pun intended. The rules of engagement had changed. Iraq was a victory, but Afghanistan is still debatable, as it lingers. In the War-On-Terror, the enemy is not traditional. The enemy does not wear uniforms and fights mostly covertly. Again…who is the enemy? Who may be trusted? And again… Congress has their nose in military business. Except lately, as the Socialists are too busy trying to counteract the President that is standing up for America as well as trying to change back to positive polarity. Today America's military is not the same as it once was as it has gone through a great number of changes including downsizing and closing of military bases. And that is a Socialist/Communist tactic for taking over an industrial nation. Now a tactic of Agenda 21. Decrease and demoralize the military.

Christian: This nation was founded on Christian principles that are as valid today as they were then. But over time and mostly within the past five decades, Christianity has been left behind, not taught and fought against. Socialism has been an instrument in distracting the younger generations. Formal, public, advance education of young adults may turn one from Christianity to worldly pursuits including Socialism/Communism. There is no God. There is only science. Moral standards may be left behind.

I give the following evidence on the founding:

The establishment of a Day of Thanks Issued by President George Washington by the request of Congress, on 3 October 1789 By the President of the United States of America, a Proclamation

Whereas it is the duty of all nations to acknowledge the providence of Almighty God, to obey His will, to be grateful for His benefits, and humbly to implore His protection and favor; and Whereas both Houses of Congress have, by their joint committee, requested me "to recommend to the people of the United States a day of public thanksgiving and prayer, to be observed by acknowledging with grateful hearts the many and signal favors of Almighty God, especially by affording them an opportunity peaceably to establish a form of government for their safety and happiness.

Now, therefore, I do recommend and assign Thursday, the 26th day of November next, to be devoted by the people of these States to the service of that great and glorious Being, who is the beneficent author of all the good that was, that is, or that will be; that we may then all unite in rendering unto Him our sincere and humble thanks for His kind

I Could Have Been One

care and protection of the people of this country previous to their becoming a nation; for the signal and manifold mercies and the favor, able interpositions of the providence in the course and conclusion of the late war; for the great degree of tranquility, union, and plenty which we have since enjoyed; for the peaceable and rational manner in which we have been enabled to establish constitutions of government for our safety and happiness, and particularly the national and now lately instituted , for the civil and religious liberty with which we are blessed, and the means we have of acquiring and diffusing useful knowledge and in general for all the great and various favors which He has been please to confer upon us.

And also that we may then unite in most humbly offering our prayers and supplications to the great Lord and Ruler of Nations, and beseech Him to pardon our national and other transgressions; to enable us all, whether in public or private stations, to perform our several and relative duties properly and punctually; to render our National Government a blessing to all the people by constantly being a Government of wise, just and constitutional laws, discreetly and faithfully executed and obeyed; to protect and guide all sovereigns and nations (especially such as have shown kindness to us) and to bless them with good governments, peace, and concord; to promote the knowledge and practice of true religion and virtue, and the increase of science among them and us, and, generally, to grant unto all mankind such a degree of temporal prosperity as He alone knows to be best.

The End

Conservative: Traditions, customs, etiquette, values, respect, manners, social graces, ritual, belief in individual freedom. Such things are not being taught and practiced as much as they once were. Such things are for the good of a free society, but not for a totalitarian society. In a free society, such things are what maintains order for the good of all especially respect. Respect is the basis for how one conducts themselves in relation to other people. Its foundation is do unto others as you would have them do unto you.

If a person has respect for themselves and others, they will perform their work well, to the best of their ability and not do just what they can get by with. They will go the extra step to finish the work with pride in what they do. Pride is both positive and negative. Pride and respect can go hand in hand and be a positive combination. Then there is false pride and also an excess of pride, both of which are negative. False pride is pretending to be proud of one's work, when one feels it is not as good as it should be. It can also be the feeling that one is better than someone else; arrogant. Excess of pride is ego driven; too much ego. There was a saying of "Whatever you do, do it well." If one respects themselves and others, they will. They will also have pride in one's self, home, surroundings and environment as in keeping clean and presentable.

However, it seems that some younger people believe that they may do as they want no manner how it affects other people. A good example of that occurred during the COVID 19 pandemic in some places. Spring Break was going to happen no matter what. It is part of the entitlement attitude. They believe they are entitled to do and say whatever and however they want with no one counteracting it. They are above the law, regulations and policies. Life owes them a free living simply because they exist and it is called social justice. They believe they are entitled to a free lunch.

Patriotic: Although some people, over the course of American history, have not been patriotic for the country they live in, which grants them freedom, there was usually a good amount of patriotism. In 1939, 20,000 attend-

I Could Have Been One

ees, at Madison Square Garden in New York City used President George Washington's Birthday for a so-called pro-American rally. It was to actually celebrate the rise of Adolf Hitler as leader of Germany. They used an image of Washington centered between two swastika flags. It was an American Socialist N.A.Z.I. event. Online reference used (rarehistoricalphotos.com/American Nazi organization rally Madison Square Garden 1939). A whole lot more than 20,000 enlisted in the American Armed Forces to fight the Nazis. Teachers taught patriotism in schools and it was taught at home. This was the Land of the Free and it was celebrated and defended. "For God and Country" was heard. Not today. Today American history is not taught to teach patriotism. The Socialist won't allow it as one cannot have patriotism to its nation because that means the patriotic will not fall in line and follow where the Socialists lead, which is to the breakdown of nations. All hail the State! As in the Communist/Socialist State.

Earns one way: What?! That is against "Entitlement". Against free welfare, free housing, free food. Free, free, free. Free lunch! Well guess what. If Socialism takes this Country, eventually all that free stuff will end and those who can will work or starve, for the sake of Sustainability.

Be of value: Value to one's self through being self-supporting providing one's own residence, food, clothing, transportation. Being of support to one's family and helping one's neighbors or those in need. Being a person practicing high moral standards. Educating one's self, to better one's life and be aware of one's world down to the local community. There are still those who want to work and not be on welfare, although they might receive more on welfare than by employment. In Socialism, one's mandated priority is to be of value to the State and not one's self.

Contribute to the community: An extension of being of value, by being involved with one's communities of faith, service organizations, government to keep it positive, children's activities such as sports or theatre and projects to assist others. Such activity helps to develop one's potential, skills and abilities. Not good as Socialism wants one to only be involved in what will advance the State. No time for such extra activities. Only approved activities will be allowed. So right now the younger generations, of adults, are given various forms of entertainment instead. Service organizations and cultural societies are declining in membership and not gaining new young members. At one time, it was a generational custom. Now the young people are mostly not interested in joining anything. The same people are continuously operating in leadership positions and becoming drained and also dying off. Some of those attending the meetings do not want to be involved as they just want the social aspect of the group. Some will be involved in the activities, but not the leadership. They do not want the responsibility or are too busy. I dare say this is such an impact that unless this changes such organizations and societies will cease to exist and this country will not be the better for it.

Anti-Communist environment: Now it is an anti-Socialism environment, which is declining due to the lack of caring by the younger generations, who are not being taught about true Socialism and think it is simply helping people.

The road to the negative:

Girls want to be Boy Scouts. "Time" online reference "boy-scouts-girls-lawsuit-history": It was the case of an eight year old girl suing the Boy Scouts, for entry into their organization, claiming they had more fun than the Girl Scouts. She wanted to do activities like camping. At least that is how I remember it. Decades ago, that girl's two older brothers were both Boy Scouts and her parents were leaders in the Scouting program. The girl would join her family at Scouting events and her parents applied for her to actually join the Boy Scouts Cub Pack, which she did. Her family was known and involved. Then the time came for an overnight camping trip and the leadership realized she was actually a girl and the ordeal began. A lawsuit was filed and lost. Now the Boy Scouts have admitted girls, transgenders and gay Scoutmasters and have gone bankrupt due to child sex abuse lawsuits. The admitted transgenders were teenage boys. There is a reason why the organizations were called the "Boy" and the "Girl" Scouts. What a mess! Admitting gay men, who practiced the lifestyle, was like giving them a play yard full of young playmates. My Scoutmasters were married. And that was way before same-sex-marriage.

Same-sex-marriage: I voted for them to have "domestic rights". Actually that should be "domestic privileges". However, marriage is for the nesting environment in which a family is produced and nurtured. It should have moral value. The gays and lesbians obtained domestic privileges, but that was not enough. They then wanted marriage, when domestic privileges already gave them the same as married couples had, except for a legal ritual giving them the married status. They pushed for that. In California, they were denied it by the majority vote of the citizens. They filed an appeal and finally were granted same-sex-marriage. Then some of them decided they wanted a church to perform the ritual. Thankfully it was explained to them, by California, that the law granted only civil marriage and not religious. So then they began to go to retail businesses known to be owned by Christians and wanting to obtain the services of such businesses such as a bakery. When denied on the basis of moral values, they sued and won. That was the attack on Christian owned businesses and freedom of religion. The gay/lesbian movement is being used by the Liberals, who are being used by the Socialists, to attack Christianity, in general. What a mess!

There are also spinoff effects. Now the U.S. government is issuing passports which have been redesigned to provide for same-sex-marriage couples. AND, if children are involved, the passport also provides for not only the birth parents, but also a second mother or father, if one of the couple is the birth parent. If the child(ren) is/are adopted, provision is made for a second mother or father. Yes, same-sex-marriage couples can adopt. And what moral values will those children be taught? What a mess!

Adults wanted to be the opposite gender than they were born as. Oh... wait...I guess that now it is adults and teens. A girl feels like a boy mentally, physically and emotionally? And vice versa. Now, with advanced science, one may physically change their sex. To me, this is another mess. Just because science provides the how there are the ethical/moral aspects of the why and when. True story. A high school student was sitting with a group of other students. Members of the group began forming opinions as to who they observed beyond themselves was heterosexual or homosexual. Some, in the group, stated that he or she over there was defiantly one or the other, but some observed were declared as "they are, but they just don't know it yet" people. Really? What a way to relax and spend free time; making judgements on a person's sexual future. What a mess!

Public restrooms can have no restrictions anymore. It is not the place of the government to decide what the people want and try to force it on them. It is the result of the voting poll place to decide that, by majority rule and even then it may, in fact, not be the result it should be. Again ethics/morals are an aspect of such decision making. But in California, the voters were not involved; only the legislature. What a mess!

Elementary school children are taught about the physical aspects of sex. Gee...no wonder teenagers sit and decide who is what. Elementary aged children do not need to know such information nor should middle school aged children unless it is provided by the parents. High school yes and it should include not just the physical, but also the mental and emotional as in cause and effect and responsibility. And porn should not be used as a visual aid!

According to some agency or organization some food item is bad for us. Enough so that it seems as though all food is bad for us one way or another. I remember people saying America was obese. Really? Where did they find all of those overweight people, in order to state the whole country was obese? The definition, by the way, is "extremely overweight". Some overweight is actually normal such as middle-age spread, of both men and women. Sometimes genetics are involved. Can bad eating habits be involved? Yes. Can a lack of health and dietary education be involved? Yes. Can common sense not be involved? Yes. Can a disorder be involved? Yes. Are there people who are grossly overweight? Yes. Are there people as skinny as a rail? Yes. Are most people somewhere between those two extremes? Yes. Does all of that follow the bell curve? I would think so. So just how did some people decide the whole country was obese and needed to go on a diet plan? Who are these people who decided they know what is best for everyone?

My guess is they are well educated, specialized, professional people, who are so focused they have blinders on and do not consider the whole picture. Therefore they do not have all the required information to make a proper decision and also qualify it and then take a proper course of action. So even food is a mess these days. What was wrong with the three previous food groups? Mama Mia! Is ice cream considered to be in the dairy or the dessert food group?

Math is now taught a different way, in some places, so if a student obtains the correct answer they still might be wrong. That is Common Core. Another Socialist idea to find the elite thinker for future grooming. No independent thinkers allowed. There is plenty of pro and con material online to study. Truth is the federal government, under a pretense, orchestrated the development of what became Common Core and presented it to the States using it as Relief from No Child Left Behind and used denial of federal funding to intimidate and used the possibility of federal funding for implementing Common Core to bribe. This was done while the State legislatures were in recess and with a deadline for accepting Common Care that was before the recess was scheduled to end. This was under the Obama Administration. Four States never adopted Common Core Standards, while five did adopt and later repealed the Standards and one State partially adopted the Standards. However, other

States also took anti-Common Core measures one way or another and there was also a lot of backlash against Common Core by both teachers and parents. What a mess!

The Speaker of the House, Pelosi, stated, "First we will pass the bill and then we will find out what is in it." Really!? That is not how the system works! But it was not read and it was passed. Pelosi also threatened the political careers of those Representatives who did not blindly follow her tactic to achieve what Obama wanted. He was implementing a Socialist plan. And it was later discovered some of what was in the Bill had nothing to do with healthcare, as in Socialist planning items to further Agenda 21. And there has been problems with the insurance system as established under the Bill since the beginning. What a mess that is!

People have to more and more get a license, a permit, a certificate or something for permission or pay a fee or tax in order to do something involving their life. Some of it is good and some not so. Overreach of government, in some cases?

The Founding Fathers did not want an overreach of government. That is why the Second Amendment was included. Nor did they intend to have career politicians spending their whole life in Congress. It was the custom, in those days, for a person to serve their country in Congress and then go home.

Personal property was once the American dream and now it is being restricted by regulation. To purchase a piece of property, it once took only a few pieces of paper and could be done seller to buyer. Now is takes a stack of paperwork and a real estate specialist due to all of the legal aspects involved, with official and certified inspectors for this and that. There is a reason for it all and it is not good.

Those who are not here legally have better opportunities for advance education than citizens do. Legal immigrants may be granted money, by the government, to start a retail business, while a citizen has to meet restrictive requirements in order to obtain the some type of business. Or so I am told, but in this upside down world I lean toward believing it.

Women and so-called minorities can sue for entrance to private educational institutions and private clubs traditionally men's, but if an institution or an organization is private and for women or minorities only, then men or white folk are not allowed. Or so it seems.

The noted New York City Saint Patrick's Day Parade, which is a cultural event, was invaded by homosexuals and other alternate sexual lifestyle people. The New Orleans Mardi Gras, which is also or was a cultural event, has become an avenue for drunkenness and sexual behavior.

Seems like every time one turns around men have been given a different… what…description? There has been macho, getting in touch with their feminine side, metrosexual, getting back to being protective and I don't know what else by now. Me, I am simply a man. Period. None of the above. I am acceptable or not and I do not care which.

What was considered polite and respectful is now considered demeaning by some women such as holding a door open for a woman. I once got a look of strong disdain from a woman when I held the door for her. I stopped opening doors for women unless I knew them. It has nothing to do with thinking a woman cannot do it herself.

More messes!

The feminist movement said women have to get out of the house and into professions. Shouldn't that be up to the woman? If a married couple has children, more money can be brought into the family budget by both being employed, but there might be expenses for childcare and transportation, for both are required. What is earned is spent. Families began to have two vehicles. Remember the "lock key" situation of children going home, after school, and spending time home along until a parent arrived. Women were to develop themselves into what the men were; the bread provider. Women became known as such. Women became independent. I am not saying women should not have a profession, if they want to. I am simply saying it is not always a simple matter. There are pros and cons and just because a women does not work outside of the home does not mean she is not a worthwhile person; that she is not an independent spirit. Also…women, volunteering for various causes, have been good for this country's cultural life; performing arts, beautification, historical, community positions, literary, etc. There are many ways for a person to be of value.

Some women began to say marriage was legalized prostitution. And there are some women who hate men. Some have reason to. Once bitten; twice shy. But not all men are like the one that caused the hate. Bad things also happen to men, in their relationships with women. By the way, the same can happen with gay and lesbian couples. In fact, it was a gay man who stated that normally gays do not stay together long, as they are always looking for another affair. That gay man had been in a relationship for decades and was the exception to the unwritten rule. His partner has now passed over. They were together until death.

There is the movement of women more and more going into various professions including those traditionally a men's such as firefighter, law enforcement, including the field of politics. Nothing wrong with that. However, the Socialists are quick to get women and minorities involved with their own movement. Even if a person is not a card-carrying Socialist, it does not mean they are not involved with and working for the Socialist cause. Even if they think they are just helping others. I would think women involve other women and minorities involve other minorities under the banner of "We have to stick together and advance our people and or our gender. All for the Sisterhood". That within itself is not a bad thing. Proper advancement has been obtained in such a manner. What is a bad thing can be how one is used to obtain the objectives and goals of an unknown entity or a front operation that appears to be very worthwhile.

I Could Have Been One

There are two types of purges; one, historical and two, physical. We have known historical purge right here in our own Country, in the destruction and removal by Liberals of Civil War reminders such as statues memorializing the bravery of men who fought for the Confederacy. Such Liberals are following one way or another what the Socialist/Communist wants, under the excuse that the reminders offend black people. It is pitting blacks against whites. Our past did indeed happen. It is there forever. Removing reminders of it does not remove the history itself. The past whether positive or negative must be learned from as to what to do or not do. There are also those writers of revisional history. They try to rewrite history according to their own agenda for a cause; a cause to change what happened in the past or delete it altogether. Before we had false news, we had false history writing. What happened in the past cannot be changed. It is there in our history. Physical is the type Bella received. Another example of physical purging is that of Russian Communist leader Joseph Stalin, who is known to have been a mass murderer, of those he felt was a threat to either himself or Communism or both, and, in 1933, imposed famine on the Ukraine killing off people because they did not agree with him.

The older generation grew up being taught not only the alphabet, spelling and sentence structure, but also hand writing. Since then, type writers evolved into memory writers. Next came processors also known as small computers. And finally computers themselves. The common element in them all is the keyboard. I am speaking of the coming about of business and personal computers.

Some people, in the field of education, believe hand writing should not be taught in school any longer, since that artful skill will not be required for anything. Therefore it is not being taught. There is also talk that one day there will no longer be any books or newspapers as all of those will be computerized. A future society is being developed based on computer technology. How will libraries change? Even though libraries are being reinvented for this and that community program, will it simply become a headquarters for such programs without the written media? As us older folks die off and are replaced by the younger generations, I guess that could happen. I guess such things as handwritten letters, typewriters or even computer typed letters will end up in museums.

For a person of one country to enter another country, by not going through the legal process, is illegal. They disobey and break the law of the country being entered. That is called a crime, by Federal law. They become a criminal by doing so. These days it seems as though such people can break the law without any repercussions as they are granted sanctuary, in cities and states called sanctuary cities and sanctuary states. Why is that allowed? By aiding and abetting, the city or state becomes a law breaker and should have repercussions taken on it. Why is it happening? Can anyone see an Agenda 21 connection?

I had heard that once upon a time the color for the Republican Party was blue and the color for the Democrat Party was red. I began to wonder why the switch. I wonder if it had to do with red being the color of the Communist Party. I found the following article.

When Republicans were blue and Democrats were red: Online reference. By Jodi Enda, SMITHSONIANMAG.COM, OCTOBER 31, 2012

Television's first dynamic, color-coded presidential map, standing two stories high in the studio best known as the home to *Saturday Night Live*, was melting. It was early October, 1976, the month before the map was to debut—live—on election night. At the urging of anchor John Chancellor, NBC had constructed the behemoth map to illustrate, in vivid blue and red, which states supported Republican incumbent Gerald Ford and which backed Democratic challenger Jimmy Carter. The test run didn't go well. Although the map was buttressed by a sturdy wood frame, the front of each state was plastic. "There were thousands of bulbs," recalled Roy Wetzel, then the newly minted general manager of NBC's election unit. "The thing started to melt when we turned all the lights on. We then had to bring in gigantic interior air conditioning and fans to put behind the thing to cool it." That solved the problem. And when election results flowed in Tuesday night, Nov. 2, Studio 8-H at 30 Rockefeller Center lit up. Light bulbs on each state changed from undecided white to Republican blue and Democratic red. NBC declared Carter the winner at 3:30 a.m. EST, when Mississippi turned red.

That's right: In the beginning, blue was red and red was blue and they changed back and forth from election to election and network to network in what appears, in hindsight, to be a flight of whimsy. The notion that there were "red states" and "blue states"—and that the former were Republican and the latter Democratic—wasn't cemented on the national psyche until the year 2000.

And everybody had to continue doing it for a long time. The 2000 election dragged on until mid-December, until the Supreme Court declared Bush the victor. For weeks, the maps were ubiquitous. Perhaps that's why the 2000 colors stuck. Along with images of Florida elections officials eyeballing tiny ballot chads, the maps were there constantly, reminding us of the vast, nearly even divide between, well, red and blue voters.

Here's something else we know: All the maps—on TV stations and websites election night and in newspapers the next morning—will look alike. We won't have to switch our thinking as we switch channels, wondering which candidate is blue and which is red. Before the epic election of 2000, there was no uniformity in the maps that television stations, newspapers or magazines used to illustrate presidential elections. Pretty much everyone embraced red and blue, but which color represented which party varied, sometimes by organization, sometimes by election cycle.

There are theories, some likely, some just plain weird, to explain the shifting palette. "For years, both parties would do red and blue maps, but they always made the other guys red," said Chuck Todd, political director and chief

White House correspondent for NBC News. "During the Cold War, who wanted to be red?" Indeed, prior to the breakup of the Soviet Union little more than two decades ago, "red was a term of derision," noted Mitchell Stephens, a New York University professor of journalism and author of *A History of News*. "There's a movie named *Reds*," he said. "You'd see red in tabloid headlines, particularly in right wing tabloids like the *Daily Mirror* in New York and the *New York Daily News*. CBS News split the country into regions and used a color-coded map, with blue for Republicans and red for Democrats. (YouTube)

Perhaps the stigma of red in those days explains why some networks changed colors— in what appeared to be random fashion—over the years. Still, there were reversals and deviations. In 1976, when NBC debuted its mammoth electronic map, ABC News employed a small, rudimentary version that used yellow for Ford, blue for Carter and red for states in which votes had yet to be tallied. In 1980, NBC once again used red for Carter and blue for the Republican challenger, Ronald Reagan, and CBS followed suit. But ABC flipped the colors and promised to use orange for states won by John Anderson, the third-party candidate who received 6.6% of the popular vote. (Anderson carried no states, and orange seems to have gone by the wayside.) Four years later, ABC and CBS used red for Republicans and blue for Democrats, but the combination wouldn't stick for another 16 years. During the four presidential elections Wetzel oversaw for NBC, from 1976 through 1988, the network never switched colors. Republicans were cool blue, Democrats hot red.

The reasoning was simple, he said: Great Britain. "Without giving it a second thought, we said blue for conservatives, because that's what the parliamentary system in London is, red for the more liberal party. And that settled it. We just did it," said Wetzel, now retired. Forget all that communist red stuff, he said. "It didn't occur to us. When I first heard it, I thought, 'Oh, that's really silly.'"

When ABC produced its first large electronic map in 1980, it used red for Republicans and blue for Democrats, while CBS did the reverse, according to Wetzel. NBC stuck with its original color scheme, prompting anchor David Brinkley to say that Reagan's victory looked like "a suburban swimming pool." Newspapers, in those days, were largely black and white. But two days after voters went to the polls in 2000, both the *New York Times* and *USA Today* published their first color-coded, county-by-county maps detailing the showdown between Al Gore and George W. Bush. Both papers used red for the Republican Bush, blue for the Democrat Gore. Why?

"I just decided *red* begins with 'r,' *Republican* begins with 'r.' It was a more natural association," said Archie Tse, senior graphics editor for the *Times*. "There wasn't much discussion about it."

Paul Overberg, a database editor who designed the map for USA Today, said he was following a trend: "The reason I did it was because everybody was already doing it that way at that point." From an aesthetic standpoint, Overberg said, the current color scheme fits with the political landscape. Republicans typically dominate in larger, less populated states in the Plains and Mountain West, meaning the center of the United States is very red. "If it had been flipped, the map would have been too dark," he said. "The blue would have been swamping the red. Red is a lighter color." But not everyone liked the shift. Republican operative Clark Bensen wrote an analysis in 2004 titled "RED STATE BLUES: Did I Miss That Memo?"

"There are two general reasons why blue for Republican and Red for Democrat make the most sense: connotation and practice," Bensen wrote.

> First, there has been a generally understood meaning to the two colors inasmuch as they relate to politics. That is, the cooler color blue more closely represented the rational thinker and cold-hearted and the hotter red more

closely red for Democrats. Put another way, red was also the color most associated with socialism and the party of the Democrats was clearly the more socialistic of the two major parties. The second reason why blue for Republicans makes sense is that traditional political mapmakers have used blue for the modern-day Republicans, and the Federalists before that, throughout the 20th century. Perhaps this was a holdover from the days of the Civil War when the predominantly Republican North was "Blue."

At this point—three presidential elections after *Bush v. Gore*—the color arrangement seems unlikely to reverse any time soon. Not only have "red states" and "blue states" entered the lexicon, partisans on both sides have taken ownership of them. For instance, RedState is a conservative blog; Blue State Digital, which grew out of Democrat Howard Dean's 2004 presidential campaign, helps candidates and organizations use technology to raise money, advocate their positions and connect with constituents. In 2008, a Republican and a Democrat even joined forces to create Purple Strategies, a bipartisan public affairs firm.

Sara Quinn, a visual journalist now at the Poynter Institute in Florida, said she sees no particular advantage to either color. "Red is usually very warm and it comes forward to the eye. Blue tends to be a recessive color, but a calming color," she said. Not that anyone thought of those things when assigning colors in 2000. Not that they think about it at all today.

"After that election the colors became part of the national discourse, " said Tse. "You couldn't do it any other way."

The End.

Personally I still believe the Socialist did not want the stigma of the color red, for the Democrat Party and finally were able to have it attached to the Republican Party.

Okay…I do believe I have covered enough upside-down examples for the reader to get the idea.

So American society is no longer a white male dominated society. Societies do change, as demonstrated by our ancestor's time periods, and hopefully for the better. Sometimes not. They do not change by generation, but over time, by new ways of doing things and new inventions and new philosophies of how people should think intruding upon traditional thinking.

There is now an orchestrated movement of change. It can turn us upside down so we will get used to change and say, "Oh well." Then when the big change comes, we will say, "Oh well." It is for the setting of aspects of life against one another such as women against men, so-called black and brown against so-called white, alternate sexual life style against traditional, non-God believer against God believer, illegal against legal, deletion of private property and totalitarian government against republic of freedom.

These are all pieces of the same puzzle that when taken all together and in view of the overall picture, one begins to see how this piece fits with that piece and that piece with those pieces and those with other pieces until the whole picture is together. A picture of hell.

In truth, the only winners in the picture are those of the elite who believe that, through the use of their ego, they know what is best for everyone in the whole wide world; on the whole globe, in every continent, from pole to pole and around the equator. They believe because all but two very small nations are represented in their United Nations organization they should govern the whole globe and without any independent nations. That all should be under their rule of law. Note: The U.N. does not call them countries or nations, but states.

They will continue to try to divide and conquer or legislate until everyone is bound and gagged by regulation until every nation is molded into their own image. In researching the U.N. membership, I noticed that although Taiwan is an independent country, for the purposes of the U.N., it is considered as represented by the U.N. member country of Communist China.

However, we must not fear the future, for God Himself holds the future in His own hands. If we have fear, we become paralyzed in the present and do nothing to have the future we want. The future we should have in following the teachings and examples of Jesus Christ, by being active to achieve that future. There is a saying, "God helps those who helps themselves." That is the aspect of our God given freewill. We can do nothing or something. Bottom line though is God holds the future and He will judge us all accordingly.

The First Epistle of Peter or First Peter also addresses trials and tribulations. (Online reference insight.org: First Peter.)

Who wrote the book?

The first word of this epistle, *Peter*, identifies the author, who called himself "an apostle of Jesus Christ" (1 Peter 1:1). He wrote this letter to a group of Christians scattered throughout the northern areas of Asia Minor, where he may have previously preached the gospel.

Peter wrote to a group of people that probably included both Jews and Gentiles. The apostle addressed the letter's recipients as "aliens" (1:1), a word indicating that Peter was speaking not just to Jews or just to Gentiles but to Christians who were living their lives in such a way that they would have stood out as aliens among the surrounding culture.

Where are we?

In this letter, Peter spoke much about persecution, which anticipated the persecution he and other Christians would endure in the final years of Nero's reign. At the time he wrote, Peter had not yet been arrested, an event that would lead to his martyrdom around AD 66–68. First Peter 5:13 indicates that Peter sent greetings from the local church—calling it

"Babylon"—but it's most likely that the apostle was writing in a common metaphor there. He used the name of the ancient Mesopotamian city as a stand-in for Rome, the modern city that, like Babylon, gave itself over to idol worship and false gods. While the fact is not recorded in the Bible, Peter has long been thought to have spent his final years serving the church in Rome. Based on the numerous references to suffering and persecution in this letter, Peter likely wrote in AD 64, just as the persecution of Christians under Nero was ramping up.

Why is First Peter so important?
First Peter focuses on the importance of believers bearing up under unjust suffering yet continuing to live well (1 Peter 2:20). In this way, 1 Peter might be called the Job of the New Testament, providing encouragement for the true believer to continue on in the way that Jesus has laid out for all His followers. The endurance Peter called these believers to is similar to Job's, a man who suffered despite his righteousness. Peter maintained that this was the kind of true perseverance that God expects from His people.

What's the big idea?
Living in close proximity to Jesus Christ for more than three years had provided the apostle Peter the best possible example of what it looked like to live in holiness amid a hostile world. More than any other man who walked the earth, Jesus modeled that lifestyle. Peter therefore pointed his readers in the best possible direction, to Jesus Himself. The apostle called Christians to "sanctify Christ as Lord" in their hearts, that believers might live and act as Jesus desires during their short time here on earth (1 Peter 3:14–18). This would include submission to authority—even unjust authority—in the government, in the home, and in the workplace. Jesus becomes the focal point for ordering one's life in the midst of trials and tribulations. By rooting their

perseverance in the person and work of Christ, believers can always cling to hope in the midst of suffering.

How do I apply this?

Unjust or unforeseen suffering is one of the great problems that grips the hearts of people today. We struggle with frustration, anger, and uncertainty when trials strange and unexpected land on our doorsteps. Too often in those most difficult moments of our lives, confusion reigns while contentment wanes; questions arise while prayer subsides.

How do you react when suffering comes?

Many crumble at the mere thought of another pain or trial. Others rise to the occasion. Most of us are probably somewhere in between. Peter's encouragement to his Christian readers is one of perseverance in faith. It isn't enough for us to simply get up every morning and trudge through each day; neither is it advisable to paste a smile on our faces and ignore troubles. Instead, the lesson of 1 Peter is to push through the troubles, recognizing their temporary presence in our lives while walking in holiness and hope as people of faith.

Additional Thoughts Referencing

I purposely did not include the following comments in the text of the page referenced due to not wanting to interrupt the continuance of the line of thought occurring at the time, for the reader. So I present those comments now.

Page 3 bottom: Please notice that I use "German" and "Nazi" together. That is because the German Army was composed of troops who were not members of the Nazi Party. They were German troops, including commanders, under the control of the Nazi high command. Some generals were career military, while some were Nazis appointed to their positions. It was the Nazis, under Hitler, who had control, with the non-Nazis following because they believed in what Hitler was doing or because they wanted to advance Germany, after the effects of World War I, or because they felt trapped.

Today is the same situation. Socialists have infiltrated elements of American life such as our government, military, schools and are establishing NGOs to organize regional activity. It is not the people who are in control, but Socialists in key positions of influence just as the members of the NAZI Party were. If the Socialists take control of the Federal Government, the situation will be as NAZI Germany described above. Therefore the people need to take control by voting for those who will stand up for our liberties and God given rights. People also need to counteract any voter fraud.

Page 13 bottom, in reference to education:

The Scopes Trial, formally known as *The State of Tennessee v. John Thomas Scopes* and commonly referred to as the Scopes Monkey Trial, was an American legal case in July 1925 in which a substitute high school teacher, John T. Scopes, was accused of violating Tennessee's Butler Act, which had made it unlawful to teach human evolution in any state funded school; Darwin's theory of evolution, which was based on human evolving from apes, with a missing link between the two species. The following is from online reference History.com. I have included it in whole so as to also give the atmosphere of the time.

In Dayton, Tennessee, the so-called Scopes Monkey Trial begins with John Thomas Scopes, a young high school science teacher, accused of teaching evolution in violation of a Tennessee state law.

The law, which had been passed in March, made it a misdemeanor punishable by fine to "teach any theory that denies the story of the Divine Creation of man as taught in the Bible, and to teach instead that man has descended from a lower order of animals." With local businessman George Rappleyea, Scopes had conspired to get charged with this violation, and after his arrest the pair enlisted the aid of the American Civil Liberties Union (ACLU) to organize a defense. Hearing of this coordinated attack on Christian fundamentalism, William Jennings Bryan, the three-time Democratic presidential candidate and a fundamentalist hero, volunteered to assist the prosecution. Soon after, the great attorney Clarence Darrow agreed to join the ACLU in the defense, and the stage was set for one of the most famous trials in U.S. history.

On July 10, the Monkey Trial got underway, and within a few days hordes of spectators and reporters had descended on Dayton as preachers set up revival tents along the city's main street to keep the faithful stirred up. Inside the Rhea County Courthouse, the defense suffered early setbacks when Judge John Raulston ruled against their attempt to prove the law unconstitutional and then refused to end his practice of opening each day's proceeding with prayer.

Outside, Dayton took on a carnival-like atmosphere as an exhibit featuring two chimpanzees and a supposed "missing link" opened in town, and vendors sold Bibles, toy monkeys, hot dogs, and lemonade. The missing link was in fact Jo Viens of Burlington, Vermont, a 51-year-old man who was of short stature and possessed a receding forehead and a protruding jaw. One of the chimpanzees–named Joe Mendi–wore a plaid suit, a brown fedora, and white spats, and entertained Dayton's citizens by monkeying around on the courthouse lawn.

In the courtroom, Judge Raulston destroyed the defense's strategy by ruling that expert scientific testimony on evolution was inadmissible–on the grounds that it was Scopes who was on trial, not the law he had violated. The next day, Raulston ordered the trial moved to the courthouse lawn, fearing that the weight of the crowd inside was in danger of collapsing the floor.

In front of several thousand spectators in the open air, Darrow changed his tactics and as his sole witness called Bryan in an attempt to discredit his literal interpretation of the Bible. In a searching examination, Bryan was subjected to severe ridicule and forced to make ignorant and contradictory statements to the amusement of the crowd. On July 21, in his closing speech, Darrow asked the jury to return a verdict of guilty in order that the case might be appealed. Under Tennessee law, Bryan was thereby denied the opportunity to deliver the closing speech he had been preparing for weeks. After eight minutes of deliberation, the jury returned with a guilty verdict, and Raulston ordered Scopes to pay a fine of $100, the minimum the law allowed. Although Bryan had won the case, he had been publicly humiliated and his fundamentalist beliefs had been disgraced. Five days later, on July 26, he lay down for a Sunday afternoon nap and never woke up.

In 1927, the Tennessee Supreme Court overturned the Monkey Trial verdict on a technicality but left the constitutional issues unresolved until 1968, when the U.S. Supreme Court overturned a similar Arkansas law on the grounds that it violated the First Amendment.

So evolution of humans may be taught in schools. The creation as stated in the Bible of course may not. It is up to the churches and Christian parents to teach how both creation and evolution coincide; God created and the human species evolved.

Page 19: "'Eisenhower' is as much and no more to the left than were Landon, Willkie and Dewey. In a two-party system, under normal conditions, both parties play as close to the center as possible. This leaves both the Republican right and the Democratic left dissatisfied but since they have nowhere else to go they exercise no leverage. At the moment, while the Republicans are thus 'left,' the Democrats are 'right.' In fact some of them are shopping around for a more conservative candidate...."

It would seem directional terms of "right" and "left" were used back in the 1950s and that the two political Parties would switch positions depending on the political factors involved at any given time, by which each Party believed they could win the popular vote. I am thinking a lot of moderate politicking was being conducted at the time, with no far right or left. Politics had not arrived at the Far Right or Far Left or Socialism versus Conservative yet. AND it truly is now Socialism versus Conservative.

Page 22 top: I could not care less what he did as the important issue is what he said. "We will bury you from within!!!!!"

That was in reference to what Nikita Khrushchev stated at the United Nations, in speaking to America. He knew of the Communist plan to take and overthrow America. Remember it was their heyday time. He was sure the Communists would succeed due to the plan's infiltrating and undermining our education and organizations and trade unions, etc.

22 bottom: It was also a time of political revolution, in the United States, as demonstrated by the anti-war riot, at the 1968 Democratic Convention, in Chicago. Anti-war protests were prevalent on college campuses. However, the one held at Kent State University, on May 4, 1970, by approximately five hundred students, resulting in the shooting and deaths of students, by the Ohio Army National Guard, was the most noted because of its tragedy. Now all of those involved, of both student and Guardsmen, including their families, have to live with that day for the rest of their lives. In the words of Forrest Gump, "That is all I am going to say about that." Reference movie *Forrest Gump*, with Tom Hanks.

The order to open fire, on the students by the military, was never given. Investigation showed the Guardsmen had never been in combat or any kind of hostile engagement much less an encounter with their own people. There was confusion and the students were throwing glass bottles at the military. A bottle landed close to a Guardsmen. He thought his unit was being fired upon and he therefore, without an order being given, opened fire and his fellow Guardsmen thought they were supposed to open fire and did so as well.

Page 23: In 1961, the Berlin Wall was constructed while Berliners were fast asleep. When they woke up the next morning, whatever side of the wall

I Could Have Been One

they went to sleep on was where they were to stay. West Berliners, in the American and English and French sectors, of post WWII Germany, could no longer travel into the Russian sector, to visit relatives and friends. Likewise East Berliners could no longer travel into West Berlin for visiting and attending cultural and sports events. There was travel between the East and West, but it was highly limited and controlled. One had to be traveling on official business. Online reference ThoughtCo "Rise and Fall of the Berlin Wall".

Although the Cold War, between the United States of America along with other western countries such as England, and the Union of Soviet Socialist Republics also known as Communist Russia now known as the Commonwealth of Independent States, began as soon as WWII ended and Russia began to isolate their occupied sector of East Germany. Soon the Wall presented both a physical and symbolic separation between Communist Russia and the "Free World". Later it would be torn down.

This is how Communists/Socialists think. They did not ask who wanted to be on what side of the wall or even inform the public there would be a wall. They just did it. They wanted and maintained control of the people. Such underhanded, deviousness can occur today, even if they say it will not. We go to sleep and they shackle us.

Page 24: Both teens and young adults are impressionable and do not have a lot of life experience. They live in the here and now sometimes not giving a care to the future, but just going through the process of trying to be independent and go one's own way. Some fail to realize their parents and grandparents and those of the older generations do have life experience to learn from. But sometimes one does not think about that, for it is as though the offspring never thinks about the fact the older generations were not always such; they were once young too. Even if the younger generation does factually realize it, they do not think about what that actually means.

That is why story telling of one's past is important to the younger generation, starting with when they are children. Stories of mistakes made, good decisions and what would have happened if the other option had been taken. Stories of good times and bad and how one enjoyed the good and endured the bad. We need to take the time to do that.

Page 25: Going to church was just something the family did, but why is that important to continue? What does all that stuff really mean anyway? I need a break. I want to just do my own thing. Therefore it needs to be taught why it is important. The child cannot just learn about Christianity. They have to be taught the meaning of Christianity and why they should follow Jesus.

A young, exceedingly intelligent man, who was intellectually burned out due to his prior position as a scientist did not believe in God and religion. He stated to me that religion is the opium of the masses. I replied it can be. However, Communism and Socialism can also be the opium of the masses and I believe it can be even more so because of its forceful techniques. Opium is addictive. So yes religion may be addictive, but in a positive way. Opium has a negative connotation. Religion operates on love and mercy, faith, hope and charity. Or at least it should. Some people might think of religious cults being forceful. Cults are not true religions as they are one person's ideology in operation for what they want to use their followers for and it can be forceful. It can be opium. Their followers follow them and not Jesus.

If the young have a good, solid foundation in Christianity, they will be able to withstand, with the help of Jesus, what the world will throw against them be it through a college professor, a coworker, a supposed friend or even a stranger in conversation. We cannot take their growing up for granted. Yes, they will physically and mentally mature, but they also need to mature emotionally and spiritually. It cannot be taken for granted that they will and leave them to their own devices in the world.

Page 25: While I was in the military, we received word that Russia was sending ships loaded with long range missiles, to Communist Cuba. This was a threat to American peace and welfare. President John F. Kennedy communicated with the U.S.S.R. President Khrushchev and finally issued orders for the US Navy to blockade Cuba against the Russian ships. If the Russian ships continued to sail for Cuba, they would be fired upon under the authority of the Monroe Doctrine, which states protection of the Americas from non-North, Central and South American sources. Khrushchev waited until the last minute to recall the ships back to their own country.

There was also a 1960s incident between the U.S. Navy and Communist China. International waters begin at three miles from a country's coastline, at least at that time. One of our naval ships was sailing outside of the three miles, off the coast of China, but within eleven miles of its coast. China contacted the ship and claimed coastal waters starting at the eleven mile mark. It instructed our ship to leave and sail beyond the eleven mile mark or be fired upon. Three Naval aircraft carrier task forces were assembled and sailed toward China and past the eleven mile mark. They commenced to sail between the eleven and the three mile mark waiting for China's shore batteries to fire on them. The batteries did not. The task forces sailed such a pattern day after day, for some time. After a decent amount of time, of challenging the Communist Chinese without incident, they sailed away to continue routine operations.

It was during the '60s that Fidel Castrol established a Communist Cuba and began to influence Central and South America. Freedom loving Cubans were braving the waters between their home country and the United States, to continue to live in freedom. It was the tide of freedom loving Cubans fleeing to the United States, from the tide of Communism in their home country.

First paragraph: The Monroe Doctrine is to be used against foreign invaders only. The freedoms granted by our own Constitution is being used against us as those same freedoms apply to even Americans who want to destroy our Constitution and Republic and way of life. Our enemy is from within.

Second paragraph: Both Communist and Socialist will push the envelope as far as they can to find out how far they can go before counteraction is presented. Remember as soon as Obama was in the Oval Office his administration wanted to establish a youth group from elementary to college level and a mandatory senior citizens community service and another reserve army? Guess what will happen under Communism/Socialism.

Third paragraph: Why were those freedom loving Cubans fleeing their own country and some dying during the flight just to come to America? What did they fear? Communism. What did they want their life to be? Lived in freedom. If we lost our freedom, where will we go? Where will they and their children and their children's children go? The Socialist takeover is for the whole world, under the United Nations.

Page 35: However, there was a school principal announcing at the first football game of the season, that government did not allow them to lead prayer, but anyone attending the game could. The whole stadium stood and prayed.

This is what I was sent in an email concerning that situation.

This is a statement that was read over the PA system at the football game at…High School…by the school Principal.

> "It has always been the custom at…High School football games, to say a prayer and play the National Anthem, to honor God and Country.
>
> Due to a recent ruling by the Supreme Court, I am told that saying a Prayer is a violation of Federal Case Law. As I understand the law at this time, I can use this public facility to approve of sexual perversion and call it 'an alternate lifestyle',

and if someone is offended, that's OK. I can use it to condone sexual promiscuity, by dispensing condoms and calling it, 'safe sex'. If someone is offended, that's OK. I can even use this public facility to present the merits of killing an unborn baby as a 'viable means of birth control'. If someone is offended, no problem. I can designate a school day as 'Earth Day' and involve students in activities to worship religiously and praise the goddess 'Mother Earth' and call it 'ecology'. I can use literature, videos and presentations in the classroom that depict people with strong, traditional Christian convictions as 'simple minded' and 'ignorant' and call it 'enlightenment'. However, if anyone uses this facility to honor GOD and to ask HIM to Bless this event with safety and good sportsmanship, then Federal Case Law is violated.

This appears to be inconsistent at best and, at worst, diabolical. Apparently, we are to be tolerant of everything and anyone, except GOD and HIS Commandments. Nevertheless, as a school principal, I frequently ask staff and students to abide by rules with which they do not necessarily agree. For me to do otherwise would be inconsistent at best and, at worst, hypocritical. I suffer from that affliction enough unintentionally. I certainly do not need to add an intentional transgression. For this reason, I shall 'Render unto Caesar that which is Caesar's', and refrain from praying at this time. However, if you feel inspired to honor, praise and thank GOD and ask HIM, in the name of JESUS, to Bless this event, please feel free to do so. As far as I know, that's not against the law...yet."

One by one, the people in the stands bowed their heads, held hands with one another and began to pray. They prayed in the stands. They prayed in the team huddles. They prayed at the concession stand and they prayed in the announcer's box!

The only place they didn't pray was in the Supreme Court of the United States of America - the Seat of "Justice" in the "one nation, under GOD."

Somehow ...remembered what so many have forgotten. We are given the Freedom OF Religion, not the Freedom *FROM Religion. Praise GOD that HIS remnant remains!*

This is a good example of Christian counteraction to anti-freedom of religion and freedom of speech laws. This is also a good example of the misuse of "separation of church and state". The First Amendment does not refer to anything about prayer not being allowed in public schools nor does it refer to anything except for the establishment of a national religion. This is also a good example of how people use the Constitution to their own agenda and twist what is meant by the wording of it. Another phase of the United States Constitution that is misused is "...for the common good."

There is another issue. Just as "separation of church and state" has led to misunderstanding either purposely or not, "prayer banned from school" has become the dominate understanding of what the Supreme Court did. It did not. The Supreme Court stated no school official may establish or mandate organized prayer and religious belief would not be forced on any student. I have two comments on that.

One, on 16 January 2020, President Trump defended students who feel they can't pray in their schools and warned school administrators they risk

I Could Have Been One

losing federal funds if they violate their students' rights to religious expression. Trump held an event in the Oval Office with a group of Christian, Jewish and Muslim students and teachers to commemorate National Religious Freedom Day. The students and teachers said they have been discriminated against for practicing their religion at school.

The U.S. Supreme Court banned school-sponsored prayer in public schools in a 1962 decision, saying that it violated the First Amendment. But students are allowed to meet and pray on school grounds as long as they do so privately and don't try to force others to do the same. Trump said the government must "never stand between the people and God" and said public schools too often stop students from praying and sharing their faith. "It is totally unacceptable," Trump said. "You see it on the football field. You see it so many times where they are stopped from praying and we are doing something to stop that." Online reference npr.org.

Two, in regards to Muslim influence on this country's educational system, Muslim countries made donations to American schools. The funding has the condition that educational material concerning the Muslim faith will be accepted by the school, for use in the classroom. Such books are, in effect, propaganda, teaching what the Muslims want American children, on into college, to believe.I read of one class in which a high school teacher who mandated that her class memorize the Five Pillars of Islam and teaching that the faith of a Muslim is stronger than the average Christian according to the federal lawsuit. It also stated the girl was forced to disparage her Christian faith by reciting the Shahada and acknowledging Mohammed as her spiritual leader. Shahada is the Islamic Creed, "There is no god by Allah, and Muhammad is the messenger of Allah." The creed is viewed as sufficient to be a conversion to Islam. Allegedly the students were also instructed that the Islamic religion is a fact, while Christianity and Judaism are just beliefs. According to a handout titled "Islam Today," the school served as apologists for the Islamic faith. The school also instructed students on "jihad," a holy war waged on behalf of Islam as a religious duty. This story and the Muslim influence is all online. (Online source Lawsuit: Public school forced my child to convert to Islam – Fox News)

Page 40: My friends were foreign students. We were together on another occasion, when some other students of my friends' home country were having a promotion for the Communist cause, in their home country. They were also fund raising. That was when I learned that people, of such a cause, are not necessarily Communist, in reality. They do not like the political/social/economic conditions of their country and would accept the financial and other assistance from either the United States or Communist Russia, who competed for alliance throughout the world.

It is the government of a country who might decide what a person hears on the news and what a person reads. Therefore that is what the person knows, which may or may not be the truth about the world or another country. And it may be that what is portrayed by a government is not what the people of that country believe and want. It is the government and not necessary the citizens that give the appearance of a country. Revolutionaries using an outside source, for assistance, may or may not be hardcore in believing the same as the assisting country. In the case of Iran, Russia wasted its money as Iran is still under Muslim control, with Muslim law.

Page 42: Chavez was very active politically fighting for farm workers' rights through the decades of the 1960s, '70s and '80s. He also influenced the 1986 Immigration and Reform Control Act, on related issues of U.S. farm workers. Online reference Wikipedia "Cesar Chavez".

Put the key words of "Cesar Chavez and Saul Alinsky" into your search engine and see all of the material that appears on the connection between those two men. Alinsky was assisting Chavez, with his organizing of the farm labor union. This does not mean Chavez himself was a Communist. It may only mean he accepted assistance from wherever he could get it.

I Could Have Been One

Page 45: In 1989, I was one of those Americans watching the television showing images of the Berlin Wall being torn down manually piece by piece as the Cold War was coming to an end, at least formally. I never thought of it ever being torn down, but it was. It came and it went twenty-eight years later.

But why was it torn down? What did the people who conducted the teardown and those who cheered them on want. What did they yearn for?

Background online reference History.com: In 1945, following Germany's defeat in World War II, the nation's capital, Berlin, was Divined into four sections, with the Americans, British and French controlling the western region and the Soviets gaining power in the eastern region. In May 1949, the three western sections came together as the Federal Republic of Germany (West Germany), with the German Democratic Republic (East Germany) being established in October of that same year. In 1952, the border between the two countries was closed and by the following year East Germans were prosecuted if they left their country without permission. In August 1961, the Berlin Wall was erected by the East German government to prevent its citizens from escaping to the West. Between 1949 and the wall's inception, it's estimated that over 2.5 million East Germans fled to the West in search of a less repressive life.

With the wall as a backdrop, President Reagan declared to a West Berlin crowd in 1987, "There is one sign the Soviets can make that would be unmistakable, that would advance dramatically the cause of freedom and peace." He then called upon his Soviet counterpart: "Secretary General Gorbachev, if you seek peace–if you seek prosperity for the Soviet Union and Eastern Europe– if you seek liberalization: come here, to this gate. Mr. Gorbachev, open this gate. Mr. Gorbachev, tear down this wall." Reagan then went on to ask Gorbachev to undertake serious arms reduction talks with the United States. Most listeners at the time viewed Reagan's speech as a dramatic appeal to Gorbachev to renew negotiations on nuclear arms reductions. It was also a reminder that despite the Soviet leader's public statements about a new relationship with the

West, the U.S. wanted to see action taken to lessen Cold War tensions. Happily for Berliners, though, the speech also foreshadowed events to come: Two years later, on November 9, 1989, joyful East and West Germans did break down the infamous barrier between East and West Berlin. Germany was officially reunited on October 3, 1990. That was after an East German official announced that East Germans could leave East Germany permanently or temporary. Gorbachev, who had been in office since 1985, stepped down from his post as Soviet leader in 1991

Even though the restrictions were officially lifted, the Germans wanted the symbol of the totalitarian government, under which the East had lived, to be destroyed. The symbol of imprisonment had to come down for the sake of freedom and liberty. The Spirit of Freedom is innate and people will have Liberty.

Page 47: Now people, in Oregon, who are fatally ill and will suffer physically, mentally and emotionally, may have an assisted death, at the time of their choosing. Would I want to do that under those conditions? Why not? Why suffer? Why just exist with no quality of life. Why exist without purpose? These were all thoughts that went through my mind in deciding how I felt about the issue. Why not just die? We all die anyway. I guess maybe assisted suicide would be better. I moved further into the thinking pattern of Liberalism and Socialism.

It sounds good just like a lot of other pragmatic ideas sound good. However, when viewed from a moral aspect, it is not so good. God has to be in the equation. Why? Because we are talking about life and death here. God gives life and it is He who should give death, to this world, for His reason and when He wants. I have wondered why God allows some people to linger and suffer. The answer I came up with is that He is also allowing them to suffer here instead of after death to this world. Now I know there are people who would be in my face thinking I just said the people they love were bad people. No, that is not what I am saying. I am saying even a good person may have something to maybe think about or get straight with loved ones or that there is just something between them and God to be settled. Of course, we have to believe in God. Perhaps some people come to such belief when they realize they are facing death. Maybe loved ones around them do as well. Maybe suffering is a last chance.

I consider myself to be a good person, at least a decent person. But I also know all of us are sinners, in some way, shape, or form one way or another. Jesus has already paid for my sins and the sins of us all. We only need to ask for His forgiveness and mercy. Maybe God uses the suffering of ill health to do that so a person may obtain a closer place to Him afterward. All things are used for the good of these who serve Him.

Of course, I could be incorrect, as I am not God and His ways are not human ways. In any case, I will take suffering here anytime, instead of the suffering of the soul in the next life.

Page 48: Concerning the establishment of Social Security Insurance. Seems like I received this in an email.

Dick Kantenberger, Gifted Education Writer, Examiner.com, History Lesson on Your Social Security Card

Just in case some of you young whippersnappers (& some older ones) didn't know this. It's easy to check out, if you don't believe it. Be sure and show it to your family and friends. They need a little history lesson on what's what and it doesn't matter whether you are Democrat or Republican. Facts are Facts.

<u>Social Security Cards up until the 1980s expressly stated the number and card were not to be used for identification purposes</u>. Since nearly everyone in the United States now has a number, it became convenient to use it anyway *and the message, NOT FOR IDENTIFICATION, was removed.*

Franklin Roosevelt, a Democrat, introduced the Social Security (FICA) Program. He promised:

1.) That participation in the Program would be Completely voluntary,

    No longer Voluntary

2.) That the <u>participants would only have to pay 1% of the first $1,400 of their annual Incomes into the Program.</u>

    Now 7.65% on the first $90,000

3.) That the money the participants elected to put into the Program would be <u>deductible from their income for tax purposes each year,</u>

    No longer tax deductible

4.) That the <u>money the participants put into the independent 'Trust Fund'</u> rather than into the general operating fund, and therefore, <u>would only be used to fund the Social Security Retirement Program, and no other Government program, and,</u>

    Under Johnson the money was moved to The General Fund and Spent

5.) That the<u> annuity payments to the retirees would never be taxed as income.</u>

    Under Clinton & Gore up to 85% of your Social Security can be Taxed

I Could Have Been One

Since many of us have paid into FICA for years and are now receiving a Social Security check every month — and then finding that we are getting taxed on 85% of the money we paid to the Federal government to 'put away' — you may be interested in the following:

Q: Which Political Party took Social Security from the independent 'Trust Fund' and put it into the general fund so that Congress could spend it?

A: It was Lyndon Johnson and the democratically controlled House and Senate.

Q: Which Political Party eliminated the income tax deduction for Social Security (FICA) withholding?

A: The Democratic Party.

Q: Which Political Party started taxing Social Security annuities?

A: The Democratic Party, with *Al Gore* casting the 'tic-breaking' deciding vote as President of the Senate, while he was Vice President of the US

Q: Which Political Party decided to start giving annuity payments to immigrants?

A: *Jimmy Carter* and the Democratic Party. Immigrants moved into this country, and at age 65, began to receive Social Security payments! The Democratic Party gave these payments to them, even though they never paid a dime into it! Page 49: At least it seemed to begin then, but it actually had begun back in 1924, in Chicago, as an organization named Society for Human Rights. (Speaking of the gay movement.)

These last five are yet again a reminder that nothing is new. It just becomes presented under a different name. We only think it is new because we, ourselves, are just hearing about it, but the older generations knows/knew better.

Page 29: 1848: The first women's rights convention is held in Seneca Falls, New York. After two days of discussion and debate, 68 women and 32 men sign a Declaration of Sentiments, which outlines grievances and sets the agenda for the women's rights movement. A set of 12 resolutions is adopted calling for equal treatment of women and men under the law and voting rights for women. And...

Page 38: I first became aware of the Chicano Civil Rights Movement, during the mid-1970s. However, that movement has its roots in the 1940s as the Mexican American Civil Rights Movement, which moved on into the '50s and '60s. And

Page 43: I have found material stating that in this country, social programs go back to 1915, in some form of State program. The Social Security Act established in 1935, during the Great Depression, of the United States, had its beginnings as the Old Age, Survivors and Disability Insurance Federal Program. It was mandated to the States they pay unemployment insurance. Therefore each State had to pass legislation to develop their own program. Out of that grew a form of an Unemployment Insurance Department, which grew to a partnership between employers and the Department, to assist those who would be collecting the insurance to find employment positions. And

Page 44: The background of illegal immigration, for this country, begins in the late 1800s, with the situation worsening in the mid-1900s. In 1875, the first federal law was passed prohibiting convicts and prostitutes from entering the country. In the mid-1880s, most Chinese were prohibited along with paupers, criminals and the mentally ill. Of course, there were still those who entered illegally.

Page 49: Political Correctness is a control mechanism and was to be used to advance Communist control of the populace. By introducing it in America, we begin to get used to having our freedom of speech censured. It is like trying to force a change of attitudes, but such changes cannot be forced. A person has to decide to clean up their language or actions, for their own self, and not out of peer pressure or policy. They have to see the reason in changing otherwise they are just going along to get along. When we get used to our speech and actions being censured, then someone else has control of us and we will fall in with whatever they want, even if it is wrong.

Page 99: He gave acknowledgement to Lucifer also known as Satan also known as the Devil. He must have admired the Devil.

While that was done by a non-Christian, it is Christians who must believe that Satan does exists and wants our souls and will use our weakness of character and others doing his bidding to entice us to wrong doing. If Christians believe in God, Jesus Christ and Heaven, then they must believe in the Satan and Hell. Jesus, His Apostles and others, in the name of Jesus, cast out demons. Demons exist and are the minions of Satan working for him to obtain souls for Hell.

I decided to end this chapter with an email that was running around the circuit. It shows aspects of what Capitalistic American is. It also shows why the Communists/Socialists want to dismantle the United States of America and delete its history. This country is the most powerful in the world and it developed under the economic system of Capitalism.

How Soon They Forget: Sent via email March 31, 2008.

When in England at a fairly large conference, Colin Powell was asked by the Archbishop of Canterbury if our plans for Iraq were just an example of empire building' by George Bush. He answered by saying, "Over the years, the United States has sent many of its fine young men and women into great peril to fight for freedom beyond our borders. The only amount of land we have ever asked for in return is enough to bury those that did not return." It became very quiet in the room.

Then there was a conference in France where a number of international engineers were taking part, including French and American. During a break one of the French engineers came back into the room saying "Have you heard the latest dumb stunt Bush has done? He has sent an aircraft carrier to Indonesia to help the tsunami victims. What does he intended to do, bomb them?"

A Boeing engineer stood up and replied quietly, "Our carriers have three hospitals on board that can treat several hundred people; they are nuclear powered and can supply emergency electrical power to shore facilities; they have three cafeterias with the capacity to feed 3,000 people three meals a day, they can produce several thousand gallons of fresh water from sea water each day, and they carry half a dozen helicopters for use in transporting victims and injured to and from their flight deck. We have eleven such ships; how many does France have?" Once again, dead silence.

A U.S. Navy Admiral was attending a naval conference that included Admirals from the U.S., English, Canadian, Australian and French Navies. At a cocktail reception, he found himself standing with a large group of Officers that included personnel from most of those countries. Everyone was chatting away in English as they sipped their drinks but a French admiral suddenly complained that, "...whereas Europeans learn many languages, Americans learn only English." He then asked, "Why is it that we always have to speak English in these conferences rather than speaking French? Without hesitating, the American Admiral replied, "Maybe it's because the Brits, Canadians, Aussies and Americans arranged it so you wouldn't have to speak German." You could have heard a pin drop

A group of Americans, retired teachers, recently went to France on a tour. Robert Whiting, an elderly gentleman of 83, arrived in Paris by plane. At French Customs, he took a few minutes to locate his passport in his carry on.

"You have been to France before, monsieur?" the customs officer asked sarcastically. Mr. Whiting admitted that he had been to France previously. "Then you should know enough to have your passport ready." The American said, "The last time I was here, I didn't have to show it." "Impossible. Americans always have to show your passports on arrival in France!"

The American senior gave the Frenchman a long hard look. Then he quietly explained. "Well, when I came ashore at Omaha Beach on D-Day in '44 to help liberate this country, I couldn't find any damn Frenchmen to show it to."

It Had No Fancy Name

Page 48: My parents and their generation used to talk about workhouses, poor houses and old people's homes.

Back then I never heard anything about such places being socialism or social justice. It all was called by the titles of the time. There were also poor farms or county farms, which dealt with agriculture instead of industry. It was just government taking care of people the best way they could find, for that time. Such places had reputations and stigma. Now everything has to have a fancy name and be under an umbrella title such as social justice. Everything is complicated. Anyway…I researched and found the following on line. It is concerning Britain, but then that is the ancestry of our Founding Fathers. Although this Country has the influence of other countries besides Britain, it was Great Britain that colonized and it was prior British citizens who gained independence from Britain and began the western movement from sea to shining sea, including those of Scotch/Irish ancestry. And what was practiced in Great Britain came here.

I copied the articles, in whole, and kept what I wanted. However, I did keep most of it so you may get as full a view of such places as possible. I also enjoy that some of the wording and spelling shows the difference between our time and the time the last article was composed. By the way, the "L" like symbol stands for "pounds", which is one of Britain's money denominations. Notice the last article goes back to the late 1700s. Nothing new. Just different.

Online: Primary Homework Help – Victorians - The Workhouse
Before 1834, poor people were looked after by buying food and clothing from money collected from land owners and other wealthy people.

The Poor Law Amendment Act of 1834, ensured that no able-bodied person could get poor relief unless they went to live in special workhouses. The idea was that the poor were helped to support themselves. They had to work for their food and accommodation. What were workhouses? Workhouses were where poor people who had no job or home lived. They earned their keep by doing jobs in the workhouse. Also in the workhouses were orphaned (children without parents) and abandoned children, the physically and mentally sick, the disabled, the elderly and unmarried mothers. Workhouses were often very large and were feared by the poor and old. A workhouse provided: a place to live, work and earn money, free medical care, food, clothes and free education for children and training for a job. The staff of a workhouse included: a Master, Matron, Medical Officer, Chaplain, porter and school teacher. Workhouses provided almost everything that was needed onsite: kitchen, bakery, dining hall, dormitories, laundry, tailors, cobbler, school rooms, nurseries, hospital, chapel, mortuary, vegetable gardens and a small farm. Why were workhouses feared by the poor and old? The government, terrified of encouraging 'idlers' (lazy people), made sure that people feared the workhouse and would do anything to keep out of it. How did they do that? What were workhouses like? Women, children and men had different living and working areas in the workhouse, so families were split up. To make things even worse they could be punished if

I Could Have Been One

they even tried to speak to one another! The education the children received did not include the two most important skills of all, reading and writing, which were needed to get a good job. The poor were made to wear a uniform. This meant that everyone looked the same and everyone outside knew they were poor and lived in the workhouse. Upon entering the workhouse, the poor were stripped and bathed (under supervision). The food was tasteless and was the same day after day. The young and old as well as men and women were made to work hard, often doing unpleasant jobs. Children could also find themselves 'hired out' (sold) to work in factories or mines.Dr Thomas Barnardo felt that workhouses were the wrong places for children and so from 1867 onwards, he led the way in setting up proper children's homes.

Online reference: London Lives Workhouses
Thomas Gibson's plan for a workhouse as included in Henry Fielding, Proposal for Making Effectual Provision for the Poor, 1753. © London Lives.

Introduction
By 1776 over 16,000 individual men, women and children were housed in one of the eighty workhouses in metropolitan London; between 1 per cent and 2 per cent of the population of London. Workhouses, institutions in which the poor were housed, fed and set to work, had by this time become the most common form of relief available to Londoners.[1] The process of creating this complex landscape of institutions, however, stretched over three centuries, and resulted in a variety of institutions that would have confounded the expectations of the men and women who established them.

The Sixteenth and Seventeenth Centuries
At regular intervals through the sixteenth and seventeenth centuries, and especially following the establishment of the Royal Hospitals (and in particular Bridewell

Hospital and Prison in 1553), Londoners attempted to create city-wide employment schemes or residential workhouses as a solution to the problem of poverty and economic dislocation. After Bridewell, which quickly evolved into the combination of a house of correction for the punishment of petty offenders and an industrial school, which it remained throughout the eighteenth century, London's next major experiment of this kind was Samuel Hartlib's Corporation of the Poor, established in 1648, which in turn built on the ideas of projectors such as Rowland Vaughn. Hartlib's experiment in collective employment, which at its most radical aspired to the creation of an egalitarian commonwealth of the poor, survived just a dozen years. By the time the foundation was given a firm legal footing as part of the Act of Settlement in 1662, it had already collapsed, though inclusion of the provisions for the Corporation in the Act itself effectively publicised the venture.[2] The same legislation also empowered Middlesex and Southwark to establish their own corporations, and in 1664 Middlesex spent £5,000 creating a new workhouse at Clerkenwell, adjacent to the house of correction. Initially the workhouse provided raw materials for the adult poor to work up at home, and accommodation for the "reception and breeding up of poor fatherless and motherless infants".[3]

The Prospect of Bridewell from John Strype's, An Accurate Edition of Stow's Survey of London (1720). © Tim Hitchcock.

In 1676 Thomas Firmin established a parallel scheme in Aldersgate for employing the poor in the City of London, and through it provided training and a stock of flax for home working. This project survived through Firmin's death in 1697, and its existence provided one model for the later Corporation of the Poor or London Workhouse. Again using the workhouse half of the house of correction at Clerkenwell, in 1688 Sir Thomas Rowe created a College of Infants, which failed after just a few years, to be replaced by the Quaker Workhouse at Clerkenwell. This workhouse was based on the ideas of John Bellers and incorporated many of the commonwealth aspirations familiar from Samuel Hartlib's writing and from continental pietism.[4]

The aspiration to create a metropolitan, or at least City-wide institution, however, reached its apotheosis in the re-establishment of the Corporation of the Poor for London - also known as the London Workhouse - in 1698.

The London Workhouse

Throughout the 1690s pressure to reform the system of poor relief and the manners (morals) of the poor grew. The Societies for the Reformation of Manners, active from 1690, employed the criminal justice system to discipline the poor, but in parallel a wider national movement to create workhouses in major cities also evolved with the related aim to "inure the poor to labour", and train up poor children to a religious and industrious life. In London from 1688 Thomas Firmin and Sir Robert Clayton organized a voluntary house-to-house collection in aid of the poor, to which the new king, William III, gave both his support and money - donating initially £2,000 in 1688, and later £1,000 a year through the 1690s to what became known as the The King's Letter Fund. Between 1694 and 1705 Parliament also considered substantial reform of the poor relief system on at least thirteen separate occasions, a process that only lost impetus with the failure of Sir Humphrey Mackworth's attempt to re-codify the poor laws in 1705. During these same years the Board of Trade, under John Locke's leadership, spent much effort enquiring into the workings of the poor laws, and attempting, but largely failing, to generate a consistent reform agenda that had setting the poor to work at its core. In the absence of effective national reform, and following the lead of John Cary and the City of Bristol, thirteen Corporations of the Poor were established on the basis of local Acts of Parliament in all the major cites of England in the decade and a half after 1696. These institutions were generally run under the auspices of local city government, and took on the character of a combined house of correction and industrial school for children, and in relation to children at least, were intended largely to replace parochial provision.[5]

London was keen to follow the Bristol example, and hoped that specific provision for the creation of a Corporation covering the area within the Bills of Mortality would be included in national legislation promoted by the Board of Trade, but when this failed in 1697, the Lord Mayor, Sir Humphrey Edwin, recommended that the Interregnum Corporation of the Poor as authorised by the Act of Settlement simply be revived.

Bridewell and Bethlem Archives, Bridewell and Bethlem, Minutes of the Court of Governors, 1738-51, BCB-21 (Box C04/3), LL ref: BBBRMG202060517.

On this basis, the City of London initially sought to create a non-residential employment scheme, of the sort Thomas Firmin had been running for twenty years; and in the Autumn of 1698 committed over £5,000 to the project, which was up and running by the early months of 1699. Two undertakers were hired, and a six week course of training in spinning wool was run for parish children. The entirely unrealistic expectation was that "any willing industrious & capeable person may earn from two shillings to four shillings per weeke & some five or six shillings per weeke". Over 400 people, primarily children, were trained, but the scheme collapsed in the summer of 1699; and the City turned instead to a residential workhouse model, leasing a house in Half-Moon Alley, off Bishopsgate Street, in August 1699. For the next dozen years the London Workhouse maintained, employed and educated substantial numbers of parish children; and punished a slew of beggars and vagrants. The house was Divined, like Bridewell, between a Keeper's Side (the house of correction) and a Steward's Side, which functioned as a residential workhouse and industrial school for poor children, which would take in parish children at a charge of 12 pence per week. In 1703 the annual report claimed that 427 children had been maintained in the preceding year, and 430 vagrants corrected. Two beadles were directly employed by the Corporation to apprehend beggars, and a bounty of a shilling per beggar or vagrant was offered for their apprehension. This was later restricted to beggars only, when the numbers of prostitutes and the disorderly grew too large.

The Corporation, however, rapidly encountered significant opposition from the parishes, which had traditionally cared for their own poor. In part this was a simple reflection of the high cost of maintaining an institutional provision. Between 1698 and 1713, a total expenditure of £34,644 was authorised in support of the Corporation, while the earnings from manufacturing proved largely illusory.

In response to these demands many parishes simply refused to collect the money assessed on them in support of the Corporation, and the conflict with the parishes (driven primarily by finance, but inflected with political divisions as well) dragged on through the 1700s. By 1708 several parishes were questioning the legal basis of the Corporation, and in that year a committee of the Court of Common Council was charged with finding some way of reducing the expenditure on the house. This committee failed to produce a clear recommendation, but in 1712, in response to a request for more funding, the Corporation was forced to change its by-laws, and drastically reduce its workhouse function. Although it survived into the nineteenth century, from 1713 it stopped taking in parish children, and restricted its educational role to boarding children sponsored by individual benefactors at a cost of £50 for City children, and £70 for children from elsewhere. From this date the London Workhouse survived almost exclusively as a house of correction.[6]

Workhouse Test Act and *Account of Several Workhouses*
As a part of the same flowering of debate on social welfare that contributed to the creation of the Corporations of the Poor, the Society for the Promotion of Christian Knowledge (SPCK) was established in 1698. During the

next two decades the Society actively supported the creation of a large number of charity schools and working charity schools across the country, and most especially in London. It also acted as a clearing house for correspondence tying local activists into a national movement for reforming the poor, and as a publishing house, producing both pamphlet literature on religion and social policy, and a large number of short moralistic pamphlets designed for consumption by the labouring poor. Following the Jacobite uprising of 1715 and the Hanoverian succession, many of the schools promoted by the Society were suspected of inculcating Jacobite principles in their students; in response the Society shifted its efforts towards facilitating the establishment of parish workhouses.

The Account of Several Workhouses, 1725. © London Lives.
The percentage of the SPCK's effort and time taken up with workhouses grew slowly between about 1719 and 1723. In 1720 the Society offered a premium to any town setting up a workhouse and gradually more and more of the Society's correspondents wrote to describe and commend local experiments. In 1722 the Society began to actively support Sir Edward Knatchbull and John Comyns in the drafting and passage of the Workhouse Test Act: "An Act for Amending the Laws relating to the Settlement, Imployment and Relief of the Poor".[7] The Act itself was a hodge-podge of poor relief clauses with little obvious direction and few new ideas. But it gave legislative expression to a new kind of workhouse based on the idea of deterrence, rather than the belief that the poor's labour could be made profitable. The Act allowed parishes to refuse to relieve any applicant who refused to enter a workhouse. More than this, it gave a governmental stamp of approval to a series of institutions recently set up in the East Midlands and Essex.

With the passage of the Workhouse Test Act and in the same year the publication of Bernard De Mandeville's damning *Essay on Charity and Charity*

Schools (1723), which argued that charity schools encouraged poor children to aspire above their station, the shift in emphasis from education in schools to industrial discipline in workhouses was complete. The publication by the SPCK of *An Account of Several Workhouses* in 1725, which gave details of the management and establishment of over forty-four workhouses and working charity schools, and noted the existence of a further seventy-seven institutions, effectively ensured that the provisions of the Workhouse Test Act would be adopted widely, indeed almost universally in the larger metropolitan parishes, in particular those of Westminster.

Parish Workhouses:
In metropolitan London the Workhouse Test Act provided the cue for the rapid expansion of parochial institutions. The earliest foundations were in the East End with Limehouse and Whitechapel establishing houses in 1724, followed St Katherine by the Tower in the following year and St Leonard Shoreditch in 1726. In 1725 in Westminster, St Martin in the Fields and St James both established substantial workhouses, accommodating several hundred paupers each; and in the following year St George Hanover Square and St Margaret followed their example. The house established by St George Hanover Square was built to a design commissioned by the SPCK from Nicholas Hawksmoor and was used as a model for many provincial houses. Over the course of the next few years most of the major urban parishes of metropolitan London created their own houses, with particularly large and important institutions being established by St Giles Cripplegate (1724), St Giles in the Fields (1725), St James Clerkenwell (1727), St Sepulchre, London Division (1727), St Andrew Holborn (1727), St Dunstan in the West (1728), St John the Evangelist (1728), and St Marylebone (1730).

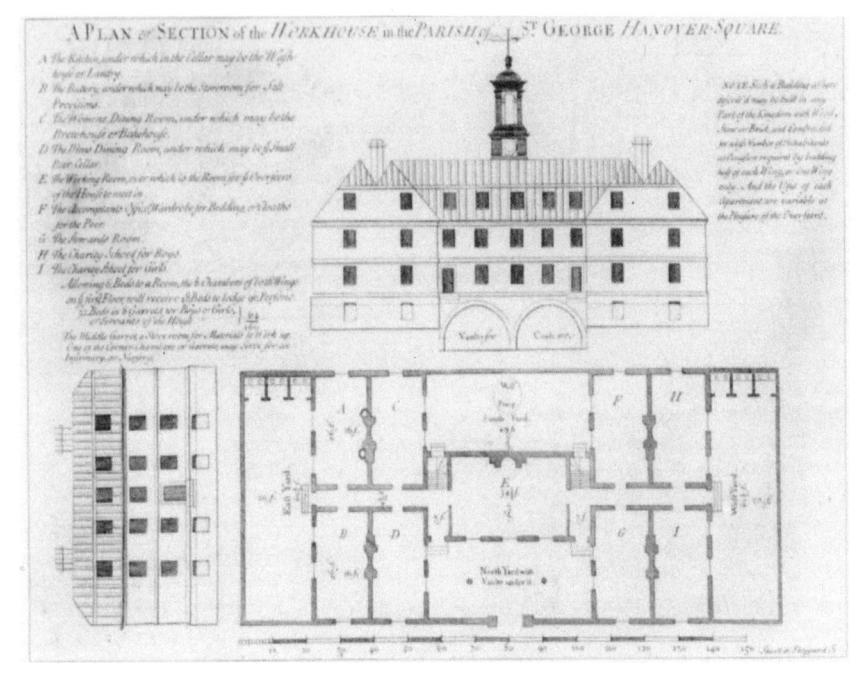

A Plan & Section of the Workhouse Belonging to St George Hanover Square, c.1724. © Trustees of the British Museum.

In the City of London itself the majority of foundations took place in the 1730s, with a series of larger establishments concentrated in the parishes *without the walls*. These included houses in Christ Church Newgate Street (1729), St Dunstan in the East (1730), All Hallows Honey Lane (1731), St Andrew Undershaft (1733) and St Bartholomew the Great (1737).[9]

Most workhouses were established in the expectation that the adult, able bodied and male poor would form the majority of the workhouse population (or family as contemporaries termed it), the hope being that the labour of such paupers could be disciplined to help subsidize the cost of the house. But within just a few years of opening, these houses were almost universally forced to restrict or even abandon work undertaken by the inmates, and to refocus their efforts on the care of the ill, the orphaned and the elderly. Within months of the opening of the house belonging to St George Hanover Square a new infirmary was under construction. Similarly, at St Margaret Westminster, in 1727 six rooms were converted into a ward for the reception of the sick, as were six more in the following year. At St Martin in the Fields, one of the largest of London's parish workhouses, this refocussing was more drawn out, but by 1736 new and separate wards were being created for the sick, smallpox patients and lying-in women.[10]

The Workhouse Cruelty, c.1731. © The British Libary.
Typical of the population that came to occupy London's workhouses was that of St Luke Chelsea, the workhouse register for which is available through this site. This indicates that throughout the century the majority of inmates were women (50 per cent), and children (30 per cent); while adult male residents (19 per cent) were restricted to elderly inhabitants and the seriously ill.

The early form of these institutions was determined in part by the published information produced by the SPCK, especially its *Account of Several Workhouses* (1725, 2nd expanded edn 1732), but many were also set up and managed by Matthew Marryott, who worked closely with the Society, and who moved from Olney in Buckinghamshire, where he had been instrumental in establishing many early provincial houses, to London in 1724. From 1725 to 1727 Marryott practically monopolised the management of the larger houses established by the parishes of London, and either directly managed or sub-contracted the running of workhouses in St Giles in the Fields, St Leonard Shoreditch, St Martin in the Fields, St George Hanover Square and both St Margaret and St James, Westminster. But a series of complaints and workhouse scandals ensured that his monopoly was rapidly eroded. It was finally broken completely following the publication of a pamphlet and ballad detailing a number of deaths in the workhouse belonging to the parish of

St Giles in the Fields between 1728 and 1731, and in particular that of Mary Whistle in 1731. As a result of this and other complaints Marryott was excluded from his role in managing several houses. He died in either late 1731 or early 1732.[11]

Workhouse Conditions
Unlike their nineteenth-century successors, eighteenth-century workhouses were not designed to be particularly unpleasant or punitive. And although they were initially set up with the adult, able-bodied (and generally male) poor in mind, they rapidly evolved to cater for young children and orphans, the elderly, and the ill. In size they could vary from a small parish house accommodating only twenty or thirty paupers, possibly managed by one of their own number, to massive bureaucratic institutions housing hundreds of people. The house belonging to St Martin in the Fields, whose register is included on this site, could accommodate 700 individuals in 1776. In most instances workhouses became general parish houses for the relief of the poor; while the larger institutions made available specialist accommodation for lying in and the provision of medical care, and for the elderly and infants and young children. Many houses also contained facilities to cope with accidents and emergencies (the parish shell or stretcher was usually stored at the workhouse), acted as parish mortuaries, and served as the venue for parish meetings and administration. For most parishes the workhouse represented the first and most important parish building after the church itself; and as such came to serve as the focus for many parish activities beyond poor relief.[12]

Typical of the larger London houses was that established by St James Westminster. The building used for the workhouse was purpose-built in 1726, and was described five years later as a "spacious brickhouse". It was built in the burial ground belonging to the parish and in the early 1730s could hold approximately 300 people, Divined among "8 Wards, viz. 4 for women, 2 for men, 1 for boys, and 1 for girls, containing 18 beds in each ward". There was also a "ward for lying-in women, into which many are brought out of the streets to be delivered [and] another ward for an infirmary".

The Wise Acre Corporation, 1804. British Museum Satires 10358. © Trustees of the British Museum.

There were fourteen members of staff, each receiving wages of between £5 and £40 per year, plus board. Besides the master (Matthew Marryott from 1727 to 1729), who was paid £40 per annum, there was also a clerk, matron, assistant matron, laundry maid, porter, schoolmistress, matron of the infirmary and general maid servant. The highest paid of these posts was that of clerk, who earned a salary of £20 a year. The employees of the house were "allowed a convenient joint of meat every day for their dinners" and dined "immediately after the rest of the family". Their responsibilities were strictly Divined between several spheres of activity. The porter, for instance, had responsibility for only three things. He ensured that all the men rose at the appointed hour in the morning, that meal times were indicated by the ringing of a bell, and that no one entered or left the house without the permission of the master. Similarly, the bread cutter was responsible for allocating "all the allowances of bread and cheese" and "such quantities of beer and coals every day ... as the governor shall direct".

Beyond these paid servants there were also numerous positions filled by the poor themselves. Each ward was looked after by a nurse recruited from among the poor, who was ordered to "thoroughly clean their respective wards and air the rooms if the weather permits"; "every morning sweep the passages and stairs leading from the floors of the respective wards, and on every Wednesday and Saturday scour the said passages and stairs and make clean the wainscot and balusters belong to the same". The nurses were also required "every morning immediately after prayers [to] make the beds and at other times of the day mend the bedding clothes and linen, and take care of them and all other things belonging to the persons under the particular charge". They looked after the sick, fetched their meals for them and notified the master or apothecary of any assistance that might be required, and for children between the ages of four and six, were expected to "dress, wash and comb them every morning and bring them clean to morning prayers, take care of them at their meals and at night ... [and] put them to bed". For these services the nurses received no wages or special allowances, but the vestry did promise to reward "'extraordinary diligence" with a small gratuity.

Below this large management structure were the inmates, who were employed by the work master, looked after in the infirmary, or delivered in the lying-in ward. Their days were regimented and controlled by both the paid and pauper staff. Every morning they were awoken by the ringing of a bell by the porter of the house, at seven in the winter and six in the summer months. Forty-five minutes was then allowed for the inmates to get up, and wash and dress themselves, before they had to be in the main hall of the workhouse for prayers read by the master. The only persons allowed to absent themselves from prayers were children under four and the bedridden. Having read prayers the master then counted the poor in the hall, taking note of their condition - whether children, aged, or infirm - while the mistress went to the various wards to list those unable to attend. The poor were then Divined into messes for the purpose of determining the amount of food necessary for the day. Once this account had been taken the poor were dismissed into the hands of the work master and mistress, or, if children between the ages of four and six, sent to the schoolmistress for instruction. Other inmates were appointed to work in the laundry, while the nurses were sent back to the wards to make the beds and clean out the rooms.

Regimen and Diet

Every morning the work master and mistress assigned "every poor person a reasonable task to perform for a day's work in proportion to the party's ability ... [or] join[ed] two or three or four in a piece of work as shall be most convenient". Under the eye of the work master and mistress the poor then started their labour, children over the age of six being sent for short periods throughout the day to the schoolmistress to be taught to read.

Westminster Archives Centre, St Clement Danes, Vestry Minutes, 1776-87, B1072, LL ref: WCCDMV362040294.

At nine in the summer and as soon as possible after prayers in the winter, breakfast was served. A bell was rung by the porter to summon the inmates, and the men and boys over six then proceeded to the "men's hall" where they were "regularly placed at tables". Likewise, the women, and girls and children under six, went to the "women's hall", where they were "served with their messes in a decent manner". The master was present throughout the meal, and saw to it that everyone was there and maintained good order: anyone absenting themselves without permission was denied one meal on the first occasion. Half an hour was allowed for breakfast, which conformed to one of three menus depending on the day of the week. On Sunday each person above six years old received five ounces of bread and a pint of beer; on Monday, Wednesday and Friday, a pint of beef broth and two and a half ounces of bread; and on Tuesday, Thursday and Saturday, a pint of mild porridge and two and a half ounces of bread. While breakfast was in progress the mistress toured the house seeing to it that bedridden inmates received their meals and were attended to by the nurses.

After breakfast everyone returned to work until, at one in the afternoon, the dinner bell was rung. Once again the poor trooped into the halls and a meal was served under the auspices of the master. Slightly more varied than breakfast, this was the main meal of the day. On Sundays, Tuesdays and

Thursdays, the poor were served ten ounces of boiled beef, five ounces of bread and one pint of beer. On Mondays each adult received a pint of peas pudding; on Wednesday, a pint of rice milk, on Fridays, a pint of frumenty; and on Saturdays a pound of plum pudding and a pint of beer. An hour was allowed for dinner, after which the poor went back to work until at least six during the winter months and until supper was served at seven during the summer. During the winter an hour was allowed between the end of the working day and supper, during which time the inmates were left to their own devices.

Supper was the least substantial and most monotonous meal of the day. On Sundays each pauper received five ounces of bread, two ounces of cheese and a pint of beer, and during the rest of the week, four ounces of bread, one and a half ounces of cheese and half a pint of beer. No particular time limit was set on the evening meal, though it had to be finished by approximately half past eight, when the master read evening prayers, sending the inmates to bed at nine o'clock.

The unvaried routine described above was put into effect on five days a week. On Saturdays the poor were allowed to cease work at five in the afternoon during the summer and three in winter. On Sundays work was largely replaced by religious devotions. After breakfast on Sundays it was the master's duty to see that "the officers of the workhouse and likewise the poor not being dissenters from the church do attend constantly and reverently on divine service". After the morning service the master was allowed to "suffer those who desire it to go abroad" as long as no one was discovered using this time and freedom in begging or in becoming "disordered in liquor". The poor had to return to the house by half past eight in the evening, and were liable to lose their right to go abroad on Sundays for up to three months for any breach of the master's standards of behaviour. Eight days a year were reserved as holidays. "Good Fridays, Christmas Day and the two next days after it and the

Monday and Tuesday in Easter and Whitsun week" were set aside from the constant round of work and meals.

The workroom at St James's workhouse, from The Microcosm of London (1808). © London Lives.

This monotonous regimen was not in itself sufficient to cope with the vagaries of workhouse life. The treatment of the sick, the pregnant, the very old and very young required further rules. The master was also given some latitude in both the punishment and reward of individuals, though as he did not have a judicial function of any kind, all punishments needed to be non-corporal, and normally took the form either of confinement in the dark hole or else the denial of food or privileges. The infirmary of St. James's workhouse was largely exempt from the orders enforced in the rest of the house, being under the authority of the surgeon, apothecary and mistress of the infirmary, and depending on the master primarily for the supply of fresh linen, clothes and cooked meals. Similarly the hours of work for the inmates employed in the kitchen and laundry were determined by the members of staff directly responsible — the cook and laundry maid.

The conditions described by the rules of St. James's workhouse were good. The ability to go out of the house on Sundays and the quality of the diet compare favourably to most other London houses. In particular, the meals provided were both reasonably varied and made up of extremely filling ingredients. The plum pudding served the inmates each Saturday was made according to the following recipe:

Poor ffolkes must be glad of Pottage. c.1700. British Museum Schriber English 68. © Trustees of the British Museum.

That to make sixteen plumb puddings there be put 15l. suet, 15q. raisins, eighteen quarts of milk, two bushels and one peck of flower, three Qrs of a pound of rice and one pound of salt each of which is to be Divined for men and women in sixteen parts.

Smaller houses made do with many fewer rules and employees, but generally sought to create precisely the kinds of conditions evident at St James.[13]

London Workhouses in 1776-7

According to the 1776-7 Parliamentary enquiry, by this date parochial institutions could be found in the following parishes. (The spelling and categorisation is reproduced as recorded in the original Parliamentary Papers, and the numbers accommodated are in parentheses.)

Contractors, Private Workhouses and Baby Farms
One clause of the Workhouse Test Act (1723) provided for parishes to contract "with any person or persons for the lodging, keeping, maintaining and imploying any or all such poor ... as shall desire to receive relief or collection from the same parish", effectively laying the legal groundwork for smaller parishes to contract out their poor relief obligations to either other parishes or private individuals.[14] This was a particularly popular strategy for the small parishes of the City of London, which normally had too few paupers to justify the creation of a house of their own.

In effect, Matthew Marryott functioned as a private contractor in this mould, normally taking full control of a parish's provision for a set sum. Others followed Marryott's example, including Thomas Mico and his wife. In 1727 Mico and Thomas Worrall contracted with St Martin in the Fields for the care of its poor, in direct succession to Marryott; Mico and his wife acting as master and mistress of the house, and employing the poor, while Worrall entered into a separate contract to keep the accounts, look after the sick poor, and manage the buying of provisions. By 1739 Mico had long since left St Martin and was contracting for the care of the poor of Enfield; agreeing "to take the men, women and children at 2s. a head per week,.... and ... to find them in meat, drink, washing soap, and firing, candles and all other necessaries".

London Metropolitan Archives, St Dionis Backchurch, Miscellaneous Parish Papers, 17th August 1707-7th September 1778, 1280A, LL ref: GLDBPM306140002.

There were many others. During the 1730s and early 1740s John Thruckstone sought contracts with London parishes for both the care of paupers in his own workhouse at Tottenham High Cross, and for the management of several parish houses. In 1733 he contracted with St Dionis Backchurch for the care of their poor, and in the following year he contracted with both St Michael Cornhill and St Helen Bishopsgate. The contract entered into between Thruckstone and St Dionis Backchurch is entirely typical. In it Thruckstone agreed to receive and maintain all the parish poor, put out children to appropriate apprenticeships, indemnify the parish against legal costs relating to settlement, and pay the costs of burial and medical care for a set sum of £167 5s per year.

In the nine years following 1733 Thruckstone applied to three more parishes for the care of their poor, St Leonard Shoreditch in 1737, St Clement Danes in 1742, and St Andrew Undershaft in 1742. Other men and couples seeking similar contracts in these decades included John Smith, Christopher Stafford, Samuel Tull, John Stoke, and Solomon Gardiner and his wife. John Smith, for instance, can first be identified as master of the workhouse belonging to St Andrew Undershaft in 1742, when the parish put his position up for re-appointment and he unsuccessfully competed with five other people for the contract for the care of the poor of that parish.[15] By 1747, he was running an independent workhouse at Tottenham High Cross, and also had a contract with St Martin Vintry. These men gradually took over the administration of a large number of London workhouses, and gradually developed a series of free-standing non-parochial houses located principally at Hoxton, Tottenham High Cross and Mile End Old Town. During most of the eighteenth century, the charges levied for the care of the poor were calibrated to the kind of pauper being supported, and could range from 1s 6d per week for a healthy pauper able to contribute to their support through labour, to 4s a week for the less physically able. By the end the century, the charges levied had become standardised at between 4s and 6s per week, per pauper.

London Metropolitan Archives, St Dionis Backchurch, Miscellaneous Parish Papers, 17th August 1707-7th September 1778, 1280A, LL ref: GLDBPM306140002.

The ways in which vestries used these houses varied from parish to parish. Some reserved these contract houses for the most dependent poor, or the insane; while others used the offer of the house as a deterrent threat against the casual poor, while allowing pensioners and established paupers to live independently in their own homes, and maintaining only a small proportion of their poor in a contract workhouse. This latter strategy allowed overseers to apply a workhouse test without actually going to the expense of maintaining those in temporary need, while also providing centralised nursing and medical care.

The size and specialised facilities available through these houses grew over the course of the century, and by the beginning of the next century took the form of a relatively few very large houses, including James Robertson's establishment at Hoxton, which by 1815 was thought to house up to 300 paupers from forty different City parishes; Thomas Tipple's pauper farm at 12 Queen's Street, Hoxton, which had 230 places and was used by seventeen City parishes; and Edward Deacon's two houses at Mile End and Bow, which between them housed 520 paupers, and served over forty City parishes.[16]

The passage of the Act for the better Regulation of the Parish Poor Children (1767), sponsored by Jonas Hanway, which required that all parish children under the age of four should be nursed in the countryside at least three miles from London and Westminster, also encouraged the development of a sub-set of contract workhouses, known as baby farms.[17] It was at a farm of this sort that the infant Oliver Twist was confined and starved.

Among the parishes included on this site, St Dionis Backchurch made extensive and long-term use of several different contract workhouses and pauper farms from 1733. Overall, the parish appears to have taken some care of the poor it housed in this manner, and the existence of series of Workhouse Inquest Minute Books (IW), recording details of the parish officers' monthly visit to the poor in several workhouses in Hoxton, gives a good insight into conditions and arrangements.

Henry Fielding's Plan

The ever more disparate nature of poor relief provision in London ensured that few projectors or politicians could contemplate a single unified solution to the issue of housing and employing the poor of the metropolis. On a national scale politicians and projectors such as William Hay and Sir Richard Lloyd had long argued for "county" workhouses, as a means of overcoming the problems associated with amateurish parochial administration and the costs of policing pauper settlement. But the only substantial advocacy of this kind of solution for London, following the failure of the London Workhouse, was produced by Henry and John Fielding. Published in the form of three separate pamphlets, they developed a broad analysis of social problems and policing in London, depicting them as facets of a single issue:

Henry Fielding's, Enquiry in to the Causes of the Late Increase of Robbers (1751)

Henry Fielding's Proposal for Making an Effectual Provision for the Poor which specifically addressed the need for a general county workhouse (1753)

I COULD HAVE BEEN ONE

John Fielding's Plan for Preventing Robberies within Twenty Miles of London (1755), published after Henry Fielding's death.

The workhouse proposed by the Fieldings combined a county workhouse for Middlesex with a house of correction. Much of the programme of reform in these pamphlets was eventually implemented in the following decades. The Middlesex-wide workhouse they proposed was designed to accommodate 5,000 paupers (3,000 men and 2,000 women), and a further 600 petty criminals in the associated house of correction. One nineteenth-century commentator, C. D. Brereton, accused Fielding of attempting to, "effect the reformation of manners and the employment of the poor, by brick and mortar, and architectural devices". [18] The house was never built, but its proposal forms part of a major building programme that eventually resulted in the rebuilding of Newgate Prison, and many of the other major carceral institutions of greater London.[19]

Notice there were not only government facilities, but also church facilities; faith based facilities.

So called civilization has always had its problem of the human condition. Some Americans want to speak badly of their Country both presently and past, but they fail to have a view of other countries who have had the same problems to overcome through the course of history. Nothing is new and America is not by itself in common situations and problems of the human condition. Wanting to improve conditions is good, but sometimes the way of improving has side effects. One situation leads to another and sometimes the other is not good.

An example is the prior condition of child labor in America. During the Industrial Revolution period from 1820 to 1870, families relocated from rural areas into the cities, in hopes of a better lifestyle. So the improvement was machine mass production. The side effect was that early industry was open to children being employed as well as the parents. Parents allowed the children to work so more money could be added to the family budget, which did not allow for much purchasing, as there was only enough money to trade for basic essentials of shelter, food and clothing.

Like the parents the children worked from sunup to sunset and had little rest. Since they could not attend school, as non-working children did, they could not obtain better employment later on. Factory conditions were not good, to say the least, and the children worked under the same unsafe circumstances as parents. Finally attention was given to child labor laws and they have improved over the decades. Working conditions, in general, also improved through legislation. Again America was not alone in this circumstance as Britain was also. And if these two countries were, my guess is that other European counties were as well.

The point is not only have women come a long way, but so has America itself. As far as prior conditions is concerned and the means of government intervention, it was not socialism. There was no free lunch. Due to inventions and technology and legislation America has made great lifestyle improvements, through Capitalism. Just because the human condition factor has not gone away does not mean that Capitalism does not work. It simply means the human condition continues on as it always will. Why? Because we are human. There is a saying of, "If it is not broken, don't fix it." If something that is not broken is fixed, then it is going to be messed up and will be broken. Improve…yes. Fix…no. What is occurring now is Socialism that will lead to Communism. And the human condition will still exist one way or another. It is not a fix or an improvement as it will cause serious circumstances, though totalitarianism. It is not perfection. There will be no utopia. There is no perfection, in this life!

In Closing

I offer the following:

I have presented the historical background of Communism/Socialism. I have shown how it operates, through infiltration and deceit and why. The possible future of Communism/Socialism has been presented, which is presently fulfilling its objectives toward its goal of world domination via the United Nations. I have also presented something of how that organization operates, to gain world control through evil means. And I have presented Christianity and its history and how it operates, through following of the teachings of Jesus Christ, for the goal of eternal life, with God.

Yes, there are Christians who are also Socialists. The current name of the organization is titled Christians On the Left. That makes it sound less negative. Why would a Christian want to be a Socialist? The only reason I can think of is that they get talked into it maybe even by a shame or guilt tactic and with the use of Bible verses. And the person does not know enough about Socialism to even realize the truth of what it actually is, which has nothing whatsoever to do with God. Using Bible verses is a bait and hook tactic. Or maybe they what to be part of the latest and greatest fad, which is now called "social justice". But true social justice is from God and all the Christian has to do is practice it, as Jesus taught it.

Genesis 32: 22-27 Jacob wrestled with a man starting in the day going through the night and into the morning. In the morning, the man touched Jacob's hip and dislocated it, but Jacob fought on. The man asked Jacob to release him and Jacob replied that he would if the man would bless him. Jacob also asked the man's name, to which the man questioned why Jacob asked such a question. And Jacob knew that it was God. Jacob's victory was not in winning the wrestling itself, but in his perseverance. Jacob stated that he had seen the face of God.

Other people throughout the Bible wrestled with God, in that they tried to be released from what God wanted of them; Job, Jonah, Jesus. Even Jesus, in the Garden of Gethsemane, wrestled with God. In Jesus' case, He wrestled with His Father concerning removing the cup, of suffering and death, Jesus was to drink, for us. "Wrestling" is a metaphor meaning to struggle concerning an issue.

Jacob's wrestling was physical. Ours' is spiritual, mental and/or emotional. Sometimes that wrestling is over a short period of time, while other times it is a long period of time. My own was long. I was a drifted away non-practicing Christian for two decades, before returning to Christianity.

Remember I grew up under Segregation. Remember I had found a religion which accepted all races. That was important to me. I had the opportunity to actually interact with Black people; to learn that they are human beings just like me with all of the elements involved in being human. For that matter, any race is. We all obviously have differences, but we are all children of God.

Maybe…just maybe God's plan for me was to use my drifting away, with freewill, to teach me what I could not have learned about different races while living under Segregation. With that being said, I dare say that I was not wrestling with God concerning that issue. I may have been wrestling with Him concerning living a good life, of being at least a good decent person. My trying to live a good life was now and then. Two decades of that, with the final years preparing me to return to Christianity.

I remember missing the celebration of Christmas. I wanted to celebrate Christmas.

But my returning to Christianity, was not when God was finished with me. I had to be renewed and that took three more decades for God to deal with me and me with myself and get me to the point of my wanting renewal. It was a preparation period. A grand total of fifty years. Five decades. Half of a century. Most of my life. I wrestled metaphorically with God. But God is still not finished with me. At least now I ask for His will to be accomplished with me. God will not be done with me, on this earth, until He decides to call me from my earthly remains, which will be when my mission in this life has been accomplished. And even then He will not be done with me, for He shall continue my existence so that I may continue to praise Him.

In the meantime, I shall continue to vote for the person who will best represent my beliefs of moral standards and to practice my Faith as a Christian Constitutional Conservative patriot, of the Republic of the United States of America. God bless America!

Will Christianity continue to exist? That depends on current Christians. Will current Christians fight via the ballot box, to elect those who are anti-Socialism and believe in True Social Justice? Will Christians teach their children about following Jesus Christ and the why and how of voting and what True Social Justice is; that it is not Socialism?. Will true Christians realize they cannot serve both men and God and choose serving God in their Christian Faith over serving Socialism for totalitarian, communitarianism control of humans? Will Christians put God back into the equation of human decision making and realize the aspects of morals and values?

Will those, who have drifted away from Christianity, come back to it in order to save their soul for the next life? Will those who have left Christianity, for whatever reason, examine that reason and realize if it was because of a person abusing their authority and betraying trust placed in them or a person being a false portrayal of a follower of Christ, that the person is not the church itself and investigate what the church itself actually is.? If one left Christianity due to not agreeing with the teachings of a church, will that one investigate other churches to find one that is agreeable?

The hearts, minds and attitudes of people must change from negative to positive, from the world to God, and they should become the best version of themselves. Even if one's heart, mind and attitudes are positive one should strive to become the best version of themselves, in having a positive purpose driven life. For Christians, it is a simple step by step disciplined program of prayer and study. There are numerous classes one may attend at churches such as Bible study, as well as courses one may obtain online or in a Christian book store. If one feels they do not have the times for such study, then churches and Christian book stores have a lot of books to read. Just do not forget prayer, for it opens the communication channel to God. I know from experience. Once it is open, keep it open. Finding, loving and enjoying God is not complicated. At least it does not have to be. Humans make it complicated sometimes.

There is no offense against God that is so great He cannot forgive it. He is greater than any offense. We have only to ask. In not asking, we are saying He is not greater than any offense and will not show mercy, which He does, and does not love us, which He does. We are denying Him the opportunity to come into our lives and that will be our downfall. Remember Jesus asked a known sinner to be an Apostle and He ate and associated with sinners. At the Last Supper Judas ate with Jesus and the other Apostle. When Jesus washed their feet, Judas was included even though Jesus knew of his betrayal. When Peter denied Him three times, He forgave him. When ten of His Apostles were not to be found during His crucifixion, He forgave them. When those who had followed Him in multitude were not to be found on the way to Golgotha "place of the skull", for crucifixion, He forgave them. We have all to gain and nothing to lose. Remember His ways are not our ways and He does everything in His time, for His reasons.

If the Socialists do establish totalitarian communitarianism, will true Christians continue to practice their faith, including in secret?. Will Christianity be passed down, by word of mouth, generation to generation, as it was in Russia and China? Christianity will exist and Jesus Christ will come again. And then…how will we be judged?

Even a sustainable society/culture will someday fall, if by nothing else than the unexpected. Just as the Berlin Wall came crumbling down and the Soviet Satellite States were released.

Jesus Christ is the Christian Church and His Church may become depressed and compressed, by humans, but it will still exist one way or another. It will survive.

Psalm 28: 3 Do not drag me away with the wicked, with the evil doers, who speak words of peace to their neighbors, but with evil in their hearts.

Do not enter the school of darkness! Fight its existence!

Addendum

The following Antifa Manual was emailed to me during June 2020. At the time, the Capitol Hill neighborhood of Seattle, Washington, had been allowed to be taken by Antifa, who threated to burn the police station. The Police Chief abandoned the station. Possibly to prevent a fire that would have traveled from district to district. The Mayor did not request the Governor activate and deploy the Washington Army Nation Guard to reinforce the Seattle Police Department. Antifa was allowed to take over the police station and barricade off six square blocks around the station, as an autonomous zone, and protected it with armed guards. Operations and living conditions, for its members, were set up. It was not just men, but also women and families. Mainly younger people.

Before the actual takeover, it was estimated 150 protestors had crowded the streets protesting against President Trump. Seattle is a far-left city and both the Mayor and the Washington State Governor are Socialist Democrats.

After establishing its territory, Antifa sent a list of demands to both the Mayor and the Governor.

There was also Antifa action that took place in Eugene, Oregon. A copy of their manual was found in "Eugene". I am assuming it was the Capitol of Oregon that it was found in. Notice the brown ring on the cover, as though a coffee cup had been set on it. The manual proclaims anyone who is not Antifa to be a fascist. Remember that the Communist and the Socialist saw Hitler as a Fascist and as competition. Fascist is totalitarian government by a dictator, while Communism is totalitarian government by a group of people; a committee.

While Antifa is composed of various left-wing groups, including anarchist who do not even believe in any form of government, notice the last section of the so-called manual is concerning the establishment of a government; a totalitarian government.

Antifa is simply the same old thing, Communism, labeled under a different name, which was used by German non-communist people in protest against Hitler. Antifa is being used by current day Communists/Socialists, for their own objects. It is not a new tactic. The Communists/Socialists will cause a problem, which seems to have been caused by someone else, and walk in saying that they have a solution. If they are allowed to implement their solution, freedom is taken away.

Now...see the following Antifa Manual.

I Could Have Been One

These pages were Dropped in Eugene on May 29, 2020 during a Riot.

THE
ANTIFA
MANUAL

Do not distribute
to any
cis white males
non-PoC
non-LGBTQ
peoples
a.k.a. fascists

Introduction

If you are reading this, it's because someone close to our movement trusted you with it. Please do not distribute to anyone who may attempt to harm or denigrate what we are doing.

This is an ANTI-FASCIST or ANTIFA manual. If you are reading this, you already know that we are a social justice movement against hatred, intolerance and bigotry.

This manual outlines where we've been, where we're at, and where we're headed within the next 100 years.

But first, to understand how we got here, we have to understand ...

White Privilege

For hundreds if not thousands of years, the cis white male power structure controlled the media and disbursement of information. First came the printing press (controlled by white males). Then came mass media such as newspapers and television (controlled by white males). But the next evolution of media was born in a time when the cis white male power structure began to lose its firm grip on the dissemination of ideas. Some of our kind have begun to infiltrate high-level positions of power in major media organizations.

And of course ... the new king of idea dissemination is Social Media. This is the new battleground for our war against fascism.

Whites, especially cis white males, have proven to be the greatest evil mankind has ever known. From Hitler to our very own Harry S. Truman (who dropped the atom bomb on Hiroshima and Nagasaki), to the slave traders of old, no one has proven to do more harm to mankind than white men.

From their murderous plundering (e.g. of the Native Americans and African slaves), white males have achieved status and power in the United States and Western Europe. Never indulge any fantasy by the fascists that white men have also cured diseases, lifted people out of poverty through western capitalism / democracy, or any other facetious claim they may make about

such men. Their gains were only achieved through rape and plunder.

Hence, cis white males have inherent privilege in our society. This is the basis on which people of color, LGBTQ, the disabled, and other groups that need protection will level the playing field and form a New World Order a.k.a. One World Government. A government by protected classes of people, for protected classes of people, for the protection and betterment of all of humanity.

Creating a Culture of Tolerance

To create a culture of tolerance, we must first eliminate all forms of hate speech. Every idea critical of our movement or our way of thinking must be condemned as: racist, homophobic, misogynist, etc.

We have the facts and history on our side. When all else fails, compare someone to Hitler. Every once in a while, one of our minority group friends will become disillusioned and speak out as a conservative a.k.a. fascist. Belittle them as delusional. They speak against their own rational self-interest.

Our color, my blackness, for example, comes first. It defines who I am. Black first, American second. Gay/Lesbian first, little person / dwarf second, American third, and so on

Crashing the Borders

Most liberals are not ANTIFA (yet), but soon they will be. Refugee crises such as those created by the situation in Syria are the ideal way to get more people of color (PoC) into America. They NEED our help. There are pictures of dead babies who have washed ashore onto beaches. Use imagery such as this to get support for expanding the PoC / minority population in the United States.

Never call any immigrant "illegal," obviously. They are "undocumented." It doesn't matter whether they came over here to smuggle drugs or if they were brought here by their parents at a young age. Migrants from Mexico and South America will play a crucial role in ANTIFA activities in the next 100 years.

By 2117, one hundred years from now, our goal is to have 70% of the US population be non-white. By then, we will hopefully

As people of color, LGBTQ, little people, the disabled, Muslims, and other minority classes slowly become the majority, we will naturally vote pro-ANTIFA politicians into office. It is, after all, only in our best interest.

After healthcare, the next target for socialization will obviously be the media. Use one of the government's only tools against big corporations: anti-trust, anti-monopoly laws - to split the media into worker-owned, ANTIFA-controlled entities.

Currently only the rich and upper middle class get to enjoy the benefits of Wall Street and all it has to offer. If the workers owned and controlled their own businesses, everyone would win (except the big fat cat CEOs who would be out of a job).

We will have to gradually raise the tax rates on both the 1% as well as the mid to upper middle class to achieve our ends. Raise the minimum wage to a livable wage, especially in places like San Francisco, Los Angeles and New York. Build homes for the homeless and confiscate foreclosed properties from banks to give to the homeless.

After media, banks and finance will be our next target, followed by technology and manufacturing.

One thing we must be sure of is to never let the white man excuse himself of his obligations to us by taking so-called "reparations." That time has surely passed, and would give the cis white male power structure an excuse to stop caving to our demands. "Oh, we gave Jamal $100k in reparations two years ago, we don't need to help him now that he's a penniless crack addict on the street now," they will surely say.

Speeding Up Progress

To achieve these ends, there are some tactics that we must use to speed our way towards progress. It's well-known that whites in America are not producing as many offspring as their counterparts. It's important to make abortion, on demand and without apology, overwhelmingly available in predominantly white communities. We must lower the bar to access birth control in these communities and use media to promulgate the image of childless white people as being sexy, hip and cool. Meanwhile the fascists on the right will continue to attempt to restrict access to abortions on demand. Middle class whites tend to have the ability to pay, even for out of state travel, to get their fetuses aborted. Currently the predominantly people of color dominated poor communities have little choice but to keep a baby to term. Even if sent into the foster system, these children will one day lay the groundwork for our eventual New World Order and One World Government.

Phase 3: New World Order

Imagine a world free of hatred and bigotry. Imagine a world where you'll never have to be called the n-word again. Imagine a world where you can be as gay as you want, and not be called a raging, dick-sucking "fa**ot." Where ANTIF ideas reign supreme and all hateful, microaggressive speech is eradicated.

One way to accomplish this will be to tag (or microchip) every human being on the planet, and they will do so voluntarily. Use the guise of entertainment and other benefits to lure the people to this end. This chip, embedded in the hand or neck, will allow ANTIFA-approved regulators to monitor the citizenry of the world. Information accessible (by waving a wand a few feet away from the chip) would be: DNA content (including % of color, genetic disadvantages, etc), political leanings (scored by past social media posts), earnings, known associates, ANTIFA status, etc. We must ensure that only ANTIFA-approved regulators can access this data, lest we veer too far into fascism ourselves.

Thus, with the wave of a wand, one would be able to tell whether that vaguely beige-ish looking person is allowed to use the term "nigga." For example, in rap lexicon it is popular to say, "where my niggas at? I got hoes in different area codes." While clearly misogynistic, a person of color has the right to use the term "nigga." ANTIFA regulators will have to determine an acceptable percentage threshold of color in one's DNA that makes it acceptable to use the term "nigga." If you are only 17% of African descent, perhaps it is not okay to use that term. Clearly if you are 1% or less of African descent, it is problematic, although some dark Asians can get away with saying it just because of how dark their skin tone is. However, if someone of, say, 80% Caucasian descent attempts to use the n-word with the "hard r," they will clearly be in violation of hate crime speech. While prison would clearly be too harsh of a punishment for such an individual, demotion of status, power and income would not be out of the question and should be the norm.

The issue of using force to achieve our ends is a tricky one. Always shout down fascist opponents. Disrupt their speeches, counter-rally their rallies. Force the media to show our side as the righteous one that it is. When it comes to the issue of terror, such men. Their gains were only achieved through rape and plunder.

Hence, cis white males have inherent privilege in our society. This is the basis on which people of color, LGBTQ, the disabled, and other groups that need protection will level the playing field and form a New World Order a.k.a. One World Government. A government by protected classes of people, for protected classes of people, for the protection and betterment of all of humanity.

Creating a Culture of Tolerance

To create a culture of tolerance, we must first eliminate all forms of hate speech. Every idea critical of our movement or our way of thinking must be condemned as: racist, homophobic, misogynist, etc.

We have the facts and history on our side. When all else fails, compare someone to Hitler. Every once in a while, one of our minority group friends will become disillusioned and speak out as a conservative a.k.a. fascist. Belittle them as delusional. They speak against their own rational self-interest.

Our color, my blackness, for example, comes first. It defines who I am. Black first, American second. Gay/Lesbian first, little person / dwarf second, American third, and so on

Crashing the Borders

Most liberals are not ANTIFA (yet), but soon they will be. Refugee crises such as those created by the situation in Syria are the ideal way to get more people of color (PoC) into America. They NEED our help. There are pictures of dead babies who have washed ashore onto beaches. Use imagery such as this to get support for expanding the PoC / minority population in the United States.

Never call any immigrant "illegal," obviously. They are "undocumented." It doesn't matter whether they came over here to smuggle drugs or if they were brought here by their parents at a young age. Migrants from Mexico and South America will play a crucial role in ANTIFA activities in the next 100 years.

By 2117, one hundred years from now, our goal is to have 70% of the US population be non-white. By then, we will hopefully

such men. Their gains were only achieved through rape and plunder.

Hence, cis white males have inherent privilege in our society. This is the basis on which people of color, LGBTQ, the disabled, and other groups that need protection will level the playing field and form a New World Order a.k.a. One World Government. A government by protected classes of people, for protected classes of people, for the protection and betterment of all of humanity.

Creating a Culture of Tolerance

To create a culture of tolerance, we must first eliminate all forms of hate speech. Every idea critical of our movement or our way of thinking must be condemned as: racist, homophobic, misogynist, etc.

We have the facts and history on our side. When all else fails, compare someone to Hitler. Every once in a while, one of our minority group friends will become disillusioned and speak out as a conservative a.k.a. fascist. Belittle them as delusional. They speak against their own rational self-interest.

Our color, my blackness, for example, comes first. It defines who I am. Black first, American second. Gay/Lesbian first, little person / dwarf second, American third, and so on

Crashing the Borders

Most liberals are not ANTIFA (yet), but soon they will be. Refugee crises such as those created by the situation in Syria are the ideal way to get more people of color (PoC) into America. They NEED our help. There are pictures of dead babies who have washed ashore onto beaches. Use imagery such as this to get support for expanding the PoC / minority population in the United States.

Never call any immigrant "illegal," obviously. They are "undocumented." It doesn't matter whether they came over here to smuggle drugs or if they were brought here by their parents at a young age. Migrants from Mexico and South America will play a crucial role in ANTIFA activities in the next 100 years.

By 2117, one hundred years from now, our goal is to have 70% of the US population be non-white. By then, we will hopefully

we do not condone mass murder. However, a tiny majority of people who happen to be Muslim have decided to blow themselves up for their cause. Clearly this is the result of hundreds of years of Western intervention by cis white males on their culture. Osama Bin Laden would not have attacked the WTC and Pentagon had we not dropped atom bombs on Japan in WWII, for example. Palestinians are clearly victims and have little to no choice than to avenge their relatives' deaths at the hands of the Israeli government. Make no mistake - Jews are a protected class of people, but we do not condone Israeli aggression against Palestinians.

Phase 4: One World Government

Our movement will eventually spread to other nations–indeed, it has already begun. Some peoples will prove excessively resistant to our brand of ANTIFA, such as those who were previously burned by Communism or failed socialist states. Make no mistake–we will prevail where others have failed. Their leaders' lust for status, power and wealth eventually led them to create layers of power full of corrupt state officials. ANTIFA have the power of the people on our side (or we will, eventually) and will not succumb to such a fate.

It is only natural that the ideologies we espouse spread throughout the globe. Starving Africans will finally be lifted out of poverty when we redistribute the wealth of the Western 1% to them (and to our brothers and sisters here at home).

Container ship after container ship will be converted to massive passenger cruise-liners and will ferry poverty-stricken brown people from around the world to the (former) United States and Western Europe. Jobs will flower aplenty at all of the world's worker-owned businesses. Those who can't work will be provided a stipend and unlimited supply of opiates, marijuana, meth and cocaine to occupy their free time.

Sound too good to be true?

It isn't. This is what we're fighting for.

This is what we believe. WE ARE ANTIFA. EITHER YOU ARE WITH US, OR YOU ARE A FASCIST.

[Please do not distribute to cis white males, non-PoC, non-LGBTQ, etc. Use common sense.]

Other Publications' Credits

The Bridge At Andau by James A. Michener, copyright © 1957. Used by permission of Penguin Random House.

Haunted Fifties, The by I.F. Stone, copyright © 1989. Reprinted by permission of Little, Brown, an imprint of Hachette Book Group, Inc. Used by permission of as well as British United Kingdom and Commonwealth use permission granted by Stone's representative Wylie Agency of London, England, per I.F. Stone Estate.

The Long Loneliness by Dorothy Day. Copyright © 1952 by Harper & Row, Publishers, Inc. Copyright renewed © 1980 by Tamar Teresa Hennessy. Used by permission of HarperCollins Publishers.

School of Darkness by Bella Dodd. Original publication by P. J. Kenedy & Sons, New York, 1954. Reprint published by and being used by permission of Angelico Press.

Behind the Green Mask by Rosa Koire, copyright © 2011. Used by permission of the author.

Jesus Was/Is Involved In Politics by Neil Mammen, copyright © 2007. Used by permission of the author.

Rules for Radicals by Saul Alinsky, copyright © 1971 by Random House. Used by permission of Penguin Random House.

All other publications are used under *Fair Use* of copyright law.